Statistics for Social and Behavioral Sciences

Advisors:
S.E. Fienberg
W.J. van der Linden

Statistics for Social and Behavioral Sciences

Neil J. Dorans
Mary Pommerich
Paul W. Holland
(Editors)

Linking and Aligning Scores and Scales

Foreword by Ida M. Lawrence

 Springer

Neil J. Dorans
Educational Testing Service
Rosedale Road
Princeton, NJ 08541
ndorans@ets.org

Paul W. Holland
Educational Testing Service
Rosedale Road
Princeton, NJ 08541
pholland@ets.org

Mary Pommerich
Monterey Bay Defense Manpower Data Center
400 Gigling Rd.
Seaside, CA 93955
USA
mary.pommerich@osd.pentagon.mil

Disclaimer: The opinions expressed by Mary Pommerich are her own and not necessarily those of the Department of Defense or the United States Government.

ETS, GRE, Praxis and TOEFL are registered trademarks of Educational Testing Service (ETS).
CLEP, COLLEGE BOARD, PSAT/NMSQT, and SAT are registered trademarks of College Board.
SAT REASONING TEST is a trademark of College Board.
ACT is a registered trademark of ACT, Inc. in the U.S.A. and other countries.

Library of Congress Control Number: 2007920470

ISBN-10: 0-387-49770-6
ISBN-13: 978-0-387-49770-9

e-ISBN-10: 0-387-49771-4
e-ISBN-13: 978-0-387-49771-6

Printed on acid-free paper.

9 8 7 6 5 4 3 2 1

springer.com

Dedication

To Kirsten.
   —N. J. D.

To Bob and Mellita
   —M. P.

To Martha
   —P. W. H.

Foreword

In their preface to the second edition of *Test Equating, Scaling, and Linking,* Mike Kolen and Bob Brennan (2004) made the following observation: "Prior to 1980, the subject of equating was ignored by most people in the measurement community except for psychometricians, who had responsibility for equating" (p. vii). The authors went on to say that considerably more attention is now paid to equating, indeed to all forms of linkages between tests, and that this increased attention can be attributed to several factors:

1. An increase in the number and variety of testing programs that use multiple forms and the recognition among professionals that these multiple forms need to be linked.
2. Test developers and publishers, in response to critics, often refer to the role of linking in reporting scores.
3. The accountability movement and fairness issues related to assessment have become much more visible.

Those of us who work in this field know that ensuring comparability of scores is not an easy thing to do. Nonetheless, our customers—the test-takers and score users—either assume that scores on different forms of an assessment can be used interchangeably or, like the critics above, ask us to justify our comparability assumptions. And they are right to do this. After all, the test scores that we provide have an impact on decisions that affect people's choices and their future plans. From an ethical point of view, we are obligated to get it right.

With the increased spotlight on linking, we have also seen interest in providing more sophisticated and complex kinds of assessment for tests designed for making high-stakes decisions. As we introduce more constructed response questions into our assessments, the challenge of linking increases. For example, when constructed response items are used as linking items, we are making the implicit claim that the raters scored the question the same way both times. How to control for differences in scoring at different administrations is a tricky business but is essential to successful linking. When test questions are scored by humans, instead of by machines, what mechanisms are needed to ensure that scores on reused test forms can be reported without a check on the stability of the scoring of the constructed response portions?

The No Child Left Behind Act of 2001 has spawned a strong market interest in formative assessments and assessments for other low-stakes decisions. We need to remind ourselves, and others, that linking issues need to play a role in assessment for lower stakes decisions. Without attention to score comparability on these formative assessments, we run the risk of giving bad instructional advice. The challenge lies in determining what kinds of standards need to apply to scores on these kinds of test.

A final challenge relates to improved communication about the practical consequences of addressing linking issues at the design phase for a testing program and as an ongoing activity in order to ensure fair and meaningful scores. We need to do a better job of helping decision-makers and policy folks understand the issues around equating and linking. We need to explain the limitations of the methods and the cost of being able to make truthful claims about score comparability.

This volume takes important steps in preparing us for these challenges. It examines foundational issues that cut across different types of linking. It delves into issues that are particularly germane to different classes of linking.

Ida M. Lawrence
ETS Senior Vice-President of Research & Development
January 2007

Preface

In 1980, an Educational Testing Service (ETS) equating conference led to a book (Holland & Rubin, 1982) that was one of first to bring professional attention to the critical statistical practice of equating. At that time, equating was a trade practiced by a small group of applied psychometricians, and equating practices were passed down from experts to novices.

Shortly after that book was published, both Neil Dorans and Paul Holland became intrigued by a simple question: When is an equating a good equating? Put another way, how do we evaluate the quality of an equating?

About 15 years later, Holland chaired a National Research Council committee that produced a report, *Uncommon Measures* (Feuer, Holland, Green, Bertenthal, & Hemphill, 1999), giving an accessible summary of informed, professional judgment about the issues involved in linking scores on different educational tests. Congressional requests to provide advice on how to link scores on tests that cover similar material was the impetus for the profession's response delivered in *Uncommon Measures*.

Around the same time, Neil Dorans and Mary Pommerich collaborated to produce a concordance between scores on the ACT® and SAT®, the two major college admissions tests in the United States (Dorans, Lyu, Pommerich, & Houston, 1997). This work led to an interest in better understanding how equating differs from other types of linkage between scores and when different types of linkage should be conducted. In time, a special *Applied Psychological Measurement* issue on concordance was co-edited by Pommerich and Dorans (2004a). Drawing distinctions among types of linkage was an important theme in that special issue.

Returning to the question of what constitutes an equating, Dorans and Holland (2000) introduced indexes for quantifying how much an equating depends on the subpopulation in which it is conducted. The importance of population invariance as a check on equatability has developed rapidly since 2001, as evidenced by a special issue on the topic in the *Journal of Educational Measurement*, edited by Dorans (2004a).

In June, 2005, Dorans and Holland organized another ETS-sponsored conference.[1] Demonstrating a shift in focus from the seminal conference held 25 years earlier, the 2005 conference focused on the more general issue of linking, of which equating was but one topic of discussion. The conference was dedicated to Professor Ledyard R Tucker,[2] one of the early theorists and practitioners of equating. The conference provided raw material for this volume.

During the 25 years between the two ETS conferences, several books addressed issues in score linking. The volume by Kolen and Brennan (2004), in its second edition, is an encyclopedic treatment of the field of equating, scaling, and linking. von Davier, Holland, and Thayer (2004b) focused on kernel equating as a unified approach that introduces several new ideas of general use in equating. In addition to *Uncommon Measures*, another report on score linking from the National Research Council is *Embedding Questions* (Koretz, Bertenthal, & Green, 1999). Finally, the work of Livingston (2004) is a user-friendly account of many of the major issues and techniques.

Where does this volume fit into the array of books that have been written about equating and linking? Simply, it is more about score linking than score equating. We place a strong emphasis on distinguishing between different kinds of linking and the inferences that can be associated with each type of linking. This volume examines the different types of linking from both theoretical and practical perspectives. Theory that ignores reality is doomed to be irrelevant. Practice that occurs without an appreciation of the theory of linking is likely to be influenced by the biases of the practitioner. This volume emphasizes the importance of both theory and practice.

Several ETS staff provided essential support. Martha Thompson organized the linking conference that was attended by 200 assessment professionals. She and Liz Brophy turned a concept into a reality. John Mazzeo, Associate Vice-President for Statistical Analysis and Research, and Ida Lawrence, Senior Vice-President of Research and Development at ETS, supported the conference. As experienced linkers, they readily endorsed production of this volume as well. The volume benefited from the administrative skills of Liz Brophy and the editorial skills of Kim Fryer.

---

[1] Linking and Aligning Scores and Scales, a conference in honor of Ledyard R Tucker's approach to theory and practice, was held at Princeton University on June 24–25, 2005.

[2] A brief history of Ledyard R Tucker's professional life can be found in Dorans (2004b).

Contents

List of Contributors

Braun, Dr. Henry I.
  Boston College
  Campion Hall
  140 Commonwealth Ave
  Chestnut Hill, MA 02467
  braunh@bc.edu

Brennan, Dr. Robert L.
  Center for Advanced Studies in
  Measurement and Assessment
  (CASMA)
  210 Lindquist Center South
  University of Iowa
  Iowa City, IA 52242-1529
  robert-brennan@uiowa.edu

Cook, Dr. Linda L.
  Educational Testing Service
  Rosedale Road
  Princeton, NJ 08541
  lcook@ets.org

Dorans, Dr. Neil J.
  Educational Testing Service
  Rosedale Road
  Princeton, NJ 08541
  ndorans@ets.org

Eignor, Dr. Daniel R.
  Educational Testing Service
  Rosedale Road
  Princeton, NJ 08541
  deignor@ets.org

Harris, Dr. Deborah J.
  ACT, Inc.
  500 ACT Drive
  P. O. Box 168
  Iowa City, IA 52243
  deborah.harris@act.org

Holland, Dr. Paul W.
  Educational Testing Service and
  Paul Holland Consulting
  Corporation
  Rosedale Road
  Princeton, NJ 08541
  pholland@ets.org

Kolen, Dr. Michael J.
  Iowa Testing Programs
  College of Education
  The University of Iowa
  224 B1 Lindquist Center
  Iowa City, IA 52242
  michael-kolen@uiowa.edu

Koretz, Dr. Daniel
  Harvard Graduate School of
  Education
  415 Gutman Library
  6 Appian Way
  Cambridge, MA 02138
  daniel_koretz@harvard.edu

Liu, Dr. Jinghua
  Educational Testing Service
  Rosedale Road
  Princeton, NJ 08541
  jliu@ets.org

Patz, Dr. Richard J.
  CTB/McGraw-Hill
  20 Ryan Ranch Road
  Monterey, CA 93940
  richard_patz@ctb.com

Petersen, Dr. Nancy S.
  ACT, Inc.
  500 ACT Drive
  P. O. Box 168
  Iowa City, Iowa 52243-0168
  nancy.petersen@act.org

Pommerich, Dr. Mary
  Defense Manpower Data
  Center
  DoD Center Monterey Bay
  400 Gigling Road
  Seaside, CA 93955-6771
  mary.pommerich@osd.pentagon.
  mil

Qian, Dr. Jiahe
  Educational Testing Service
  Rosedale Road
  Princeton, NJ 08541
  jqian@ets.org

Sawyer, Dr. Richard
  ACT, Inc.
  500 ACT Drive
  P. O. Box 168
  Iowa City, IA 52243-0168
  richard.sawyer@act.org

Thissen, Dr. David
  L. L. Thurstone Psychometric
  Laboratory
  Department of Psychology
  University of North Carolina at
  Chapel Hill
  CB#3270 Davie Hall
  Chapel Hill, NC 27599-3270
  dthissen@email.unc.edu

von Davier, Dr. Alina A.
  Educational Testing Service
  Rosedale Road
  Princeton, NJ 08541
  avondavier@ets.org

Walker, Dr. Michael E.
  Educational Testing Service
  Rosedale Road
  Princeton, NJ 08541
  mwalker@ets.org

Yao, Dr. Lihua
  CTB/McGraw-Hill
  20 Ryan Ranch Road
  Monterey, CA 93940
  lihua_yao@ctb.com

Yen, Dr. Wendy M.
  Educational Testing Service
  80 Garden Court #202
  Monterey, CA 93940
  wyen@ets.org

1 Overview

There are six parts to this volume. The first part, *Foundations*, sets the stage for the remainder of the volume, providing an historical perspective on score linking, definitions of types of score linkage, and background information on data collection designs, linking methods, and related assumptions. The remaining five parts deal with different types of linking scenario.

In the not too far past, linkings of any sort were treated as equatings. In this volume, we use equating to refer to the pinnacle of linking, the type of linkage that is sought, rarely achieved, and too often mistakenly presumed to have been attained. Equating is what large-scale testing programs engage in when they use large representative samples of examinees, sound data collection practices, and appropriate methods to link test editions built to the same set of specifications. Equating adjusts for differences in difficulty that occur with the use of different sets of similar test questions. Equating ensures that examinees are treated fairly. Part 2, *Equating*, focuses on linking scenarios in which the assumptions of equating are met.

A slightly different linking scenario arises when a testing program implements some form of change to their test, and wants to link scores across the old and new versions. The change might be in content, test administration conditions, or mode of administration. The change might be small or large. Testing programs that are in transition due to changes of any nature must face the question of whether scores from the previous version of the test can be viewed as interchangeable with scores from the new version of the test. Part 3, *Tests in Transitions*, discusses linking issues associated with this scenario.

Another linking scenario occurs when there is an interest in linking scores across related but distinct tests. Typically, the tests measure similar constructs, are administered to similar kinds of examinees, and are used for the same purpose, but differ in terms of specifications and perspective. Part 4, *Concordance*, deals with linking issues associated with this scenario.

An alternate linking scenario arises when there is an interest in making comparisons of performance across different levels of difficulty for a given construct. In the realm of K-12 testing, test scores are often compared across grades even though test content and test populations differ. Linkages of this sort must ensure that the comparisons are meaningful despite the changes in content and examinees. Part 5, *Vertical Scaling*, discusses linking issues associated with this scenario.

The final linking scenario considered in this volume occurs when there is an interest in linking group-level scores to individual-level scores. For example, the accountability movement has triggered an interest in making meaningful quantitative comparisons across scores on the National Assessment of Educational Progress and assessments designed to measure whether individuals meet state standards. Part 6, *Linking Group Assessments to Individual Assessments*, looks at linking issues under this scenario.

In the final chapter of this volume, *Postscript*, we briefly review the transitions that occur from Parts 2 to 6. We take note of the diversity of perspective within parts. We discuss the descent of linking from the ideal state of equating to the realities faced by professionals who have to operate in arenas where the need for comparability is great and the capacity to achieve it is limited. We address the inevitable conflict that occurs when expectations exceed professional capabilities.

Part 1: Foundations

The title of this part, *Foundations*, is self-descriptive. Each of the two chapters sets a foundation for later parts of this volume. In *A Framework and History for Score Linking*, Paul Holland notes that linking scores or scales from different tests has a history about as long as the field of psychometrics itself. This chapter is organized around a typology of linking methods that distinguishes among predicting, scaling, and equating, providing useful distinctions for subsequent chapters. Appropriate historical facts are woven into the narrative to help show the relationship between the methods.

In *Data Collection Designs and Linking Procedures*, Michael Kolen describes commonly used designs for collecting data and statistical procedures for linking scores. Features of testing situations that influence linking are divided into the following categories: test content, conditions of measurement, and examinee population. Common data collection designs and their variations are considered. Statistical linking methods also are described, with a focus on the required statistical assumptions.

Together these two foundational chapters present a frame of reference for the subsequent parts, which discuss different types of linking in some detail.

2 A Framework and History for Score Linking

Paul W. Holland[1]

Educational Testing Service and Paul Holland Consulting Corporation

2.1. Introduction

For two tests, a *link* between their scores is a transformation from a score on one to a score on the other. The scores being linked might be raw scores or scaled scores (Angoff, 1971). Linking transformations can be developed in a variety of ways that reflect the similarities and differences between the tests as well as the uses to which the links are to be put. Several frameworks have been suggested for organizing the variety of links that are used in practice. For example, see Flanagan (1951), Angoff (1971), Mislevy (1992), Linn (1993), Feuer, Holland, Green, Bertenthal, and Hemphill (1999), and Dorans (2000, 2004d). In addition, Kolen (2004a) and Kolen and Brennan (2004) reviewed and synthesized several frameworks.

This chapter is concerned with a framework developed in Holland and Dorans (2006) that builds on this prior work. In addition, it gives a brief account of the history of score linking. Along with the next chapter by Kolen, it provides a setting for subsequent chapters in this volume that appear in the part of this volume on equating (Part 2), tests in transition (Part 3), concordance (Part 4), vertical linking (Part 5), and linking scales from group assessments to scales used to report scores on individuals (Part 6).

The term *linking* refers to the general class of transformations between the scores from one test and those of another. Linking methods can then be divided into three basic categories called *predicting*, *scale aligning*, and *equating*. Scale aligning will be shortened to *scaling* when convenient.

---

[1] The opinions expressed in this chapter are those of the author and not necessarily of Educational Testing Service.

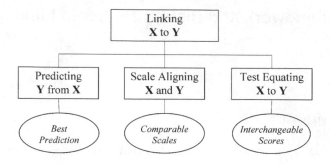

Figure 2.1. The three overall categories of test linking methods and their goals.

Figure 2.1 illustrates the three basic categories of linking and their purposes.

Each of these basic categories contains subcategories that share common objectives and that are distinct from the objectives of the methods in the other categories. It is important to distinguish among these basic categories because they are often seen as similar or identical when in fact they are not. Testing professionals need to understand these differences and the circumstances when one category is more relevant than another and, when necessary, to be able to communicate these distinctions to test users. Figures 2.2, 2.3, and 2.4 illustrate the several subcategories within the basic categories of predicting, scale aligning, and equating.

It is sometimes useful to distinguish between score linkings that are *direct* and those that are *indirect*. A direct link functionally connects the scores on one test directly to those of another. An indirect link connects the scores on two tests through their common connection to a third test or scale. The categories of predicting and equating usually produce direct links, whereas the various subcategories of scale aligning typically produce indirect links. These distinctions are mentioned when appropriate.

2.2. Predicting

Predicting is the oldest form of score linking and it has been confused with the other methods of score linking since the earliest days of psychometrics. By the dawn of the 19th century, Legendre, Gauss, Laplace, and their scientific contemporaries understood how to use least squares methods to fit curves to solve problems in astronomy. By the end of that century, linear regression methods had been applied to a variety of social and psychological phenomena as well. Notable among these pioneers was Galton, who first observed the effects of regression to the mean (Stigler, 1986). Thus, the use of linear regression methods to predict the scores on one test or measurement from those of another is probably the oldest approach taken for linking scores. A version of predicting, called *projection*, is closely related to certain forms of scaling and equating. Both predicting and projecting are described in this section.

Figure 2.2 illustrates the subcategories within the overall linking category of predicting.

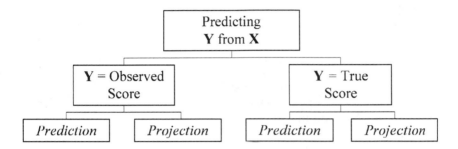

Figure 2.2. The types of linking methods within the overall linking category of *predicting*.

2.2.1. Predicting Observed Scores

The goal of predicting is to predict an examinee's score on one test from some other information about that examinee. This other information might be a score on another test or the scores from several other tests and it might include demographic or other information. For this reason, there is always an asymmetry between what is predicted and what is being used to make the prediction. The predictors and the predicted quantity might be different both in number and character. This asymmetry is evident even in the case of predicting one test score, $\mathbf{Y}$, from another, $\mathbf{X}$. In this simplest case, it has been known since the 19th century that the usual linear regression function for predicting $\mathbf{Y}$ from $\mathbf{X}$ is not the inverse of the linear regression function for predicting $\mathbf{X}$ from $\mathbf{Y}$ (Galton, 1888). This is a basic aspect of the asymmetry between the predictor score and the predicted score. It is highlighted in requirement (c) of Section 2.4.1.

If $\mathbf{X}$ and $\mathbf{Y}$ denote the scores on the two tests for examinees who are from a population, $\mathbf{P}$, then denote the conditional expectation (or conditional mean/average) of $\mathbf{Y}$ given $\mathbf{X}$ over $\mathbf{P}$, by

$$E(\mathbf{Y} \mid \mathbf{X} = x, \mathbf{P}). \tag{2.1}$$

This conditional expectation is a standard method for predicting $\mathbf{Y}$ from $\mathbf{X}$. If $\mathbf{X}$ has the value x, then the equation $y = E(\mathbf{Y} \mid \mathbf{X} = x, \mathbf{P})$ predicts y to be the value of $\mathbf{Y}$. The prediction of $\mathbf{Y}$ from $\mathbf{X}$ is an example of a direct link between the scores on the two tests.

Unless $\mathbf{Y}$ is functionally dependent on $\mathbf{X}$, there is always some amount of *error* or uncertainty in any prediction. The error in this prediction is how far $E(\mathbf{Y} \mid \mathbf{X} = x, \mathbf{P})$ is from the actual value of $\mathbf{Y}$; that is, the difference

$$\mathbf{Y} - E(\mathbf{Y} \mid \mathbf{X} = x, \mathbf{P}). \tag{2.2}$$

The conditional expectation is the *best* predictor of $\mathbf{Y}$ in the sense that any other predictor of $\mathbf{Y}$ from $\mathbf{X}$, say $y = \mathrm{Pred}(x)$, will have a larger expected squared error in expression (2.2); that is,

$$
\begin{aligned}
&E\left[\left(\mathbf{Y} - \mathrm{Pred}(x)\right)^2 \mid \mathbf{X} = x, \mathbf{P}\right] \geq \\
&E\left[\left(\mathbf{Y} - E(\mathbf{Y} \mid \mathbf{X} = x, \mathbf{P})\right)^2 \mid \mathbf{X} = x, \mathbf{P}\right] = \mathrm{Var}(\mathbf{Y} \mid \mathbf{X} = x, \mathbf{P}),
\end{aligned} \tag{2.3}
$$

as shown in Cramér (1946), Parzen (1960), and others.

The conditional variance in Equation 2.3 is also called the conditional *prediction error* in the context of predicting $\mathbf{Y}$-scores from $\mathbf{X}$-scores. Other types of predictor or prediction method minimize other measures of prediction error, a subject too large for us to do much more than merely mention. For example, see Blackwell and Girshick (1954), Parzen (1960), or the discussion of best linear predictors in Holland and Hoskens (2003).

Using regression methods, both the conditional expectation, $E(\mathbf{Y} \mid \mathbf{X} = x, \mathbf{P})$, and the conditional prediction error can be estimated from data in which examinees are sampled from $\mathbf{P}$ and tested with both $\mathbf{X}$ and $\mathbf{Y}$. Discussions of regression methods are so widely available that no more details are given here about the variety of possibilities; for example, see Moore and McCabe (1999) or Birkes and Dodge (1993).

An appropriate use of predicting to make a link between two tests arises when an examinee's score on one test is used to predict how he or she will perform on another test. An example is the use of PSAT/NMSQT® scores to forecast how an examinee will perform on the SAT® a year or so later. For example, periodically a year's worth of SAT data from students who have taken both tests is used to estimate the conditional distribution of SAT scores given the corresponding (verbal or mathematical) PSAT/NMSQT score (see Educational Testing Service, 1999). This conditional distribution predicts the range of likely performance on the SAT given an examinee's PSAT/NMSQT score. If these predictions are applied to examinees who are similar to those in the population from which the prediction equations are derived, then they are likely to be useful. For examinees who are very different from those whose data were used to estimate the conditional distributions, these predictions are less likely to be accurate.

2.2.2. Projecting Distributions of Observed Scores

Related to predicting individual scores on a test is the problem of *projecting distributions of scores* on one test from those on another test. In this case, as described earlier for predicting a score on $\mathbf{Y}$ from a score on $\mathbf{X}$, data obtained from a sample of examinees who take both $\mathbf{X}$ and $\mathbf{Y}$ is used to estimate the conditional distribution of $\mathbf{Y}$ given $\mathbf{X}$ on a particular population, say $\mathbf{P}$. Denote the conditional cumulative distribution function (cdf) of $\mathbf{Y}$ given $\mathbf{X} = x$ in $\mathbf{P}$ by

$$\Pr\{\mathbf{Y} \le y \mid \mathbf{X} = x, \mathbf{P}\}. \tag{2.4}$$

The data can be used to estimate the cdf in Equation 2.4. Now suppose that in another population, say $\mathbf{Q}$, there are data for the distribution of $\mathbf{X}$, but not for $\mathbf{Y}$. If the distribution of $\mathbf{X}$ in $\mathbf{Q}$ is somewhat different from that of $\mathbf{X}$ in $\mathbf{P}$, it might be desired to *project* the distribution of $\mathbf{X}$ in $\mathbf{Q}$ to obtain an estimate of the cdf of $\mathbf{Y}$ in $\mathbf{Q}$, $F_{\mathbf{YQ}}(y)$, using methods that are based on the formula

$$F_{\mathbf{YQ}}(y) = \Pr\{\mathbf{Y} \le y \mid \mathbf{Q}\} = \mathrm{E}[\Pr\{\mathbf{Y} \le y \mid \mathbf{X}, \mathbf{P}\} \mid \mathbf{Q}]. \tag{2.5}$$

In Equation 2.5, the outer expectation (or averaging) is over the distribution of $\mathbf{X}$ in $\mathbf{Q}$. Strictly speaking, Equation 2.5 is valid only if the conditional distribution of $\mathbf{Y}$ given $\mathbf{X}$ is the same in both $\mathbf{P}$ and $\mathbf{Q}$; that is, if

$$\Pr\{\mathbf{Y} \le y \mid \mathbf{X} = x, \mathbf{P}\} = \Pr\{\mathbf{Y} \le y \mid \mathbf{X} = x, \mathbf{Q}\}. \tag{2.6}$$

Equation (2.6) is a type of *population invariance* assumption because it requires the conditional distribution that holds for one population to also hold for another population. Assumptions that are identical to Equation 2.6 also arise in various cases of scaling and equating. Population invariance assumptions, like Equation 2.6, pervade all aspects of scaling and equating where there are missing data in the sense that in the above example the data for **Y** in **Q** are missing.

An important example of projecting a score distribution arises when **X** and **Y** are both given to a sample of examinees in Year 1, and then in Year 2, only one of them, say **X**, is given. To predict what the distribution of **Y** would have been had it also been given in Year 2, projection methods provide a way of doing this. They are based on Equation 2.5, with **P** representing the data from Year 1 and **Q** representing the data in Year 2. The need for the population invariance assumption in Equation 2.6 is quite evident in this example.

Pashley and Phillips (1993) provided an example of projecting scores from the International Assessment of Educational Progress (IAEP) to the scale of the National Assessment of Educational Progress (NAEP). Williams, Rosa, McLeod, Thissen, and Sanford (1998) gave a detailed discussion of an example of projecting scores from a state assessment to the NAEP scale, which is the focus of the chapters by Braun and Qian (Chapter 17), Koretz (Chapter 18), and Thissen (Chapter 16).

So far, the discussion has concerned only prediction methods that directly link observed scores on the tests to each other. There are other forms of prediction worthy of mention for completeness (e.g., methods that use observed scores to predict *true scores*).

2.2.3. Predicting True Scores

The oldest version of predicting true scores from observed scores is Kelley's formula that predicts the true score on **Y** from the observed score on **Y** (Kelley, 1927). This idea was generalized in Wainer et al. (2001) to the prediction of true scores on one test from the observed scores on it and some other tests. They referred to the predicted true scores as *augmented scores*. Holland and Hoskens (2003) considered the problem of predicting true-scores from observed scores where the true-scores come from one test, **Y**, and the observed scores come from another test, **X**. They showed that the usual linear regression function, which predicts the observed scores of **Y** from the observed scores of **X**, is an appropriate predictor of the true score of **Y**, but that the usual measure of prediction error from linear regression is too large and needs to be adjusted by the reliabilities of the two tests.

2.2.4. Summary

It was recognized very early that prediction methods were not satisfactory ways of creating *comparable scores*, as the early forms of scale aligning were called. Thorndike (1922) and Otis (1922) gave the first arguments for why linear regression was not a satisfactory method of finding comparable scores. Later, Flanagan (1951) emphasized the lack of symmetry of regression functions, thereby connecting regression methods to the failure to satisfy requirement (c) of Section 2.4.1. The distinction between prediction and equating has been repeatedly reaffirmed over the years; see Hull (1922), Flanagan (1939, 1951), Lord (1950, 1955, 1982), Angoff (1971), Mislevy (1992), Linn (1993), and Holland and Dorans (2006).

2.3. Scale Aligning

The methods of aligning scales are the second oldest group of linking methods. The need to make scores on different tests comparable (i.e., scaling) and the invention of methods to do it has a history almost as old as the field of psychometrics itself. Procedures for scaling were initially called methods for creating comparable scores. Kelley (1914) discussed problems with the methods proposed in Starch (1913) and modified in Weiss (1914) and Pinter (1914) for putting into comparable units the Ayers and the Thorndike methods of scoring of handwriting. Pinter had a sample of handwriting from examinees who had been judged using both methods. Weiss advocated setting the means of the scores on both tests equal to 50 by a multiplicative factor. Kelley showed that this method could give absurd results in various circumstances and proposed, instead, to use standard scores as comparable measures (i.e., to subtract the mean and divide by the standard deviation of each measure). Using standard scores to scale tests has been used widely since that time. Treating standard scores as equivalent leads to the method of linear equating. Kelley explicitly titled his article "Comparable Measures" and used the terms *equate* and *equating* to refer to the results of setting comparable scores equal.

The influential textbook by Kelley (1923) had a chapter titled "Comparable Measures" in which he (a) again showed that the method proposed by Weiss (1914) can lead to absurd results, (b) asserted that Galton had, decades earlier, used a version of standard scores to compare quantities that are measured on different scales, (c) advocated standard scores and showed that they equal the ratio method only when special conditions hold, and (d) discussed the equal successive percentiles method to define comparable scores; this is an early form of equipercentile equating (Equation 11 in Kelley). Kelley referred to even earlier uses of the equal successive percentile method in Otis (1916, 1918).

These references suggest that by the time of the US entry into World War I, those who worked with test data had some familiarity with both the linear and the equipercentile methods of scaling the scores from different tests. von Davier, Holland, and Thayer (2004b) quoted Kelley (1923) to indicate that he was aware of the dual influence of examinee ability and test difficulty on test scores and this needed to be accounted for in scaling tests.

The goal of scale aligning is to transform the scores from two different tests onto a common scale. Scaling transformations take scores from two different tests, **X** and **Y**, and put them onto a common scale. Such aligned scales imply an indirect linking of the scores on **X** and **Y**. More specifically, the implied linking is found by taking a score on **X**, transforming it to the common scale, and then inverting the **Y**-to-scale transformation to find the corresponding value for **Y**. The result is an indirect link from scores on **X** to those on **Y**. All methods of scale aligning can create indirect links between tests in this way.

It should be emphasized that although the implied indirect links always exists, their meaningfulness depends on many factors, and the indirect link is rarely the main purpose for putting **X** and **Y** onto a common scale.

The subcategories of scaling form a continuum starting with situations where the tests measure different constructs all the way to those where the tests measure similar constructs. The next five subsections briefly describe the six types of scaling along this continuum. Figure 2.3 illustrates the subcategories within the overall linking category of scale aligning.

2.3.1. Battery Scaling: Different Constructs and a Common Population of Examinees

When two or more tests that measure different constructs are administered to a common population, the scale scores for each test can be transformed to have a common distribution for this population of examinees (i.e., the *reference population*). Kolen (2004a) denoted this case as *battery scaling*. Battery scaling has been used for many years. Flanagan (1951) described it in an educational testing context, but its roots can be traced back at least to Kelley (1914), where the scores on the different tests were given the same mean and variance in the reference population. Kelley (1923) and Angoff (1971) referred to scores from tests that measure different constructs but that are scaled so that they have the same distributions on a common population as *comparable measures* (Kelley, 1923) or *comparable scores* (Angoff, 1971).

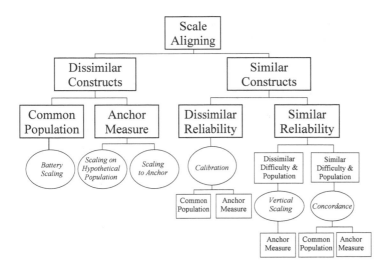

Figure 2.3. The types of linking method within the overall linking category of *scale*.

The data collected for battery scaling is usually either (a) a sample of examinees, all of whom take all of the tests, or (b) several equivalent (i.e., random) samples of examinees from a common population who take one or just some of the tests. In this way, all of the tests are taken by equivalent groups of examinees from the reference population. Thus, for each test being scaled, **Y**, the data can be used to estimate the cdf of **Y** over the reference population, **P**; that is,

$$F_{\text{YP}}(y) = \Pr\{\mathbf{Y} \leq y \mid \mathbf{P}\}. \tag{2.7}$$

Y is then put on the common scale by a transformation of the form

$$s = S(F_{\text{YP}}(y)), \tag{2.8}$$

where $S(u)$ is an arbitrary *scaling function* selected to give the scaled version of **Y** a particular distributional form. A common example of such a scaling function is the inverse of the Normal or Gaussian distribution so that the distribution of the scaled scores is approximately Gaussian (Kolen & Brennan, 2004).

The value of making the scales of different tests comparable in this special sense is that examinees will correctly interpret differences in the scores across the battery of tests. A higher score on one test will indicate better performance on that test when compared to a lower score on another test (relative to the population **P**). Effectively, comparing scaled scores becomes the same as comparing percentiles in the reference population when the scales have been aligned this way. Measures or scores on comparable scales could be useful for comparing the strengths and weaknesses of examinees who are similar to those in the reference population. For examinees who are different from those in the reference population, such interpretations might not be as useful.

Although the scales on the different tests are made comparable in this special sense, the tests measure different constructs. The implied indirect link between the scores on the different tests, described earlier, can be used to indicate comparable performance on the different tests (relative to the reference population), but it has no meaning as a way of transforming a score on a test of one construct into a score that is an appropriate measure for another construct.

The recentering of the SAT scale is an example of battery scaling (Dorans, 2002). The scales for the SAT-verbal (SAT-V) and SAT-mathematical (SAT-M) scores were redefined so as to give the scaled scores on the SAT-V and SAT-M the same distribution in a reference population of students tested in 1990. The redefined score scales replaced the original score scales, which had been defined for a reference population tested in 1941. The new score scales enable a student whose SAT-M score is higher than his SAT-V score to conclude that he/she did in fact perform better on the mathematical portion than on the verbal portion, at least in relation to the students tested in 1990. When the scales of tests are not aligned in this way, such inferences are not necessarily accurate. As the population of students taking the SAT becomes less like the reference population tested in 1990, the simple interpretation of better performance on one test compared to another, based solely on the scaled scores, will become less accurate. Finally, it should be obvious that the indirect link between the SAT-M and SAT-V has no meaning as a way of turning a score on one of these tests into a score on the other.

2.3.2. Anchor Scaling: Different Constructs and Different Populations of Examinees

An important approximation to battery scaling arises when two or more tests that measure different constructs are administered to *different* populations and a common measure (the *anchor measure*) is available for all of the examinees in these different populations. *Anchor scaling* refers to this general class of scaling method. Mislevy (1992) and Linn (1993) used the term *statistical moderation* to refer to cases of anchor scaling.

In the typical application of anchor scaling, it is possible for one or more of the tests being scaled to be completely inappropriate for the examinees taking some of the other tests. Language examinations provide good examples of this: A test of French is inappropriate for examinees who are unfamiliar with French. In other situations, examinees might choose which test to take based on the courses they have taken in school. Because of these selective factors, the samples of examinees taking the different tests are usually *not equivalent*, and the anchor measure is the information used to both measure and to adjust for this. Anchor scaling necessarily involves incomplete test data because some tests are given to certain subgroups of examinees, but not to all of them. Anchor scaling is an *approximation* to battery scaling because of the potential inequivalence of the samples of examinees taking each of the tests. In contrast, when different samples of examinees take different tests for battery scaling, these samples are designed to be *equivalent* samples of examinees.

The inequivalence of the samples used in anchor scaling requires the scaling methods used to make assumptions about the anchor measure that are not easily evaluated. The more strongly the anchor measure is related to the different tests being put on a common scale, the more satisfactory the resulting scale alignment will be, but other than that, little more can be said in general.

2.3.2.1. Scaling on a Hypothetical Population

There are two distinct ways that the anchor measure is used in anchor scaling. The first approach is very similar to projecting score distributions, discussed in Section 2.2. This approach has no commonly accepted name, so Holland and Dorans (2006) proposed identifying it as *scaling on a hypothetical population* (SHP). To outline this approach and to relate it to projecting score distributions, suppose that $\mathbf{Y}$ denotes a test to be scaled and $\mathbf{A}$ is the anchor measure. The data for the examinees taking $\mathbf{Y}$ and $\mathbf{A}$ are used to estimate the conditional distribution of $\mathbf{Y}$ given $\mathbf{A}$ in the population of examinees (denoted by $\mathbf{P_Y}$) who take test $\mathbf{Y}$. As indicated earlier, $\mathbf{P_X}$ and $\mathbf{P_Y}$ might be different for different tests, $\mathbf{X}$ and $\mathbf{Y}$. As in Section 2.2, denote the cdf of this conditional distribution by

$$\Pr\{\mathbf{Y} \leq y \mid \mathbf{A} = a, \mathbf{P_Y}\}. \tag{2.9}$$

Next, this estimated conditional distribution is averaged over a hypothetical distribution for $\mathbf{A}$, the distribution of $\mathbf{A}$ in the *hypothetical* population, $\mathbf{P}$, to obtain an estimate of the cdf of $\mathbf{Y}$ in the hypothetical $\mathbf{P}$; that is,

$$\Pr\{\mathbf{Y} \leq y \mid \mathbf{P}\} = \mathrm{E}[\Pr\{\mathbf{Y} \leq y \mid \mathbf{A}, \mathbf{P_Y}\} \mid \mathbf{P}]. \tag{2.10}$$

In Equation 2.10, the outer expectation is over the distribution of $\mathbf{A}$ in the hypothetical population. These cdfs are found for each of the tests being scaled. The estimated cdf for Y on the hypothetical population, defined in Equation 2.10, is then treated as if it is *the* cdf of Y on a common population. Once this is done, the problem is regarded as the simpler case of battery scaling and the same scaling techniques are used from that point forward.

As in the case of projection in Section 2.2, in order for Equation 2.10 to hold, a population invariance assumption, similar to Equation 2.6, must hold. The weaker the correlation between the anchor measure and the test, the less likely it is for this population invariance assumption to hold, even approximately.

It should also be pointed out here that there is nothing in the above analysis that requires the anchor measure to be a single score or number; it could involve more than one score, as the next example illustrates.

The construction of the hypothetical population is critical to the success of this method because the linking is population dependent. Although a variety of hypothetical populations might be posited in a particular setting, they are unlikely to be equally plausible. Great care needs to be exercised in the construction of the population.

An example of SHP is given by the scaling of the various subject area tests of the SAT. Typically, students take the SAT, and then some of them might take one or more subject tests. All of these scores are then presented as part of their college admissions materials, and the results of the subject tests for different examinees are treated as if they are on comparable scales. In this application, the SAT-V and SAT-M scores are used as the anchor measures. The hypothetical population is taken to be the population on which the SAT-V and SAT-M scales were established. SHP is closely related to poststratification equating, mentioned in Section 2.4.

2.3.2.2. Scaling to the Anchor

The second approach to anchor scaling also has no commonly accepted name, so Holland and Dorans (2006) identified it as *scaling to the anchor* (STA). In this approach, the data for the examinees taking test Y are used to estimate a function linking scores on Y to those on A using the data from P_Y. This is done for each of the tests to be scaled and these linking functions are used to put each of the tests onto the scale of the anchor measure. Strictly speaking, in order for STA to be valid, the estimated linking functions for each test should not depend on the choice of the population used for each linking. This is a population invariance assumption similar those mentioned in Section 2.4.3 for chain equating.

Linn (1993) indicated that the STA approach was used to bring comparability to scores on tests that are specific to particular schools in a school district. The anchor measure is a common districtwide examination score, and the scores from the locally developed tests in each school are put on a common scale using the STA approach to anchor scaling.

One difference between STA and SHP is that for STA, the measure needs to be a single score or number, whereas, indicated earlier, the SHP can operate on multiple sets of scores. See McGaw (1977) and Keeves (1988) for more discussion of STA, where it was referred to as an example of *moderation*.

2.3.3. Vertical Scaling: Similar Constructs and Similar Reliability, But Different Difficulty and Different Populations of Examinees

Tests of academic subjects targeted for different school grades might be viewed as tests of similar constructs that are intended to differ in difficulty—those for the lower grades being easier than those for the higher grades. It is often desired to put scores from such tests onto a common overall scale so that progress in a given subject can be tracked over time. This type of scaling is called *vertical scaling* (Kolen & Brennan, 2004). It has been called other things as well. For example, Angoff (1971) called it *calibrating tests at different levels of ability* and the term *vertical equating* is also used.

A topic, such as mathematics or reading, when considered over a range of school grades, has several subtopics or dimensions. At different grades, different aspects, or dimensions, of these subjects are relevant and tested. For this reason, the constructs being measured by the tests for different levels might differ somewhat, but the tests are often similar in reliability.

Vertical scaling shares some features with anchor scaling (Section 2.3.2). In particular, the tests to be scaled are, to some degree, inappropriate for all but one or a few grades, so the samples of examinees who take each test are not equivalent in the sense that they are for battery scaling (Section 2.3.1). However, due to the range of ages and grades that are usually involved, there is rarely an appropriate anchor measure that is available for every examinee. Instead, the tests given to neighboring grades might share some common material that can serve as an anchor test that connects a pair of tests for different grade levels but not all of the tests being scaled. This common material will be different for different pairs of tests given to neighboring grades. Methods such as SHP and STA, described briefly in Section 2.3.2, might be used to put the tests given to neighboring grades onto a common scale, and these can then be connected up to form an overall scale for the entire vertical system of tests. Item response theory (IRT) is also used to link these scales. See Kolen and Brennan (2004), Petersen, Kolen, and Hoover (1989), and the chapter by

Kolen (2006) for more discussions of these and other methods used in vertical scaling.

There is usually a close connection between the material tested in a given test and the curriculum for that grade. For this reason, vertical scaling might be sensitive to population differences, such as school grade or age. For example, scaling a fourth-grade reading test to a fifth-grade reading test on a sample of fifth graders is likely to disagree somewhat with the link obtained from a sample of fourth graders. For more discussion of these issues, see the chapter by Kolen (2006), as well as Harris, Hendrickson, Tong, Shin, and Shyu (2004), Hoover, Dunbar, and Frisbie (2001), and Kolen (2003). Chapters by Harris (Chapter 13), Patz and Yao (Chapter 14), and Yen (Chapter 15) discussed issues in vertical scaling in depth. For an illustration of vertical scaling, see Williams. Pommerich, and Thissen (1998).

Vertical scaling can be viewed as producing indirect links between the scores on the different levels of the tests, but these links are of less interest than the comparisons of scores on the same scale for the same student on the different tests in order to measure his or her learning and growth.

2.3.4. Calibration: Same Construct, Different Reliability, and the Same Population of Examinees

Kolen and Brennan (2004) indicated that in the test-linking literature, the term *calibration* is used in a variety of senses. In Angoff (1971), it referred to vertical scaling (Section 2.3.3). In Petersen et al. (1989), *calibration* referred to the estimation of item response theory (IRT) item parameters so that they were on a common scale. This usage is standard in the IRT literature (Lord, 1980; Thissen & Wainer, 2001; Yen & Fitzpatrick, 2006). In Linn (1993), *calibration* referred to methods of score linking for tests that measure the same constructs but that have different statistical characteristics—in particular, different reliability *or* difficulty.

Here the term *calibration* is used to refer to situations in which the tests measure the same construct, have similar levels of difficulty, but differ in reliability (usually test length). To add to the confusion, Angoff (1971) regarded this use of calibration as an example of *equating* tests of differing reliability; in this framework, *equating* is reserved for tests of equal or at least very similar reliability. The classic case of calibration in the sense used here is scaling the scores of a short form of a test onto the scale of its full or long form.

For calibration, there might be some ambiguity as to whether the linking is direct or indirect. The short form is often derived from the long form so that it usually makes more sense to scale from the less reliable test to the more reliable one than vice versa. It is intuitively obvious as well that simply putting the scores of the short form onto the scale of a more reliable long form cannot increase the actual reliability of the short form.

2.3.5 Concordances: Similar Constructs, Difficulty, and Reliability

Sometimes the tests to be linked all measure similar constructs, but they are constructed according to different specifications. In most cases, they are similar in test length and reliability. In addition, they often have similar uses and might be taken by the same examinees for the same purpose. The use of the linking is to add value to the scores on both tests by expressing them as if they were scores on the other test. Concordances represent scalings of tests that are very similar but that were not created with the idea that their scores would be used interchangeably. See Pommerich and Dorans (2004a) for a thorough discussion of many aspects of concordances.

Many colleges and universities accept scores on either the ACT® or SAT for the purpose of admissions decisions, and they typically have more experience interpreting the results from one of these tests than the other. Dorans, Lyu, Pommerich, and Houston (1997) reported a concordance table or function that linked the scores on each of these two tests to each other. This concordance was based on data from more than 100,000 examinees who had taken both tests within a restricted time frame. If their applicants were not widely different from those in this large sample, this concordance enabled admissions officers to align cut-scores on these two similar but somewhat different tests better than they could have using the limited data typically available to them.

Because the tests being linked measure somewhat different constructs and are constructed in different ways, concordances are potentially sensitive to the population of examinees whose data are used to estimate the concordance function. Dorans and Holland (2000) and Holland and Dorans (2006) argued that when the data indicate that substantially different concordance functions hold for large subpopulations of examinees (e.g., males and females), separate concordance functions ought to be considered for these groups, lest one group be disadvantaged by the use of a pooled concordance function for all. Dorans (2004d) discussed this point for the ACT and SAT. In practice, separate concordances might not be feasible for a variety of reasons, including a perceived unfairness in high-stakes uses of the tests.

Concordances are examples of scalings that produce direct links between the scores on the two tests.

Chapters by Pommerich (Chapter 11), Sawyer (Chapter 12), and Dorans and Walker (Chapter 10) addressed concordances in more detail. The chapters by Brennan (Chapter 9), Eignor (Chapter 8), and Liu and Walker (Chapter 7) addressed linking issues for testing programs in a state of transition, either with regard to mode of administration or test content. These linkages might be concordances, calibrations, or equatings.

2.4. Equating: Same Construct and the Same Intended Difficulty and Reliability

Equating is the third category of linking methods in this framework. All linking frameworks define equating as the strongest form of linking between the scores on two tests. In this chapter, equating represents the end point of a continuum that begins with methods that make no assumptions about the relationships between the tests being linked (prediction and battery scaling) and proceeds to methods that are appropriate for linking tests that are very similar (concordances and equating). Equating might be viewed as a form of scaling in which very strong requirements are placed on the tests being linked.

The purpose of equating is to allow the scores from each test to be used interchangeably, as if they had come from the same test. This purpose puts strong requirements on the two tests and on the method of linking. Among other things, the two tests must measure the same construct at similar levels of difficulty and reliability.

The earliest example of equating alternative forms of the same tests is not known to this author, but there is an early example of alternative forms that *were not equated*: the Army Alpha Test used by the American army during World War I. By the end of 1918, the army had tested over 1.7 million men using the Alpha and Beta. The Alpha was targeted for examinees who could read and write English and the Beta was for those who could not. Yoakum and Yerkes (1920) gave a detailed description of both instruments. They indicated that the Alpha had five different test forms: "To avoid . . . the risk of coaching, several duplicate forms of this examination have been made available" (p. 18). Thus, by this early date, test security issues had already led to the use of alternate forms, at least for the Alpha. Yoakum and Yerkes said little about how the alternate forms of the Alpha were constructed, but the following passage suggests that they used random assignment of test items to forms to help ensure the similarity of the alternate forms. "All five forms of the group examination were used in the pre official trial of the tests. The differences in forms were so slight as to indicate the success of the random method of selecting items" (p. 8).

Under appropriate conditions, assigning test items to forms at random will produce nearly parallel test forms that are similar but not identical in difficulty. In the next sentence, Yoakum and Yerkes indicated that the five forms were not exactly equivalent: "Form B proved more difficult than the other forms" (p. 8).

Nothing more is said about the issue of Form B's difficulty, and in all probability, scores on the different forms of the Alpha were treated as sufficiently similar so that they were not equated, even though the linear and equipercentile methods for doing so were known and available by that time.

Of greater concern to the army statisticians was the comparability of scores achieved on the Alpha and Beta versions of the test. A special sample of military personnel was tested with both, and these data were used to put the Alpha and Beta on a common 7-point scale (A, B, C+, C, C−, D, D−). Because these two tests were quite different in terms of format and questions asked, this was a case of battery scaling rather than of test equating. Indeed, Thorndike (1922) referred to three distinct scalings of the Alpha and Beta.

The example that Kelley criticized in 1914 was also a form of battery scaling rather than equating. The two methods of assessing handwriting were very different scoring methods and would not, in current terminology, be construed to be alternative forms of the same test. The problem that interested Pinter (1914) and Starch (1913) was to measure the accuracy/stability of these different handwriting measures. Kelley referred to an earlier work by Woodworth (1912), which used standard scores to combine the results of several tests. Otis (1918) was also interested in the problem of combining test results when the tests were on quite different subjects: spelling, arithmetic, synonyms, proverbs, and so forth. Thus, these early uses of comparable scores were not to equate scores in the sense used here, but, rather, as intermediate battery scalings needed to solve other problems.

Terman and Merrill (1937) discussed their revised edition of the Stanford-Binet test. Two alternative forms of the new edition were produced, but they were not equated directly. Rather, both were treated separately and the scores of each one put on the IQ scale using battery-scaling methods. In the next edition of the Stanford-Binet test, the second form was eliminated because it was rarely used.

Thus, the need, or at least the desire, to equate scores on alternate forms of the same test probably arose decades after the invention of scaling methods and of the two standard methods for equating: the linear and equipercentile methods. In 1938 two forms of the College Board's SAT tests were given in the same year, and the need to equate them became evident by 1940. Early versions of anchor-test equating were used to remove the effect of differential form difficulty for the SATs in 1941. In 1942 the SAT verbal and math scales were linked back to the verbal scale established in April 1941; all linkings subsequent to 1942 were equatings (Donlon & Angoff, 1971; Dorans, 2002). Lord (1950, 1955) credited Ledyard R Tucker with devising the anchor-test methods used to equate the SATs during the 1940s; these methods, in various versions, continue to be used.

Test equating is a necessary part of any testing program that continually produces new test forms and for which the uses of these tests require the meaning of the score scale be maintained over time. Although they measure the same constructs and are usually built to the same test specifications or test blueprint, different editions or forms of a test almost always differ somewhat in their statistical properties. For example, one form might be harder than another, so without adjustments, examinees would be expected to receive lower scores on the harder form. A primary goal of test equating for testing programs is to eliminate the effects on scores of these unintended differences in test form difficulty. For many testing programs, test equating is necessary to be fair to examinees taking different test forms and to provide score-users with scores that mean the same thing, regardless of the tests taken by examinees (Angoff, 1971; Kolen & Brennan, 2004; Petersen et al., 1989).

In testing programs with high-stakes outcomes, it cannot be overemphasized how important it is that test equating be done carefully and accurately. The released scores are usually the most visible part of a testing program, even though they represent the end point of a long test production, administration, and scoring enterprise. An error in the equating function or score conversion function might change the scores for many examinees. The credibility of testing organizations has been called into question over test equating problems, in ways that rarely occur when, for example, flawed test questions are discovered in operational tests. Chapters 5, 6, and 4 by Cook, von Davier, and Petersen, respectively, in this volume addressed issues related to equating.

2.4.1. What Makes a Linking an Equating?

All forms of test score linking involve some of the same ingredients. These include (a) two or more tests and rules for scoring them, (b) scores on these tests from one or more samples of examinees, (c) an implicit or explicit population of examinees on which linking takes place, and (d) one or more methods of estimating or calculating the linking function. What distinguishes test equating from other forms of linking is its demanding goal of allowing the scores from both tests to be used interchangeably for any purpose.

In the context of a testing program that continually produces new test forms that are required to produce scores on the same scale, test equating is often regarded as the first part of a two-step process by which scores on new tests are put onto the reporting scale. The first step is the computation of the *equating function*, $y = e(x)$, that links the raw scores on a new test, $\mathbf{X}$, to those of an old test, $\mathbf{Y}$—the so-called *raw-to-raw equating*. The second step is the conversion of these equated $\mathbf{X}$ raw scores to the reporting scale. In practice, there is an old form conversion function that maps the raw scores of the old test, $\mathbf{Y}$, to the scale, call it $S = s(y)$. The old form conversion function is composed with the equating function, $e(x)$, to put the raw scores of $\mathbf{X}$ onto the reporting scale; that is, the new form conversion function is $s(e(x))$.

An alternative approach is to use the methods of IRT to find a direct conversion of $\mathbf{X}$-scores to the common IRT scale rather than going through an old test, $\mathbf{Y}$. This method, in principle, does not even require an old test, but could involve portions of several old tests. Discussion of this approach is beyond the scope of this chapter. Instead, the focus here is on equating functions.

Dorans and Holland (2000) outlined five requirements that are widely viewed as necessary for test equating to be successful. The order in which these requirements are listed corresponds roughly to the order of their appearance in the literature.

a. *The equal construct requirement*: The tests should measure the same constructs.
b. *The equal reliability requirement*: The tests should have the same reliability.
c. *The symmetry requirement*: The equating function for equating the scores of $\mathbf{Y}$ to those of $\mathbf{X}$ should be the *inverse* of the equating function for equating the scores of $\mathbf{X}$ to those of $\mathbf{Y}$.
d. *The equity requirement*: It should be a matter of indifference to an examinee to be tested by either one of two tests that have been equated.
e. *The population invariance requirement*: The choice of (sub)population used to estimate the equating function between the scores of tests $\mathbf{X}$ and $\mathbf{Y}$ should not matter; that is, the equating function used to link the scores of $\mathbf{X}$ and $\mathbf{Y}$ should be *population invariant*.

Both formal and informal statements of subsets of these five requirements appeared in a variety of earlier sources, including Lord (1950), Angoff (1971), Lord (1980), Petersen et al. (1989), and Kolen and Brennan (2004). Kolen (Chapter 3, Section 3.2) pointed out the importance of common conditions of measurement as well as common content as a requirement for equating.

In practice, requirements (a) and (b) mean that the tests need to be built to the same specifications and administered under the same conditions of measurement, whereas requirement (c) precludes regression methods for predicting **Y**-scores from **X**-scores from being a form of test equating. Lord (1980) indicated that requirement (d) explains why both requirements (a) and (b) are needed. Requirement (d) is, however, hard to evaluate empirically and its use is primarily theoretical (Lord, 1980; Hanson, 1991). Furthermore, requirement (e), which is easy to use in practice, also can be used to explain why requirements (a) and (b) are needed (Holland & Dorans, 2006). Dorans and Holland (2000) used requirement (e) to develop quantitative measures of equitability. Their measures indicate the degree to which equating functions depend on the subpopulations used to estimate them.

The other cases of score linking are likely to violate at least one of the five requirements for equating. Concordances are used with tests that measure similar but different things and do not share common test specifications. Although they might have a similar difficulty and reliability, they will satisfy requirement (a) only approximately and this might be detected by the failure of requirement (e) and possibly requirement (d). Tests that are vertically scaled might be on such different aspects of a school subject that requirement (a) is not satisfied, at least when the gap between the grades is large and the differences in difficulty might be so great that, regardless of attempts to scale them appropriately, examinees will definitely prefer one test over the other, thus violating requirement (d) and probably requirement (e) as well. Calibrating a short form to a long form violates requirement (b) and is likely to violate requirements (d) and (e).

The tests that are scaled by either battery scaling or anchor scaling are usually measures of different constructs by design so that requirement (a) is not satisfied. Furthermore, scaling tests of different constructs will also tend to fail to satisfy requirements (d) and (e) for important subgroups of examinees. The direct and indirect linkings that arise in scaling are invertible, so requirement (c) is usually satisfied.

Finally, prediction methods need not satisfy any of the five requirements. The asymmetry between predictors and outcomes violates requirement (c). Furthermore, requirements (a) and (b), measuring the same construct and being equally reliable, affect only the quality of the prediction; less related or less reliable tests make poorer predictors of the scores on another test. Requirement (d) plays no role in prediction. Finally, it often makes sense to include subgroup membership as predictors to improve prediction. This incorporates population sensitivity directly into the prediction, whereas equating functions should not depend on subpopulations, according to requirement (e).

The difference between prediction and equating has been pointed out repeatedly over the last century. To give an example that shows how test equating and predicting can work together but do different things, suppose the scores from one testing program are used to predict some outcome variable, such as first-year college grades, using regression methods. In this case, the test score is being used as a predictor. It is routine to use the equated scores that come from different test forms as interchangeable values of the predictor. The predictions benefit from a prior test equating because test equating eliminates the need to distinguish between the scores on the various forms of the test that are used as predictors. This application occurs every time test scores from a testing program are used as predictors in validity studies. However, the predicted average grades from the test score would never be construed as an *equating* of test scores and first-year grades.

2.4.2. A Crucial Consideration for Scale Aligning and Equating

There is one common concern for all of the methods that are grouped under categories of scale aligning and equating. Appropriate attention must be given to the control of differential examinee ability in the linking process. To be clearer about this, suppose that two different tests are given to two different groups of examinees. In the two distributions of resulting scores, there are two ever-present factors that can influence the results, regardless of how similar the score scales of the tests appear. One is the relative *difficulty* of the two tests (which is what test scaling and equating is concerned about) and the other is the relative *ability* of the two groups of examinees on these tests (which is a confounding factor that should be eliminated in the linking process). In scaling and equating, the interest is in adjusting for differences in test characteristics and in controlling for possible examinee differences in ability when making these adjustments.

There are two distinct ways that the separation of test difficulty and differential examinee proficiency is addressed in practice. The first is to use a common population of examinees and the other is use an anchor measure. These approaches were mentioned in the discussion of scaling aligning in Section 2.3. Using the same examinees explicitly controls for differential examinee ability (i.e., they are the same examinees and have the same proficiencies). A variant of the use of a common set of examinees is to use two equivalent samples of examinees from a common population. On the other hand, when it is not possible to have samples of examinees from the same population, their performance on an anchor measure or set of common items can quantify the differences between two distinct, but not necessarily equivalent, samples of examinees. The use of an anchor measure leads to approaches that can be more flexible than the use of common examinees (Holland & Dorans, 2006).

2.4.3. A Brief Outline of Equating Methods

Numerous methods have been developed over the years for scaling and equating tests. In the next two subsections they are organized according to whether the data collection design involves a common population or common items. The focus here is on *observed-score procedures* that directly transform (or link) the scores on **X** to those on **Y**, because these methods are the most directly related to the estimation of equating functions. True-score methods are mentioned in passing. Kolen (Chapter 3, Section 3.5) provided a more extensive consideration of methods and data collection designs.

Figure 2.4 organizes the subcategories within the overall linking category of equating.

2.4.3.1. Procedures for Equating Scores on a Common Population

Holland and Dorans (2006) discussed three data collection designs that make use of a common population of examinees: the single group (SG), the equivalent group (EG), and the counterbalanced (CB) designs. They all involve a single population, **P**. Most of this section applies easily to both the EG and SG designs. The CB design is more complicated and is omitted; for more on the CB design, see Kolen (Chapter 3), von Davier et al. (2004b), Angoff (1971), and Kolen and Brennan (2004).

Several procedures have been developed for estimating equating functions using a common population. Underlying any linking method is a *target population* of examinees, following the usage in von Davier et al. (2004b). The target population is the population for which the equating function is supposed to apply. For data collection designs that use a common population, this is also the target population. In this chapter, **T** denotes the target population of examinees.

The cdf of the scores of examinees in the target population, **T**, on test **X** is denoted by $F_T(x)$; and it is defined as the proportion of examinees in **T** who score at or below x on test **X**. More formally, $F_T(x) = \Pr\{\mathbf{X} \leq x \mid \mathbf{T}\}$.

The equipercentile definition of *comparable scores* is that x (an **X**-score) and y (a **Y**-score) are *comparable* in **T** if $F_T(x) = G_T(y)$. This means that x and y have the same percentile in the target population, **T**. When the two cdfs are continuous and strictly increasing, the equation of $F_T(x)$ and

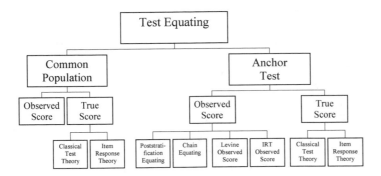

Figure 2.4. The types of linking methods within the overall linking category of *test equating.*

$G_T(y)$ can always be satisfied and can be solved for y in terms of x. This equipercentile function is used for equating, concordances, vertical scaling, battery scaling, and calibration. For equating, the influence of **T** should be small or negligible, and, in that case alone, the transformed **X**-scores are *interchangeable* with the **Y**-scores.

It is sometimes appropriate to assume that the two cdfs, $F_T(x)$ and $G_T(y)$, have the same shape and only differ in their means and standard deviations. In this case, it can be shown that the equipercentile function is the *linear linking function*. The linear linking function can also be derived as the transformation of **X**-scores that gives them the same mean and standard deviation on **T** as the **Y**-scores have.

The linear linking and equipercentile functions were introduced in the first two decades of the 20th century as methods of scale aligning. Both of these functions satisfy the symmetry requirement (c) of Section 2.4.1; that is, linking **Y** to **X** is the inverse function for linking **X** to **Y**.

The linear linking function can be viewed as the linear part of the equipercentile function (see von Davier et al., 2004b, for more details). The remainder is the nonlinear part of the equipercentile function. In the *kernel equating* method of equating (von Davier et al., 2004b), the equipercentile function and the linear linking function are shown to be two members of a two-parameter family of equipercentile functions that interpolate smoothly between these two special cases.

Although there is really only one linear linking function for the SG or EG designs, the equipercentile function can depend on how $F_T(x)$ and $G_T(y)$ are made continuous or *continuized*. Test scores are typically integers, such as number-right scores or rounded formula scores. Because of this, the inverse function is not well defined; that is, for many values of p, there is no score y for which $p = G_{\mathrm{T}}(y)$. This is not due to the *finiteness of real samples*, but, rather, to the *discreteness of real test scores*. To get around this, two methods of continuization of $G_{\mathrm{T}}(y)$ are in current use.

The first is very old (Otis, 1916) and uses linear interpolation to make $G_{\mathrm{T}}(y)$ piecewise linear and continuous; see Kolen and Brennan (2004). The second approach uses Gaussian kernel smoothing to continuize the discrete distributions; see Holland and Thayer (1989) and von Davier et al. (2004b). This results in a continuously differentiable $G_{\mathrm{T}}(y)$. Prior to continuizing the cdfs, several authors recommended presmoothing the discrete distributions of scores (Kolen & Brennan, 2004; Kolen & Jarjoura, 1987; Livingston, 1993; von Davier et al., 2004b). In presmoothing data, it is important to achieve a balance between a good representation of the original data and smoothness. Smoothness reduces sampling variability and a good representation of the data reduces the possibility of bias.

Levine (1955) used classical test theory to derive a procedure designed to equate the true scores of **X** to those of **Y**. For a more detailed discussion of true-score equating, see Kolen and Brennan (2004). Hanson's theorem (Holland & Dorans, 2006) uses classical test theory to formalize the first four equating requirements of Section 2.4.1 and from them to derive the linear equating function as the only linear solution. Holland and Dorans also showed how Hanson's theorem shows the relationship among the linear linking function, linear regression, and true-score equating in the case of calibration (Section 2.3.4).

Lord (1980) introduced nonlinear versions of true-score equating using IRT (Kolen & Brennan, 2004).

2.4.3.2. Procedures for Linking Scores Using Common Items

The use of common items to control for differential examinee ability arises when there are two populations of examinees, **P** and **Q**, rather than just one. In this situation, **X** and a set of common items (or anchor test) **A** are taken by examinees from **P** while **Y** and **A** are taken by examinees in **Q**. Examinees take **A** and either **X** or **Y**. This is called the nonequivalent groups with anchor test or NEAT design in Holland and Dorans (2006). Kolen (Chapter 3, Section 3.5) called it the common-item nonequivalent groups design. The NEAT design is widely used because it can give greater operational flexibility than the approaches using common examinees. Examinees need only take one test, and the samples need not be from a common population.

This flexibility comes with a price, however. For one, the target population is less clearcut for the NEAT design. Which is it, **P** or **Q** or something else? For another, the use of the NEAT design always involves making additional assumptions to allow for the missing data in the NEAT design: **X** is never observed in **Q** and **Y** is never observed in **P**.

Braun and Holland (1982) proposed that for the NEAT design, the target population be what they called the *synthetic population* created by weighting **P** and **Q**. They denoted the synthetic population by $\mathbf{T} = w\mathbf{P} + (1 - w)\mathbf{Q}$, which means that distributions (or moments) of **X** or **Y** over **T** are obtained by first computing them over **P** and **Q**, separately, and then averaging them with w and $(1 - w)$ to get the distribution or moments over **T**. The definition of the synthetic population forces the user to confront the need to create distributions (or moments) for **X** on **Q** and **Y** in **P**, where there are no data. This is why assumptions must be made about the missing data in the NEAT design.

There are three distinct sets of assumptions about the missing data that have been used to estimate observed-score equating functions for the NEAT design. These are the (a) *post-stratification equating* type, (b) *chain equating* type, and (c) *Levine* type discussed in detail in Holland and Dorans (2006). These three sets of assumptions all have the form that some aspect of the equating is the same for populations **P** and **Q**. The first two types of assumption can produce both the linear linking and equipercentile functions, whereas the Levine type, being based on classical test theory, only produces a linear function that need not be a linear linking function that describes the linear portion of the equipercentile function.

In general, the three sets of assumptions result in different equating functions; however, when $\mathbf{P} = \mathbf{Q}$, all three sets of assumptions result in the same linear or nonlinear equating functions.

For the NEAT design, there are also linear and nonlinear true-score equating functions available that use either classical test theory or IRT (Kolen & Brennan, 2004).

In the next chapter, Kolen describes various data collection designs and the methods used for equating and other types of linking in greater detail.

2.5. A Brief Note on the Theory of Equating

The theory underlying test equating has evolved slowly over the years. The methods called observed-score test equating can be viewed as simple adaptations of scale-aligning methods to the problem of equating tests. This includes the linear and equipercentile methods discussed in Section 2.3.1, as well as the methods adapted to the anchor-test designs discussed in Section 2.3.2. Levine (1955) was the first application of classical test theory to the problem of equating tests, and Lord (1980) first applied IRT to test equating. Other attempts to give a theoretical foundation to test equating include Morris

(1982), Hanson (1991), and van der Linden (2000). Hanson's theorem (Holland & Dorans, 2006) is the earliest result that derives an equating function from formalizations of conditions that are related to the five equating requirements in Section 2.3.1.

Flanagan (1951) was careful to indicate the potential sensitivity of linking functions to the groups and samples used to form them. He even went so far as to state, "Comparability which would hold for all types of groups—that is general comparability between different tests, or even between various forms of a particular test—is strictly and logically impossible" (p. 758). This negative position is rather different from that taken later by Angoff (1971), who stated that equating relationships should be population invariant, or in his words, "...the resulting conversion should be independent of the individuals from whom the data were drawn to develop the conversion and should be freely applicable to all situations" (p. 563). Thus, both the requirement of population invariance for equating and its denial have roots that are at least 50 years old. See Kolen (2004b) for more on the history of population invariance and test equating. See also Chapters 6, 4, 12, and 10 by von Davier, Petersen, Sawyer, and Dorans and Walker, respectively, in this volume for discussions of what to do if population invariance fails to be met.

Acknowledgments. Many colleagues have helped me learn about test equating and scaling. Perhaps the most important is my colleague and co-author Neil Dorans, who has been a strong source of information and opinion for many years. In writing this chapter, I have borrowed heavily from parts of our chapter on linking and equating for the fourth edition of *Educational Measurement.* Many thanks go to Robert Brennan, Michael Kolen, Nancy Petersen, Mary Pommerich, and to my ETS colleagues, Tim Davey, Alina von Davier, Daniel Eignor, Kim Fryer, and Samuel Livingston, for their detailed reviews and comments on the material that led to this chapter.

3   Data Collection Designs and Linking Procedures

Michael J. Kolen[1]

The University of Iowa

3.1. Introduction

Scores on tests are linked using statistical procedures on data that have been collected in a systematic way. The outcome of a linking study is one or more statistically based linking functions that relate scores on one test or form to scores on another test or form. The purposes of the present chapter are to describe commonly used designs for collecting data and statistical procedures for linking scores.

The score linking situations considered are those in which scores from the tests or forms to be linked are expressed on a common metric and used for common purposes. These situations are restricted in this chapter to the linking of tests that are intended to measure the same or similar constructs. With reference to the Holland and Dorans (2006) and Holland (Chapter 2) description of types of linking method, only test form equating and concordance are considered. Predicting and scale aligning for tests measuring dissimilar constructs and vertical scaling in the Holland and Dorans (2006) and Holland (Chapter 2) framework were not considered. Vertical scaling was considered further in Patz and Yao (Chapter 14), Harris (Chapter 13), and Yen (Chapter 15). Linkages involving aggregate-level data are not addressed in this chapter. The interested reader should consult chapters by Thissen (Chapter 16), Braun and Qian (Chapter 17), and Koretz (Chapter 18).

---

[1] The opinions expressed in this chapter are those of the author and not necessarily of the University of Iowa.

In this chapter, the features of testing situations that influence linking are described. Equating and linking tests that are intended to measure similar constructs are distinguished. Common data collection designs and their variants for equating and for linking tests that are intended to measure similar constructs are considered. Statistical linking methods are described.

3.2. Features of Testing Situations

There have been various frameworks developed in recent years for distinguishing among and developing terminology for different types of linking (e.g., Feuer et al., 1999; Holland, Chapter 2; Holland & Dorans, 2006; Kolen & Brennan, 2004, Chapter 10; Linn, 1993; Mislevy, 1992; and the special issue of *Applied Psychological Measurement* edited by Pommerich & Dorans, 2004). The Holland and Holland and Dorans frameworks are the most up-to-date. Even these frameworks, and the associated terminology, do not emphasize important features of linking situations that are important for discussing linking designs and methods. For this reason, notation and terminology used in this chapter are in some cases different from those in typical usage.

In distinguishing among linking designs, it is important to acknowledge that the entire context of test administration affects scores on tests and can influence linking functions. For the purposes of this chapter, these features are considered in three categories: test content, conditions of measurement, and examinee population.

3.2.1. Test Content

An examinee's score on a test depends on the content of the test. Test content is considered broadly here as tasks that are presented to examinees. Standardized tests are developed with clearly defined content and statistical specifications that delineate the content areas, intended cognitive complexity, and item types to be included on a test. Features such as length of reading passages, complexity of diagrams, specifications for writing prompts, and so forth are carefully delineated in such specifications. Test specifications are an essential blueprint for test construction that provides an operational definition of test content.

3.2.2. Conditions of Measurement

Scores also depend on the conditions under which the test is administered, referred to here as *conditions of measurement*. Some of these conditions are under the control of the test developer, such as the instructions, booklet layout, answer sheet design, timing, scoring procedures, aids such as calculators, mode of administration (e.g., computer or paper-and-pencil), how items are displayed on a computer screen, and so forth. Conditions of measurement not under the direct control of the test developer include the stakes associated with test performance, the reasons an examinee is taking a test, and the type of test preparation activities.

3.2.3. Examinee Population

In aggregate, scores on tests differ for different examinee populations, such as those defined by gender, race, geographic region, or month of administration. Linking functions can differ from one examinee population to the next. Recent work has been done on examining the dependence of linking functions on examinee population. Much of this work was summarized in the special issue of the *Journal of Educational Measurement* edited by Dorans (2004a).

3.2.4. Construct Measured

The construct measured by a test clearly depends on the content of the test. The construct also depends on the conditions of measurement. For example, a test given under highly speeded administration conditions likely measures a different construct than a test given with ample time for all examinees to finish. The construct also can depend on the examinee population. For example, an English language reading comprehension test would likely measure a different construct for English language learners than for native English speakers.

3.3. Types of Linking Considered

Alternate forms of a test are built to the same test specifications. Alternate forms have nearly identical content features and differ only in the particular items that appear on the alternate forms. In operational administrations, alternate forms typically are administered under common conditions of measurement. As the term is used in the present chapter, *test form equating* can be conducted when the test content and conditions of administration for the alternate forms to be equated are held constant. Using this restrictive definition of equating, scores on alternate forms of carefully constructed multiple-choice tests, such as the ACT® assessment multiple-choice tests, can be equated. Equating designs and methods were also considered in Cook (Chapter 5, Section 5.2), von Davier (Chapter 6, Section 6.2), Holland (Chapter 2, Section 2.4.3), and Petersen (Chapter 4).

By this definition of equating, the term *equating* is *not* appropriate for linking tests that are intended to measure similar constructs. Situations that are *not* equating include linking scores on tests that differ in content and/or conditions of measurement.

Table 3.1 provides some examples of linking situations. The upper left-hand cell of this 2 × 2 table illustrates equating, where the content and conditions of measurement are the same for the tests to be linked.

The lower right-hand cell gives situations in which both the content and conditions of measurement are not the same. This situation is typical of many in which scores on tests that are intended to measure similar constructs are linked. For example, linking scores on the mathematics test of the ACT assessment to scores on the mathematics test of the SAT® involves tests of somewhat different content that are administered under somewhat different conditions of measurement. These sorts of linking have traditionally been referred to as concordances and they are considered in Dorans and Walker (Chapter 10), Pommerich (Chapter 11), and Sawyer (Chapter 12).

Some situations exist in which the tests differ in conditions of measurement but not in content. Examples are given in the lower left-hand portion of Table 3.1. One example is linking scores on a linear computer-based test and a paper-and-pencil test, where the same items are given in the two administration modes. This sort of situation was considered further in Eignor (Chapter 8) and Brennan (Chapter 9). There are also situations in which tests differ in content but not in conditions of measurement. Examples are given in the upper right-hand portion of Table 3.1. One example is the revision of test content specifications when there are no changes in administration conditions. This sort of situation was considered further in Liu and Walker (Chapter 7) and Brennan (Chapter 9).

All of the situations just mentioned are referred to in this chapter as examples of *linking tests intended to measure similar constructs*. In the Holland and Dorans (2006) and Holland (Chapter 2) linking categorization, the upper left-hand cell of Table 3.1 is referred to as test equating. The other three cells describe variations of what is referred to as scale aligning. In the Holland and Dorans (2006) and Holland (Chapter 2) linking categorization, equating is said to produce equivalence tables, whereas scale aligning is said to produce concordance tables.

Table 3.1. Examples of situations for linking scores on tests that differ in content and/or conditions of measurement

		Content	
		Same	Not same
Conditions of measurement	Same	Alternate forms of multiple-choice tests of the ACT Assessment	Old and new versions of a test when there has been a shift in test content, but not in administration conditions
		Alternate forms of the multiple-choice tests of the SAT	Scores for examinees who choose to take different questions on a test that allows examinee choice about which questions to answer
	Not Same	Computer-based linear and paper-and-pencil tests, when no changes are made to test content	ACT Assessment and SAT Reading achievement tests from two different publishers
		A constructed response test before and after a change in scoring rubric, assuming that the examinees are unaware of the change	Computer-adaptive and paper and-pencil tests. Tests administered in different languages

3.4. Linking Functions and Features of Testing Situations

Linking functions depend on the content of the tests, the conditions of measurement, and the population features of linking situations. The designs for data collection for linking exert control over these features of the testing situation.

Consider that scores on Test X and Test Y are to be linked. A score on Test X is represented by X and a score on Test Y is represented by Y. Linking functions depend on the content of Test X, CX, and the content of Test Y, CY. Linking functions also can depend on the population of examinees. In most situations, examinees for a linking study are sampled from an actual population, P, that differs from the target population, T, on which the linking function is ideally defined.

Linking functions also can depend on the conditions of measurement for Test X, *MX*, and Test Y, *MY*. The conditions of measurement in linking studies can differ from conditions of measurement that are considered ideal, *IX* for Test X and *IY* for Test Y.

To emphasize that linking functions can depend on all of the features of testing situations, the statistical notation for linking functions used in this chapter carries all of these important features. Consider a study in which data are collected and scores on Test X and Test Y are linked. In this study, the random-variable test score on Form X with content *CX* administered under conditions of measurement *MX* is symbolized as $X_{CX,MX}$, with particular score (realization) $x_{CX,MX}$. For Test Y with content *CY* administered under conditions of measurement *MY*, the random variable is $Y_{CY,MY}$. Using *link* for a general linking function, the notation that is used to specify a function for linking scores on Test X to scores on Test Y in a particular population, *P*, is

$$link_{Y_{CY,MY}|P}(x_{CX,MX}).$$

This function can be read as a function in population *P* for linking a score on Test X with content *CX* administered under conditions of measurement *MX* to scores on Form Y with content *CY* administered under conditions of measurement *MY*. This notation makes it clear that the linking function depends on the examinee population, the content of each test, and the conditions of measurement for Test X and Test Y.

Now also consider a situation in which the conditions of measurement are ideal and the target population, *T*, is used to define the linking function. Using similar notational conventions, this ideal linking function is specified as

$$link_{Y_{CY,IY}|T}(x_{CX,IX}).$$

Thus, this ideal linking function can differ from the actual linking function,

$$link_{Y_{CY,MY}|P}(x_{CX,MX})$$

on the population of examinees and on the conditions of measurement for Test X and Test Y.

When scores on test forms are equated, it is assumed that the content of Form X is the same as the content for Form Y, so that

$$CX = CY = C.$$

When equating, it is also assumed that the conditions of measurement for Form X and Form Y are the same, so that

$$MX = MY = M .$$

When equating using operational administrations, it is assumed that the actual conditions of measurement are ideal, so that

$$MX = MY = IX = IY = I .$$

When scores on tests that are intended to measure similar constructs are linked, it is assumed that the content of Test X and Test Y are different, so that

$$CX \neq CY .$$

In these situations, it also is assumed that the conditions of measurement for Test X and Test Y are different, so that

$$MX \neq MY .$$

When scores on test forms are equated or scores on tests are linked using special administrations or data collections, it is assumed that the actual conditions of measurement are different from the ideal conditions of measurement so that

$$MX \neq IX , \; MY \neq IY , \text{ and } IX \neq IY .$$

Although likely oversimplifications, these assumptions are used to highlight the importance of test content and conditions of measurement and to help compare and contrast the various designs.

3.5. Linking Designs

Commonly used designs for data collection in equating (Kolen & Brennan, 2004) are considered in this section. Counterparts of these designs for linking tests that are intended to measure similar constructs, as well as some variations, are also considered. In this section, a design is discussed first as it is used in equating and then as its counterparts and variations are used to link tests intended to measure similar constructs.

3.5.1. Random Groups Design for Equating

The random groups design for equating is diagrammed in Figure 3.1. In this design, examinees are randomly assigned Form X or Form Y. A spiraling process is often used with this design. In one method for spiraling, the alternate forms are alternated when the forms are packaged. When the booklets are handed out, the first examinee receives Form X, the second examinee receives Form Y, the third examinee receives Form X, and so on. This process leads to comparable, randomly equivalent groups taking Form X and Form Y. With the random groups equating design, the tests can be administered during standard operational administration conditions. Holland (Chapter 2, Section 2.4.3) would consider this design to be a common population design.

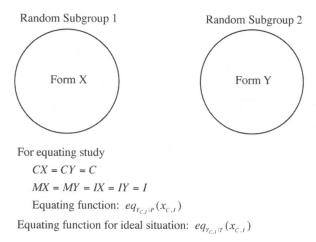

Random Groups Equating

Random Subgroup 1   Random Subgroup 2

Form X   Form Y

For equating study

$CX = CY = C$

$MX = MY = IX = IY = I$

Equating function: $eq_{Y_{C,I}|P}(x_{C,I})$

Equating function for ideal situation: $eq_{Y_{C,I}|T}(x_{C,I})$

Figure 3.1. Diagram for random groups equating design.

Because this is an equating, it is assumed that the content of Form X and Form Y is the same, so $CX = CY = C$, as indicated in Figure 3.1. In an equating study using this design, the conditions of measurement for Form X and Form Y typically are identical to one another when both forms are administered in the same testing rooms under operational testing conditions. Although situations exist to the contrary, the conditions of measurement are the same for Form X and Form Y and are considered ideal when the design is implemented in an operational administration. Thus, $MX = MY = IX = IY = I$, as indicated in Figure 3.1. Using eq to refer to an equating function, which is a special type of linking function, the actual equating function from the equating study is denoted $eq_{Y_{C,I}|P}(x_{C,I})$, and the ideal equating function is denoted as $eq_{Y_{C,I}|T}(x_{C,I})$, as shown in Figure 3.1. A comparison highlights that the conditions of measurement for the two forms are the same (and ideal) when equating with the random groups design. The only difference between the two equating functions is due to population. There is much evidence in the literature (see the special issue of the *Journal of Educational Measurement* edited by Dorans, 2004a) that equating functions depend little on population, so there is reason to expect that, in practice, the actual and ideal equating functions will be very similar.

In the random groups equating design, the difference between group-level performance on the two forms is taken as a direct indication of the difference in difficulty for the two forms. Various statistical procedures, which require only minimal statistical assumptions, are available to estimate equating functions that equate scores on Form X and Form Y.

3.5.2. Random Groups Design and Variations for Linking

A random groups design can be implemented for linking tests that are intended to measure similar constructs. This design is illustrated in Figure 3.2. One way that Figure 3.2 differs from Figure 3.1 is that *test* replaces *form*. To apply this design to linking, examinees are randomly assigned to be administered Test X and Test Y. Holland (Chapter 2, Section 2.4.3) would consider this design to be a common population design.

Random Groups Linking

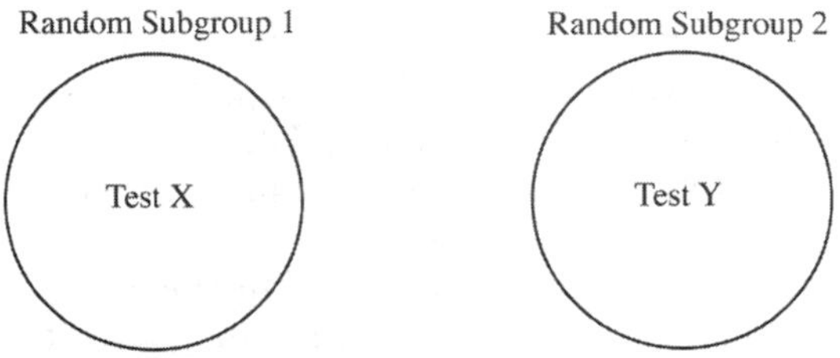

Random Subgroup 1   Random Subgroup 2

Test X   Test Y

For linking study
$CX \neq CY$
$MX \neq MY, MX \neq IX, MY \neq IY, IX \neq IY$
Linking function: $link_{Y_{CY,MY}|P}(x_{CX,MX})$
Linking function for ideal situation: $link_{Y_{CY,IY}|T}(x_{CX,IX})$

Figure 3.2. Diagram for random groups linking design.

Compared to random groups equating, the random assignment can be much more difficult to implement when the conditions of measurement for Test X and Test Y differ. For example, if the time limits for Test X and Test Y differ, it would be difficult to administer both tests in the same room. As another example, it would be difficult to administer a computer-based test and a paper-and-pencil test in the same room. In these linking situations, examinees could be assigned to take Test X or Test Y ahead of time. Students assigned to Test X would take the test in one room and students assigned to Test Y would take the test in another room.

Given these administration complications, Test X and Test Y, in general, cannot be administered in a standard operational administration when using this design. In this case, a special linking administration is needed. If the conditions of measurement in the linking study differ from those used operationally, then the conditions of measurement in the linking study likely differ from the ideal conditions of measurement. In addition, the examinees included in the linking study, out of necessity, might not be representative of the target population of examinees.

For the linking design illustrated in Figure 3.2, it is assumed that Test X and Test Y differ in content, so $CX \neq CY$. In addition, the conditions of measurement for Test X and Test Y differ from one another because each test is different and each is administered under its own conditions of measurement. Because the linking typically requires a special data collection, the conditions of measurement likely differ from ideal conditions of measurement. Thus, as indicated in Figure 3.2, in general, $MX \neq MY$, $MX \neq IX$, $MY \neq IY$, and $IX \neq IY$. The linking function from the linking study, $link_{Y_{CY,MY}|P}(x_{CX,MX})$, can differ from the ideal linking function, $link_{Y_{CY,IY}|T}(x_{CX,IX})$, due to differences in content, differences in conditions of measurement for the tests, and differences in population. When Test X and Test Y differ in content, there is evidence in the literature to suggest that the linking relationship will depend on the population (see the special issue of the *Journal of Educational Measurement* edited by Dorans, 2004a).

To avoid the problems of having to assign students within a school to take different tests, a variation of this design is sometimes used where random assignment is conducted at the school level. This design is referred to as the *random groups design—randomization by school*. In this variation, a list of schools to be included in the study is constructed and the schools are randomly assigned to take either Test X or Test Y. Note that the unit of randomization is the school. To achieve reasonable linking precision, the number of students that must be tested is, in general, too large to be practicable.

3.5.3. Single Group Design with Counterbalancing for Equating

The single group design with counterbalancing for equating is illustrated in Figure 3.3. In this design, each examinee takes Form X and Form Y, in counterbalanced order. Counterbalancing is needed because examinee performance can differ depending on whether a form is taken first or second, due to such factors as practice and fatigue. One randomly chosen subgroup of examinees is administered Form X first. A second randomly chosen subgroup is administered Form Y first. Holland (Chapter 2, Section 2.4.3) would consider this design to be a common population design.

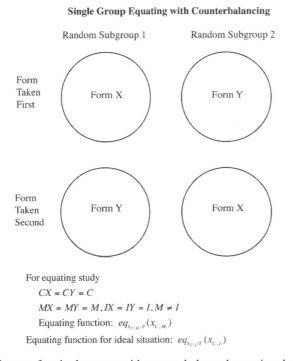

Single Group Equating with Counterbalancing

Random Subgroup 1   Random Subgroup 2

Form Taken First   Form X   Form Y

Form Taken Second   Form Y   Form X

For equating study

$CX = CY = C$

$MX = MY = M, IX = IY = I, M \neq I$

Equating function: $eq_{Y_{C,M}|P}(x_{C,M})$

Equating function for ideal situation: $eq_{Y_{C,I}|T}(x_{C,I})$

Figure 3.3. Diagram for single group with counterbalanced equating design.

A special study is required when using this design, because examinees normally do not take two test forms in operational administrations. One way to administer the forms in this design is to construct test booklets that contain both forms. Half of the booklets contain Form X followed by Form Y. The other half of the booklets contains Form Y followed by Form X. The booklets are packaged in a spiraled manner and distributed in such a way that the first examinee in a room is administered Form X first followed by Form Y, the second examinee is administered Form Y followed by Form X, and so forth. The first and second forms are administered under separate time limits.

Refer again to Figure 3.3. The portion of the design labeled *form taken first* is identical to the random groups design shown in Figure 3.1. Thus, equating could be conducted using only the form taken first. To take full advantage of this design, data from the *form taken second* are used. However, the form taken second is administered under atypical conditions of measurement. In practice, examinees do not take two forms of a test. Thus, the data on the test taken second can be used only if the equating relationship for the form taken second can be shown to be the same as the equating relationship for the form taken first. If these equating relationships differ, then a *differential order effect* is said to occur. If this effect is substantial, then the data on the test administered second might need to be disregarded.

When alternate forms of a test are equated, there is little reason to expect that differential order effects occur because the content of the two forms is the same and the only difference in conditions of measurement is test order. When a differential order effect does not exist, the data from the two orders can be pooled. In this case, each examinee has scores on two forms, and serves as his or her own control. Consequently, for a particular sample size, this design leads to much more precise estimates of equating relationships than does the random groups design.

The single group design with counterbalancing is administered in a special study, which can lead to the conditions of measurement for this design being different from those for an operational administration. These different conditions of measurement can lead to differences between the equating function estimated in this design and the ideal equating function.

When equating with this design, it is assumed that the content of the two forms is the same, so $CX = CY = C$, as indicated in Figure 3.3. Assume that there is no differential order effect, so that the conditions of measurement for Form X and Form Y are considered the same. Thus, as indicated in Figure 3.3, $MX = MY = M$, where M represents the conditions of measurement in the study. In the ideal situation, $IX = IY = I$, where I represents the ideal conditions of measurement. Because a special study is used, the conditions of measurement for the study likely are different from the ideal conditions of measurement. Thus, in general, with this design, $M \neq I$. In this situation, as indicated in Figure 3.3, the equating function for an equating study is denoted as $eq_{Y_{C,M}|P}(x_{C,M})$ and the ideal equating function is denoted as $eq_{Y_{C,I}|T}(x_{C,I})$.

This notation illustrates that the equating function for the equating study differs from that for the ideal equating function due to differences in conditions of measurement and differences in examinee population.

In some situations, what Holland (Chapter 2, Section 2.4.3), Holland and Dorans (2006), and Kolen and Brennan (2004) referred to as a single group design might be considered. In the single group design, examinees are administered the two tests to be equated, but the order of administration is not counterbalanced. The portion of Figure 3.3 for random subgroup 1 is an example of this design, where all of the examinees take Form X followed by Form Y. When order effects exist, there is no way to estimate their magnitude or to adjust the equating relationship for the effect of order when using the single group design. Thus, it is difficult to justify the use of the single group design in practical equating contexts.

3.5.4. Single Group Design with Counterbalancing and Variations for Linking

The single group design with counterbalancing for linking is illustrated in Figure 3.4. One way that Figure 3.4 differs from Figure 3.3 is that *test* replaces *form*. In this linking design, the content of the two tests is assumed to differ, so $CX \neq CY$, as indicated in the figure. This design can be particularly difficult to administer when linking two tests that are intended to measure similar constructs. Typically, in this situation the conditions of measurement are different for the two tests (i.e., $MX \neq MY$), so it is not possible to administer both tests in the same room. Holland (Chapter 2) would consider this design to be a common population design.

For example, suppose that Test X is a paper-and-pencil test and Test Y is a computer-based test. It likely would not be feasible to administer both modes in the same testing room at the same time. Instead, examinees are assigned to condition ahead of time, and special procedures are used for when and how the examinee takes each of the assigned tests in the order required by the design.

Proper administration of this design requires that examinees be randomly assigned to condition (*test taken first*) and that the tests be administered appropriately. In addition, it is necessary to assess whether differential order effects occur. It seems much more likely that differential order effects will be present when linking tests that are intended to measure similar constructs than when equating test forms, because the conditions of measurement for the two tests differ. For example, the effect of first taking a computer-based test on subsequent scores on a paper-and-pencil test likely differs from the effect of first taking a paper-and-pencil test on subsequent scores on a computer-based test. If so, then a differential order effect occurs, and the data for the test taken second might need to be disregarded. However, disregarding data from the test administered second leads to a serious loss in linking precision.

As indicated near the bottom of Figure 3.4, when linking Test X to Test Y using the single group design with counterbalancing for linking and its variations, test content differs, the conditions of measurement differ for Test X and Test Y, and these conditions of measurement differ from the ideal conditions of measurement. Also, as indicated at the bottom of Figure 3.4, the linking function from the study, $link_{Y_{CY,MY}|P}(x_{CX,MX})$, differs from the ideal linking function, $link_{CY,IY|T}(x_{CX,IX})$, due to differences in content, differences in conditions of measurement for the tests, and differences in examinee population.

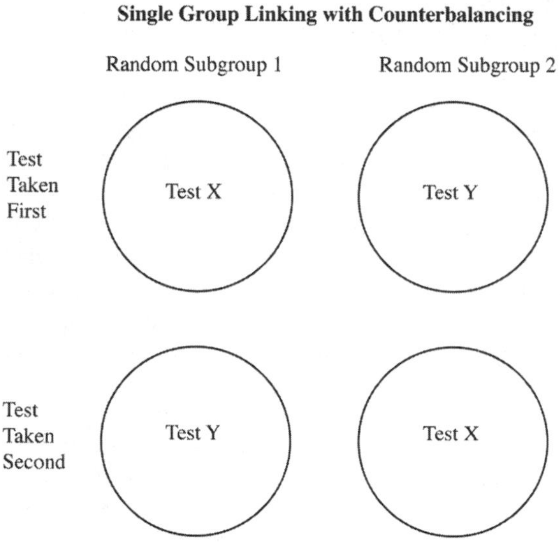

Single Group Linking with Counterbalancing

Random Subgroup 1   Random Subgroup 2

Test Taken First   (Test X)   (Test Y)

Test Taken Second   (Test Y)   (Test X)

For linking study

$CX \neq CY$

$MX \neq MY, MX \neq IX, MY \neq IY, IX \neq IY$

Linking function: $link_{Y_{CY,MY}|P}(x_{CX,MX})$

Linking function for ideal situation: $link_{Y_{CY,IY}|T}(x_{CX,IX})$

Figure 3.4. Diagram for single group with counterbalancing linking design.

Because of the serious practical difficulties in administering the single group design with counterbalancing in many linking situations, variations of this design often are used in practice. In one variation, the random assignment to condition is done by school. This design is referred to here as the *single group design with counterbalancing for linking—randomization by school*. For example, using a random selection procedure, one set of schools is assigned to be administered Test X first and a second set of schools is assigned to be administered Test Y first. In this case, school is the unit of randomization, which leads to substantial loss of precision when assessing whether there is a differential order effect. If a differential order effect cannot be ruled out, then a linking function calculated by pooling data would not necessarily control for differences in conditions of measurement for the ideal as compared to the actual linking functions.

Another variation of this design is one in which examinees are found who have taken both of the tests to be linked, with examinees found who have taken the tests in both orders. This design is referred to here as the *single group design with counterbalancing for linking—naturally occurring groups*. This sort of design is used, for example, to link scores on the ACT assessment to scores on the SAT exam. Pommerich (Chapter 11), Dorans and Walker (Chapter 10), and Sawyer (Chapter 12) considered situations in which this design is used. In this design, some examinees are found who have taken one test first and other examinees are found who have taken the other test first. The time between administrations can vary, as can the test forms. In addition, the population of examinees who take the two tests can differ considerably from the general population of test-takers. In this design variation, differences in conditions of measurement as compared to ideal conditions can differ widely and are, for the most part, uncontrolled.

The single group design, where all of the examinees take the tests in the same order, also might be considered for use in linking. If this design is used, the linking function will be affected by order effects by an unknown amount, making it difficult to justify the use of the single group design for linking.

3.5.5. Common-Item Nonequivalent Groups Design for Equating

The common-item nonequivalent groups design for equating is illustrated in Figure 3.5. This design is used when only one form can be administered per test date. In this design, Form X and Form Y have a set of items in common. Examinee Group 1 takes Form X and examinee Group 2 takes Form Y. The two groups of examinees might test on different test dates. With this design, examinee Group 1 is considered to differ systematically from examinee Group 2. This design was referred to as the nonequivalent groups anchor test (NEAT) design by Holland (Chapter 2, Section 2.4.3).

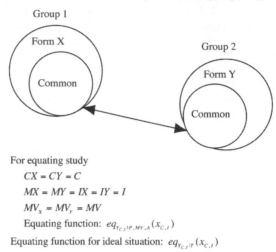

For equating study

$$CX = CY = C$$

$$MX = MY = IX = IY = I$$

$$MV_X = MV_Y = MV$$

Equating function: $eq_{Y_{C,I}|P,MV,A}(x_{C,I})$

Equating function for ideal situation: $eq_{Y_{C,I}|T}(x_{C,I})$

Figure 3.5. Diagram for common-item nonequivalent groups equating design.

This design has two variations. When the score on the set of common items contributes to the examinee's score on the test, the set of common items is referred to as internal. Typically, these items are interspersed among other scored items. When the score on the set of common items does not contribute to the examinee's score, the set of items is referred to as external. Typically, external common items are administered in a separately timed section.

Scores on the common items provide direct information on how the performance of examinee Group 1 differs from the performance of examinee Group 2. The set of common items is chosen to proportionally represent the total test forms in content and statistical characteristics. To ensure that the common items behave the same way on the two forms, each of the common items is identical on the two forms and is in a similar position in the test booklet.

When conducting equating using this design, strong statistical assumptions are required to disentangle form differences from examinee group differences. Especially when there are large group differences, the set of assumptions chosen can have a substantial effect on the equating results.

Because this is an equating study, the content of Test X and Test Y are the same (i.e., $CX = CY = C$) as shown in Figure 3.5. The measurement conditions for Form X and Form Y often can be considered to be the same and ideal when this design is conducted in operational administration so that $IX = IY = MX = MY = I$, as indicated in Figure 3.5.

The actual equating relationship depends on the set of common items. Let V represent score on the common items, let MV_X represent the conditions of measurement for the common items as administered with Form X, and let MV_Y represent the conditions of measurement for the common items as administered with Form Y. Assume that the context of the common items is the same for Form X and Form Y and that the common items accurately reflect the content of the total scores. In this case, it seems reasonable to assume that the conditions of measurement are the same for the common items, regardless of test form. Denoting the common conditions of measurement as MV ($MV_X = MV_Y = MV$). The actual equating relationship also depends on the set of assumptions that are made, denoted as A.

Notation for the equating function is expressed in Figure 3.5 as $eq_{Y_{C,I}|P,MV,A}(x_{C,I})$. The ideal equating function does not depend on the common items, because it is a relationship between scores on Form X and Form Y. So, the ideal equating function is expressed as $eq_{Y_{C,I}|T}(x_{C,I})$ in Figure 3.5. Comparing these two functions highlights that the conditions of measurement for the two forms are the same (and ideal) when equating with this design using operational administrations. The diffcrences between the two equating functions are due to differences in population and the statistical assumptions used to estimate the equating function.

3.5.6. Anchor-Test Nonequivalent Groups Design for Linking

The *anchor-test nonequivalent groups design* illustrated in Figure 3.6, used to link tests that are intended to measure similar constructs, has similarities to the common-item nonequivalent groups design. In this design, Test X is administered to one group, Test Y is administered to a second group, and an anchor test, Test V, is administered to both groups. A major requirement in the common-item nonequivalent groups design for equating is that the content of the common items adequately represents the content of Form X and Form Y. When the content of Test X and Test Y differ, it is impossible for the common items to adequately represent the content of both Tests X and Y. Thus, the common-item nonequivalent groups design cannot be used when linking tests that are intended to measure similar constructs. Instead, the anchor-test nonequivalent groups design, which does not require that the anchor test have the same content as Test X and Test Y, is used. Linking using this design would fall under the category *concordance* using an anchor measure in the framework presented by Holland (Chapter 2).

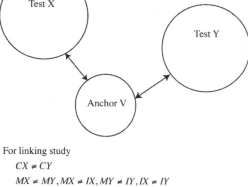

For linking study

$CX \neq CY$

$MX \neq MY, MX \neq IX, MY \neq IY, IX \neq IY$

$MV_X = MV_Y = MV$

Linking function: $link_{Y_{CY,MY}|P,MV}(x_{CX,MX})$

Linking function for ideal situation: $link_{Y_{CY,IY}|T}(x_{CX,IX})$

Figure 3.6. Diagram for anchor-test nonequivalent groups linking design.

In the anchor-test nonequivalent groups design, it is crucial that the conditions of measurement for the anchor test are the same for the group taking Test $X(MV_X)$ and Test Y (MV_Y). Otherwise, examinee group differences are completely confounded with differences in conditions of measurement for the two groups. So, in Figure 3.6, $MV_X = MV_Y = MV$.

In linking using this design, the conditions of measurement for Test X and Test Y typically differ from one another. In these studies, the conditions of measurement for Test X and Test Y also could differ from ideal conditions of measurement. For this reason, the actual linking function in Figure 3.6 is $link_{Y_{CY,MY}|P,MV,A}(x_{CX,MX})$. The ideal linking function in Figure 3.6 is $link_{Y_{CY,IY}|T}(x_{CX,IX})$, which makes explicit that the ideal conditions of measurement for Test X can differ from the ideal conditions of measurement for Test Y. By comparing these functions, it can be seen that the actual function can differ from the ideal function due to differences between the actual and the ideal conditions of measurement for Test X, differences between the actual and the ideal conditions of measurement for Test Y, and differences in population. The assumptions

(A) can also contribute to differences between these two functions. As is made clear in the discussion of statistical methods later in this chapter, it is unlikely that the statistical assumptions made in this linking design hold in situations where Test X and Test Y differ in content and the group of examinees taking Test X differs substantially from the group of examinees taking Test Y.

3.6. Linking Procedures

In this section, statistical procedures for equating alternate forms and linking scores on tests intended to measure similar constructs are considered. Equating and linking methods were described in detail elsewhere (e.g., Holland & Dorans, 2006; Kolen & Brennan, 2004), so only an overview is provided here.

As described earlier, the score linking situations considered were those in which scores from the tests or forms to be linked are expressed on a common metric and used for a common purpose. To address these situations, only *symmetric* statistical linking functions were considered (see Holland, Chapter 2).

In this section, overviews of traditional and item response theory (IRT) methods for equating are presented. Then the application of some the methods to linking tests that measure similar constructs is considered.

3.6.1. Traditional Statistical Methods for Equating

The intent of traditional methods of equating is for scores on alternate forms to have the same score distributional characteristics in a population of examinees, after the scores are transformed to a common scale. *Mean equating* results in scores having the same mean on the common scale. Using a linear transformation, *linear equating* results in scores having the same mean and standard deviation on the common scale. Using a nonlinear transformation, *equipercentile equating* results in scores on alternate forms having approximately the same score distribution on the common scale. Focus in this section is on equipercentile methods.

Equipercentile equating functions are defined for a population and for tests given under particular conditions of measurement. Define F_T as the cumulative distribution of scores on Form X in population T, G_T as the cumulative distribution of scores on Form X in population T, G_T^{-1} as the inverse of G_T, and $x_{C,I}$ and $Y_{C,I}$ as defined earlier. Based on results presented by Braun and Holland (1982), when scores are continuous, Form X and Form Y measure content *C*, and the forms are administered under ideal conditions of measurement *I*, the equipercentile equating function for population *T* can be expressed as

$$eq_{Y_{C,I}|T}\left(x_{C,I}\right) = G_T^{-1}\left[F_T\left(x_{C,I}\right)\right].$$ (3.1)

By substituting different subscripts in Equation 3.1, the function can be defined for other populations or for other conditions of measurement. For example, the equipercentile equating function for forms administered under other than ideal conditions of measurement, *M*, to examinees from population *P* is expressed as

$$eq_{Y_{C,M}|P}\left(x_{C,M}\right) = G_P^{-1}\left[F_P\left(x_{C,M}\right)\right].$$ (3.2)

Estimates of the cumulative distribution functions can be used with Equations 3.1 and 3.2 to produce an estimated equating function.

Because scores on tests typically are discrete, a procedure is used to *continuize* scores so that the equations can be applied. Traditionally, percentiles and percentile ranks are used to continuize scores. If scores are integers, percentiles and percentile ranks can be thought of as continuizing scores by uniformly spreading the score density at an integer score over the range $x - .5$ to $x + .5$. von Davier, Holland, and Thayer (2003) provided an alternate scheme for continuizing scores referred to as the *kernel method*. Using the kernel method, the score density at an integer score is spread using a Normal distribution. Either of these approaches leads to continuous scores that can be equated using Equations 3.1 and 3.2.

Smoothing methods often are used with estimates of equipercentile equating functions to reduce sampling error. In *presmoothing*, the score distributions are smoothed. The *log-linear smoothing method*, which is summarized by Kolen and Brennan (2004) and by von Davier et al. (2003), is an often-used presmoothing method. In *postsmoothing*, the equipercentile function is smoothed directly. The *cubic spline postsmoothing method* described by Kolen and Brennan is an often-used postsmoothing method.

3.6.1.1. Random Groups and Single Group with Counterbalancing Designs

After data are collected using the random groups design, equipercentile equating, continuization, and smoothing procedures are applied. For the single group design with counterbalancing, after deciding on whether data from the forms taken second can be used, similar procedures are followed.

3.6.1.2. Common-Item Nonequivalent Groups Design

Traditional equating methods using the common-item nonequivalent groups design (referred to as the NEAT design by Holland, Chapter 2) are more complicated. In this design, statistical assumptions are required to disentangle form and group differences.

In one class of methods, sometimes referred to as *poststratification methods*, the following nontestable assumptions are made: the regression of *X* on *V* is the same in examinee Group 1 and Group 2 and the regression of *Y* on *V* is the same in Group 1 and Group 2. In the *Tucker linear method*, assumptions are made regarding linear regressions. In the *frequency estimation equipercentile method*, assumptions are made regarding nonlinear regressions. A synthetic population is defined as a combination of the populations from which Group 1 and Group 2 are sampled. The equating function is based on this population. The assumptions made in poststratification methods seem less likely to hold when Group 1 and Group 2 differ substantially in proficiency.

Smoothing methods can be applied when conducting the frequency estimation equipercentile method. von Davier et al. (2003) summarized a log-linear smoothing in the context of the kernel method. Kolen and Brennan (2004) summarized a cubic spline postsmoothing method in which a cubic spline function is fit to the unsmoothed equipercentile equivalents.

In another class of methods for linear equating, referred to as *Levine methods*, an assumption is made that true scores on *X* and *V* in Group 1 are perfectly linearly correlated and that true scores on *Y* and *V* in Group 1 are perfectly linearly correlated. This assumption seems less likely to hold when the common items measure a construct that differs from the construct measured by the alternate forms.

A third class of traditional methods for the common-item nonequivalent groups design are *chained methods*. In these methods, *X* is linked to *V* in Group 1, *V* is linked to *Y* in Group 2, and these two linkings are chained together. A *chained linear method* and a *chained equipercentile method* have been developed.

3.6.2. IRT Statistical Methods for Equating

Unidimensional IRT models assume that examinee proficiency can be described by a single latent variable, θ, and that items can be described by a set of parameters or curves that relate proficiency to probability of correctly answering the item (Lord, 1980). Unidimensional IRT models have been developed for use with test items that are dichotomously scored or polytomously scored. IRT models are based on strong statistical assumptions. The θ-scale has an indeterminate location and spread. For this reason, one θ-scale sometimes needs to be converted to another linearly related θ-scale. If summed scores are to be used, there are two steps in IRT equating (Kolen & Brennan, 2004). First, the θ-scales for the two forms are considered to be equal or are set equal. Then summed score equivalents on the two forms are found.

In many situations, the parameter estimates for the two forms are on the same θ-scale without further transformation. The typical situation in which a transformation of the θ-scale is required is in the common-item nonequivalent groups design when Form X and Form Y parameters are estimated separately.

After the parameter estimates are on the same scale, *IRT true-score* and *IRT observed-score* methods can be used to relate summed scores on Form X to summed scores on Form Y. In IRT true-score equating, the true-score on one form associated with a given θ is considered to be equivalent to the true score on another form associated with that same θ.

Item response theory observed-score equating uses the item parameters estimated for each form along with the estimated distribution of ability for the population of examinees to estimate the distributions of summed scores for Form X and Form Y. Standard equipercentile equating procedures are used to equate these two smoothed distributions. As Holland and Dorans (2006) noted, IRT observed-score equating can be viewed as an equipercentile equating of presmoothed score distributions that are consistent with the assumptions of an item-level response model.

Any application of unidimensional IRT models requires that all of the items measure the same unidimensional proficiency, that the item responses are conditionally independent, and that the relationship between proficiency and probability of correct response follows the particular IRT model used.

3.6.3. Methods for Linking Tests Intended to Measure Similar Constructs

Tests intended to measure similar constructs often are linked using the same statistical methods used for equating. However, certain complications need to be addressed.

In some circumstances, when using equipercentile methods, presmoothing methods can be difficult to apply because the distributions might be expected to be irregular. For example, in linking scores on the ACT and SAT, integer-scale scores on the two tests are linked. For some test forms, the use of integer-scale scores can cause certain scale scores to be reported more often than adjacent scale scores because of the way the conversion to integers happens to be applied. In these situations, the scale score distribution is expected to be irregular. Such expected irregularities can lead to complications with presmoothing methods. For this reason, Kolen and Brennan (2004) used postsmoothing methods to link scale scores from different tests.

Item response theory methods can be used only in those situations in which the tests that are linked can be considered to measure the same proficiency and in situations in which item-level response data are available. For example, IRT methods would not be used to link ACT and SAT scores, because the tests do not measure the same proficiency and item-level data are typically unavailable when the tests are linked.

The statistical procedures for linking scores on tests intended to measure similar constructs with the anchor-test nonequivalent groups design (referred to as the NEAT design by Holland, Chapter 2) often are the same statistical procedures as those for equating alternate forms with the common-item nonequivalent groups design. In applying these procedures, it is important that the anchor test be administered under the same conditions of measurement for the two tests, otherwise the linking results will be misleading. For example, consider linking a paper-and-pencil to a computer-based test using the anchor-test nonequivalent groups design. Suppose that the examinees taking the computer-based test take the anchor test on the computer and that the examinees taking the paper-and-pencil test take the anchor test under paper-and-pencil conditions. In this case, group differences are completely confounded with mode of administration effects, and it is impossible to use data collected to disentangle these effects. To disentangle these effects, it would be necessary to administer the same anchor test to both groups under the same conditions of measurement. For example, a paper-and-pencil anchor test might be administered to both groups.

When using the anchor-test nonequivalent groups design, it is important to consider the effects of violations of statistical assumptions. Recall that poststratification methods require that regressions of X on V and Y on V be the same for the groups taking Test X and Test Y. The chained methods require an assumption of population invariance of the links between Test X and anchor Test V and between anchor Test V and Test Y. These assumptions are less likely to hold as the extent of the differences in content or administration conditions for Test X and Test Y increase and to the extent that the differences in the proficiencies of the group taking Test X and Test Y increase. When using IRT methods with this design, an assumption is made that all items on Test X, Test Y, and the anchor test measure the same proficiency. This assumption is unlikely to hold for most situations in which scores on tests that measure similar constructs are linked.

When using the anchor-test nonequivalent groups design for linking scores on tests of different content, the anchor test cannot adequately represent the content of both Test X and Test Y. In this case, the linking results likely depend on the particular anchor chosen. If possible, the linking can be conducted using different anchor tests and the sensitivity of the linking to choice of anchor test assessed. In addition, the standard methods might be modified to accommodate the use of multiple anchors in a single linking.

3.7. Summary and Conclusions

Notation and terminology were used in this chapter to distinguish among designs, linking functions, and linking results. The notation incorporated population, conditions of measurement, and content. This notation makes explicit those factors on which linking functions depend. Terminology used with equating designs was expanded from typical terminology to distinguish between designs used in linking and equating. For example, the use of the term *common-item nonequivalent groups design* for equating and the term *anchor-test nonequivalent groups design* for linking tests that measure similar constructs serves to highlight the substantial differences between these designs (Holland, Chapter 2, referred to both of these designs as the NEAT design). In particular, in equating, the content of the set of common items represents the content of Form X and Form Y, whereas when linking tests intended to measure similar constructs, the content of the anchor test typically does not represent the content of both Test X and Test Y. Further developments in notation and terminology should serve to better distinguish among different linking situations, to display important differences among the designs, and to highlight the effects of factors such as content, conditions of measurement, and population on linking results.

When conducting equating, Form X and Form Y have the same content and typically are administered under the same conditions of measurement, providing significant statistical control. Equating can be expected to provide reasonable results, and the statistical assumptions required for conducting equating can be expected to hold reasonably well in a variety of situations.

When linking scores on tests that are intended to measure similar constructs, Test X and Test Y typically have somewhat different content and are administered under different conditions of measurement to examinees from populations that differ from the target population. Thus, there is significantly less statistical control exerted in these situations than in equating situations. In addition, data collection designs often are very difficult to implement properly and statistical assumptions often are violated. Because of these complications, linking of scores on tests that measure similar constructs likely depends on the examinee population and on the conditions of measurement.

Because of these dependencies, the sensitivity of linking functions to variations in conditions of measurement and population should be assessed. If there is substantial variation, then either reporting different linking relationships for different conditions of measurement and populations or not reporting the relationships should be strongly considered. In any case, when presenting the results of linking, test content, conditions of measurement, and population should be clearly specified.

Acknowledgments. The author thanks Robert L. Brennan, Neil J. Dorans, and Mary Pommerich for their detailed reviews and comments on earlier versions of this chapter.

Part 2: Equating

In *Equating: Best Practices and Challenges to Best Practices*, Nancy Petersen provides a succinct review of what she considers to be best practices in equating, followed by a consideration of circumstances that can waylay equatings.

Linda Cook, in *Practical Problems in Equating Test Scores: A Practitioner's Perspective*, also considers some of the daunting challenges facing practitioners. She discusses three major stumbling blocks encountered when attempting to equate scores on tests under difficult conditions: characteristics of the tests to be equated, characteristics of the groups used for equating, and characteristics of the anchor tests.

Alina von Davier addresses potential future directions for improving equating practices in *Potential Solutions to Practical Equating Issues*. She provides a brief introduction to kernel equating and addresses the potential utility and controversy surrounding assessment of the population sensitivity of equating functions.

As a set, these three authors provide interesting practical and theoretical perspectives demonstrating that even the most tractable form of linking, equating, is not without challenges.

4 Equating: Best Practices and Challenges to Best Practices

Nancy S. Petersen[1]

ACT, Inc.

This chapter addresses best practices and challenges to best practices in equating. While in places, I comment on or refer to the chapters by von Davier (Chapter 6) and Cook (Chapter 5), the focus is on best practices in equating and challenges to these best practices that we face today.

4.1. Equating

First, let me recap what equating is and why we do it. Most testing programs use multiple forms of the same test, primarily for security reasons. Although different forms for a given test are built to be very similar in content, format, type, and range of difficulty of the questions asked, the actual questions used might all be different in each form. Thus, two forms of a test cannot be expected to be precisely equivalent in level and range of difficulty. As a consequence, any comparison of raw scores on the two forms of the test would be unfair to the people who happened to take the more difficult form.

Whenever scores on different test forms are to be compared, it is necessary that they be equivalent in some sense. Statistical procedures, referred to as equating methods, have been developed to deal with this problem. Equating methods are empirical procedures for establishing a statistical relationship between raw scores on two test forms; this relationship can be used to express the scores on one form in terms of the scores on the other form. When equating is successful, it becomes possible

---

[1] The opinions expressed in this chapter are those of the author and not necessarily of ACT, Inc.

to measure examinees' growth, to chart trends, and to compare or merge data, even when the separate pieces of data derive from different forms of a test with somewhat different item characteristics (Petersen, Kolen, & Hoover, 1989). The purpose of equating, then, is to establish, as nearly as possible, an effective equivalence between raw scores on two test forms such that scores from each test can be used as if they had come from the same test.

Because equating is an empirical procedure, it requires a design for data collection and a rule for transforming scores on one test form to scores on another. Viewed simply as an empirical procedure, an equating method imposes no restrictions on the properties of the scores to be equated or on the method used to determine the transformation. It is when we contemplate the purpose of equating and try to define what is meant by an effective equivalence between scores on two test forms that it becomes necessary to impose restrictions (Petersen et al., 1989).

In practice, equating is used to fine-tune the test construction process; that is, we use statistical procedures to correct for small variations in difficulty between multiple forms of a test that are built to the same blueprint (the same content and difficulty specifications) so that the scores on the multiple forms can be used interchangeably. To achieve this goal of interchangeable scores, strong requirements must be put on the blueprints for the two tests and on the method used for linking the scores.

There are five requirements that are widely viewed as necessary for a linking to be an equating (Holland & Dorans, 2006):

a. *The equal construct requirement*: The two tests should both be measures of the same constructs (latent traits, skills, abilities).
b. *The equal reliability requirement*: The two tests should have the same reliability.
c. *The symmetry requirement*: The equating transformation for mapping the scores of Form Y to those of Form X should be the *inverse* of the equating transformation for mapping the scores of X to those of Y.
d. *The equity requirement*: It should be a matter of indifference to examinees whether they are tested with Form X or Form Y.
e. *The population invariance requirement*: The equating function used to link the scores of Form X and Form Y should be the same regardless of the choice of (sub)population from which it is derived.

These five requirements are often treated as criteria for evaluating whether or not two tests can be, or have been, successfully equated. They also provide an intuitive "theory" of test equating. Holland (Chapter 2, Section 2.4.1) treated these requirements in greater detail.

For practical purposes, is sufficient to say that the equal construct and equal reliability requirements mean that the tests to be equated need to be built to the same content and statistical specifications. The symmetry requirement excludes the use of regression methods for test score equating. The equity requirement might be used to explain why both the equal construct and equal reliability requirements are needed (Lord, 1980). If the two tests measure different constructs, examinees will prefer the one on which they believe they will score higher. The equity requirement is, however, hard to evaluate empirically and its use is primarily theoretical (Lord, 1980; Hanson, 1991). The population invariance requirement, on the other hand, is easy to apply in practice and it also can be used to explain why the equal construct and equal reliability requirements are needed. If the same blueprint is not used to construct the two tests, then the conversions will certainly differ for different groups of examinees. For example, a conversion table relating scores on a mathematics test to scores on a verbal test developed on data for men would be very different from one developed from data on women, because in our society women tend to do less well than men on mathematics tests.

4.2. Best Practices

What contributes to a good equating? The primary things that contribute to a successful equating are choice of data collection design, quality and similarity of the tests to be equated, characteristics of the anchor test in relation to the tests to be equated, sample sizes and examinee characteristics, and choice of analysis methods (Holland, Dorans, & Petersen, 2006).

4.2.1. Data Collection

Data collection is the most important aspect of any equating study. Ideally, the data should come from a large representative sample of motivated examinees that is divided in half, either randomly or randomly within strata, to achieve equivalent groups. Each half is then administered either the new or the old form of the test (Holland et al., 2006); that is, an equivalent groups design is the preferred design. In practice, however, an anchor test (a set of items or a test taken by both groups) should be included in the design as a contingency in case the spiraling does not work (see Figure 4.1). If the spiraling does not work, then we can still conduct an equating using a nonequivalent groups anchor test design (Kolen &

	TEST		
SAMPLE	Old Form X	New Form Y	Anchor V
P_1	✓		✓
P_2		✓	✓

Figure 4.1. Equivalent groups design with optional anchor test.

Brennan, 2004). Anchor designs were discussed in more detail in Kolen (Chapter 3, Section 3.5).

4.2.2. Total Tests and Anchor Tests

The old and new test forms should be reliable measures of the same construct, built to the same test blueprint. Preferably, an external anchor test (a separately timed test) is available that is highly related to both the old and new test forms. Scores on the anchor test are used to adjust for any differences in ability that might have occurred randomly between groups and for any differences in difficulty between the test forms. The content and difficulty level of the old form, the new form, and the anchor test should be appropriate for the targeted population.

It is generally considered good practice to have the anchor test be a miniversion of the old and new test forms (Holland et al., 2006). That means it should be similar in difficulty to and mirror the content of the tests that are being equated. This is done to boost the correlation of scores on the anchor test with those of the old and new forms. High reliability also helps increase this correlation. For item response theory (IRT) linking methods, it is also desirable to have the anchor-test items cover a broad range of difficulty.

In practice, internal anchors (items common to both tests being equated) are often used. External anchors are seldom feasible due to the increased time required for administration or test structure. (Most tests do not consist of multiple, separately timed sections.) However, context effects become a possible issue with the use of internal anchors. To minimize these effects, common items should be placed, as nearly as possible, in the same location within each test form.

4.2.3. Equating Process

Once the data are available, it is often useful to presmooth the cumulative distributions, especially when samples are small (Livingston, 1993; Skaggs, 2004). Ideally, samples are large enough to make presmoothing optional. It is informative to equate with several different models, including both linear and equipercentile models. With an equivalent groups design, equipercentile and linear methods can be compared using the standard error of equating, which describes sampling error, and the difference that matters (DTM), an effect size that can be used to assess whether differences in equating functions have practical significance (Holland & Dorans, 2006). The magnitude of the DTM depends on the intended use of the scores and the scale units of the test. If the departures from linearity are less than the DTM and less than what would be expected due to sampling error, the linear model is often chosen for its ease of implementation. Otherwise, the more general equipercentile model is selected.

When an anchor test is used, differential item functioning (DIF) analyses should be run to evaluate whether the items on the anchor test are performing in the same way in both the old and new form samples. In addition, an item analysis should be run for all items on both the new and old forms to see if they are performing as expected. If they are not, it is often because of a quality control problem such as a miscoded key.

An equating should be checked for its reasonableness (Holland et al., 2006). How do we determine reasonableness? We compare the raw-to-scale score conversion for the new form to those obtained for previously administered forms. Is the new form conversion an outlier? Is it consistent with other difficulty information (such as mean percent correct) that might be available for that form and other forms that have been administered in the past? Do the more difficult forms tend to have higher raw-to-scale score conversions than the easier forms? Is the performance of the new form group consistent with the performance of other groups that are expected to be similar to it? For example, in testing programs with reasonable volumes and relatively stable populations, it is reasonable to expect that the new form sample will have scale score summary statistics similar to those obtained at the same time the year before. If the test has a passing score, then the pass rates should be relatively stable from year to year.

4.3. Challenges to Best Practices

There can be many challenges to a successful equating. Random assignment of test forms to large samples of motivated examinees is not always possible. Total-test and anchor-test reliability are not always as high as desired. Internal anchors with few items might not be very reliable. Anchor tests, especially external anchors, might not be highly correlated with the tests being equated. As noted by Cook (Chapter 5), all of these can present daunting challenges for the practitioner faced with providing equivalent scores on multiple forms of an assessment.

4.3.1. Choice of Data Collection Design

Some data collection designs can pose threats to sound equating. For example, test security is an issue for many high-stakes admissions, certification, and licensure tests. To help maintain test security, many of these testing programs want to give a new test form at every administration. As a result, they do not want to use an equivalent groups design because it requires readministration of an old test form for equating purposes. Instead, as Cook (Chapter 5) noted, they prefer to use a common-item or anchor-test design (see Kolen, Chapter 3, Figures 3.5 and 3.6 for pictorial depictions of these designs) so that only a subset of items is readministered for equating purposes. Consequently, these nonequivalent groups anchor-test designs (referred to as the NEAT design in Holland, Chapter 2) are often used in practice because of the flexibility they provide. Figure 4.2 demonstrates that the NEAT design looks just like an equivalent groups design with anchor test except that the samples **P** and **Q** are from different subpopulations of the total population of test-takers and might differ in significant ways. Thus, use of the NEAT design requires statistical procedures to adjust for ability differences between groups. The adjustments are based on assumptions. The assumptions might be unsound.

		TEST	
SAMPLE	Old Form X	New Form Y	Anchor V
P	✓		✓
Q		✓	✓

Figure 4.2. Nonequivalent groups anchor test design.

In fact, because of test security concerns, more and more testing programs want to move beyond the NEAT design to select the set of common items from multiple old forms to further reduce the chances that any test-taker has previously seen any item on the test. In pool equating (see Figure 4.3), item parameters are estimated after administration and then fed into a pool of active items for use in future test form assembly. Depending on whether the new form contains any items without parameter estimates, IRT preadministration or postadministration equating methods are used to equate the new form to the old base form, which is composed of previously calibrated items from the pool. (IRT preequating can only be performed if all items in the new form have been previously calibrated.) In pool equating, unlike in traditional observed-score equating, the anchor items used in building a new form do not need to come from a single old form and they do not need to be included in the base form in order to be used as anchor items. IRT equating is more flexible than observed-score methods in that it can be used to manufacture potential solutions for missing data designs like these. However, IRT analyses are more complex to conduct than observed-score equating procedures; more importantly, IRT methods make more assumptions than observed-score methods. With IRT, it is necessary to evaluate the choice and the fit of the IRT model to the data. Otherwise, the validity of the potential solution might be suspect.

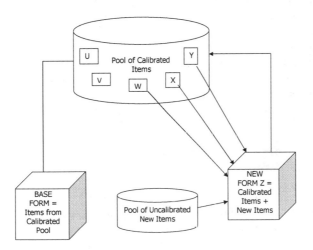

Figure 4.3. Pool equating.

The anchor items in a NEAT design are typically embedded within sections of scored operational items to help conceal their presence. In addition, the anchor or common items should be located in the same item positions within both total tests to reduce their susceptibility to context effects that might diminish their utility as measures of ability. If there are few common items, the anchor might be relatively unreliable and less useful for identifying differences in ability between samples and differences in difficulty between the test forms.

Small samples yield suspect equating results. As von Davier (Chapter 6, Section 6.4) noted, smoothing might help if the sample sizes are moderate. Nevertheless, smoothing might be of little help with samples of less than 50 (Skaggs, 2004). In such cases, it might be necessary to make strong assumptions about the equating function. For example, there might be no option other than to assume that the equating function is the identity function or that it differs from the identity function by a constant estimated from the data.

The synthetic equating function proposed by von Davier (Chapter 6, Section 6.4), which is defined as the weighted average of the identity equating function and the equating function based on the small sample, holds some promise. This type of function has been used previously in practice and, at ACT, Inc. we recently had an equating where we contemplated doing this. von Davier's formal explication of this procedure is an advance in the field.

With the NEAT design, the old and new form samples might perform very differently on the anchor test. When group differences in ability are large, different equating methods might yield different conversions unless the scores on the anchor test are highly related to scores on both total tests. In general, dissimilar conversion lines are indicative of problems with the data and additional quality control should be initiated to verify the results. Sometimes, in practice, the psychometrician has little control over the choice of data collection design and the selection of old and new form samples. Sometimes, in practice, a data processing error is made.

4.3.2. Psychometric Properties of the Total Tests and Anchor Test

Test characteristics affect the quality of equating. Use of pretested items in test assembly results in higher quality exams. Tests containing untried items might end up with fewer scorable items than planned. Shorter, less reliable tests are hard to equate because a greater portion of their score variability is noise. More importantly, tests composed of many untried items can turn out to be different in length, content, difficulty, and reliability from the tests to which they are to be equated; these factors make equating more difficult. Tests composed primarily of unpretested items might turn out to be too easy or too difficult for the intended population; this results in data that do not facilitate linking to other tests because the distributions are so skewed and relationships with other scores are attenuated.

Anchor tests provide a common score across groups that can be used to adjust for group ability differences before adjusting for test difficulty differences (Holland et al., 2006). Short anchor tests tend to result in unreliable scores and lower correlations than desired with total-test scores. Low correlations might also occur when the content of the anchor test differs from that for the total tests. Context effects can impair the comparability of common items across forms. Anchors that are too easy or too hard for the intended population produce skewed score distributions that present challenges for equating.

4.3.3. Samples

Use of unrepresentative and unmotivated samples undermines equating. Only members of the population of interest should be included in equating samples. To the extent possible, equating samples should also be representative of the intended population. When equating data are collected via special studies rather than operational administrations, incentives are needed to ensure that examinees will take the test seriously.

Equating cannot be done effectively using small samples. The smaller the sample size, the more restricted is the class of plausible equating methods. Smoothing score distributions works with moderate-sized samples, but it is not effective with very small samples, especially when we are unsure of how representative the sample is of the intended population.

Large ability differences between the anchor-test samples, .25 standard deviation units or higher, tend to yield situations in which equating becomes difficult to impossible unless the anchor is highly related to both tests to be equated.

4.3.4. Problems in Implementation

Most of the difficulties in real-life equating settings are due to problems in data collection.

The samples are too small, unmotivated, and/or unrepresentative of the population for which the test is intended. For some testing programs, especially those used to measure employability skills, it is difficult to gather data on the population of interest. Job applicants differ for different jobs and for different companies in significant ways. Therefore, it is basically impossible to gather data routinely on a representative sample of job applicants or on some other well-defined stable subsample for analysis purposes.

Sometimes the test administrators do not spiral the booklets as intended, messing up our equivalent groups design. Then if we have not included some common items so that we can use a NEAT design as a backup, we cannot equate, as we do not have data that can be used to conduct analyses to separate group ability differences from difficulty differences in the tests.

Sometimes the developers include very few common items in the total tests. Then if the samples turn out to be very disparate in ability, performance differences between groups are not adequately represented by differences on the common items.

In all of these situations, the equating issues might be further exacerbated by issues related to test construction—the new form contains mainly unpretested items and turns out to differ significantly in difficulty from the old form; the content specs were changed; or the administration format was changed (e.g., for a listening test, the scenario was presented via text in the old form and by both text and orally in the new form).

4.3.4.1. An Example of a Very Challenging Equating

Until recently, the College Board Biology Achievement Test equating described in Cook (Chapter 5) and Cook and Petersen (1987) was the most memorable equating I have encountered in my 30 some years of equating (that and one for a Praxis II® Subject test with a sample size of three). However, those equatings were relatively straightforward compared to an equating situation recently encountered at ACT, Inc.

We were asked to equate four field test forms of a reading test for non-English speakers. Summary data for the base (old) form and the four new field test forms are shown in Table 4.1. The base form was administered in a foreign country to well-educated, white-collar workers who have had access to a great deal of English-language training. The new field-test forms were administered in the United States to recent immigrant, blue-collar workers who have had limited access to English-language training. The two groups performed very differently on the common-items and on the total tests.

The reading tests consisted of 30 items; however, there were only 7 items common across forms for use as an anchor. This is far fewer than the general rule of thumb that the number of common items should be the greater of 20 items or 20% of the test length. Now with a test of only 30 items, it is understandable why there are fewer than 20 common items, but only 7? That is too few to provide a reliable score.

The four field-test forms were supposed to be spiraled. We never did figure out why Form RFT1 had twice as many test-takers as the others. Given the disparity in sample sizes, the spiraling could not have gone as planned.

The four field-test form groups scored approximately 1.3 standard deviation (SD) units lower than the old form group on the common items and 1.6 SDs lower on the total test. The mean scores on the new forms corresponded to approximately 41% of the maximum score, whereas the mean score on the base form corresponded to approximately 65%. The reading field tests were very speeded, with approximately 40% of the test-takers running out of time.

Table 4.1. Reading for non-English speakers: Field-test raw score (RS) summary statistics

| Reading | Base form[b] | Field-test forms[a] | | | |
		RFT1	RFT2	RFT3	RFT4
Sample size	559	323	149	146	141
RS mean	20.3	10.9	12.2	11.3	13.0
RS *SD*	4.9	5.2	5.2	5.3	5.5
No. of operational items	30	30	30	30	30
KR-20	0.83	0.83	0.81	0.82	0.84
Common items mean	4.0	2.3	2.4	2.3	2.3
Common items *SD*	1.5	1.4	1.3	1.3	1.2
No. of common items	7	7	7	7	7
Correlation[c]	0.79	0.78	0.65	0.70	0.77

[a]The field test forms were administered to test-takers in the United States. Each field test form contains 23 pretest items plus 7 items in common with the base form.

[b]The base form is the current operational Form. The base form was administered to test-takers in a foreign country.

[c]Correlation between common items and unique items.

Consequently, we informed the client that we were unable to perform an actual equating for the field tests because the basic assumptions underlying the various equating models were violated. Rather, we provided a conversion table for use in scoring the field-test data based on our best professional judgment. We also informed the client that the field-test data were not suitable for estimating the statistical properties of the pretest items prior to inclusion in new forms because of the small number of test-takers for three of the field-test forms, the small number of common items, the disparate performance of the groups, and the high not-reached rate on the reading tests.

This is a new assessment, still under development. The client is now in the process of planning a new field-test study. Along with that, we have asked the client to decide who their primary market is so we can determine the targeted test-taking population for the test. We will then try to sample from this population for our next field test. If the group from the foreign country is typical of the targeted test-taking population and if the group from the United States is typical of the American test-taking population, then the client actually needs to consider developing a different assessment for use in the United States. The current assessment is much too difficult for this particular American test-taking population. If they want to test in the United States, they really need to develop a different assessment or they need to determine if there is a white-collar job market in the United States for a test of reading for non-English speakers. If the group from the foreign country is typical of the targeted test-taking population, then the current reading test appears to be of suitable difficulty for this population.

4.4. Discussion

For large-scale testing programs such as the ACT and the SAT®, most operational equatings come close to meeting the five criteria for an equating. These programs have large volumes, relatively stable test specifications, a relatively stable test-taker population, a well-designed data collection plan, and a large well-defined test-taker group used for item/test analysis and equating. They also pretest items prior to operational use and give a new form at every administration. In addition, these programs have sufficient data to evaluate questions such as whether scrambled section orders affect equating results and whether equatings are invariant for major subgroups. If not, they have been able to define a major stable subpopulation used for analysis purposes. For example, for the Biology Achievement Test (Cook & Petersen, 1987; Cook, Chapter 5), we solved the problem of subpopulation sensitivity by defining the analysis population for all future equatings to be seniors taking the test in the fall. So from then on, we only administered and equated new Biology forms using data from seniors who took the test in the fall; and, we only expected population invariance to hold for subgroups of that "analysis" population rather than for the whole test-taker population.

However, most testing programs are not so lucky. Many licensure and certification programs have small volumes, and small item pools, major security problems and they cannot readily pretest. It can be difficult when working on a small or new testing program to know when you have done a "good" equating. For new testing programs, it might be difficult to specify an analysis population on whom you can initially actually collect data for equating purposes. Often, you have to use whoever is willing to pay for the test; those users' examinees might differ in significant ways from each other, such as with the reading exam for non-English speakers example. To improve security, many testing programs want to assemble tests from calibrated item pools in order to minimize the number of common items from any one old form in a new form even though the exam might only be given to a couple of hundred examinees at best in a year, making item calibration problematic. To reduce cheating, clients might also want to scramble items within a test form, even though context effects can cause comparability problems across scrambles. However, no matter what, when all is said and done, we are expected to do our magic and produce scores.

Perhaps the psychometrician's oath should be essentially the Hippocratic Oath: Do no harm. That is the most important goal of equating. Not only have we produced the best equating possible for all possible test forms or subgroups, but, given all of the problems we might have encountered, we have also produced the best linking the client can afford with minimal negative impact on any subset of examinees. Thus, I disagree with von Davier (Chapter 6, Section 6.3) as to her solution for population sensitivity. I would never recommend to a client that they use different conversions for different subgroups that took the same test or the same test items. I view a test score as the result of a "measurement," like taking your temperature with a calibrated thermometer, rather than as strictly an "estimate" of a latent ability parameter. I do not want to be the one to go in front of a judge to say that it is fair to give different scores to two examinees who took exactly the same questions and answered them in the same way. We are not talking about "test use" here. In test use, when we are essentially making a prediction about how someone will perform in the future, there might be times when it is appropriate, and legal, to use individual or subgroup information in addition to test performance in the decision-making process. However, when we are equating, we are not talking about test use; we are talking about how we report scores for a test or a collection of items. The results of our equating analyses might indicate that our equating is not population invariant. In which case, I believe we should revisit our test blueprint, our definition of the analysis population, how scores will be used, and how we treat/talk about our equating results. However, I do not see it as a reason to score the test differently for different groups. I believe the only way to be fair to individuals in scoring the test is to report scores on the test in the same way for everyone. We might use the scores from a test differently for different groups, but I believe there should only be one way to report scores for any given collection of test items.

4.5. Summary

All in all, I think the theory of equating is in good shape. We can continue to tweak it, and von Davier's Chapter 6 presented some good examples of how we can further refine our equating procedures. However, it is difficult to deal with the test development and data collection problems we face in practice, especially now that the world is our marketplace.

I do feel that there is still a need for more comprehensive empirical investigations. Some of the various challenges we face in practice could be explored further via systematic investigations of the appropriateness of different equating procedures in a variety of realistic settings. These empirical investigations have their predecessors, such as the comprehensive studies conducted in the early eighties by Marco, Petersen, and Stewart (1983) as well as other studies cited in Kolen and Brennan (2004). A variety of factors could be manipulated in a series of studies that examines the robustness of both newer approaches like kernel equating (von Davier, Holland, & Thayer, 2004b) and older linear and nonlinear methods. Foremost among these factors would be the magnitude of ability differences between samples as measured by the anchor items and the shape of the score distributions. What is the minimum number of anchor items that we really need to capture ability differences between groups? In addition, it would be worthwhile to manipulate difficulty differences between the total tests and the anchor, as well as the reliability of the total score and the anchor score. Correlations of the anchor score with total score and with sample size should be manipulated and studied. Ideally, real data would be used as the starting point for these studies.

The results of the studies reviewed by Cook (Chapter 5) plus the equating example discussed in Section 4.3.4 clearly show that it is impossible to separate fully the effects of samples, tests, and common items on equating results. Therefore, as Cook and Petersen (1987) noted years ago, as long as it is still necessary to attempt to develop comparable scores in practical testing situations, equating will remain in large part not just a science but also an art.

5 Practical Problems in Equating Test Scores: A Practitioner's Perspective

Linda L. Cook[1]

Educational Testing Service

5.1. Introduction

Most major testing programs, particularly large-scale or high-stakes testing programs, require the construction and administration of multiple forms of the same test. There are several reasons for this requirement. One reason is that many testing programs (e.g., the ACT® or the SAT®) administer tests on a fairly large number of testing dates per year. In addition, for security reasons, testing programs such as these rarely administer an examination more than once. Consequently, in order to protect the security of the tests and meet the demands of an examinee population for flexible testing dates, the construction and administration of alternate forms of the same test is a necessary requirement for operating these programs.

One thing that most major testing programs have in common is that it is imperative that scores on the multiple forms of the tests that are administered on the different test dates be completely interchangeable. Because it is virtually impossible to construct multiple test forms that are equivalent in level and range of difficulty, test scores on the different forms must be equated using some statistical procedure. Numerous procedures have been described and researched to accomplish both the equating and, when equating is not advisable, the alignment of the scales underlying the test scores. These equating and scale-alignment procedures have been discussed in great detail in a number of important publications (see, e.g., Angoff, 1984; Kolen & Brennan, 2004, Holland, Chapter 2; Kolen, Chapter 3). However, a review of these publications leaves the

---

[1] The opinions expressed in this chapter are those of the author and not necessarily of Educational Testing Service.

reader with a clear sense that there are many difficult situations in which there is a need to equate or align scales on different test forms or tests and in which the usual procedures might provide questionable results.

Cook and Petersen (1987) begin their review of problems related to using conventional and item response theory (IRT) equating methods in what they refer to as "less than optimal circumstances" by saying that "many psychometricians view score equating as a subjective art with theoretical foundations because the true relationship between scores on different forms of the same test is never known in practice." They continue by saying, "Furthermore, actual data never satisfy the assumptions of the various equating models" (p. 225).

The art, and science, of equating has advanced considerably since Cook and Petersen published their article in 1987 in which they described the many problems and issues that they encountered as practitioners equating scores on the SAT and the College Board Achievement Tests (now called the SAT Reasoning Test™ and the SAT Subject Tests™). The recent work on assessing the population sensitivity of equating functions that has been published in a special issue of the *Journal of Educational Measurement* (JEM) edited by Dorans (2004a) is an excellent example of the insightful analysis and scientific approach that is now being brought to bear on the practical issues related to linking test scores. In addition, *Test Equating, Scaling, and Linking* by Kolen and Brennan (2004) and *The Kernel Method of Test Equating* by von Davier, Holland, and Thayer (2004b) are examples of recent and substantial contributions to what we know today about the science of score linking.

In spite of the important advances that have been made in analyzing and understanding some of the issues and problems related to score linking, and particularly score equating, there remain many daunting challenges for the practitioner who is faced with providing equivalent scores on multiple forms of an assessment in situations that sometimes include one or more of the following conditions: test forms that differ in content, difficulty, and reliability, new and old form samples that differ in important characteristics, and anchor tests, used to adjust for sample differences, that have specifications that differ from the tests to be equated. (See Kolen, this volume, for details of how anchor tests are used.)

The purpose of this chapter is to discuss some of the more important conditions that can lead to "stumbling blocks" that a practitioner might have to face as she attempts to develop equivalent or interchangeable scores. Because of the prevalence and importance of the nonequivalent groups anchor test (NEAT) design and because of the complexities of implementing this design, most of the discussion in this chapter naturally focuses on equatings based on a NEAT data collection design. The chapter will provide a general discussion of this data collection design and some issues related to using the design, followed by a discussion of three major stumbling blocks encountered when attempting to equate scores on tests under difficult conditions: characteristics of the test forms to be equated, characteristics of the groups used for equating, and characteristics of the anchor tests.

5.2 The Nonequivalent Groups Anchor Test Design

Equating designs typically have two important components. One component is a design for data collection and the second is a statistical model used to equate scores on the tests of interest. The nonequivalent groups anchor-test design is used to collect data in situations in which it is not possible to administer the tests to be equated to the same or randomly equivalent groups. Consequently, when using a NEAT design, the groups taking the new form (the test form to be placed on scale) and the old form (the test form that has been previously placed on scale) of the test to be equated differ from each other, typically in level of skills or abilities measured by the test. Section 2.4.3 in Holland (Chapter 2) described this design. The NEAT design was also described in Kolen (Chapter 3, Section 3.5; see especially Figures 3.5 and 3.6). Usually the new and old form groups take the tests of interest on different test dates. The anchor test, or set of common items, is administered along with, or as part of, the new and old forms of the test and is used to evaluate the differences in the ability levels between these groups and to estimate or help create distributions of scores on the two forms to be equated for the common population for the test. (See von Davier et al., 2004b, for a discussion of how these distributions are created.) Observed-score methods typically used with anchor-test designs are the chained equipercentile method and the Tucker and Levine observed-score linear methods (see Figure 2.4 in Holland, Chapter 2, Section 2.3.4). True-score methods such as Levine true score and IRT methods are also used. For IRT procedures, the anchor test is used to place the item parameter estimates for the two test forms on the same scale prior to score equating. (See Kolen, Chapter 3, Section 3.5; Kolen & Brennan, 2004; Petersen, Cook, & Stocking, 1983; von Davier et al., 2004b, for a description of these equating models.)

The anchor test can be included within the total test (internal anchor) or it can be administered separately from the total test (external anchor). (Kolen's Chapter 3 in this volume contains visuals for both the internal anchor or common items design [Figure 3.5] and the external anchor design [Figure 3.6].) As mentioned previously, anchor-test designs are probably the most prevalently used designs in practice and the most difficult designs to implement. One reason that anchor-test designs are difficult to implement has to do with the fact that these designs work best when certain conditions hold: similarity of new and old form samples, similarity of the two test forms to be equated, and a close relationship between scores on each of the forms to be equated and the anchor-test scores. Consequently, when equating scores on two test forms using an anchor-test design, "... it is necessary to determine how similar the test forms are with respect to content, difficulty and reliability. It is also necessary to determine the extent to which the anchor test mirrors the properties of the total tests. It is also important to gather as much information as possible about the extent to which the samples to be used in equating are similar in composition and ability and are representative of the population for which the test is intended"(Cook & Petersen, 1987, p. 225).

Although the issues related to differences in equating samples, differences in the characteristics of the new and old forms, and differences in the relationship between the anchor test and the total tests are listed here as separate issues, it is important to point out that these are not independent issues; instead, they are very much intertwined. For example, it is quite possible for two test forms to appear to be very parallel when given to one set of equating samples, but yet exhibit quite discrepant properties when given to a second set of equating samples. This dependency between the characteristics of the assessment and the characteristics of the group taking the assessment is also a concern when evaluating the characteristics of the anchor test. These issues and how they interact will be discussed in the next sections of this chapter.

5.3. Characteristics of the New and Old Forms

A fundamental requirement of all test equating procedures is that the multiple forms of the test to be equated must be as similar as possible in all important aspects (e.g., length, reliability, difficulty, content). Kolen and Brennan (2004) began the test development section of their chapter on practical issues in equating with a quote from Mislevy (1992). According to Mislevy, "Test construction and equating are inseparable. When they are applied in concert, equated scores from parallel test forms provide virtually exchangeable evidence about students' behavior on the same general domain of tasks, under the same specified standardized conditions. When equating works it is because of the way the tests are constructed"(p. 37). Angoff (1984) discussed a definition of equated scores and emphasizes that "...equating, or the derivation of equivalent scores, concerns itself with the problem of unique conversions which may be derived only across test forms that are parallel—that is, forms that measure, within acceptable limits, the same psychological function" (p. 86).

One of the key points made in the equating literature (see, e.g., Angoff, 1984; Kolen & Brennan, 2004) is the notion of population or subpopulation invariance; that is, scores on two forms of a test should exhibit a relationship that does not depend on the particular groups of examinees used to derive the relationship. As Dorans (2004e) pointed out, the notion of population invariance depends both on the tests to be equated and the samples that are used to carry out the equating. Dorans stated, "Lack of invariance in an equating function indicates that the differential difficulty of the two tests is not consistent across the two groups. Note that invariance can hold if the relative difficulty changes as a function of score level in the same way across subpopulations. If, however, the relative difficulty of the two tests interacts with group membership or there is an interaction among score level, difficulty, and group, then invariance does not hold" (p. 49).

The point to emphasize in this discussion is that population invariance— a recommended criterion for evaluating the quality of equating results that can be evaluated by checking whether the results for the equating based on a particular population hold for subpopulations—is well known to be related to differences in the characteristics of the test forms to be equated (see Dorans, 2004e). Kolen (2004b) summarized the implications of these differences for population invariance by making use of two different sets of study results. He referred to several studies (Angoff & Cowell, 1986; Dorans & Holland, 2000; Harris & Kolen, 1986) in which the researchers determined that parallel test forms given to randomly equivalent subgroups of a population basically produced score conversions that were invariant across these subgroups. On the other hand, Kolen pointed out a number of studies that were designed to link nonparallel assessments that resulted in linking functions that were dependent on the subpopulation of examinees (Dorans, 2000; Dorans & Feigenbaum, 1994; Dorans & Holland, 2000; Houston & Sawyer, 1991). Kolen made the point that the results from the Dorans and Holland study showed that the larger the differences between the content of the tests to be linked, the more the linkings appeared to be population dependent.

According to Kolen (2004a) and Dorans (2004e), parallelism of test forms is an important principle for good test equating, and if it is suspected that the test forms might not be as similar as they should be to provide the basis for interchangeable scores, then it is particularly important to make sure that the groups used to derive the equating or linking transformations are as similar as possible in all aspects measured by the test forms. It is appropriate at this point to consider the consequences of this statement for a large-scale testing program.

At first glance, the requirement of parallel forms, and reasonably comparable equating samples, as a basis for the development of equivalent scores seems very logical and obtainable for most large-scale testing programs. However, the development and maintenance of parallel test forms over a period of time might not always be possible for a testing program. The maintenance of parallel test forms would not be such a critical issue were it not for the fact that, as pointed out earlier, most large-scale testing programs use an anchor-test data collection design because it is difficult for them to collect equating data using a single group or a randomly equivalent groups data collection design. Consequently, many large-scale testing programs are frequently in the position of deriving equivalent scores on tests using groups that might not be similar in ability or other characteristics. This situation might not present a challenge to the testing program as long as the test forms to be equated are very similar in characteristics, but what about situations when test forms are not parallel?

Sometimes the need to administer nonparallel test forms in a testing program cannot be avoided. For example, the testing program might decide that it needs to revise the current testing battery to better align the assessments with current educational practices or to take advantage of technological advances in measurement. There are a number of notable examples of these types of change. Testing programs such as the SAT, ACT, and PSAT/NMSQT® have had the content of their tests revised periodically to better reflect changes to curricula and so forth. In most of these situations, the linking across forms with altered test content has been considered to result in equivalent scores (see Liu & Walker, Chapter 7, for one such illustration). In addition, the introduction of computerized testing in testing programs such as the GRE® and the TOEFL® necessitated some form of score linking between the nonparallel paper-and-pencil and computer-adaptive versions. In this situation, the linking cannot be assumed to constitute an equating, but, instead, it can be considered a calibration in the sense defined by Holland (Chapter 2, Section 2.3.4). See the chapter by Eignor in this volume for more discussion of issues involved in making the transition from one mode of administration to another. Brennan (Chapter 9) discussed both Chapter 8 by Eignor and Chapter 7 by Liu and Walker in his consideration of issues faced by tests in transition. Kolen (Chapter 3, Section 3.2) formally incorporated conditions of administration into his treatment of linking and equating.

Given the results of some of the studies cited earlier in this chapter (Dorans, 2000; Dorans & Feigenbaum, 1994; Dorans & Holland, 2000; Houston & Sawyer, 1991), it would seem prudent for practitioners facing the need to link scores on nonparallel assessments to do the best they can to ensure that the equating samples are representative of the target population for the test and that the samples are as similar as possible in the skills and abilities measured by the test.

As mentioned earlier, there is an interaction between the tests to be equated and the characteristics of the samples to be used in the equating. It is quite possible for test forms to exhibit the properties of parallelism when given to one pair of equating samples and to behave as nonparallel test forms when administered to a second pair of equating samples. This point will be explored further in the next section of this chapter, which focuses on issues related to differences in equating samples.

5.4. Characteristics of the Groups Used for Equating

Kolen and Brennan (2004) have pointed out that the effect of the group used for equating depends on the data collection design. They discussed the fact that when the test forms are carefully constructed to be parallel to each other and when the groups used to equate these test forms are randomly equivalent and representative samples, the equating relationship appears to be group independent (i.e., invariant across groups; see Angoff & Cowell, 1986; Harris & Kolen, 1986.) These authors continued by pointing out that for anchor-test designs, large differences between the old and new form groups "…can cause significant problems in estimating equating relationships, both for traditional and IRT equating methods." (See Cook & Petersen, 1987; Harris, 1993; Skaggs, 1990; Skaggs & Lissitz, 1986.) Kolen and Brennan (2004) explained these results by making the point that large differences in mean ability or distribution of ability of the equating samples can lead to the failure of the assumptions of any equating model to hold.

It is important, at this point, to note that equating samples can exhibit a number of different sampling characteristics. For one, the samples can be either representative or nonrepresentative samples of the target population for the test. For example, a nonrepresentative sample of the target population of the test might be a sample of students who take the test in a special study and consequently might not be as motivated as students from the target population who took the test under standard testing conditions. The samples might also be representative of a different population than the target population. For example, this situation might occur if samples selected for the equating have been exposed to an academic curriculum other than the curriculum that the intended population for the test will be exposed to. Finally, it is possible that the new and old form samples, themselves, might each be representative of different populations. This situation could occur, for example, if the new and old form groups took the tests at different points in time during the academic year when a particular content series in a course was being taught.

In practice, nearly all of the above-described situations are encountered from time to time. The equating studies reviewed in this chapter, and prevalent in the equating literature, involve all of the situations just described. However, the last situation—new and old form samples from different populations—is one of the most problematic situations for score linking procedures and is one that can only occur with a NEAT data collection design.

One approach to the problem of disparate equating samples in anchor-test designs is to attempt to match the new and old form samples using some type of matching variable (e.g., anchor-test scores). Matching, as a possible solution to the problems created by disparate equating samples, was a topic researched at Educational Testing Service (ETS) in the late 1980s. The studies were reported in a special issue of *Applied Measurement in Education* (APM) that was edited by Dorans (1990b). Matching was alluring because of the repeated observation that equating methods tended to converge to the same answer when old and new form samples were close in ability. In other words, different linear observed-score methods would tend to give the same linear linking function, and different curvilinear observed-score methods would tend to give the same nonlinear linking function. By matching the old and new form sample such that they had identical distributions of anchor-test scores, a convergence of results would be obtained. In essence, matching is an inefficient brute-force way of doing what Tucker and frequency estimation do elegantly (see Dorans, 1990a, for description of methods). The research documented in this special issue found that matching procedures provided inconsistent results; that is, some of the studies found the equatings resulting from the matching procedures to be quite acceptable and other studies found that the procedures did not produce successful equating results at all. This seemed, in part, to be a function of the specific equating methods employed in the various studies, but the results were also most surely related to the nature of the samples (i.e., whether they were representative samples from a particular population and whether the new and old form samples were samples from the same population).

Skaggs (1990), in his discussion of the ETS studies, commented, "The five articles in this special issue address what I think is the single most important of these factors,[2] namely, the problem that different populations of examinees who take a test may not produce the same

---

[2] The factors discussed by Skaggs were reliability of the tests to be equated, properties of the anchor tests, ability levels of the samples, and types of test to be equated.

equating function. This problem is actually a symptom of a larger concern, namely, that the same test can mean different things to different people" (p. 105). Skaggs continued by pointing out the many dimensions on which equating samples might differ, such as reading ability, recency of instruction, test anxiety, the number of hours of sleep the night before a test, etc. He urged more work on determining a causal explanation for how dimensions, such as these, interact to impact examinees' test scores. What is implied by Skaggs' comments is that equating samples that differ on the dimensions he describes are quite likely unrepresentative samples from the target population. Also, the samples may differ sufficiently on the characteristics described by Skaggs that they may not even be samples from the same target population.

Skaggs' concerns about group characteristics impacting equating designs become even clearer when one considers that a complicating factor for large-scale testing programs using anchor-test designs is that these testing programs offer multiple administrations of a test and, consequently, the new and old form groups used for equating usually take the test on different administration dates that can be a number of months or even several years apart. As Cook and Petersen (1987) pointed out, "The possibility exists that they [the groups used for equating] may not be subgroups from the same population. If this situation exists, the equating function obtained from such a design may be very problematic" (p. 228).

Cook and Petersen (1987) described a study carried out by Cook, Eignor, and Taft (1985), which was later published in the *Journal of Educational Measurement* (Cook, Eignor, & Taft, 1988). This study examined the results of equating two forms of a biology achievement test, which had been constructed to be reasonably parallel to each other in both content and statistical properties, but which differed slightly in test length. For their study, Cook et al. (1985) used one old form sample and two different new form samples. The old form sample was randomly selected from a fall administration of the test. One new form sample was randomly selected from a spring administration of the test and the second sample was randomly selected from a fall administration. Cook et al. (1985) noted that students taking the biology test in the spring were able students who had recently completed a course in biology. They pointed out that students taking the test in the fall were less able students who mostly had not formally studied biology for 6–18 months.

Table 5.1 contains summary statistics from Cook et al. (1985) that describe the performance of the three samples on the two forms of the biology test (the old form contained 99 items and the new form contained 95 items), the anchor test (58 common items included in the total score on both the new and old forms of the test), and the correlation of the anchor test with the total test. As Cook and Petersen (1987) pointed out, the new and old form fall samples were very similar in performance on the 58-item anchor test. The performance of the two fall samples on the 58 common items can be contrasted with that of the spring sample, which performed much better on this same set of items. Item difficulties for the 58 common items contained in the new and old biology test forms correlated .99, which indicates that they measure biology, as defined by the specifications, in the same way for the two fall samples. The same set of items measures biology in a different way for the spring and fall groups, as evidenced by a correlation of .74 for their item difficulties. Cook and Petersen pointed out that "... it is quite likely that the two biology test forms, even though constructed to be very parallel, measure different skills or constructs depending upon whether they are administered to a spring or fall group" (p. 230).

Table 5.1. Biology test raw score summary statistics[a]

Form	Sample size	No. of items	Mean	*SD*	*r*
Fall old form	2,408	99	46.33	18.26	.96
Anchor test		58	25.62	11.42	
Spring new form	3,892	95	53.71	17.61	.97
Anchor test		58	32.89	11.42	
Fall new form	3,653	95	44.74	17.56	.96
Anchor test		58	25.65	11.27	

[a] Raw score summary statistics for the total test taken by the two new form samples and for the common items taken by all of the samples can be directly compared. Due to differences in test difficulty and test length, summary statistics for the old form should not be compared with those for the new form.

Cook and Petersen (1987) continued the discussion of the Cook et al. (1985) work by pointing out that these authors also investigated the impact of the various new and old form sample combinations on the equating results. Cook et al. equated the two biology test forms to each other using Tucker, Levine, and equipercentile equating methods (see Angoff, 1984). IRT true-score equating based on the three-parameter logistic model (Lord, 1980, p. 193) was also used. See Chapter 2 by Holland (especially Section 2.4.3), and Chapter 3 by Kolen in this volume for details about equating methods. All equatings were carried out using (a) the spring new form/fall old form combination and (b) the fall new form/fall old form combination. Information provided in Table 5.2 gives the results of the equatings in the form of summary statistics obtained for the spring total group. Examination of the data shown in Table 5.2 indicates the different equatings using the spring new form fall old form combination resulted in scaled-score means at least 15 points higher than those based on the fall new form/fall old form combinations.

Cook and Petersen (1987) asked several questions about these results. "Are the equatings discrepant due to the differences in ability level of the new and old form samples, or are they discrepant because the test is measuring different (nonparallel) constructs for the spring and fall groups?" (p. 230). Another closely related question is: Will the equating transformation determined by, for instance, using two samples from the fall population, produce the same results as an equating transformation determined using two samples from the spring population? This second question was investigated by Cook (1984).

Cook (1984) equated two different forms of the biology test using new and old form samples from fall administrations and the equating was then repeated using new and old form samples from spring administrations. Although the spring and fall groups differed in level and dispersion of ability, the two spring samples used for the equatings were similar to each other, as were the two fall samples.

Table 5.2. Scaled-score summary statistics for the biology exam resulting from combinations of equating method, and equating sample, using the 58-item common-item set [a]

| | Equating method | | | | | |
| | Linear | | Equipercentile | | IRT | |
	Mean	SD	Mean	SD	Mean	SD
Fall new-form sample/ fall old-form sample–58 items	569	103	567	103	568	103
Spring new–form sample/ fall old–form sample–58 items	585	104	582	102	586	102

[a]Raw score frequency distributions used to compute scaled-score summary statistics were obtained from the spring total group ($N = 23{,}405$).

Cook and Petersen (1987) provided the rounded results of the equatings carried out by Cook (1984) using the spring/spring and fall/fall samples. They showed that the equating transformation determined using the spring/spring combination results in reported scores that were 10 points higher, through most of the score range, than those obtained by a transformation determined using the fall/fall samples. As Cook and Petersen pointed out, these results provided an indication that the spring and fall groups taking the biology test might not be subgroups from the same population and that the biology test is quite likely not measuring the same thing for these two populations.

In the above-described situation, the slight differences in equating results, taken in conjunction with the correlation of .74 reported earlier between item difficulties obtained in the spring and fall samples, indicate that the spring groups might be samples from one population and the fall groups might be samples from a different population. The different populations might be defined by the groups' different levels of preparedness for taking the biology test; that is, the spring equating results are based on new and old form samples from one population and the fall equating results are based on new and old form samples from a second population. As mentioned previously, the spring and fall test-takers most likely represent different populations.

Although this situation caused problems for the equating, it is less problematic than the situation in which the new form group is taken from one population (e.g., a spring administration) and the old form group is taken from a different population (e.g., the fall administration). Recall that Cook et al. (1985) found that when parallel forms of the biology test were equated using new and old form groups that took the tests on different administration dates (i.e., were subgroups from different populations), all equating results were seriously affected. They concluded that the differences in equating results were brought about by differences in the new and old form samples. They attributed the differences in the groups to the differences in the recency of their course work and hypothesized that this difference in recency of course work interacted with test content.

The Cook et al. (1985) study is certainly a worse-case scenario. The results of their study do, however, highlight the necessity of choosing equating samples very carefully. When these samples cannot be selected such that they are similar in the abilities measured by the tests to be equated or when the samples are not representative of the target population, extreme caution must be taken in interpreting the results of the equating study. The next section of this chapter will explore how the characteristics of the anchor test (common items) interact with the characteristics of the groups used for equating and how this influences the equating results.

5.5. Characteristics of the Anchor Test (Common Items)

A number of important considerations exist for choosing a set of anchor-test items. It is clear that anchor tests need to be long enough to provide reliable scores and long enough so that the scores on anchor tests can be highly correlated with scores on both the new and old forms of the tests. Klein and Kolen (1985) investigated the relationship between anchor-test length and accuracy of results obtained using the Tucker conventional linear equating method. The test used was a certification test that contained 250 multiple-choice items. These researchers, using data from a fall administration of the test, separated examinees into similar and dissimilar ability-level groups. Within each group, they equated the test to itself several times using the Tucker method and anchor tests of 20, 40, 60, 80, and 100 items. The results of their study indicated that when groups are similar in ability, anchor-test length has little effect on the quality of equating. However, when the groups used for equating differ in level of ability, the length of the anchor test becomes very important. Klein and Kolen concluded that, "When the tests being equated were very similar, or in this particular case, identical, and the groups of examinees very similar, substantially more accurate equating was not obtained by lengthening the anchor. However, longer anchors did result in more accurate equating when the groups of examinees were dissimilar" (p. 10).

When considering the length of common item sets, Kolen and Brennan (2004) pointed out, "When using the common-item nonequivalent groups design, common-item sets should be built to the same specifications, proportionately, as the total test if they are to reflect group differences adequately. In constructing common-item sections, the sections should be long enough to represent test content adequately" (p. 271).

Klein and Jarjoura (1985) evaluated the importance of the content representation of the anchor test when using two conventional linear equating methods. They equated a 250-item multiple-choice test to itself through three intervening links or anchor tests. The success of the equating was judged by how closely the identity relationship of equating a test to itself was recovered. For the representative chain of equatings, they used three 60-item anchor tests, all representative of the content of the total tests. For the nonrepresentative chain, the first anchor consisted of 101 items, the second of 105 items, and the third of 60 items. Only the 60-item anchor was representative of the total-test content: All anchors were similar to the total test in average difficulty. Both Tucker observed-score and Levine true-score equating methods were used.

Based on the results of their study, Klein and Jarjoura (1985) concluded that it was quite important to use content representative anchors with nonrandom groups. According to these authors, "...when nonrandom groups in a common-item equating design perform differentially with respect to various content areas covered in a particular examination, it is important that the common items directly reflect the content representation of the full test forms. A failure to equate on the basis of content representative anchors may lead to substantial equating error" (p. 205).

The points made by Klein and Jarjoura (1985) are particularly salient when considering the results of the Cook et al. (1985) study mentioned in the previous section of this chapter. In another part of their study, Cook et al. contrasted the results of using four different anchor tests to equate the biology achievement tests. They used the 58 common items originally chosen for the equating, a 36-item anchor test that was constructed by content experts to represent concepts in biology least likely to be affected by differences in recency of course work, a 29-item anchor test with item difficulty indexes (delta values) that changed the least for the spring and fall groups, and 29 common items for which item difficulty indexes changed the most for these two groups. The results of the equatings based on the different sets of common items are shown in Table 5.3. These results are in the form of summary statistics for the spring total group that have been derived using the equatings based on the four different anchor tests used with the spring/fall and fall/fall new form/old form sampling combinations.

Table 5.3. Scaled-score summary statistics for the biology exam resulting from combinations of the equating method, common-item set, and equating sample[a]

Spring new form sample/fall old form sample	Equating method					
	Linear		Equipercentile		IRT	
	Mean	SD	Mean	SD	Mean	SD
58 items	585	104	582	102	586	102
36 items	579	102	574	102	581	103
29 items (smallest differences in deltas)	539	103	541	103	545	102
29 items (largest differences in deltas)	624	105	608	99	619	97

[a]Raw score frequency distributions used to compute scaled-score summary statistics were obtained from the spring total group ($N = 23{,}405$).

Cook and Petersen (1987) discussed the results of the equatings and pointed out, "...that when the groups differ in level of ability (spring/fall samples), the different anchor tests yield very disparate equating results. However, when the groups are similar in level of ability (fall/fall samples), the various anchor tests yield equating results that are in close agreement" (p. 234). These authors concluded that these findings in conjunction with the Klein and Jarjoura (1985) findings, "...strongly indicate that when groups differ in level of ability (as they typically do in anchor test designs), special care must be taken when selecting the set of common items constituting the anchor test" (p. 234).

Kolen and Brennan (2004) discussed the results of the Cook et al. (1985) study and concluded that, "...even after the more obvious effects [position effects, order of response alternatives, context effects] are controlled, common items might still perform differently across administrations" (p. 272). They urged that common items be screened for differences in functioning across the groups taking the new and old forms and that, as mentioned earlier, common-item sets be long enough that items that do not behave the same across groups can be dropped from the set of common items without impacting the representativeness of the common-item set. Actually, when new and old form groups are samples from different populations and differ in characteristics as greatly as the spring and fall groups used in the biology test equatings differed (Cook et al.), no amount of screening of the common items is likely to improve the situation and it simply might be impossible to choose an anchor test that will result in a satisfactory equating.

5.6. Conclusions

The purpose of this chapter was to discuss some of the practical issues, or stumbling blocks, that psychometricians who are interested in developing comparable scores on multiple forms of assessments frequently encounter. Most of the discussion in the chapter centered on the use of traditional equating methods with a nonequivalent groups anchor-test data collection design. The results of the studies reviewed in this chapter demonstrate very clearly that if the goal of the testing program is to produce equivalent scores on multiple forms of an assessment and an anchor-test data collection design is to be routinely used, then great care must be taken in (a) constructing the test forms, (b) choosing the new and old form groups to use in the equating, and (c) constructing the anchor test. The results of the studies reviewed in this chapter clearly show that it is impossible to separate the impact on equating results of the three components: samples, test, and common items. These three components of an equating design clearly interact with each other in a complex way that impacts the equating results.

One point made in the chapter is that an important definition of equated scores is that the equating function demonstrates population invariance; that is, an equating function must remain the same regardless of the subgroup from the total population used to derive it. Given that most large-scale testing programs administer tests on multiple testing dates and, by necessity, use anchor-test data collection designs, the likelihood of new and old form groups differing in some significant way that will impact the equating results is very high. Consequently, it would seem imperative to develop and institutionalize rigorous methods for evaluating the equating results as part of the ongoing equating process. One important tool in this evaluation would be the routine investigation of the invariance of the equating results for all major subgroups of the population. In addition, for testing programs that administer content-bound tests at different points in the academic year, it would be very useful to investigate whether equating functions developed using, say, spring groups and then again using fall groups, are reasonably equivalent. If these two functions are not equivalent, it might be necessary to examine carefully what is meant when one talks about the intended population for the test.

The practical problems addressed in this chapter are among those that are frequently encountered when equating tests. A great deal of research has been done recently that has advanced the science of equating. However, as long as it is still necessary to attempt to develop comparable scores in practical testing situations, equating will require sound judgment on the part of professionals trained in the proper use and interpretation of methods and procedures (see Kolen, Chapter 3) as well as an understanding of distinctions among different types of linking (see Holland, Chapter 2).

Acknowledgment. The author wishes to thank Daniel Eignor for his review and insightful and constructive comments.

6 Potential Solutions to Practical Equating Issues

Alina A. von Davier[1]

Educational Testing Service

I work on problems in statistics that I can solve.
—Rupert Miller (Stanford, Department of Statistics) to Paul Holland, circa 1964

6.1. Introduction

Test equating methods are used to produce scores that are interchangeable across different test forms that are built to the same specifications (Holland, Chapter 2; Holland & Dorans, 2006; Kolen, Chapter 3). It is the most stringent form of score linking because it claims score *interchangeability*, not merely comparability, as do concordances and predictions (see Holland & Dorans and Holland, Chapter 2, for more details and definitions of types of score linking). Other types of score linking might use the same computations as test equating but do not result in scores that are interchangeable. A linking typically does not qualify as an equating when the test forms are not constructed to the same specifications or when the test forms measure different constructs. Test equating places several stringent requirements on the content and statistical properties of the test forms and on the samples of test-takers involved and is vulnerable to deviations from these requirements. These deviations might result in scores that are not interchangeable. In these circumstances, the intended test equating becomes a weaker form of test linking and the lack of interchangeability of scores can lead to unintended unfairness to some test-takers.

A good equating is like good cooking: It starts with good ingredients, the right tools, sound knowledge, and a bit of talent. Some "stumbling blocks to equating" (Cook, Chapter 5) appear when the assumptions

---

[1]The opinions expressed in this chapter are those of the author and not necessarily of Educational Testing Service.

required by an equating method are not fulfilled—for example, when the population invariance assumption fails (Dorans & Holland, 2000). Other stumbling blocks arise when the samples available for equating are too small and when large differences exist in the abilities of the groups that take the two test forms to be equated. In these situations, the equating issues are further exacerbated by poor test or anchor-test construction. In an attempt to address these stumbling blocks, researchers have measured the impact on equating of failures of assumptions (population invariance studies, studies on the quality of the anchor) and have developed new strategies to cope with design and data difficulties (equating with small samples, new approaches to anchor-test construction, and new equating models).

This chapter outlines some of this new research and discusses how it can improve test equating practice.

Before embarking on this investigation of the usefulness of new methodologies, we need to remember that, so far, no systematic theory of test equating has been outlined. Over the years, methods have been developed in response to the need to create comparable test scores in practical circumstances. In order to evaluate these methods, Dorans and Holland (2000), Holland and Dorans (2006), Kolen and Brennan (2004), and Lord (1980) have laid out a framework that defines a good equating procedure. This framework is based on the following five *requirements* on the test forms and on the equating functions: the same construct, equal reliability, symmetry, equity, and population invariance requirements. "This is not much of a theoretical underpinning for test equating," said Dorans and Holland (2000, p. 283). Moreover, many of these requirements are vague or arguable. In addition, in most situations, a failure of any of these requirements is hard to detect using the available data. The combination of the lack of a theory and difficulties in detecting bad equating results in practical settings create a challenging situation for a practitioner.

The research overviewed in this chapter is mostly focused on observed-score equating methods and investigates the following equating issues:

1. The population sensitivity of equating functions
2. Small samples equating
3. Addressing the differences in ability of the two groups of test-takers by matching on an anchor test and by constructing the anchor test in nontraditional ways
4. Addressing the stability of the equating results by implementing new equating models such as kernel equating (KE) and by applying the KE framework

The rest of the chapter is structured in six sections, with the first introducing the notation, the next four addressing the above-described issues, and, finally, providing the conclusions and discussion.

This overview of problems and solutions in equating does not directly address the conflicts that might arise between the demands of the testing industry and strong statistical and psychometric practice. To paraphrase the motto of the chapter: "I work on statistical problems that I can solve."

6.2. Observed-Score Equating Methods

In this section I introduce notation and lay out a framework for the discussion of equating. See also Kolen (Chapter 3) for a related discussion.

There are two test forms to be equated, X and Y, and a target population, T, on which this is to be done. The data are collected in such a way that the differences in the difficulty of the test forms and the differences in the ability of the test-takers that take the two forms are not confounded. There are two classes of data collection designs for equating: (a) designs that allow for common people (equivalent groups, single group, and counterbalanced designs) from a single target population of examinees T (see Livingston, 2004, for a slightly different view and definition of a target population) and (b) designs that allow for common items (the nonequivalent groups with an anchor-test design or NEAT design, also referred to as the common-item or anchor-test design) where the tests, X and Y, are given to two samples from two test administrations (populations), P and Q, respectively, and a set of common items, the "anchor test," is given to samples from both these populations). See also Figures 3.5 and 3.6 in the chapter by Kolen (Chapter 3, Section 3.5). The target population, T for the NEAT design, is assumed to be a *weighted average* of P and Q. P and Q are given weights that sum to 1. This is denoted by $T = wP + (1 - w)Q$.

Many observed-score equating methods are based on the *equipercentile equating function*. It is defined on the target population, T, as

$$e_{Y,T}(x) = G_T^{-1}(F_T(x)), \tag{6.1}$$

where $F_T(x)$ and $G_T(y)$ are the cumulative distribution functions (cdfs) of X and Y, respectively, on T. In order for this definition to make sense and to ensure that the inverse equating function also exists, it is also assumed that $F_T(x)$ and $G_T(y)$ have been made strictly increasing and continuous or "continuized."

Several important observed-score equating methods might be viewed as only differing in the way the continuization is achieved. The traditional equipercentile equating method (percentile rank method) uses linear interpolation of the discrete distribution to make it piecewise linear and, therefore, continuous. The KE method uses Gaussian kernel smoothing to approximate the discrete histogram by a continuous density function.

Equipercentile equating leads to linear equating if one assumes that $F_T(x)$ and $G_T(y)$ are continuous and have the same shape while differing in mean and variance. The linear equating function, $\text{Lin}_{Y;T}(x)$, is defined by $\text{Lin}_{Y;T}(x) = \mu_{YT} + \sigma_{YT}((x - \mu_{XT})/\sigma_{XT})$, where μ_{XT}, and μ_{YT}, and σ_{XT}, and σ_{YT} are the means and standard deviations of X and Y on T, respectively.

In von Davier et al. (2004b), it is shown that any equipercentile equating function can be decomposed into the corresponding linear equating function and a nonlinear part.

The next four sections describe several stumbling blocks to equating, some of the research conducted to address them, how the results of these research studies might improve equating practice, and identify research that still needs to be conducted.

6.3. Addressing the Fairness Issue: Population Invariance of Equating Functions

The practical equating concern addressed in this section is the lack of fairness towards subgroups of examinees that may occur when the assumption of population invariance of an equating function does not hold across subpopulations. I discuss this topic from several perspectives.

6.3.1. Definitions and Measures of Population Differences in Equating

One of the five requirements of score equating functions mentioned earlier is that equating should be population invariant; that is, the function computed should not be sensitive to the examinees whose data are used to compute it. Because strict population invariance is often impossible to achieve, Dorans and Holland (2000) introduced a measure of the degree to which an equating function is sensitive to the population on which it is computed. The measure, the root mean square difference (RMSD), compares linking functions computed on different subpopulations with the linking function computed for the whole population. The RMSD index was initially developed for the single group and equivalent groups designs. It was extended to other equating designs and methods in von Davier et al. (2004a).

Although the concept of invariance in equating and linking can be traced back to 1950 (Kolen, 2004b), in recent years there was a significant increase in this research. Most of the studies have focused on the detection of population differences in equating and linking (Angoff & Cowell, 1986; Dorans & Holland, 2000; Harris & Kolen, 1986; Segall, 1995; von Davier et al., 2004a) and on the development of tools for making decisions (Dorans & Feigenbaum, 1994; Holland, Liu, & Thayer, 2005; Liu & Holland, 2006; Moses, 2006; von Davier & Manalo, 2006).

Dorans (2004e) introduced *score equity assessment* (SEA) to describe studies of test fairness that include differential prediction and differential item functioning (DIF). He provided an overview of the evolution of fairness assessment and placed the study of the population sensitivity of equating functions at the core of score equity. He recommended the routine investigation of subgroup dependence of the equating functions. I also believe that measures of population sensitivity of equating results should be routinely employed in operational work (similarly to the way that DIF analyses are now routine operational procedures). This is especially important when new tests or changes to the tests are introduced. The procedure could be automated and embedded in system software and might provide a flag if the population invariance assumption is violated at particular score points. However, establishing a flag requires a criterion. In the following subsections more details on establishing criteria are presented.

How could population invariance indexes help practitioners achieve better equating results? Such indexes are a first step in the process of ensuring fair equating results. The next subsection discusses how to judge the information provided by population invariance indexes.

6.3.2. Criteria for Detecting Subpopulation Differences in Equating Functions

There are at least three different questions one might ask about a particular measure of population sensitivity: (a) Does the amount of observed population sensitivity matter? (b) Is the amount of observed population sensitivity statistically significant or is it just noise? (c) What characteristics of the data, tests, and test-takers lead to population dependence?

To address question a, we might make use of the *difference that matters* (DTM), introduced by Dorans and Feigenbaum (1994). The DTM for a testing program depends on its reporting scale. For example, if the unit of a score scale is one point, then a difference between equating functions larger than a half-point on this scale means a change in the reported score, and this fact might establish the DTM for that particular program. All differences in equating results can be compared to the DTM to judge if they matter. However, the population invariance index, RMSD, introduced by Dorans and Holland (2006), needs to be compared to a *standardized* DTM, which is the DTM divided by the same quantity as the denominator in the RMSD. Some of the recent studies that made use of the DTM criterion for detecting population sensitivity are: Dorans, Holland, Thayer, and Tateneni (2003), Liu, Cahn, and Dorans (2006), von Davier and Wilson (2005), and Yang (2004).

The studies that address question b focus on computing the accuracy of the population invariance indexes. Moses (2006) computed the standard errors (*SE*) for the RMSD index for the KE and showed how to compute the analytical formulas for the *SE* in the KE framework, using a standard large-sample approach. Other approaches compute the empirical *SE* of the RMSD for various equating functions using jackknife techniques (von Davier & Manalo, 2006).

Some studies (Holland et al., 2005; Liu & Holland, 2004) examined how population invariance indexes vary with differences between the tests and the subpopulations of test-takers. This allows us to define "a large value" of these indexes in terms of known factors that influence these indexes (question c).

How do these different criteria help practitioners achieve better equating results? All three types mentioned are valuable and are not mutually exclusive. Each provides information that can aid important decisions for ensuring a fair assessment. For example, the difference between the DTM and the *SE* is similar to the difference between clinical significance and statistical significance as used in medicine: One can have a statistically significant population dependence that will not matter to the test-takers or might have a DTM that is not statistically significant given the data at hand. One the other hand, comparing an RMSD index value to those typically found for parallel tests of given reliability can indicate when a observed RMSD value is typical of that type of testing program.

6.3.3. Implications of Population Sensitivity of Equating Functions

What should be done when the population invariance assumption is violated? This case can easily arise with concordances (see Dorans & Holland, 2000; Holland & Dorans, 2006; Dorans & Walker, Chapter 10; Pommerich, Chapter 11; Sawyer, Chapter 12). However, suppose that it occurs in an equating situation.

The psychometrician can consider examining potential violations of the equating requirements by applying the above described criteria. There are several areas that might be investigated: (a) *Test development*. Should population dependence be expected given the manner in which the tests are constructed? Do the tests measure the same construct? Are the tests equally reliable? (b) *The characteristics of the population dependence*. Is this the first occurrence of a subgroup dependence of the equating function in this assessment? How much does the equating function depend on the subpopulations? At which scores does this dependence occur? Does the dependence matter to the test-takers? (c) *The statistical significance*. Is the observed population dependence statistically significant? Are the subgroups large enough that the equating functions for the subgroups are reliably different?

If this is a first-time occurrence and if no explanation can be found given the testing process, the psychometrician might decide to monitor past and future forms of this particular assessment. If this population dependence recurs or if it is too serious to be ignored, then more radical solutions might be considered. Linking functions between two tests can be computed and the scores on the tests can be linked using them, even when population invariance fails to hold to a sufficient degree. In this situation, however, it is appropriate to claim less for the linking between the two tests: The link might be appropriate for the target population as a whole but inappropriate for some identifiable subgroups. In particular, in order to be fair to different groups of examinees, it might be necessary to consider using *different* links between the tests for different subpopulations of examinees.

Holland and Dorans (2006) gave the following example. Suppose that there are two subgroups of test-takers, two tests to be linked, and one subgroup of test-takers has lower scores on X than the other subgroup but that the *reverse* holds for the other test, Y. They concluded that when a reversal holds, the lower scoring group is always disadvantaged by the use of the total-group linking function. When tests that are built to the same specifications are equated, the possibility of reversals is rare. For the forming of concordances, however, reversals are more likely and should be monitored for major subgroups.

Dorans (2004e) recommended using SEA and population dependence of equating functions "to distinguish between equating and weaker forms of linking" and said:

> Some have argued in the K-12 arena that scores from different tests are simply exchangeable. Despite cogent arguments to the contrary (see Feuer, Holland, Green, Bertenthal, & Hemphill, 1999), this belief lingers. [...] Does it matter to a boy or a girl [...] which test or version of a test they take? If the answer is yes [...], then the presumption of exchangeability is not supported by the data. Inferences that depend on this presumption may be suspect. Some weaker form of linking is more appropriate, and separate concordances for males and females are more equitable than ignoring existing linking differences. (p. 65)

However, the use of *different* links (in situations where equating is actually expected) for different subpopulations of examinees is a controversial solution (see Petersen, Chapter 4). Is it fair to have two people taking the same test, performing similarly, and receiving different scores based on the subgroups to which they belong? This concern needs to be balanced with the unfairness that reversals can create.

6.3.4. Discussion and Future Research Directions

The suggestions for the above-described strategies are not only statistical but also involve program policy. A particular program will need to weigh the consequences of any decision for the test-takers and test users. It is better to avoid such situations by careful planning of test development and equating designs that lead to fair equating results. For more details, see Dorans (2004e), Petersen (Chapter 4, Section 4.2), and Kolen (2003).

To make the study of population sensitivity more practical, I recommend continuing to search for indexes of population dependence that do not require the various subgroups equatings. When there are multiple subpopulations, examination of the subgroups equatings with the existing indexes is time- and labor-intensive. Dorans and Holland (2000) provided an example of such a simplifying method. See Holland et al. (2005) for an illustration of how this simplified method can reduce computations without losing sensitivity to population differences in equating.

6.4. Addressing the Small-Samples Issue: Synthetic Linking Functions

The equating of test scores is subject to sample characteristics. If the sample is large, the equating relationship in the sample might represent accurately the equating relationship in the population. The smaller the sample, the more likely that the equating function computed for that particular sample will differ from the equating function in the population. Both sampling error and bias can influence the quality of the equating. Hence, the impact of small sample size on equating is compounded when the samples are not representative.

The practical equating issue addressed here is what to do when the samples are small.

The research in this area has focused on three topics: the use of presmoothing of the discrete data prior to equating (Livingston, 1993; Skaggs, 2004), the use of the identity function instead of equating (Harris & Crouse, 1993; Skaggs, 2004), and the use of a weighted average of the identity and a linear equating function without presmoothing (Kim, von Davier, & Haberman, 2006).

Livingston (1993) examined the effectiveness of log-linear presmoothing (Holland & Thayer, 1987, 2000) with small samples in an equivalent groups design with an anchor test. He found that the benefits of presmoothing were greatest when the sample was small, but that the number of moments in the observed distribution that should be preserved in the smoothed distribution might depend on the sample characteristics.

Skaggs (2004) studied equating of the passing score using samples ranging from 25 to 200 in an equivalent groups design with no anchor. He observed that the standard errors of equating became smaller as the sample size increased, but that the equating bias did not change much as a function of sample size. For samples as small as 25, no equating is likely to do less harm to examinees than some form of equating, but for samples in the 50–75 range, some form of equating was preferable to no equating. Generally, using log-linear models that fit the first two or three moments of the observed distribution produced smaller standard errors than did the unsmoothed equating, as Livingston (1993) found.

Kim et al. (2006) focused on the NEAT design, which is relatively uncommon in the literature on small-samples equating. In the NEAT design, the anchor test is supposed to adjust for the differences in ability in the two groups. However, in small samples, this adjustment might not be accurate. They introduced a compromise between the identity function (no equating) and an estimated equating function computed on the small sample. The *synthetic linking* function is defined as the weighted average of an estimated equating function and the *identity function* $(ID(x) = x)$ or no-equating.

$$\text{syn}_Y(x) = we_y(x) + (1 - w)ID(x), \tag{6.2}$$

where w is a weight between 0 and 1. They showed that under an appropriate choice of the weight w, the synthetic function meets the symmetry requirement of an equating or linking function mentioned earlier.

The identity function might be a good choice when test specifications are well defined and the test forms are close to being parallel (see also Lawrence & Dorans, 1990; Skaggs, 2004), even when the equating samples are neither representative nor large enough. The mean of the equating results from the synthetic equating function is the weighted average of the mean of the identity and of the estimated equating function. This will reduce the bias in the identity equating function. At the same time, the new linking function will always contain less noise than the estimated equating function:

$$\mathrm{Var}(\mathrm{syn}_y(x)) = w^2\mathrm{Var}(e_y(x)) + (1-w)^2\,\mathrm{Var}(ID(x)) + 2w(1-w)\mathrm{Cov}(e_y(x), ID(x)) \quad (6.3)$$
$$= w^2\mathrm{Var}(e_y(x)).$$

One limitation of this approach is that the two tests should have the same length for the identity function to make sense. In addition, if the test forms are not nearly parallel, the bias introduced by the identity function might be too large.

In Kim et al. (2006), two types of real test data were used that differed in the reliability of the tests and the anchor. For the estimated linking function they used chained linear equating. Chained linear equating was also used as the criterion based on about 10,000 cases. Smaller samples were randomly drawn from the two (nonequivalent) groups. When sample sizes were small (less than 25), the synthetic function did a better job than the estimated chained linear function. For samples as small as 10 or 25, the synthetic equating function was preferable to either not equating or using the chain linear method alone.

If historical data exist, w, in the synthetic function, can be viewed from the perspective of variance components. The weight on the identity should increase as sample variance increases and as year-to-year test variability decreases. In the absence of historical data, the weight can be a function of the difference in the abilities in the two groups, the correlation of the tests and the anchor, the reliabilities and the difference in difficulty of the two forms, and the sample size (see also Kolen & Brennan, 2004, p. 289).

Equating with small samples requires the user to depend on *assumptions* because there is less guidance from the data. The synthetic equating function illustrates how to use assumptions to achieve more stable results. When the test forms are constructed to be nearly parallel, the bias introduced by an identity equating is not expected to be large. The synthetic function allows more flexibility than simply not equating when the samples are small. In a similar way, presmoothing with log-linear models makes assumptions to compensate for the lack of data.

However, assumptions can be wrong, so it is important to know their consequences. Would using empirical data to construct a replacement for the identity function be better? Would the equating results be more stable if a log-linear model is used that fits only the mean of the sparse observed distributions? Perhaps collateral information about the test items could be used to augment the total-test scores, as Mislevy, Sheehan, and Wingersky (1993) proposed?

More research is needed before we can conclude whether the use of the synthetic function relying on the identity function makes matters better or worse. Follow-up studies of the work of Kim et al. (2006) can investigate the synthetic function under various circumstances, including those in which the identity function might introduce a significant bias. It is natural to suggest comparing versions of the synthetic function to the use of log-linear models with few parameters in terms of bias and variability.

6.5. Addressing Differences in Ability in the Two Populations of the NEAT Design

The practical equating issue here is to equate scores for test forms that are taken by groups that exhibit *large* differences in ability (see Cook, Chapter 5). In the NEAT design, the anchor test, taken by the two groups of test-takers, is used to adjust for the differences in ability in the two groups. Previous research in this area has focused on three topics: the use of the anchor test to create similar or matched groups (Kolen, 1990; Lawrence & Dorans, 1990; Livingston, Dorans, & Wright, 1990), the use of other variables to create matched groups (Liou, Cheng, & Li, 2001; Wright & Dorans, 1993), and, recently, the creation of anchor tests that maximizes their correlation with the tests to be equated (Sinharay & Holland, 2006).

When there are only small differences between the two samples of examinees used in the NEAT design, all linear equating methods tend to give similar results, as do all nonlinear equating methods (see Kolen, 1990; von Davier, 2003; von Davier et al., 2004a). To the extent that a NEAT design is almost an equivalent groups design with anchor test, the need for the anchor test is minimized. This is the main argument behind the *matching-on-the-anchor procedure*. When matching on the anchor is carried out, the distributions of the anchor in the two matched groups will be the same (Kolen, 1990; Lawrence & Dorans, 1990; Livingston et al.). If the distributions of the anchor in the two groups are the same, all comparable (equipercentile versus linear) observed-score equating methods will give the same result (von Davier, 2003). However, Cook and Petersen (1987) and Livingston et al. (1995) noted that although all the equating functions agree, their agreement might correspond to an incorrect equating function due to bias.

In order for the matching-on-the-anchor procedure to work, the anchor has to behave in the two groups similarly to the two tests, X and Y (see also Cook, Chapter 5). Other research focused on matching groups on variables other than the anchor (Wright & Dorans, 1993). Matching both on the anchor and on other variables seems to be promising.

When the two samples are very different in performance, the use of the anchor test becomes critical; it is the *only* means of separating the *differences between the abilities* of the two groups of examinees from the *differences between the two tests* that are being equated (see Holland & Dorans, 2006). The most important properties of the anchor test are its integrity and stability over time and its correlation with the scores on the two tests being equated (Holland & Dorans). It is important for the correlation to be as high as possible. Because of their part-whole relationship with the other tests, internal anchors have high correlations with the total tests.

Petersen et al. (1989, p. 246) and von Davier et al. (2004a, p. 33) indicated that the higher the correlation between scores of an anchor test and scores on the tests to be equated, the better the anchor test is for equating. The importance for equating of this correlation raises the question: Does the usual advice of making the anchor test a "mini-version" of X and Y actually increase this correlation? The requirement that the anchor test should be representative of the content of the total test has been shown to be an important requirement by Klein and Jarjoura (1985). If the difficulties of the items in the full tests are spread over a range of values, does that mean that the difficulties of the anchor-test items should be spread over the same range? The results reported in Sinharay and Holland (2006) suggested that this might not be true. These authors examined whether the spread of item difficulties should be the same as that of X and Y. They show that an anchor test with a narrow spread of item difficulty might perform as well (in terms of accuracy and precision in equating) as one consisting of items with a wider spread of difficulties. In a series of simulation studies, they explored the relations between scores on a total test and an external anchor test for different types of anchor test, based on generated data from one- and two-dimensional logistic item-response models. Their main finding is that an anchor test with a narrow spread of item difficulties located near the mean of the difficulties of the total tests has the highest correlation with the total tests for almost all of the situations considered.

How can this research improve test equating? When there are large differences in ability in the two populations in the NEAT design, equating can be a challenge.

Matching on the anchor and/or on other variables that correlate with the tests are procedures that require more research and the results need to be interpreted carefully. As mentioned earlier, all of the equating functions might agree to an incorrect (biased) equating function. If a demographic variable is used, then one might ask if the result is an equating and if the test scores are interchangeable. What role would the subpopulation dependence of the equating function play in choosing a person characteristic as a matching variable? More research is necessary to shed light on these issues.

One interpretation of Sinharay and Holland (2006) is that although it is important that anchor tests match the content and overall difficulty of the total tests, it is less important to match the spread of the item difficulties of the total tests. If further research bears out their preliminary findings, then their work suggests that test developers need not attempt to make the distribution of item difficulties look like a miniversion of the distributions for the total tests and can focus on matching test content and overall difficulty.

6.6. Addressing the Stability of Equating Results: Kernel Equating and Applications

In the practice of equipercentile equating, psychometricians have typically used the *percentile rank method* (that uses linear interpolation to make the cdfs in Equation 6.1 continuous) for equating test forms with score distributions that differ in shape. One of the consequences of this method is that the linearly interpolated cdfs and the equating function have kinks; that is, the functions are not smooth (see Kolen & Brennan, 2004, Figures 2.4, 2.5, and 2.10). Moreover, if there are no examinees at a particular score, the percentile rank method is not well defined. In order to address these issues, past research focused on procedures for smoothing the data prior to equating (presmoothing), procedures for smoothing the equating function (postsmoothing), alternative procedures for continuizing the cdfs, and new equating functions.

In my opinion, the issue of stability and quality of equating results is best addressed by providing the following: (a) a coherent and formal equating process; (b) better methods of continuizing the discrete distributions, F and G, in order to be able to compute the equating function from Equation 1; (c) useful measures of statistical accuracy; and (d) equating models that are appropriate for particular test designs. In the next subsection I will briefly describe the kernel equating method and indicate how it accomplishes the four above mentioned aspects.

6.6.1. The Gaussian Kernel Method

Holland and Thayer (1989) and von Davier et al. (2004b) viewed all observed-score test equating as having five steps or parts, each of which involves distinct ideas: (1) presmoothing of the score distributions; (2) estimation of the score probabilities on the target population; (3) continuization of the presmoothed discrete score distributions; (4) computing the equating function; and (5) computing the standard error of equating and related accuracy measures. They applied this framework to describe kernel equating (KE); see von Davier et al. (2004b) for details and for a detailed description of KE.

The main advantage of the KE framework is that it brings together these steps into an organized whole rather than treating them as disparate problems. KE exploits presmoothing by fitting log-linear models to score data, and it incorporates the presmoothing into Step 5 of the framework, where KE provides new tools for comparing two or more equating functions and to rationally choose between them.

Kernel equating is an equipercentile equating procedure in which the discrete score distributions are made continuous using Gaussian kernel smoothing rather than linear interpolation. By varying the bandwidth values in Step 4, KE can approximate the traditional equipercentile and the linear equating methods. The bandwidths are positive constants that manipulate the weight placed on the Gaussian kernel and that can be chosen to achieve various purposes. When "optimal" bandwidths are chosen, KE will closely approximate the traditional equipercentile equating method. When the bandwidths are large (10 times the standard deviation of the scores or larger), the continuized distributions will be nearly Gaussian and the KE functions are effectively linear. Thus, linear equating can be regarded as special case of equipercentile equating in the KE framework.

In the KE framework, von Davier et al. (2004b) introduced the standard error of the difference (the SEED) between two equating functions. The SEED has several practical uses such as rationalizing the linear/nonlinear decision, implementing a new approach to the counterbalanced design, comparing chained and poststratification equating methods in the NEAT design, or aiding the comparison among other observed-score equating methods (von Davier & Kong, 2005). The various uses of the SEED do not require KE, but the SEED is a natural part of the KE framework and von Davier et al. (2004b) showed how to apply it for these purposes.

Several research studies (Han, Li, & Hambleton, 2005; Mao, von Davier, & Rupp, 2006; von Davier et al., 2006) focused on evaluations of KE and on comparisons of KE with other observed-score and true-score equating methods. Among other things, these studies indicate that KE can closely approximate traditional equating methods well. These studies used the newly developed KE-Software (Educational Testing Service, 2006).

6.6.2. Applications of the KE Framework

Recent studies have taken advantage of the formal and coherent formulation of the KE process and have focused on the application of KE to particular equating issues.

Moses, Yang, and Wilson (2005) explored the use of KE for integrating and extending two procedures (Hanson, 1996; Lawrence & Dorans, 1990) proposed for assessing the statistical equivalence of two test forms in which the same items have been scrambled into different orders.

Other applications of the KE framework are Moses (2006), which computed the standard error of population invariance indexes, and Moses and Holland (in press), which extended the KE computations to situations in which the data are not presmoothed.

The KE framework is also used to *construct* hybrid equating function that combine a linear equating function from one source with an equipercentile function from another. An example is a nonlinear generalization of the Levine linear observed-score equating function. The Levine linear method does not yet have a curvilinear analogue, and there is no version of KE that approximates the Levine function. Nevertheless, the Levine linear method is often computed in practical applications for comparison purposes. Under some circumstances, it is more accurate than other linear methods (see Petersen, Marco, & Stewart, 1982).

von Davier, Fournier-Zajac, and Holland (in press) used the KE framework to construct a hybrid equating based on the Levine linear method. The new function preserves the nonlinear characteristics from the KE poststratification and the linear form from the classical Levine observed-score equating.

With the five steps of the KE framework identified, other research has focused on replacing the original proposals from von Davier et al. (2004b) with alternatives to create new equating processes. One of these proposes alternative continuization methods: Wang (2004) continuized the discrete probability distribution by using the polynomial log-linear function (from the presmoothing step), divided by the area under it, in order to ensure that it is a probability distribution function. The method is called the continuized log-linear (CLL) method. As a potential alternative to the Gaussian kernel, Holland (personal communication, July 26, 2005) discussed the possibility of using a logistic kernel. One of the advantages of the logistic kernel is that the analytical form of the derivatives required for computing the SEE and the SEED is very simple. At the same time, given the modular character of KE-Software (Educational Testing Service, 2006), it would be very easy to implement it in parallel with the Gaussian kernel.

6.6.3. Discussion and Future Research Directions

How do these new equating models address the issues of stability of the equating results? The nonlinear Levine function is a new equating method that might allow the known benefits of the Levine linear function (Petersen et al., 1982) to apply to cases where nonlinear equating is required. There are situations in which the tests and the anchor are very carefully constructed, but the two test score distributions differ in shape (see von Davier, Holland, et al., 2006). In such a case, a nonlinear version of the Levine function is desirable.

One reason for seeking alternatives to continuization with a Gaussian kernel is that the use of the Gaussian kernel leads to lower values of the higher order cumulants of the continuous distribution than those of the original discrete distribution (Holland & Thayer, 1989; von Davier et al., 2004b). So far, this reduction in the cumulants has not been shown to have any practical implication. The Wang (2004) proposal of CLL might provide a possible alternative to kernel smoothing because it directly computes the cdfs from the fitted loglinear model.

The new accuracy method introduced in the KE framework, the SEED, has direct practical uses: It can aid the decision between linear and nonlinear equating functions, between equating functions that are based on different assumptions, such as the poststratification and chained equating (see Kolen & Brennan, 2004; von Davier et al., 2004b), or between the linear methods used in the NEAT design. The SEED is a statistical tool that has the potential of being extended to other applications—possibly as a decision aid between log-linear models.

The KE method has been around for almost 20 years, and despite the obvious theoretical and practical advantages, it is still not part of the operational practice. Many practitioners are intimidated by the theoretical description of KE. Actually, many practitioners do not explicitly use linear interpolation, but a conversion table, with averaged values between score points. The KE method, although a differentiable function that differs from the linear interpolation, agrees closely to the equipercentile function, which uses linear interpolation at almost all score points when an appropriate bandwidth is selected. This is fortunate and unfortunate at the same time. It is fortunate to have the equating functions agreeing, but it is unfortunate because it gives practitioners no reason to change. Researchers and policy makers need better arguments to convince practitioners, such as emphasizing the availability of KE accuracy and diagnostic measures, the modularity of the KE framework that translates into a modular software package, and the easy-to-use interface of KE-Software (Educational Testing Service, 2006). Moreover, the KE framework has the potential of introducing automatic procedures with incorporated automatic decision steps to reduce the routine work of the psychometricians and data analysts.

In my opinion, studies of alternative continuization methods and of hybrid functions are of a more theoretical than practical interest in the near future. From the practical point of view, I believe that research focused on decision aids and automatic equating procedures is necessary. Developing or refining indexes, such as the SEED for aiding in the process of comparing equating function, indexes for deciding among log-linear models in the presmoothing procedures, or attempts to improve the fit of the loglinear models (and therefore to improve the stability of equating results) in regions of the score range that matter to a particular program are of importance in equating practice. In addition, we should focus on expanding the research on the KE method to scale drift and to tests with complicated distributional shapes. Additionally, researchers should focus on finding more efficient ways to teach and explain the KE method and to engage more practitioners in evaluating procedures and approaches.

6.7. Discussion

This chapter summarizes my selection of the current research directions in equating that show some potential in addressing issues encountered in the practice of equating.

For the sake of coherence, I decided to focus on observed-score equating only. Equating that uses item information and is based on item response theory models has its own challenges, including those mentioned in Cook and Petersen (1987), von Davier and Wilson (2006), Hambleton, Swaminathan, and Rogers (1991), Kolen and Brennan (2004), Lord (1980), and Petersen et al. (1983, 1989).

Here I discussed several equating topics: the population dependence of equating functions, the equating in small samples, the adjustments needed when the groups of test-takers differ in ability, and the stability of equating functions provided by the KE method.

The main point that this chapter makes is that there is a continuous effort to address scientifically the practical issues of equating and that research does not take place in an ivory tower, but is responsive and related to practical problems.

Another point made here is that the equating process always involves policy decisions in addition to the statistical ones and that the responsibility for fair assessments needs to be shared between the leaders of the program and the psychometricians who advise them.

Currently, when more and more standardized testing is used for assessing competencies in different domains nationally and internationally, we are also discovering more challenges to ensuring that the process and the results are fair and accurate. In turn, these challenges and these new social implications open the door to more research in support of fair assessments, both in improving the test construction process and in advancing the statistical methods involved.

Acknowledgments. The author thanks Neil Dorans, Mary Pommerich, Paul Holland, Dan Eignor, and Tim Moses for their comments on the previous versions of the chapter and for interesting discussions on different topics addressed in this presentation.

Part 3: Tests in Transition

Educational testing programs are often in a state of transition. Changes in curriculum lead to changes in assessments. Sometimes modes of administration change.

Jinghua Liu and Michael Walker in *Score Linking Issues Related to Test Content Changes* address score linking issues associated with content changes to a test in general. They use the College Board's new SAT® data to illustrate how to evaluate the linkage between the scales of the new test and the old test from different perspectives. Among the criteria they use is subgroup linking invariance to assess the equatability of the new SAT to the old SAT.

In *Linking Scores Derived Under Different Modes of Test Administration*, Daniel Eignor discusses linkings between tests given under different modes of administration. He notes that transitional linkings in general might be viewed as equatings, calibrations, or concordances. The reasons why the linking between scores from computer adaptive tests and paper-and-pencil tests cannot be considered to be equated are discussed. Examples from the literature are given.

Robert Brennan synthesizes the issues raised in the two preceding chapters in *Tests in Transition: Discussion and Synthesis*. He suggests that the field of psychometrics needs a theoretically coherent and practically useful integration of equity and subpopulation invariance, and he begins to lay the foundation for that integration.

7 Score Linking Issues Related to Test Content Changes

Jinghua Liu and Michael E. Walker[1]

Educational Testing Service

7.1. Introduction

This chapter addresses issues of score scale continuity in the event of changes to a test. A testing program needs to evolve from time to time to strengthen its alignment with school reform, curriculum changes, and changes in the test-taking population. The College Board's SAT Reasoning Test™ (referred to as the SAT®) provides an excellent example of such evolution. The SAT has been reconfigured several times since its debut in 1926. All of the changes represented attempts to update the SAT to reflect contemporary school curricula, to reinforce educational standards and practices, to maintain test fairness for the increasingly diverse test-taking population, and to enhance the test's effectiveness as an admissions tool (Lawrence, Rigol, Van Essen, & Jackson, 2003).

Changes to a test can be multifaceted, including changes in test content, test statistical specifications, and mode of administration. Content changes can involve topic coverage (e.g., the 2005 revision to the SAT to cover third-year college-preparatory math), item format, and item type changes (e.g., the elimination of analogy items and quantitative-comparison items from the SAT in 2005; the introduction of student-produced response items to the SAT math section in 1994), test length (e.g., 67 items on the 2005 SAT critical reading section vs. 78 items on the previous SAT verbal section), and the relative emphasis given to each aspect of the measured domain (e.g., the heavier reliance of the 2005 revision to the SAT on reading vs. vocabulary, as compared with the previous SAT). Content changes can also include adding a new measure to the existing test battery

---

[1] The opinions expressed in this chapter are those of the authors and not necessarily of Educational Testing Service.

(e.g., the addition of a writing section to the SAT in 2005). Changes to test statistical specifications can involve changes to test difficulty and the distribution of item difficulty (e.g., the item difficulty distribution of the SAT verbal section shifted from a bimodal to a unimodal distribution in 1994). Other changes are related to the modes of test administration, such as adjusting the timing of the test, allowing calculator use, moving from paper-and-pencil to computer-based testing and from fixed to adaptive testing, and so on.

Whenever a test undergoes changes in content, specifications, or administrative conditions, the question of score comparability arises. Although the difference between scores on the old and revised tests might fall along a wide continuum, we can nevertheless identify three distinct categories:

1. The revisions are minor enough that we can render the scores on the two versions essentially interchangeable through test score equating.
2. The revised test differs too greatly from the original test for equating; but the relationship between the two tests is strong enough to establish a concordance relationship.
3. The revisions are so substantial that the two tests cannot be said to measure the same construct, in which case, not even a concordance is warranted.

Essentially, this chapter discusses how to evaluate score comparability, test equatability, and scale continuity for tests in transition.

At some point early in the redesign process, before we begin to investigate issues of score comparability, the testing organization must make a conscious decision about what is most important in the test revision. In some cases, the desire to maintain the meaning of the reported scores might be paramount. In some cases, the intended characteristics of the revised score scale (e.g., constant standard errors of measurement along the scale) drive everything else. In still other cases, matching the test coverage to the current curriculum or ensuring that the item types reflect current teaching practice is most important. The determination of this most important factor will have strong implications for the rest of the redesign process. Therefore, staff at the testing organization should give much thought to this decision. They need to ask themselves what the organization wants to achieve with the new test and what the constraints are. All of the revisions and data collections should be guided by this redesign principle. We will emphasize this point throughout the chapter.

In this chapter, we use data from linking the new SAT critical reading to the old SAT verbal for illustrative purposes. Section 7.2 addresses the kinds of linking issue we might care about for tests in transition and the criteria we might utilize to determine the equatability of a new test to an old test. Section 7.3 discusses considerations for data collection, using the data collection design employed in the Spring 2003 new SAT field trial as an example. Section 7.4 describes how we evaluate whether the new test is equatable to the old test. Finally, Section 7.5 summarizes the findings and research implications.

7.2. Major Linking Issues for Tests in Transition

The equating process links scores from different editions of the same test (e.g., SAT math to SAT math). Equating adjusts for differences in difficulty of nearly parallel forms that are built to the same explicit content and statistical specifications and administered under the same conditions. The goal of equating is to ensure that scores from different editions of a test can be used interchangeably. Concordance, on the other hand, links two different tests that measure similar constructs (e.g., SAT math to ACT® math). Concordant scores are not interchangeable. What about tests in transition? Should the link between an old test and a revised test be considered an equating or a concordance? (See Holland, Chapter 2 for a further discussion of linkage types and factors that make a linking an equating.)

The first question is what the major goal is for the new test. For example, the College Board made it very clear at the beginning of the redesign stage for the new SAT, which was launched in March 2005, that the new critical reading score should be fully equatable to the old verbal score and that the new math score should be fully equatable to the old math score. This goal guided the development of the new SAT throughout the entire redesign process: It limited the scope of changes considered for the test, guided the design of the field trial and the analysis of the data, and directed the responses to the research findings. The importance of setting priorities for the different characteristics of the new test early in the redesign process cannot be overemphasized.

In the case of the SAT, the College Board wanted the scores from the revised test and the original test to be considered as equivalent and the linkage between them to be an equating. Thus, the statistical analysts on the redesign team directed their attention to assessing the extent to which the revised test met the conditions for score equating. If those conditions were not met with the original prototypes, then the test revision would be modified so that the conditions were met.

Other testing programs might wish to emphasize the measurement of a recently introduced topic in the core curriculum. In this situation, the research would include item analysis and construct validation efforts to ensure that the new test items adequately represented the new subject matter. The research might also focus on the dimensionality of the new measure. The revised test might be modified to obtain sufficient content coverage. Secondary efforts would examine the relationship between the old and the revised tests to aid in the determination of how the scale for the revised test might best be set.

This chapter primarily addresses score linking issues, although testing programs face many other considerations when redesigning a test. Using the SAT as an example, the remainder of this section first outlines the changes made to the test in 2005. Next, it reviews some of the characteristics that distinguish equating from other forms of score linking. Finally, the section lists the specific research questions examined to determine if the new SAT could be considered equatable to the previous, or old, SAT, given the extent of the revisions.

7.2.1. Changes to the New SAT Critical Reading in 2005

The SAT assesses how students apply what they have learned in high school to analyze and solve problems that they will likely encounter in college. The 2005 changes to the test were initiated to "strengthen the alignment of the SAT to the instructional practices in today's classroom and to address the importance of writing skills" (College Board, 2005, p. 6).

Table 7.1 summarizes the changes that were made to the content and timing of the SAT verbal and reading sections. The major content changes to the old verbal (OV) section involve the replacement of analogy items by additional short reading passages. The total length of the section has been reduced to 67 items from the previous 78 items, a 14% reduction. The new section represents increasingly heavier reliance on a reading construct, with approximately 72% reading comprehension items, as compared to 51% in the OV section. The name of the section has changed from *verbal* to *critical reading* (CR) to emphasize the change in focus.

The major content changes for the math section included the elimination of the quantitative comparison items from the old math (OM) section and the expansion of content to cover third-year college-preparatory math. The new math (NM) section contains 54 items, as compared 60 items. The number of student-produced response items remains at 10, but the number of five-choice items increased to 44 from the old 35. Correspondingly, the proportion of five-choice items in the test has increased to 81% from 58%.

Another significant change is the addition to the test battery of a new writing section, containing multiple-choice questions and a student-written essay. Test timing has also been changed. The writing section consists of two multiple-choice sections (one 25-min and one 10-min) and one 25-min essay section.[2] The CR and NM sections contain three sections each: two 25-min sections and one 20-min section (in comparison, the OV and OM sections each had two 30-min sections and one 15-min section). The variable section, which is primarily used to obtain pretest statistics or equating data from motivated examinees, has changed to 25 min for the

Table 7.1. Comparison of content specifications between the CR and OV sections

	CR[a]		OV[b]	
	No. of items	% of total test	No. of items	% of total test
Item type				
Analogy	0	0	19	24
Sentence completion	19	28	19	24
Passage-based reading	48	72	40	51
Total	67		78	
Reading item content				
Extended reasoning	36–40	54–60	28–32	36–41
Literal comprehension	4–6	6–9	4–5	5–6
Vocabulary in context	4–6	6–9	4–7	5–6
Reading content categories				
Humanities	8–12	12–18	8–12	10–15
Social studies	8–12	12–18	8–12	10–15
Natural sciences	8–12	12–18	8–12	10–15
Literary fiction	8–12	12–18	0	0
Human relationships	0	0	8–12	10–15

[a]Time allotted = 70 min.
[b]Time allotted = 75 min.

new SAT from 30 min for the old SAT. The total testing time for the new SAT has increased to 3 hr 45 mins from the previous 3 hr for the old SAT.

Any or all of the above listed changes could affect the psychometric characteristics of the test. Given the College Board's stated goal of maintaining the equivalence of the new test with the old, the proposed

---

[2]Although the introduction of the writing test constituted the greatest change in the SAT, it will not be discussed in this chapter, which focuses on linking the scores for the new SAT critical reading section to the scores for the old SAT verbal section.

changes immediately gave rise to several questions pertaining to the CR section:

1. Does the replacement of analogy items with short reading passages, the heavier reliance on a reading construct, and reallocation of time to reading items versus nonreading items change the construct enough to make equating impossible?
2. Does the CR section (which was shortened to 67 items and 70 min vs. 78 items and 75 min for the OV section) change the properties of the test enough to make equating impossible?
3. Does the introduction of a writing section with an essay alter the testing context enough to affect the equatability of the CR scores to the OV scores?

To answer the above questions, it is necessary to know what characteristics of a test will affect the equating process. This topic is discussed next.

7.2.2. Requirements for Equating

Equating is considered the strongest type of linking. Researchers in the field have devoted much energy toward providing a definition of what constitutes an equating of test X to test Y. Lord (1980) specified four requirements that must be met for equating:

1. *The same construct.* The two tests must measure the same construct.
2. *Equity.* Once two test forms have been equated, it should not matter to the test-taker which form of the test is administered.
3. *Symmetry.* The equating transformation should be symmetric. The equating of X to Y should be the inverse of equating Y to X.
4. *Subpopulation invariance.* The equating transformation should be invariant across subpopulations from the same population.

In addition to these requirements, Dorans and Holland (2000; see also Holland, Chapter 2) added another requirement for test equating, which one could argue is implicit in Lord's equity requirement above (although see Dorans and Holland for an interesting discussion of this point):

5. *Equal reliability.* Test X and test Y should have equal reliability.

Kolen and Brennan (2004) focused on the degree of similarity of two linked tests, indicating that, in order for the linking to be considered equating, the tests must be the same with respect to four features. In addition to the requirement of equal constructs mentioned above, the authors added:

6. *The same inferences.* The two tests must share common measurement goals and be designed for use to reach the same kinds of conclusion.
7. *The same population.* The two tests should have the same target population.
8. *The same measurement characteristics/conditions.* The tests should have the same specifications, be administered under the same conditions, and be equivalent in their psychometric properties.

The above listed requirements are not mutually exclusive. For example, Requirement 8, which is discussed further in Kolen's chapter (Chapter 3, Section 3.2), can subsume Requirement 5. Dorans and Holland (2000) indicated a link between Requirements 4 and 5, although the authors showed that high reliability rather than equal reliability is more essential to equating. Holland's chapter (Chapter 2, Section 2.4.1) should be consulted for a further discussion of equating requirements. Although other researchers have offered slightly different linking taxonomies, we believe that the above eight characteristics adequately summarize the consensus of the field.

The goal of equating is to produce exchangeable test scores. If all of the eight of the requirements hold exactly, then most experts in the field would agree that equating is possible. Unfortunately, the eight requirements never hold exactly, except perhaps in the most trivial of cases. Thus, the situation becomes one of degree: Are the requirements met sufficiently such that the scores on two tests can be considered equivalent within a reasonable amount of error? Dorans and Holland (2000) and Kolen and Brennan (2004) offered numerical indexes that can be useful in answering this question. Later in this chapter, we present the analyses performed in the context of the new SAT to determine whether the revised test could be considered equivalent to the previous version.

If the above conditions are not met sufficiently, then the relationship between the two tests cannot be considered equating. For example, even though the new test could be put on the same scale as the old test, if the new test has substantially lower reliability (such that Requirements 5 and 8 and possibly Requirement 2 are not met), then the new test could be considered calibrated to the old test but not equivalent to it (Holland, Chapter 2; Holland & Dorans, 2006). Even though the new test is designed for the same purpose and has the same reliability and difficulty, if the new test measures a similar but not identical construct (such that Requirements 1, 2, 4, and possibly 8 are not met), then the two tests can be concorded but not equated. A concordance will allow translation of one test score to the metric of the other test score for a specific population of examinees, although this relationship will not necessarily hold for another population. Perhaps the most familiar example of a concordance is the one between the

SAT and the ACT. Although both are designed to aid in college admissions decisions, the two tests are built to different specifications based on slightly different theoretical perspectives. Chapters 10, 11, and 12 by Dorans and Walker, Pommerich, and Sawyer, respectively, in this volume treat issues related to concordance in great detail.

If the difference in constructs between the new and old tests is drastic enough, even a concordance is not possible. Perhaps the best that can be hoped for is a scaling that allows comparisons of the scores in terms of percentile ranks. This type of scaling was accomplished between the SAT verbal and math scales by the 1990 recentering (Dorans, 2002).

The distinctions made above are not so much in terms of the arithmetic operations used to link two tests, because the methodology often remains essentially the same regardless of whether all of the requirements for equating are met. The major differences among the different types of linkage involve the interpretation of the resulting test scores. In our particular example, the College Board wanted to ensure that SAT users could interpret scores on the new test in the same way that they had interpreted scores on the old test. For that reason, it became essential that the eight requirements be met as nearly as possible. The following subsection briefly discusses some of the criteria that we used to determine the extent to which the new SAT met the eight requirements listed earlier.

7.2.3. Criteria to Determine Equatability of the New SAT

In practice, the evaluation of the eight requirements listed earlier involves extensive analysis, both statistical and conceptual. Our investigation of the revisions to the SAT could be divided into the following major categories:

1. *Construct similarity.* To achieve equating, the tests must measure the same construct. A good first step is to compare test specifications. Are the test blueprints similar enough to justify the linkage between the two tests? This comparison should include both the explicit content specifications and statistical specifications and is made at the beginning of the new test development to provide preliminary information on the degree to which the two tests measure the same construct.

2. *Empirical relationship between the old test and the new test.* What is the correlation between scores on the two tests for each measure? Is the correlation strong enough for test equating? Does the correlation approach the reliability of the test? Is this correlation invariant across important subgroups? In the case of the SAT, is the correlation between the OV and OM sections equal to the correlation between the CR and NM section? (Although equality of correlations cannot

demonstrate equality of constructs from old to new tests, lack of equality can call the equal constructs assumption into question.)

3. *Measurement precision*. What is the reliability of the new test compared to the old test? Does the new test exhibit the same measurement precision as the old test across the range of the scores?

4. *Subgroup invariance*. Does the new test and the old test rank important subgroup means in the same order? Is the linking from the new test to the old test invariant across important subgroups?

7.3. Considerations for Data Collection Design

Setting equatability as the goal does not necessarily ensure that the new test can be equated to the old test. Data need to be collected and extensive analyses need to be conducted to evaluate whether the equatability goal is achieved. This section describes what data need to be collected, data collection designs, and what issues need to be considered to evaluate the linkage issues for a test in transition.

7.3.1. Linking Designs

In the ideal linking design, both tests would be administered in their entirety to the same group of test-takers who are representative of the test-taking population under operational conditions. In such a single group administration, we could estimate item and test characteristics as well as the correlation between the two tests under an entire test context that simulates an operational situation. We also could link the two tests using the most powerful and statistically preferred design.

Unfortunately, such a design is not always feasible given practical constraints, such as test length and different administration modes. In the case of the SAT, for example, the testing time is 3 hr for the old test and more than 3 hr 30 min for the new test. Adding time for material distribution and collection, instruction, and breaks, the total sitting time for two test batteries given on the same day would have been more than 7 hr 30 mins. If, on the other hand, the two test batteries had been given on two different days, with one test administered per day, the design would have required two school days. In any case, it was unrealistic to expect schools or students to make such large time commitments. In addition, differential carryover (e.g., fatigue, practice) might have affected results. Therefore, it was necessary to make some modifications.

In this chapter, we describe the two designs that were employed as part of the Spring 2003 new SAT field trial. Kolen (Chapter 3) described data collection designs and linking procedures in some detail, including the designs and procedures described in this chapter.

7.3.1.1. Design 1: Equivalent Groups Design

One modification involved the administration of each test battery in its entirety to different but equivalent groups of test-takers. A spiraling process involving packaging test books in sequences (1, 2, 1, 2,...) was employed in order to yield equivalent groups. This design provided information on performance of each test component in the context of the entire test battery, allowing us to link the new test to the old test through equivalent groups and to evaluate item statistics and test statistics under circumstances that simulate an operational situation.

Design 1 in the field trial employed this modification, the equivalent or random groups design. This type of design is described by Kolen's Figure 3.1 (Chapter 3). The top portion of Table 7.2 summarizes the different booklets in Design 1. Booklets 1 and 2 contained a complete old SAT battery including the OV and OM sections. The two booklets were designed to determine to what degree the field-trial sample represented the ability of a typical SAT population and to serve as the old form to which the new test would be linked. Booklets 3 and 4 contained the entire new SAT prototype battery, including the CR, NM, and writing (NW) sections. The sections were interspersed in these booklets, approximating the section ordering of an operational form.[3]

7.3.1.2. Design 2: Counterbalanced Single Group Design

Through the equivalent groups design, we were able to link the tests and obtain test and item characteristics, with the exception of the correlation between tests. Therefore, we needed another modification, which involved administering both versions of each test component or construct measure,

---

[3]Each operational form of the SAT also includes a variable section, which might contain pretest items or anchor items to use for equating. The forms used in Design 1 of the field trial also included variable sections containing either math or verbal/critical reading items. These sections were identical across the old and new SAT forms; by examining performance on these sections, we could assess whether the design produced old and new form groups that were truly equivalent in ability. If the groups turned out not to be close enough in ability, the variable sections could serve as anchor tests for use in linking the old and new forms via a non-equivalent groups anchor test (NEAT) design (see Kolen's Figure 3.6, Chapter 3). Thus, the field trial contained a third equating design in addition to the equivalent groups and single group designs.

Table 7.2. Summary of the design in the Spring 2003 new SAT field trial

Design	Test administered[a]	Purpose
1. Equivalent groups		
Book 1	Entire old SAT + Variable Sect. 1	Link the new SAT prototype to the old SAT.
Book 2	Entire old SAT + Variable Sect. 2	Evaluate item characteristics (difficulty, etc.).
Book 3	Entire new SAT + Variable Sect. 1	Evaluate test characteristics (reliability, conditional standard error
Book 4	Entire new SAT + Variable Sect. 2	of measurement, speededness, etc.).
2. Single group		
Book 5	OV then CR	Link the new SAT prototype to the
Book 6	CR then OV	old SAT.
Book 7	OM then NM	Construct comparability (correlation
Book 8	NM then OM	between new and old measures, correlation with other variables, dimensionality analysis, etc.).

[a]Variable Sect. 1 contains math items; Variable Sect. 2 contains verbal/critical reading items. See Footnote 3 in the text.

one old and one new, to the same group of test-takers. This additional design provided information on the relationship between the old version and the new version on one test component or construct measure, allowing us to evaluate construct comparability, including the correlation between new and old tests, subgroup invariance of regressions, dimensionality analysis, and so on. To control for order effects, counterbalancing was used.

Design 2 in the field trial was an example of a counterbalanced single group design (see Kolen's Figure 3.3. in Chapter 3). Each book in Design 2 (shown in the lower portion of Table 7.2) contained just two versions of one component. For example, Booklets 5 and 6 both contained OV and CR sections, but in a counterbalanced order. Similarly, Booklets 7 and 8 contained OM and NM sections. The counterbalanced designs allowed identification of potential fatigue effects or other effects related to the order in which the tests were given. Because the old SAT did not have a writing section, we focused in this chapter on linking the CR section to the OV.

7.3.2. Sample Size Considerations

A crucial determinant of the success of a linking study is the ability to identify and to acquire a large enough sample that is representative of the current test-taker population. Three basic considerations underlie the target sampling allocation: adequate representation to ensure measurement precision, adequate representation of subgroups of examinees, and economic constraints. This chapter does not directly examine economic constraints, although these constraints did have an impact on what could be done.

The sample-size requirements for any research design are driven by the desired amount of precision. Sample size has a direct influence on the error in estimation (of linking functions, of population parameters, and so on). The formulas typically applied in the context of equating to compute standard errors of equating (SEE) can be used to estimate the sample size required to achieve a given level of linking precision. The standard errors will be referred to here as standard errors of linking (SEL). Similarly, maximum values of the SEL or of proportions can be used to determine the appropriate sample size for estimating these quantities within a given tolerance level. Subgroup representation, including either ethnic groups or English as a second language groups, is also important across all designs. Minimum numbers need to be met for proper psychometric analyses, including score equity assessment (Dorans, 2004e).

7.3.2.1. Sufficient Sample Size to Estimate Linking Precision

If equipercentile methods are used in any linking situation, then the shapes of score distributions, the degree of linking precision required, and the effects of smoothing affect the required sample size (Kolen & Brennan 2004). The SEL can be used to specify the sample size required to achieve a given level of linking precision for a particular linking design and method. Ideally, linking errors should be small and not make a significant contribution to error in reported scores. The researcher must decide how much error is tolerable.

Lord (1982) provided an approximate equation for estimating the standard errors of random groups equipercentile linking. Based on a simplified version that assumes normality (Petersen, Kolen, & Hoover, 1989), Kolen and Brennan (2004) provided an equation for estimating sample size for random groups equipercentile linking. If we assume equal sample sizes for the two groups, the equation becomes

$$N_{\text{group}} \cong \frac{2[P(x_i)/100][1 - P(x_i)/100]}{u^2 \phi^2}, \tag{7.1}$$

where N represents the sample size needed for each group (i.e., both groups combined would contain $2N$ individuals), u is the desired error of linking in standard deviation units, and ϕ is the ordinate of the standard normal density at the unit normal score z, below which $P(x_i)/100$ of the cases fall.

Lord (1982) also provided an approximate equation for estimating the standard errors of single group equipercentile linking. If we again assume normality, we can derive the following equation for estimating sample size:

$$N_{group} \cong \frac{2(1-\rho)[P(x_i)/100][1-P(x_i)/100]}{u^2\phi^2}, \qquad (7.2)$$

where ρ is the correlation between the old and new tests. Note that as ρ approaches 1.0, the needed sample size becomes smaller and smaller. Note, too, that when ρ is zero, the needed sample size is the same as for the random groups equipercentile linking method.

In the field trial, for example, it was decided that any absolute error less than 10, which is less than 10% of one standard deviation of the SAT scale (110), would be adequate for the purposes of this study, given the economic constraints. In Design 1, where an equivalent groups design was employed, we used Equation 7.1 to estimate that a minimum of 4,850 people would be required in each group to achieve a maximum SEL of 10 scaled score points between z-scores of −2.5 and +2.5 (i.e., for roughly the middle 99% of test scores, assuming normality). Design 2 involved administrations of component tests from different batteries using a counterbalanced single group design. If the new test were to be considered equatable to the old test, then the correlation of the two tests would need to approach the reliability of the test (i.e., .92 for the OV and OM sections). To obtain a conservative estimate of the sample size needed to estimate the single group linking functions with adequate precision, a minimum correlation of .80 between the two tests to be equated was assumed.[4] Under these conditions, a maximum SEL of 10 scaled score points between z-scores of −2.5 and +2.5 (i.e., for roughly the middle 99% of test scores, assuming normality) would require a minimum of 975 people in the group for an equipercentile linking function and a single group design.[5]

---

[4] Given the reliabilities of the SAT sections and the Writing Subject Test, a correlation this low between an old and a new section would be evidence that the two sections are not equivalent.

[5] This approximation is based on the assumptions that the scaled scores on the old and new sections are normally distributed, with standard deviations of 110.

7.3.2.2. Sufficient Subgroup Sample Size

Given the need for a minimum of 975 people in each group and a proportional representation in the sample (7.8% of the sample needed to be Hispanic and Asian students), the projected minimum sample size for each subgroup in Design 2 was 75 per spiral. Spirals in Design 2 were arranged in counterbalanced pairs. Assuming no unequal carryover effects, the projected minimum sample size was 150 per counterbalanced spiral pairs for Hispanic and Asian students. This sample size is insufficient for computing correlations and conducting separate linkings by subgroups.

Because investigating population invariance is crucial to determining whether the old and new tests are equatable, we recommended oversampling students in certain ethnic groups in Design 2 (i.e., recruit schools in California to ensure a sufficient number of Hispanic and Asian students and to ensure that either African American, Asian, and/or Hispanic students comprised at least 20% of the sample). We also recommended increasing the required sample size from a minimum of 975 to 3,000. Therefore, each counterbalanced spiral pair would have a projected minimum sample size for each subgroup of 1,200. These numbers are sufficient to perform single group linkings with acceptably small SEL and power to allow for the examination of population invariance.

In addition, we need to consider sample-size requirements based on precision of parameter estimation, (e.g., means, percentile ranks, correlation) and on statistical power considerations (Walker & Liu, 2002).

7.4. Equatability Analyses

In this section, the equatability analyses are illustrated by using the new SAT as an example. First, we compare the test specifications or blueprint between the old test and the new test. Second, we assess the empirical relationship between the old test and the new test. Third, we compare the reliability and conditional standard error of measurement (CSEM) of the new test to the old test. Finally, we apply score equity assessment (SEA) to evaluate the equatability of the new test to the old test by looking at the linking invariance across gender groups.

7.4.1. Comparison of Test Specifications Between the New SAT and the Old SAT

To achieve equating, the test must measure the same construct. A good first step is to compare test specifications, including item type, number of items per type, total number of items, item content, testing time, test difficulty, and so on. The comparison of test specifications could include comparisons of both the content specifications and statistical specifications between the new test and the old test.

Table 7.1 summarizes the content comparison between the OV section and the CR section. The OV section measured verbal reasoning via three items types: analogy (24% of items were this type), sentence completion (24%), and passage-based reading questions (51%). The reading content was balanced across four domains: humanities, social studies, natural sciences, and human relationships. The OV section had 78 items in total and was administered in 75 min.

The CR section replaced analogy items with additional short reading passages, resulting in approximately 72% reading comprehension items, as compared to 51% in the OV section. The name of the section was changed from verbal to critical reading to emphasize this change in focus. The reading content questions came from the same four domains, as earlier. The CR section had 67 items and was administered in 70 min.

Statistical specifications for the SAT state the means and standard deviations for the item difficulty. In addition, SAT statistical specifications call for a specific number of items at each difficulty level. The same proportion of items were maintained at each difficulty level; the mean and standard deviation of item difficulties on the new SAT were very close to those on the old test.

7.4.2. Empirical Relationship Between the Old and New Tests

Once we compare the specifications between the new and the old tests, we need to check the observed relationships between the scores. To achieve the score interchangeability provided by a useful equating, the correlation between the two tests must be high. Dorans (2000, 2004d) defined an index called reduction in uncertainty (RiU) to measure the statistical certainty of a dependent variable from a predictor variable. Let r represent the correlation coefficient between the two variables, then reduction in uncertainty is defined as

$$RiU = 1 - \sqrt{1 - r^2}.$$
$$(7.3)$$

When $r = 0$, there is 0% reduction; when $r = 1$, there is 100% reduction. Where should the threshold be for a predictor to serve as a valid surrogate for the variable being predicted? Dorans (2004d) suggested that for test-score linkage in high-stakes settings, it is reasonable to require at least 50% of uncertainty reduction in one observed score resulting from the other observed score. Correspondingly, a correlation coefficient of at least

.866 is needed to reduce the uncertainty by at least 50%. As measured in score units, a correlation of .866 or higher between two score vectors indicates that the two score vectors are probably close enough to equate if they measure the same thing (Dorans, 2004d).

The correlation between OV and CR scores was calculated for 3,126 students who took both the OV and CR sections in the single group design. As shown in Table 7.3, the observed-score CR-OV correlation was .912, with RiU = 59%, which reduces the uncertainty more than 50%, suggesting that the CR and OV sections are probably closely enough related to support an equating relationship.

The correlation between the OV and OM sections was compared to the correlation between the CR and NM sections. Both correlations rounded to .79 for the field-trial samples taking the entire test batteries in Design 1 (N = 5,240 for the old test and N = 2,065 for the new test). The equality of these correlations suggests that the old test and the new test might measure the same construct. This evidence is necessary but not sufficient.

Table 7.3. Comparison of observed-score correlations between the new SAT and old SAT from Design 2 in the Spring 2003 new SAT field trial

Old test	New test			
	CR Sect. 1	CR Sect. 2	CR Sect. 3	CR Total
OV Sect. 1	.818	.803	.783	.863
OV Sect. 2	.817	.812	.795	.870
OV Sect. 3	.747	.746	.726	.796
OV Total	.860	.851	.831	.912

7.4.3. Comparison of Measurement Precision on the Old and New Tests

7.4.3.1. Reliability

Dorans and Holland (2000) considered the equal reliability requirement for test equating, that is, tests that measure the same construct but differ in reliability should not be equated. This is a necessary but not sufficient condition for equating. In addition, high reliability on both tests is needed to ensure that the equated scores are informative enough to be accepted by test users (Dorans, 2004d).

Table 7.4 presents the reliability estimates on the new and old tests that were given in Design 1. In addition, a set of reliability ranges from six operational SAT forms given during 2001–2002 is summarized to serve as a baseline. As can be seen, the reliability estimates for the CR section were all above .90 across different computation methods. These reliability estimates were comparable to the reliabilities of the test forms given during 2001–2002 and they were virtually identical to the reliability estimates of the old test administered in the field trial. All other things being equal, a longer test is supposed to be more reliable. However, both the raw score reliability estimates and the scaled score reliability estimates of the CR section are quite high and are comparable to the old test, even with a considerably reduced number of items (67 items in the CR section vs. 78 items in the OV section). This might be attributed to several factors: First, the test would be more internally consistent with one item type eliminated, which would result in a higher reliability. Second, compared to sentence completion items and critical reading items, the analogy item type has relatively lower reliability (Liu, Feigenbaum, & Cook, 2004). Replacing an item set of lower reliability with an item set of higher reliability results in an increase in the overall reliability of the test. Another possible explanation is that a lack of motivation on the part of some test-takers is hard to distinguish from low ability. Both could increase the variability of item performance and correlations among items. These increases could give the appearance of higher reliability.

Table 7.4. Comparison of reliability coefficients between the new SAT and the old SAT from Design 1 in the Spring 2003 new SAT field trial

		New SAT	Old SAT	Range of SATs from 2001–2002
Verbal/critical reading				
Variance-component	Raw	.93	.93	.93–.94
Kristof	Raw	.91	.92	.92 .93
IRT	Raw	.93	.93	.93
IRT	Scaled	.91	.91	.92

The correlations obtained from Design 2 between the CR and OV sections (.912) approached the reliability estimates of the new and old tests. Given the assumptions of classical true-score theory, the true-score correlation between the old and new tests was close to unity for the CR-OV pair. This finding provides evidence that the old test and the new test might be measuring the same constructs.

7.4.3.2. Conditional Standard Errors of Measurement

In addition to the reliability comparison, we also compared the measurement precision at each score level between the old and new tests. Plots of the item response theory (IRT) scaled-score CSEM values are shown in Figure 7.1. This figure shows the CSEM values of the new test CR section compared to the CSEM values of the old test OV section given in the field trial and the CSEM values of the six operational SAT forms given in 2001–2002.

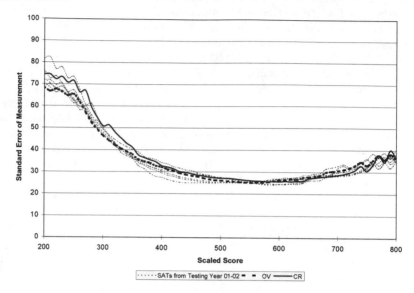

Figure 7.1. Comparison of the CSEM between the CR and OV sections.

An examination of the CSEM values of the new CR section compared to the OV section shows that the CR section appeared to have CSEM values very similar to the OV section between score range 350 and 800. Below score 350, however, some measurement power was lost. The CR CSEM curve is intertwined with the CSEM curves of the baseline forms across the entire score range, but there was variation across individual forms.

7.4.4 Score Equity Assessment

As mentioned earlier one of the requirements for test score equating is population invariance; that is, the score equating function should be the same across subpopulations of the total population as it is in the total population (Dorans, 2004e; Dorans & Holland, 2000; Lord, 1980). Dorans (2004e) further modified the framework of equating invariance and introduced the concept of SEA, which focuses on whether scores that are supposed to be used interchangeably are in fact interchangeable. The key question is whether the test measures what it measures in the same way for different subpopulations as it does for the full population (Dorans, 2004e,

p. 48). SEA uses population invariance of linking functions across important subgroups, such as gender groups or ethnic groups, to assess the degree of interchangeability of scores.

In this subsection, we apply SEA to evaluate score equity of the new SAT from the perspective of population invariance. Because this study is published elsewhere, we are just summarizing the methodology and major findings here. For details, see Liu, Cahn, and Dorans (2006).

7.4.4.1. Equatability Indexes

The equatability indexes used in this chapter are the standardized root mean square difference (RMSD) and the root expected mean square difference (REMSD), developed by Dorans and Holland (2000). Dorans and Holland (2000) suggested using the RMSD to quantify the differences between the subpopulation linking functions and the total population linking functions at a given score value and using the REMSD to summarize overall differences between the linking functions.

7.4.4.1.1. Root Mean Square Difference

The two tests to be linked are denoted by X (new test) and Y (old test), and the observed scores from these two tests are denoted by x and y, respectively. Therefore, at each X score level, the RMSD is defined as

$$\text{RMSD}_{(x)} = \frac{\sqrt{\sum_j w_j \left[e_{Pj}(x) - e_P(x) \right]^2}}{\sigma_{YP}}, \qquad (7.4)$$

where $e(x)$ represents the linking function that transforms scores of form X to the raw score scale of form Y, and $w_j = N_j / N$ denotes the relative proportion of examinees from P that are in P_j so that $\sum_j w_j = 1$.

Note that in Equation 7.4, the divisor σ_{YP} is used to quantify the sum of differences between the total population and subpopulation linked raw scores in standard deviation units. In the present study, the linkings converted the raw scores into scaled scores on the College Board's familiar 200–800 scale. Because most readers understand and readily interpret values on this scale, a modified version of Equation 7.4 was used, which expressed the differences in SAT scaled-score units (SSU) rather than in standard deviation units:

$$\text{RMSD}_{(\text{SSU})} = \sqrt{\sum_j w_j \left[s_{P_j}(x) - s_P(x) \right]^2}, \tag{7.5}$$

where $s_P(x)$ represents a scaling that transforms raw scores of form X to the SAT score scale through the linking of form X to form Y for the total population and $s_{P_j}(x)$ represents the corresponding scaling function for the subpopulation P_j. These scaling functions for X are obtained by concatenating the linking function, $e_P(x)$, with the scaling for form Y, $s(y)$.

7.4.4.1.2. Root Expected Mean Square Difference

To obtain a single number summarizing the values of RMSD(x), Dorans and Holland (2000) introduced a summary measure, REMSD by averaging over the distribution of X in P:

$$\text{REMSD} = \frac{\sqrt{E_P \left\{ \sum_j w_j \left[e_{P_j}(x) - e_P(x) \right]^2 \right\}}}{\sigma_{YP}} = \frac{\sqrt{\sum_j w_j E_P \left\{ \left[e_{P_j}(x) - e_P(x) \right]^2 \right\}}}{\sigma_{YP}}, \tag{7.6}$$

where $E_P\{\cdot\}$ denotes averaging over this distribution. Similarly, we modified Equation 7.6 and put this summary measure on the 200–800 scale:

$$\text{REMSD}_{(\text{SSU})} = \sqrt{E_P \left\{ \sum_j w_j \left[s_{P_j}(x) - s_P(x) \right]^2 \right\}} = \sqrt{\sum_j w_j E_P \left\{ \left[s_{P_j}(x) - s_P(x) \right]^2 \right\}}. \tag{7.7}$$

To evaluate the relative magnitude of the RMSD and REMSD, Dorans and Feigenbaum (1994) proposed the notion of score differences that matter (DTM) in the context of linking an SAT form to another SAT form. On the SAT scales, scores are reported in 10-point units (200, 210, ...,780, 790, 800). For a given raw score, if the unrounded scaled scores from two separate linkings differ by fewer than 5 points, then the scores ideally should be rounded to the same reported score. Dorans, Holland, Thayer, and Tateneni (2003) adapted the above indexes, used in SAT practice, to other tests and considered the DTM to be half of a score unit for unrounded scores. In the present study, the DTM was defined as half of an SAT score unit, 5 points.

7.4.4.1.3. Percentage Indexes

In addition to using the RMSD and RESMD, we make use of the percentage of raw scores (PS) for which the total and subpopulation unrounded conversions differed by more than 5 points and the percentage of examinees (PE) for whom these conversions create scores that differed by more than 5 points. The two stringent indexes provide straightforward insights into a lack of invariance as a percentage of score range and of test-takers.

7.4.4.2. Population Invariance in Linking the CR Prototype to the OV Section

In this study, the SEA on the two old SAT forms was conducted first to obtain a baseline. The two forms were given in the same SAT administration. The spiraling procedure used in the SAT administration and the large numbers of test-takers taking each form usually ensure equivalent groups in the same administration. Therefore, form X was linked to form Y through an equivalent groups design in each of the groups: total, male, and female test-takers. The results revealed that the RMSD values were smaller than 5 across the entire scale. The two percentage indexes, PS and PE, were 0 for both male and female test-takers (Liu et al., 2006). In summary, no evidence was found to question the score equity with respect to gender on this particular linkage. This finding was consistent with the results of the study by Dorans and Holland (2000).

The correlation between the OV and CR sections was calculated by using data obtained from Design 2. As shown in Table 7.5, the observed-score CR-OV correlations for the total, male, and female test-taker groups were .912 (RiU = 59%), .900 (RiU = 56%), and .921 (RiU = 61%), respectively. These correlations are all larger than .866, reducing uncertainty more than 50%. The reliability estimates for both tests were .93. Hence, the estimated true-score correlations were about .981, .968, and .990 for the total, male, and female groups, respectively. The magnitudes of these numbers suggest that the two tests measure the same construct in nearly the same way within the three groups.

The equatability assessment was then carried out on the new SAT prototypes administered in the field trial and compared to the baseline. The linking results reported here were conducted using the equivalent groups design in Design 1, in that it was the same design used in the baseline analysis and contained the entire test battery as in a real test administration. Linkings were conducted in each of the three groups.

Table 7.5. Formula score descriptive statistics in the CR and OV sections from Design 2 in the Spring 2003 new SAT field trial

Test-takers	N^a	r	RiU
Total	3,126	.912	59%
Male	1,548	.900	56%
Female	1,578	.921	61%

^{a}The summation of male and female sample sizes might not be equal to the sample size of total group due to nonresponses.

Figure 7.2 displays the differences in linking results of the CR section to the OV for each pair: male test-takers versus total test-takers and female test-takers versus total test-takers. As illustrated in Figure 7.2, female test-takers would have had slightly higher scores in the middle portion of the score scale and lower scores at the ends of the score scale if the female-only conversion was used. Conversely, male test-takers would have obtained slightly lower scores in the middle range and higher scores at the ends of the score range if the male-only conversion was used. However, the differences were less than 5 scaled-score points across the entire score range.

Figure 7.3 depicts RMSD values compared to the DTM line at each score level. As seen in Figure 7.3, the RMSD fell below the DTM line virtually across the entire score range. The REMSD value of approximately 3 was below the DTM of 5.

Table 7.6 summarizes the differences between each subgroup conversion and the total group conversion. In general, Table 7.6 shows that male test-takers would have obtained a lower mean with a male-only conversion than they had with the total group conversion (standardized difference of −0.03), whereas female test-takers would have obtained a higher mean with a female-only conversion than they had with the total group conversion (standardized difference of 0.02). The PS was 3.5 and 1.2 for male and female test-takers, respectively; and the PE was 0.7 and 0.4 for males and females, respectively. In summary, the SEA on the CR section exhibits a slightly larger degree of departure compared to the baseline, but the lack of invariance across gender groups was not enough to cause any concern.

A similar set of analyses was performed on the linkage from the NM to the OM sections in the field trial, and the results demonstrate that population invariance holds across gender groups for the math section as well (Liu, Feigenbaum, & Dorans, 2005). The observed-score correlations between the NM and OM sections were .922 (RiU = 61%), .923 (RiU = 62%), and .918 (RiU = 60%) for the total, male, and female groups, respectively. These values all reduce the uncertainty more than 60%, suggesting that the two tests measure the same construct in nearly the same way within the three groups. The divergences of the subgroup conversions from the total group conversion fell within the range of 5 points. The REMSD value in the new math prototype was 1.71, much smaller than the DTM value and even smaller than the baseline REMSD (2.37).

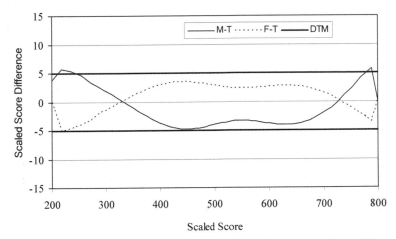

Figure 7.2. Scaled-score differences by gender in linking the CR to OV sections in the 2003 Spring new SAT field trial.

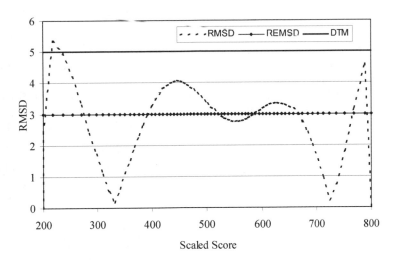

Figure 7.3. RMSD by gender in linking the CR to OV sections in the Spring 2003 new SAT field trial.

Table 7.6. Summary statistics of scaled-score based on total group conversion and subgroup conversion in linking the CR to OV sections in the Spring 2003 new SAT field trial

	Total	Male	Female
Sample size	9,194	3,801	5,374
%		41.34%	58.45%
Total group conversion			
Mean	479.4	477.9	480.4
SD	107.8	111.0	105.3
Subgroup conversion			
Mean		474.9	482.8
SD		110.0	105.8
Subgroup conversion mean - Total conversion mean		−3.0	2.3
Standardized mean difference		−0.03	0.02
% Raw scores with unrounded scaled-score difference ≥ 5		3.5	1.2
% Examinees with unrounded scaled-score difference ≥ 5		0.7	0.4

7.4.4.3. Summary of Score Equity Assessment

Equatability analyses were conducted on the linkage of the CR to OV sections. Analyses were performed by comparing the new test to the old test on test specifications, reliability, and empirical relationships. Score equity assessment was examined by employing population invariance measures.

The content specifications on the new test do suggest dramatic changes from the old test. With the elimination of analogy questions and the changes in total test length, the coverage for different content categories has shifted in the new test.

The reliability estimates on the new test were high (above .90) for the CR section. Those values were very close to the reliability on the old SAT given in the field trial, and they fell within the reliability range based on SAT operational forms. Therefore, equal reliability as a necessary condition for equating is met.

The strength of the empirical relationship between the new test and the old test was assessed. The observed-score correlation between the CR and OV sections was .912, with RiU = 59%. The correlation was higher than .866 with an uncertainty reduction of more than 50%, the threshold suggested by Dorans (2000, 2004a) as a criterion to equate the two score sectors. The high correlation is a necessary condition, but not a sufficient condition for score equating.

Score equity assessment was performed to determine the degree to which the linking relationship was invariant across gender groups. The results suggest that linking the CR to OV sections was invariant across gender groups.

Scores on one test can be considered successfully equated to scores on another test only *with respect to some population or populations*. One can invariably define other populations for which the scores on the two tests in question are not exchangeable. In this study, the ethnic group sample sizes were too small to support sound linkings at the ethnic subgroup level to yield valid inferences about population invariance. Examination of score equity across ethnic groups requires further data collection and study.

Based on the equatability analyses from the field trial, it appears that linking the CR and OV sections might meet the equating requirements. All of the evaluations discussed in this chapter involved field-trial data, except for the content and statistical specification comparisons. Now that the new test is operational, we can examine invariance with the actual SAT population. The gender analyses can be repeated on the operational data. More importantly, we can use the data to examine invariance in other subgroups, such as ethnic groups, language groups, region groups, and so on.

7.5. Discussion

When a testing program undergoes changes, researchers need to determine how to link the scores on the new test to the scores on old test. How do they evaluate the linkage between the two score vectors? To what degree do the revisions change the construct to be measured and, therefore, make the linking relationships dependent on the subpopulations? Is it best to break the old scale completely and set up a new scale? Can a concordance be established between the new test and the old test? Or is it possible to equate the new test to the old test?

Linking issues for tests in transition are different from most of the other issues studied in score linking research. In the latter situation, there are usually two existing tests to be linked, such as the SAT and ACT. When researchers try to link these two tests, they usually first choose an appropriate link type and methodology and then link the scores, evaluate the linking quality, and make recommendations (Pommerich, Hanson, Harris, & Sconing, 2004). The existing tests basically determine the linking type, and it is not possible to change the relationship between the two tests. Linking issues for tests in transition are different in that researchers can influence the types of linking. As emphasized earlier, a decision needs to be made about what is most important at an early stage of test revision. If equating the new test to the old is crucial, then all of the revisions and data collections should be guided by this principle. For example, the new SAT would need to maintain the same specified difficulty level and the same specified item discrimination as the old SAT. In addition, the specified item difficulty distribution would need to be the same as the old one proportionally. Further, the content specifications should not shift substantially.

Setting equatability as the goal does not necessarily ensure achieving it. Careful data collection needs to be designed and conducted. It is crucial to collect data on a common group of test-takers who take both the new and the old tests in order to assess the empirical relationship between the two tests. Important factors such as linking precision and sample sizes for both the total group and important subgroups need to be taken into consideration.

After data collection and score linking, one needs to determine the most appropriate linking to use and to evaluate its quality. In this chapter, we developed a set of criteria including content and reliability comparisons, the strength of the relationship between the old and the new test scores, and population invariance across important subgroups. Content comparisons can be done at the early stage of the new test development process. Factor analysis and structural equation models can be used to assess the new test construct in relation to the old. High enough correlation is essential to reduce uncertainty. A correlation of .866 with a reduction in uncertainty of at least 50% can be used as a threshold. In addition to the relationship between the old and new tests, the relationship among components in the test might also reveal some important clues as to the comparability of the test scores. Population invariance provides another useful tool to evaluate score equatability. If there is an interaction between the test difficulty and group membership, then invariance does not hold and the employed linking cannot be considered equating.

8 Linking Scores Derived Under Different Modes of Test Administration

Daniel R. Eignor[1]

Educational Testing Service

8.1. Introduction

All established testing programs that develop computer-based versions of paper-and-pencil tests, particularly computer-adaptive tests (CATs), typically need to link the scores derived from the two administration modes. Linking is necessary because computer-based and paper-based testing will likely occur together, at least for some transition period. Further, even if paper-and-pencil testing can be immediately phased out when the computer-based test (CBT) is introduced, scores from the computer-based version will, in many cases, need to be reported on the scale that existed for the paper-and-pencil test until such time that paper-based scores are no longer accepted.

All of the above considerations necessitate that a linking study between scores from the two modes of test administration be conducted. Typically, the scores from the newer computer-based mode of administration will be linked to scores from the paper-and-pencil mode of administration and the scores from the two administrations will be reported as if they were interchangeable. The degree to which the linked computer-based and paper-and-pencil scores can be treated as interchangeable will depend on a number of different factors, the most important being the nature of the computer-based test itself.

The purposes of this chapter are twofold: (a) to clarify when a linking of scores between a computer-based test and a paper-and-pencil test can be considered to result in scores that are interchangeable and (b) using

---

[1]The opinions expressed in this chapter are those of the author and not necessarily of Educational Testing Service.

available literature on the topic to provide descriptions of the ways one might design a linking study to relate scores on computer-based and paper-and-pencil-based tests.

8.2. Background

Holland and Dorans (2006) developed general definitions for a wide variety of linking methods, three of which will be important in the context of relating scores on computer-based and paper-and-pencil tests: equating, calibration, and concordance. (See Holland, Chapter 2, for a detailed discussion of types of linking.) Equating is used to refer to linking between two test forms that measure the same construct at the same level of difficulty and with the same level of reliability. Equated scores can be treated as being truly interchangeable. Calibration is used to refer to linking between two test forms that measure the same construct at approximately the same level of difficulty, but with different levels of reliability. Calibrated scores are typically treated as though they were interchangeable, although there are real questions as to whether this is appropriate. The use of a common reported score scale with scores from tests that have been calibrated actually encourages score users to use the results as if they came from an equating because there will be nothing about the nature of the scale that will help users understand that a calibration and not an equating has been done. Concordance is used to refer to linking between two different tests that measure similar constructs with somewhat similar levels of difficulty and reliability. Scores that have been concorded cannot be treated as being interchangeable.

In addition to the above definitions, it will be useful to employ two additional terms that are similar to those used by Hanson, Harris, Pommerich, Sconing, and Yi (2001): sets of equivalent scores and sets of scores that are equivalent in appearance only. A weak definition of sets of equivalent scores is that the two sets share the same raw score mean. A stronger definition is that the two sets share the same raw score mean, variance, and distribution of scores. Sets of scores that are identical in appearance only share the same raw score mean or, in the stricter sense, the same raw score mean, variance, and distribution of scores, but the scores themselves do not convey the same meaning. The scales for the two tests have been aligned, but the nature of the scores has not changed. As an example, two sets of scores might have the same raw score mean, variance, and distribution, but two scores that appear to be the same might not measure with the same level of precision; that is, the two scores might not have the same conditional standard error of measurement.

The term "linear CBT" is often used to describe a paper-and-pencil form that is administered via computer. All that differs is the mode of administration. Linkings of scores from paper-and-pencil and linear CBT modes are expected to be equatings. Whether the scores can be appropriately treated as interchangeable is an empirical question. In other instances when CATs are created, the assumption of strict interchangeability of scores from the two modes will be less appropriate. When linking scores on CATs and paper-and-pencil tests, the relationship between the scores from the two modes can at best be characterized as a calibration. Finally, there are instances in which the new computer-based test has been purposely constructed to differ from the paper-and-pencil test, either through the employment of innovative item types or through the updating of test content. In this situation, scores from the two modes cannot be considered to be interchangeable, although score users might want cut-scores on the computer-based test to be aligned with cut-scores on the paper-and-pencil test. In such a case, a concordance relationship could be established between scores across the two modes of administration. In sum, depending on the relationship between scores on paper-and-pencil and computer-based versions of the test, a linking between scores from the two modes can potentially be considered as an equating of the scores, a calibration of the scores, or a concordance between the scores. It should be noted that linear and curvilinear linking procedures, typically applied in the equating context, can also be used to calibrate scores or to bring about a concordance between scores. Most often, a curvilinear procedure, such as equipercentile linking, is employed in these contexts.

Regardless of the actual form of the linking between the scores from the two modes of administration, a data collection design must be employed to collect data to conduct the linking. (See Kolen, Chapter 3, for a description of data collection designs and a discussion of the importance of measurement conditions to linking.) Data collection designs for linking tests that are described in the literature (see also Angoff, 1984) were developed for parallel or close to parallel forms of examinations given via the same administration mode, most typically the paper-and-pencil mode. Applications of these designs to link scores derived from different modes of administration have, at times, provided results that are questionable. Questionable linkages have particularly occurred when one score is derived from a CAT and the other score is derived from a paper-and-pencil administration. As a result, variations on the standard designs in Angoff (1984) have sometimes been employed. For instance, straightforward implementation of the single group counterbalanced design in which the computer-based and paper-and-pencil tests are given contiguously in the same testing session has often produced linking results of a questionable nature. By administering the tests in a noncontiguous fashion, acceptable linking results have been produced.

In the sections that follow, a number of topics relevant to linking scores across different modes of administration will be discussed. In the next section, issues that cause scores from paper-and-pencil and certain computer-based versions of tests to lack the level of comparability brought about by an equating will be discussed. The focus will be on CATs and paper-and-pencil tests. The following section will discuss implementations of data collection designs in the context of linking scores derived from different modes of administration. Linking studies of this nature that have been documented in the literature will be discussed. Finally, the last section of the chapter will provide a summary and reflections on the linking of scores derived from different modes of test administration.

8.3. Comparability Issues Involving Scores from Computer-Based and Paper-and-Pencil Tests

The focus of this section will be on issues that cause linked scores on CATs and paper-and-pencil tests not to be comparable at the level brought about by an equating. First, however, it is useful to talk about comparability issues in the context of linking scores on linear CBTs and paper-and-pencil tests. When the same form is administered in the linear CBT and paper-and-pencil modes, the only thing that can keep scores from being equivalent across modes is the manner in which the items are presented on screen. Mazzeo and Harvey (1988) discussed many of the item presentation issues that might cause differences between scores on linear CBTs and paper-and pencil tests utilizing the same form. An updated discussion of item presentation issues is found in Pommerich (2004). Probably foremost among the issues here is how to present reading passages and items on screen. With linear CBT and paper-and-pencil versions of different test forms, scores can be affected by differences in difficulty caused by the different modes of presentation and by differences in difficulty across items. Both can keep the two sets of raw scores from being equivalent. However, the resulting scores in most instances can be linked and reported on the same reported score scale.

Score comparability issues are not a concern when forming concordances between scores on tests, be they scores on linear CBT and paper-and-pencil tests or scores on CAT and paper-and-pencil tests, because the tests in question are typically not designed to yield comparable scores. As pointed out, however, in the chapters on concordance in this volume, not all concordances are of equal quality. Typically, there will be no attempt made to report scores on a common scale. Care must be taken, however, to ensure that score users do not treat the related scores as though they were equivalent (i.e., to substitute the paper-based aligned score for a particular computer-based score in the score reporting process). Although the scales may be lined up, the scores do not mean the same thing.

Comparability issues are of concern when linking scores on CATs and paper-and-pencil tests, and a number of recent articles in the literature have focused on this issue. Perhaps the most comprehensive treatment of these issues can be found in Wang and Kolen (2001). Kolen and Brennan (2004) provided a somewhat briefer but still thorough treatment of the issues, some of which are discussed below. If these issues did not exist, it might be possible to consider a linking between scores on a CAT and a paper-and-pencil test to constitute an equating. Much of the earlier literature on the topic of linking these sorts of scores did consider the linking to constitute an equating; see Eignor (1993), McBride, Corpe, and Wing (1987), and Segall (1995).

Perhaps the first issue that comes to mind is not really an issue at all. It has to do with whether the scores from CATs and paper-and-pencil tests can be considered comparable because of possible content differences. Modern item selection algorithms used with CAT, such as those described by Stocking and Swanson (1993) or van der Linden and Reese (1998), ensure that the content coverage across the two tests is comparable, although the comparability will likely be proportional in nature, given that CATs are typically shorter than paper-and-pencil exams. Eignor, Stocking, Way, and Steffen (1993) discussed how content specifications can be treated in CATs when using the Stocking and Swanson approach so as to have the content parallel that of a paper-and-pencil test.

Test administration conditions that differ between the CAT and paper-and-pencil form might contribute to a lack of comparability. CATs are given under conditions where examinees must respond to the current item before they can receive the next item, and they are not allowed to go back and review or change items to which they have previously responded. In paper-and-pencil format, examinees can skip items and can go back and review or change previously provided responses to items.

The manner in which CAT and paper-and-pencil tests are scored can also contribute to a lack of comparability. Whereas paper-and-pencil tests are typically either number-right or formula scored, with CATs the final score is an item response theory (IRT)-based ability estimate. Typically, the ability estimate is based on a sum of weighted item responses, whereas the number-right score from the paper-and-pencil test (or, in some instances, a corresponding ability estimate) is based on a sum of unweighted item responses. Also, not reached items are treated very differently in CATs than they are in paper-and-pencil tests (see Way, Eignor, & Gawlick, 2001).

Psychometric characteristics of the CAT and paper-and-pencil tests also contribute to the lack of comparability of scores. With certain fixed-length CATs, the test length is set to yield the same level of overall reliability as the paper-and-pencil test in a representative group of examinees. Although this should ensure comparable overall standard errors of measurement (in that representative group), it in no way ensures that the conditional standard errors of measurement are equivalent. This will be true for comparisons made using observed scores (paper-and-pencil) and estimated true scores (CAT). This situation violates one of the assumptions of equating, the equity assumption, and, in particular, second-order equity (see Holland, Chapter 2; Kolen & Brennan, 2004). The equity criterion, in general, requires that it should be a matter of indifference as to which of two linked forms an examinee takes. This translates into very specific requirements about the level of precision to which scores on the two forms are measured. Second-order equity requires that examinees at a given ability level be measured with the same level of precision on the two test forms. In order for this to happen at a particular ability level, the conditional standard errors of measurement must be equivalent. The manner in which the fixed-length CAT was constructed will in no way ensure this is the case. Hence, with fixed-length CATs, second-order equity cannot be said to have been met.

With variable-length CATs, the length of the CAT is set to yield a specific level of precision. The CAT, however, is likely to provide greater precision than the paper-and-pencil test at any selected ability level.

Thus, the differing psychometric characteristics of the CAT and paper-and-pencil test lead to a lack of comparability of scores, such that the linked scores cannot be considered to be equated. This is why the term *calibration* has been used in this chapter to characterize the linking of scores on CATs and paper-and-pencil forms. After calibration, the sets of scores can be said to be equivalent in appearance only. Finally, on a very superficial level, there is no way that linked scores on a CAT and a paper-and-pencil form can lead to indifference on the part of an examinee as to which form she takes. Certain examinees will simply prefer to take the CAT, whereas others will prefer to take the paper-and-pencil form.

For a complete treatment of the issues leading to a lack of comparability between CAT and paper-and-pencil scores, the reader is referred to Wang and Kolen (2001). The issues discussed in the previous paragraphs are simply those that this author feels are the most important to emphasize.

8.4. Mode of Presentation Linking Designs

In the material that follows, taken in part from Eignor and Schaeffer (1995), the three most frequently used data collection designs for equating paper-and-pencil forms of an exam are discussed in the context of linking scores from computer-based and paper-and-pencil exams. These data collection designs are (a) the random groups design, (b) the single group counterbalanced design, and (c) the nonequivalent groups anchor test design. (See Kolen, Chapter 3, for detailed descriptions of these data collection designs.) Applications of these designs in a linking context will first be discussed, followed by a discussion of some modifications to these designs to deal with the peculiarities of computer-based administrations. These data collection designs will be discussed in the three linking contexts mentioned in Section 8.2: (a) equating linear CBT and paper-and-pencil scores, (b) calibrating CAT and paper-and-pencil scores, and (c) establishing a concordance relationship between linear CBT or CAT scores and paper-and-pencil scores where the computer-based test was not designed to be parallel to the paper-and-pencil test. Studies from the literature employing these data collection designs will be discussed where appropriate.

Table 8.1 provides a listing of the studies to be discussed, classified by data collection design and the type of linking employed. The studies are further broken down into those that attempted to demonstrate that the scores from the two modes of administration were equivalent and those that linked scores without checking their equivalence. Although no claim will be made that the studies listed represent the full set of studies that have been conducted, they are the studies that the author was able to locate, and they do provide an indication of the small amount that has been done to date in this area.

Before discussing these designs and related studies, it should be noted that the samples used in the linkings should be representative of the population to which the linking relationships will ultimately be applied. In the paper-and-pencil context, the samples should be representative of the population with respect to the distribution of the attribute being measured. With computers, other variables, such as level of computer familiarity, enter into the picture. In this case, the samples used in the linking need to be representative of the population with respect to both the attribute being measured and the level of computer familiarity or experience. This will be a particular issue when a CBT is to be introduced for the first time. Unless there are suitable practice materials and a viable tutorial, the examinees used in the linking study will likely not have the level of familiarity that examinees who take the test operationally will have. In this case, standards set on the CBT as a result of the linking study will likely demonstrate higher passing rates operationally than demonstrated in the linking samples. Determining appropriate linking samples in the computer-based testing context will necessitate a consideration of additional variables beyond those considered in the paper-and-pencil context.

Table 8.1. Summary of linking studies reviewed

		Data collection design		
		Random groups	Single group counterbalanced	Nonequivalent groups anchor-test
Equating	Equivalent scores established	Poggio, Glasnapp, Yang, & Poggio (2005)	Mazzeo, Druesne, Raffeld, Checketts, & Muhlstein (1991); Sykes & Ito (1997)	—
	Score equating performed	Schaeffer, Reese, Steffen, McKinley, & Mills (1993)	—	—
Calibration	Equivalent scores established	Eignor, Way, & Amoss (1994); Lunz & Bergstrom (1995)	Schaeffer, Steffen, Golub-Smith, Mills, & Durso (1995)	—
	Score calibration performed	Segall (1995); Segall & Carter (1995)	Eignor (1993); McBride et al. (1987)	Lawrence & Feigenbaum (1997)
Concordance	Equivalent scores established	Not possible	Not possible	Not possible
	Concordance tables produced	—	Jiang (1999)	—

8.5. Random Groups Design

8.5.1. General Discussion

One of the most frequently used data collection designs for studying whether scores from computer- and paper-based modes of administration are equivalent or for actually linking scores derived under these modes has been the random groups design. Such a design allows for straightforward statistical tests for differences in mean performance between groups across modes. Such hypothesis testing typically requires relatively large sample sizes. If the hypothesis test demonstrates no significant differences in mean performance across modes, then this might provide some initial indication that the two sets of scores are equivalent and linking can be viewed as unnecessary. To be certain that linking is unnecessary though, the test for mean differences in performance should be followed by a check of score distributions and score variances. Jaeger (1981) discussed how the Kolmogorov-Smirnov two-sample test of the equality of cumulative distribution functions (Smirnov, 1948) can be used to check for equivalent score distributions. Hanson (1996) discussed how log-linear models can be used to check on the equivalency of score frequency distributions. Finally, Segall (1995) discussed how an F-ratio test can be used to test for differences in score variances across the two modes of administration. If any of these statistical tests provide an indication that linking is necessary, the sample sizes needed to do the tests will prove useful because the random groups linking design requires relatively large sample sizes to keep linking errors at an acceptable level. (See Lord, 1950, for a discussion of these sorts of errors in the context of equating.) It should be mentioned that for all of the studies of this sort that have been reviewed in this chapter, only the test for differences in mean performance has been employed.

In addition to relatively large sample sizes, this data collection design requires a good deal of control over the examinees involved in the study. For instance, if the CBT is seen as an innovative form of assessment, examinees who have been randomly assigned to take the paper-and-pencil test might be disappointed and drop out of the linking study. Differential dropout is a major threat to this design because the two groups might no longer be comparable in ability. Hence, this design is better employed under conditions in which scores count, and the paper-and-pencil test provides a suitable avenue to attaining a valued outcome.

One distinct advantage of using a random groups design is that the same form can be given to both groups. In the case of equating a linear CBT to a paper-and-pencil test, each group would receive the same form via the different administration modes. In this situation, the linking does not need to take into account differences in difficulty due to different items. The linking must take into account only differences in difficulty brought about by administering the items via different modes.

In the case of calibrating scores on a CAT and a paper-and-pencil form, the above is not exactly true. If scores on the paper-and-pencil form used in the calibration have been reported on a scale separate from the raw score scale, as should be the case if there are multiple paper-and-pencil forms, then scores on the CAT have typically been reported on the same scale. This is done through use of a "reference form" that is part of the CAT system (see Eignor et al., 1993). The reference form has been previously given in a paper-and-pencil mode. In addition, items on the reference form will have been calibrated using the IRT model employed with the CAT and the item parameters placed on the IRT parameter scale for the bank. The initial score derived from the CAT will be an estimated ability score. Using this estimated ability and the item parameter estimates for the reference form, an estimated true score on the reference form can be derived. Estimated true scores on the reference form can then be linked with observed scores on the test given in the paper-and-pencil mode. One of the benefits of the random groups design is that it might be possible to administer the reference form from the CAT system in a paper-and-pencil format. So, as is the case with the linear CBT of the same content as the paper-and-pencil form in the equating context, the calibration of scores does not need to take into account differences in difficulty across test forms. However, it will need to take into account a much more expansive set of possible causes for differences in scores. Possible causes for these differences were discussed previously in this chapter.

Two final comments should be made about equating CBT and paper-and-pencil forms in the context of the random groups design. An advantage of this design in this context is that the same form can be given to both groups. This, however, does not need to be the case. Two different forms, say A and B, with A given as a CBT and B in paper-and-pencil mode, can be used instead. If A and B have previously been equated in paper-and-pencil format, then equated scores can be used for B in the subsequent linking across modes. In this situation, all that can differ across forms are the levels of difficulty caused by mode of administration. The above scenario does not seem to have been used in actual studies however. In the studies reviewed, Forms A and B have not previously been equated in paper-and-pencil format. Hence, the linking of A given via computer and B given via paper-and-pencil has to take into account differences in difficulty across forms due to both the use of different items on the forms and the use of the different modes of administration.

The other comment of relevance is related to how and when testing in the two modes can take place. In the context of equating two paper-and-pencil forms, randomization is usually brought about by packaging the test books in a spiraled order, and the two tests are administered simultaneously, usually in the same room. This is typically not the case when equating a CBT to a paper-and-pencil form; having computers in the same room where the paper-and-pencil test is taken could prove to be distracting. Hence, random assignment to conditions will need to be done in some other way than through spiraling, and the two groups will need to be separated for testing purposes. Also, in most situations, there will not be enough computers to test all of the examinees in the CBT group simultaneously. Instead, testing will need to be done over some time period. As long as additional learning does not take place during this time period for the CBT group, this arrangement would appear not to cause a problem. In fact, as will be seen in the discussion of the single group counterbalanced design in Section 8.6, this window of testing needed for the computer-based test can provide distinct benefits if testing is done properly.

8.5.2. Equating Studies Done with the Random Groups Design

Most times when researchers employ the random groups data collection design to study the comparability of scores from linear CBT and paper-and-pencil forms, a formal equating is not conducted. Instead, the same form is administered in both modes and statistical tests or informal checks of differences in mean scores are employed, and if the means are different, emphasis is placed on changing conditions under which the linear CBT is administered to ensure equivalent scores. For example, the administration of passage-based reading items on the computer might need to be altered so as to parallel to the extent possible the way such items are given in paper-and-pencil mode.

Mazzeo and Harvey (1988) provided a review of a large number of studies done prior to 1988 that employed the random groups design to study the equivalence of scores across linear CBT and paper-and-pencil administration of the same form. A wide variety of testing contexts are covered. The study by Schaeffer et al. (1993) to be discussed in Section 8.6.3 illustrates the practice of altering administration conditions to bring about equivalent scores. A more recent application of this data collection design with linear CBT and paper-and-pencil versions of tests can be found in Poggio et al. (2005). Finally, for a meta-analysis of some 30 studies employing the random groups design in studying scores on linear CBTs and paper-and-pencil tests, see Mead and Drasgow (1993).

In all of these studies, only differences in mean scores were looked at, and no attention was paid to possible differences in score distributions, which could imply that a formal equating study might still have needed to be conducted.

8.5.3. Calibration Studies Done with the Random Groups Design

A number of studies have been conducted that have employed the random groups design to look at comparability of scores between CATs and paper-

and-pencil tests. In certain of these studies, formal linking or calibration studies have not been conducted. Instead, IRT-based ability estimates have been derived from both modes of administration and their means directly compared. In other situations, calibration studies have been conducted to allow the derived scores from the two modes, which could not be directly compared, to be used (more or less) interchangeably. Following are some examples of both kinds of study. Eignor et al. (1994) employed the random groups design to look at whether sets of scores for the National Council of State Boards of Nursing Licensure Examinations (NCLEX), which were given in both computer-adaptive and paper-and-pencil modes, could be considered to be equivalent. Formal statistical hypotheses tests were conducted for differences in mean performance, using 1-PL IRT ability estimates, and for differences in passing rates, using log-linear models. In almost all cases, no significant differences in performance or passing rates were found. The study reported in Eignor et al. (1994) was somewhat unique in that the plan was to immediately replace the paper-and-pencil version with the computer version, and both exams were administered at the same time, with scores on both counting for licensure purposes. The focus of the study was on demonstrating that there would be no falloff in candidate performance with the switch in test modes.

Lunz and Bergstrom (1995) used a similar approach in one of a series of studies the authors conducted with the Board of Registry Certification Examinations for medical technologists. Examinees were randomly assigned to either CAT or paper-and-pencil conditions and equivalent mean performance across modes was taken as an indication that calibration of scores from the two modes of administration was not necessary. In this study, 1-PL model ability estimates were compared across the modes of administration.

It should be noted that in both the Eignor et al. (1994) and the Lunz and Bergstrom (1995) studies, no attempt was made to study the distributions of scores across the tests given in the two modes. Depending on the IRT model and calibration program employed, such a comparison might not be so straightforward. Also, even if means, variances, and distributions of scores could be established to be equivalent across modes, this would be in appearance only, as the scores would have different psychometric properties across the two modes.

For certain of the studies that employed the random groups design with CAT and paper-and-pencil versions of the same test, an actual calibration of the scores took place. Segall (1995) discussed the use of this design in linking scores on tests that are part of the Armed Services Vocational Aptitude Battery (ASVAB) and that involve computer-adaptive and paper-and-pencil counterparts of these tests. Segall and Carter (1995) discussed the planned use of the same design in calibrating scores on computer-adaptive and paper-and-pencil versions of certain tests that are part of the General Aptitude Test Battery (GATB).

In both contexts, an equipercentile procedure with smoothed frequency distributions was employed to bring about the calibration that created the conversion between scores from the two modes. What is noteworthy about both of these studies is that ability estimates from the CAT were linked directly to number-right scores on the paper-and-pencil form. It was not possible to transform scores from one of the administrations to allow a comparison of means or, for that matter, means, variances, and distributions.

8.6. Single Group Counterbalanced Test Design

8.6.1. General Discussion

With the single group counterbalanced design, all examinees take both the computer-based and paper-and-pencil versions of the test. Unlike with the random groups design, two separate tests must be used, that is, the computer and paper-and-pencil tests cannot be different versions of the same test form. In most early applications of this design, the tests were given sequentially in one testing session. A random half of the total group took the computerized test first and the remaining half took the paper-and-pencil version first. In this design, the first test taken might provide practice for the second test, thereby raising scores on the second test above what they would have been had the second test been given by itself. Fatigue might also lower performance on the test taken second. However, the relationship derived from the scores from the first administration of either version is what is of interest (i.e., the scores without practice or fatigue effects). This linking relationship could be estimated by ignoring the data from the second administrations and treating the first administrations as though they were obtained from a random groups design. However, the strength of the counterbalanced design is the potential to combine data from both administrations, thereby providing a much more precise estimate of the linking relationship than could be obtained from a random groups linking using the data from the tests administered first in each order. Another possible strength of this design is that it will likely be good for examinee motivation, given that the highest score is counted across the two testing opportunities, and everybody is provided the opportunity to take the test on computer. Both of these situations have the potential for helping with the possible dropout problem.

One key limitation of the counterbalanced design has to do with the conditions that must be met before the data can be combined and used. The procedure for combining counterbalanced design data makes some explicit assumptions about the nature of "order effects." An order effect in this context refers to the average change in scores, be it an increase (from practice) or a decrease (from fatigue), to be expected from the first administration to the second administration. The equations used for estimating equating parameters using all of the data assume that such order effects are in the same direction for both testing orders and are proportional to the standard deviations of the tests. The requirement that the average signed changes be equal in standard deviation units is usually difficult to meet in practice. It should be noted that the equations referred to are those in Angoff (1984); other counterbalanced linkings based on less restrictive assumptions have been discussed by Holland and Thayer (1990) and von Davier, Holland, and Thayer (2003), but have not been considered in the present context.

When the equations in Angoff (1984) are the focus and nonproportional order effects are present, then typically only data from the first administration of each test, treated as coming from a random groups design, can be used for linking purposes. Because the number of examinees in the counterbalanced design is usually small, in hope that the data from the orders can be combined, a linking based on only the first administration of each test will typically not be precise enough for operational use and additional data will need to be collected. See Kolen (Chapter 3, Section 3.5) for an additional discussion of these types of issue.

In more recently conducted linking studies using this design, the tests could not be given sequentially in one testing session because the availability of computers precluded the testing of all examinees in the computer mode at the same time. This situation has in many ways proven to be a blessing in disguise. If the timing between the two tests is such that there is no possibility of either practice or fatigue effects, then having two separate orderings of the versions of the test is no longer necessary. In most studies that have capitalized on this, the paper-and-pencil version of the test has been given first. The study done by Schaeffer et al (1995), discussed later in this section, is in this tradition.

Another possibility is to consider use of the full-blown counterbalanced design, but not worry about specific order effects. For instance, in the Eignor (1993) study, examinees were randomly assigned to a testing order. Paper-and-pencil testing was scheduled for the middle of the testing window. Examinees assigned to the computer-first condition could pick a specific day to test on the computer prior to the paper-and-pencil testing day, whereas examinees assigned to the paper-and-pencil-first condition could pick a specific day to test on the computer after the paper-and-pencil testing day. The testing window was established by considering how long a period between the first and second administrations could exist without being concerned that subsequent learning had taken place. Because testing in both modes was done on different days, practice and fatigue effects were viewed as being, for the most part, nonexistent, allowing data from the two modes to be combined. Although the above scenario would seem to be a viable way of collecting data with the counterbalanced design, two things happened in the Eignor (1993) study that caused difficulties: (a) test proctors at sites did not always use the rosters provided to randomly assign examinees to testing orders and (b) some test proctors chose to test certain examinees in both modes on the same day. Given all of this, a compromise was reached whereby linking was done separately in the two orders and then the separate linkings were averaged. In doing so, however, the advantage of being able to use the combined data to do a more precise linking was lost.

Finally, it is possible here to test for differences in the means across the test modes. However, unlike with the random groups data collection design, any statistical test applied in this context would need to take into account the repeated-measures nature of the data.

8.6.2. Equating Studies Done with the Single Group Counterbalanced Design

The studies that made use of the single group counterbalanced design in the equating context typically looked at whether sets of scores on the same form across modes could be considered to be equivalent rather than carrying out formal equating studies. In their review of earlier studies (i.e., prior to 1988) that compared linear CBT and paper-and-pencil versions of tests using the counterbalanced design, Mazzeo and Harvey (1988) found that order effects can be very different across orders, with such effects being considerably larger for the computer version when the paper-and-pencil test is administered first than vice versa. In these studies, however, the two ordered tests were always given sequentially in one testing session.

Mazzeo et al. (1991) looked at the comparability of computer linear and paper-and-pencil versions of the CLEP® General Examinations in Mathematics and English Composition. Because the number of available participants was small, the researchers chose to make use of a single group counterbalanced design. For a given sample size, greater precision in linking is gained from this design than from a random groups design, or from an anchor-test design, to be discussed later in this chapter. In the first round of data collection, Mazzeo et al. found the presence of order effects for both examinations. Modifications were made to the computer delivery system and then a second round of testing was undertaken with the two tests being given sequentially in one session. No order effects were found for English Composition so that the data could be pooled and average performance across the two modes could be compared. The differences in means were viewed as being nonsignificant, which implied that scores from computer administrations could be reported on the paper-and-pencil scale. In the case of Mathematics, order effects were still present and, hence, the data were not pooled for comparison of the means. Looking at means from only the first administration of each of the two tests, the differences were substantial. Rather than using this data to link the tests (sample sizes were extremely small), the authors suggested that further investigation and modification take place in an attempt to remove order effects.

Sykes and Ito (1997) employed a single group counterbalanced design to look at the equivalence of 1-PL model ability estimates across a linear CBT and a paper-and-pencil version of a licensure examination. When comparing the ability estimates, the authors found a significant order by mode of administration interaction effect such that there was a significant difference in ability estimates across modes when the paper-and-pencil form was administered first, but no significant difference in paper-and-pencil and computer-based ability estimates when the computer-based form was given first. In this study, the two tests were given sequentially in a single session. It is interesting to note that in the Mazzeo et al. (1991) study, the larger mean differences within order were found when the CBT was given first, but in both orders the test taken second had the higher mean. Hence, the Sykes and Ito results differ from the Mazzeo et al. results. The Mazzeo et al. results seem in part to be due to practice effects. Sykes and Ito hypothesized that their results had to do with examinee expectations of a positive experience taking a new CBT. When examinees received the CBT first, their expectations were immediately met and there was no later falloff in performance when taking the paper-and-pencil test. This was not true for the reverse ordering.

8.6.3. Calibration Studies Done with the Single Group Counterbalanced Design

There are three examples in the literature of calibration studies that made use of the single group counterbalanced design, or a variant of it. Two studies calibrated scores across CATs and paper-and-pencil forms. One study calibrated scores between a CAT and a linear CBT.

Schaeffer et al. (1995) used a variant of the single group counter-balanced design, where only a single ordering was used, to look at the comparability of scores from the CAT and linear CBT forms for the GRE®

General Verbal, Quantitative, and Analytical tests. In Schaeffer et al. (1993), the authors had established that scores were comparable across linear CBT and paper-and-pencil versions of these tests via a random groups design. (The ultimate goal here was to move the paper-and-pencil GRE General tests to CAT. The researchers chose to do this via a two-step process.) Each of the three CBTs, one for Verbal, one for Math, and one for Analytical, is given in two sections. Hence, to take all three CBTs, an examinee would end up taking six sections. Six scrambles, different orders of these sections, were created, and a Verbal, Quantitative, or Analytical CAT was given in the seventh or last position of each of these scrambles. (Two scrambles had the Verbal CAT, two had the Quantitative CAT, and two had the Analytical CAT.) An example of one scramble follows: V1 A2 Q1 V2 A1 Q2 VCAT. As can be seen, two sections of nonverbal material were given between V2 and VCAT, and this was true for all spirals. Although all sections were given in one session, practice effects were mitigated through the presence of two sections that contained different content prior to the CAT. This provides some justification for only using a single ordering where the linear CBT is always given first, followed by the CAT.

Schaeffer et al. (1995) used the results to create estimated true score to reported score conversion tables for the CATs and then compared them to the observed score to reported score conversion tables for the linear CBTs. For the Verbal and Quantitative CATs; these tables were viewed as being sufficiently comparable in nature that the linear CBT conversion tables could be used with the CATs. However, this did not prove to be the case for the Analytical CAT. Additional data were collected, via a "true" single group counterbalanced design, where the three GRE General CATs were given along with the Analytical linear CBT. The Analytical CAT was given first in one order, followed by the other two CATs, and then the Analytical linear CBT. In the other order, the Analytical linear CBT was given first, followed by the Verbal and Quantitative CATs, and then the Analytical CAT. It was found that, on average, the Analytical CAT scores were significantly higher than the Analytical linear CBT scores; hence, a calibration of scores on these tests was undertaken using an IRT true-score procedure. The linking results were then applied and the Analytical linear CBT reported score conversion was used with the Analytical CATs.

McBride et al. (1987) used the single group counterbalanced design to calibrate CAT and paper-and-pencil scores on selected tests from the Adaptive Differential Aptitude Test. Linear and equipercentile linking methods were employed. The equipercentile method was chosen in each case, because those results were superior to the linear linkings. In all linkings, the ability estimates on the CAT were linked directly to the number-right scores on the paper-and-pencil version. The authors did not discuss any analyses of scores in the two separate orders, and it appears that data were pooled across the orders. Hence, it must be assumed that order effects were not viewed as being a problem. Finally, it is not surprising that the equipercentile method was viewed as superior to the linear method with these linkings, given that number-right scores and ability estimates were used in the linking. For any test scored via IRT and then scored in a conventional fashion, the relationship between number-right and ability scores is nonlinear.

Finally, Eignor (1993) did a linking study between SAT® CAT prototypes in verbal and mathematics and their paper-and-pencil counterparts using the single group counterbalanced design. Many of the details of this study have been discussed in a previous section of this chapter. Noteworthy in this study is that the form used as the reference form in creating estimated true scores on the CAT was also used to generate the raw scores on the paper-and-pencil version. Eignor compared final raw to scale conversions for the CATs and the paper-and-pencil forms, where the CAT estimated true scores were linked to paper-and-pencil observed scores. Differences between the two conversion tables for particular raw scores were then scrutinized for verbal and for math. These conversions turned out to differ more than was expected, given the use of the same paper-and-pencil form to create scores. In retrospect, this is perhaps not surprising, given that the CAT reference form simply transforms ability estimates to a different metric. Differences between modes will still be evident after applying the transformation of the CAT ability estimates to the estimated true-score scale.

8.6.4. Concordance Studies Done with the Single Group Counterbalanced Design

A computerized version of the Test of English as a Foreign Language™ (TOEFL®) was planned in order to introduce new item types that took advantage of computer administration, add an essay to the Writing section, and change the structure of the Reading and Listening sections. All of these changes made the sections of the new test significantly different from the comparable sections of the old paper-and-pencil test. Consequently, a calibration of scores between the sections could not be considered. Hence, new scales were defined for each of the sections of the new test and also for the total score. After much discussion, it was decided that the Listening section and the Writing multiple-choice section of the new test would be CATs, whereas the Reading section would be what is referred to as a linear-on-the-fly test (LOFT; see Carey, 1999). Note that Kolen and Brennan (2004) referred to such tests as computer-based randomized tests.

A LOFT was chosen for Reading because it was felt that the level of item dependence among items within passages precluded the use of item-level CAT, and the details of testlet-based CAT had not been worked out at that time. Given that reporting scales were going to be discontinued for the paper-and-pencil test, there was interest in providing users with some idea as to where to set the cut-scores on the sections of the new test. Hence, it was decided that concordance relationships would be established to provide approximate cut-points on the computerized test sections that corresponded to the cut-points on the old paper-and-pencil test sections. The examinees in the study took the paper-and-pencil form at a TOEFL operational administration and then took the computerized form shortly afterward, in a nonoperational setting. Because order effects were expected to be minimal to nonexistent, only one order of the single groups counterbalanced design was used.

Aware that concordance relationships are particularly sensitive to the groups used to create them (Dorans & Walker, Chapter 10; Kolen & Brennan, 2004; Pommerich, Chapter 11; Pommerich & Dorans, 2004; Sawyer, Chapter 12), it was decided to estimate population score distributions on the computerized sections and use what could be assumed to be "representative of the population" distributions on the paper-and-pencil sections to create the concordance for each section. This represents the unique feature of this study and is documented in Jiang (1999). The paper-and-pencil population distribution was based on a national sample of 50,000 examinees that were representative of the complete population that had taken the paper-and-pencil test. The study sample of 7,057 examinees was a subset of the 50,000. From the paper-and-pencil population distribution along with the study-sample paper-and-pencil and computerized test distributions, an estimated population distribution was created for each computer-based test section. Then using the observed paper-and-pencil population distribution for each section along with the estimated population distribution for the corresponding CBT section and equipercentile linking, concordances were created and approximate cut-scores were provided for the new test sections. Actually, what is described above is a simplification of what was done in that the estimation of the computer population distributions was treated in a multivariate fashion and all section distributions were estimated simultaneously rather than one by one. However, it is useful to think of the estimation in the univariate context because of its similarity to frequency estimation observed-score linking (see Kolen & Brennan, 2004). It should be noted that all of this work was motivated by the belief that the use of the population distributions in the concordances would provide more appropriate computerized test section cut-points than if the concordances had been based on the distributions provided by the study sample of 7000+

examinees. One issue of concern though was whether the examinees in the study sample were sufficiently familiar with computer-based testing to adequately represent the group of examinees who would later be taking the computerized test in an operational setting. Even though a fairly extensive tutorial accompanied the new CBT, there were concerns about computer familiarity. In many of the other studies described in this chapter, computer familiarity does not seem to have been considered an issue.

8.7. Anchor Test: Nonequivalent Groups Design

8.7.1. General Discussion

An anchor-test design represents an alternative to use in lieu of collecting large examinee samples for the random groups design. In this context, an anchor-test design would involve two groups of examinees that are usually nonequivalent in ability. Under one possible scenario, one group would receive the CBT followed by the anchor test and the other group would receive the paper-and-pencil version followed by the anchor test. Under the other possible scenario, the anchor test would be given first in both groups, followed by the two tests for which scores will be linked. The anchor test could be a parallel form of the tests or it could be a shortened version of them. Additionally, the anchor test could be administered to both groups in either paper-and-pencil format or in computer-based format. Both groups would need to take exactly the same anchor test in exactly the same position and in exactly the same mode. It is this additional "wrinkle" that makes it difficult to conduct linkings when the test and anchor are to be given consecutively in one testing session. For one order, the test and the anchor would need to be given in different modes. Given this complication, this is not a design that would likely be considered in the linking of linear CBT and paper-and-pencil forms of an exam, where other designs work well. Given the necessity that the anchor test be parallel to both of the tests precludes the use of this design for test concordance purposes. Hence, this design would most likely be employed when calibrating scores on CAT and paper-and-pencil versions of an exam.

It should be noted that items could possibly be located to constitute an anchor test that operated in the same fashion regardless of the mode of administration. If this were possible, the anchor could be given via computer or via the paper-and-pencil mode. This is a design that has been employed in linking the scales of similar tests given in different languages, such as the English and Spanish versions of the SAT (Angoff & Cook, 1988). Note that the Spanish version was not a direct translation of the

English version; rather, the tests were constructed separately to test the same content. The anchor test in this case was made up of a separate set of items that were not part of either of the two tests. However, in this particular situation, nothing prevents the anchor items from being internal to the tests themselves. If this is the case, concerns about the influence that the tests have on the anchor when the anchor is given last or the influence that the anchor has on the tests if the anchor is given first likely become nonproblems. Further, although this scenario would seem to best hold when linking linear CBTs to their paper-and-pencil counterparts, if one is willing to seed the common items into the CATs, nothing would prevent this scenario from being used in the linking of CATs and paper-and-pencil versions of the test. Here everything hinges on establishing that the common items function in the same way when given in the computer and paper-and-pencil modes. This would need to be established prior to the linking study itself.

Like the single group counterbalanced design, the linking relationship of interest with this design is between scores on CAT and paper-and-pencil versions of the test that are uncontaminated by the effects of taking the anchor test. Given this, it makes some sense to give the anchor test after the tests for which scores are to be linked. Also, if the anchor test was given first, the possibility of nonequivalent practice effects exist. If it could be established that the groups were equivalent in ability, as might be the case if they were random groups from the same population, then when the anchor appeared last, it could be disregarded and the linking relationship estimated from the data from the two tests administered first. However, as with the single group counterbalanced design, the strength of the anchor-test design is that under certain conditions, the data from the tests to be linked and the anchor test can be used in combination to provide a more precise estimate of the linking relationship of interest than could be obtained using the random groups design with a comparable sample size (i.e., disregarding the anchor test).

The statistical theory behind the anchor-test design is based on some key assumptions regarding anchor-test performance. Specifically, the anchor test needs to be a comparable measure of the construct being assessed for both groups in the design. Scores on the anchor test must represent the same attribute being measured, apart from possible group differences in performance on that attribute. Such a condition implies that any order effects associated with the anchor test need to be the same for both groups. Thus, difficulties associated with the anchor test might not necessarily be circumvented by giving the anchor test after the two test versions for which scores are to be linked.

Possible order effects associated with giving the anchor test last or possible practice effects associated with giving the anchor test first become a nonproblem if the tests and the anchor are not given sequentially in one testing session. The time period between administration of the anchor and the tests to be linked would need to be such that no learning took place during the period. Also, if the anchor and the tests are given on separate occasions, the problem that the anchor will be given in a different mode than one of the tests in question also becomes a nonproblem. In fact, one study took advantage of just this sort of arrangement.

One possible concern about the anchor test and the tests to be linked being given on separate occasions is whether this causes any of the assumptions underlying the nonequivalent groups anchor test design to be violated. After all, when this design and the single group counterbalanced design are discussed in the literature, the treatments have either the test and the anchor, or the two ordered tests, administered contiguously in a single testing session. However, it is often the case in the context of equating forms of paper-and-pencil tests that the external anchor is administered at a different point in time than either of the tests to be equated. An example of this occurs with certain SAT II Subject Tests that are equated through external anchors consisting of SAT verbal and SAT math scores. Not only are the SAT scores from administrations at a different point in time than the SAT II adminstration, but the SAT scores themselves are from multiple different administrations. In sum, in the context of linking scores given in different modes, as long as the time period between the anchor administration and the test administration (or the two ordered test administrations) is such that no intervening learning of the test content can occur, noncontiguous administrations would appear not to cause problems with respect to underlying assumptions.

Finally, it should be noted that statistical tests of differences in performance across the two modes of administration are not possible with this design if the groups are nonrandom groups. If the groups are random in nature and the anchor is given last, the data from the anchor can be disregarded for hypothesis testing purposes. It is unclear what benefits could be derived from including the anchor items with the test items in doing statistical tests with random groups.

8.7.2. Calibration Studies Done with the Anchor Test Design

Lawrence and Feigenbaum (1997) used an anchor-test design to link a computerized-adaptive version of the SAT to the paper-and-pencil test. The SAT CAT and test linking described earlier in this chapter (Eignor, 1993) was never used for operational purposes. In the period between 1993 AND 1997, the CAT system was improved upon by, for instance, putting in appropriate item exposure controls. Also, the SAT was revised during this period of time. In addition, the College Board made a decision that an SAT CAT would be used operationally with students who were seeking placement into talent search programs such as the Johns Hopkins Center for Talented Youth. Hence, it was felt that a linking study needed to be done with scores from the new SAT CAT system prior to operational implementation. The linking or calibration study was done using data from regular SAT examinees, although the test was later to be targeted for talented youth.

To conduct the study, the researchers identified a group of examinees who had taken a paper-and-pencil SAT form at an operational SAT test administration. A subset of these examinees was invited to take a CAT version of the test 1 month later; those who subsequently took the CAT formed one of the nonrandom groups. The other nonrandom group was made up of those examinees from the original group who took another operational paper-and-pencil SAT 1 month later. Scores for these two groups were calibrated making use of an anchor-test design where the score from the original operational SAT administration was used as the anchor score. Distributions were smoothed via log-linear procedures and then the chained equipercentile method (see Kolen & Brennan, 2004; Kolen, Chapter 3) was used to link the scores from the CAT and the paper-and-pencil test. New conversion tables were created for the CAT and compared to the paper-and-pencil conversion tables that existed for the paper-and-pencil form taken in the second administration. (As described earlier, with the CAT, the estimated abilities were transformed into estimated true scores on a reference form that already had a raw to scale conversion table.) The magnitude of the differences in the conversion tables for both verbal and math ranged from 0 to 20 scaled-score points. It is interesting to note that the magnitude of differences from the Eignor (1993) study, done using a different CAT system and data collection design, were also between 0 and 20 scaled-score points, and the nonzero differences in the conversion tables were in the same relative spots on the raw score scales in both studies. However, although the differences in the two studies were in the same direction for verbal, they were in opposite directions for math. Lawrence and Feigenbaum (1997) had a number of concerns about their study, including possible differential motivation levels between the examinees who took the CAT and those who took the subsequent SAT, for which scores were reported as usual. However, it should be noted that the examinees who took the CAT were given the option of keeping their scores or having them canceled. This should have helped to eliminate, to some extent, possible motivational differences.

8.8. Summary

A number of issues surrounding the linking of scores on computer-based and paper-and-pencil tests were discussed in this chapter. The linking relationship between the tests could be characterized as being an equating, a calibration, or a concordance, depending on the nature of the CBT. The linking for which the most issues surface involves scores on CAT and paper-and-pencil forms of a test. Although users would like to be able to use the scores from these two sorts of test interchangeably, as would be the case if the linking of these scores could be viewed as an equating, such a linking can be considered to be, at best, a calibration, primarily because it cannot be shown to satisfy the equity requirement of equating. This, however, has not stopped score users from treating calibration results as if they were equating results. In fact, because the calibration process typically yields scores that are reported on the same scale, it is only logical that users will treat the calibrated scores as if they were equated scores. At present, it is not exactly clear what the consequences are of treating a calibration in this context as if it were an equating. It might very well prove to be the case that such scores should be related via a concordance table. Separate scales would exist for the forms and there would be less inclination to use the results as if they came from an equating. However, unless specifically cautioned, users will often use the scores related via a concordance table as if they were equated scores, even though the scales themselves will likely be different. Pommerich (Chapter 11) expressed similar concerns with concordance tables.

The population invariance requirement for the equating of scores was not specifically discussed in this chapter. However, a number of reviewed studies took a look at the effects of linking transformations on subgroups. These include the studies done by Poggio et al. (2005), Schaeffer et al. (1993, 1995), Eignor et al. (1994), Segall (1995), and Lawrence and Feigenbaum (1997). In all of these studies the (sub)population invariance property was not specifically investigated because separate subpopulation linkings were not undertaken. This is partly because the invariance checking procedures (see Dorans & Holland, 2000) had not been developed at the time that most of the studies were done. It would be particularly interesting to see whether linkings between CATs and paper-and-pencil tests, which have been shown not to satisfy the equity requirement, also do not satisfy the population invariance property. This would add additional strength to the assertion made in this chapter that the linking between scores on a CAT and a paper-and-pencil test does not qualify as an equating.

A significant portion of the chapter dealt with data collection designs necessary to link scores on CBTs and paper-and-pencil tests. This was done in hope that the chapter might provide some guidance to other practitioners faced with similar linking situations. It was seen that the random groups design provides a mechanism for linking scores on these tests that is basically free from the influence of practice or fatigue effects, or order effects in general. It was also shown, however, that nontraditional applications of the other designs, whereby tests to be linked are not given consecutively in one testing session, also provide viable options for linking scores.

One final caveat is in order. Much of the material in this chapter was based on the author's personal experiences in linking computer-based and paper-and-pencil forms of tests and on the experiences documented in 11 articles located in the literature. This is clearly too small a set of articles on which to draw general conclusions of any sort, and it might prove to be the case when further studies are conducted that certain of the conclusions in this chapter might need to be altered. In fact, this has already happened, given that in earlier work this author and other authors considered the linking of scores on CATs and paper-and-pencil tests to qualify as equatings, whereas more recent work, such as the work of Wang and Kolen (2001), has shown this not to be the case. Finally, it should be pointed out that the number of studies in the literature addressing linking of this sort, and the related problems, will never be voluminous in nature because testing programs most often do these sorts of study only once, or perhaps a small number of times, as the programs are transitioned from paper-and-pencil to computer-based testing.

Acknowledgments. The author thanks John Mazzeo and Lin Wang for their reviews of a draft version of this chapter.

9 Tests in Transition: Discussion and Synthesis

Robert L. Brennan[1]

University of Iowa

In educational settings that focus primarily on student achievement, testing programs are almost always in a state of transition, or they should be! Over time, changes occur in curricula and student populations. It follows that if a testing program is to reflect what is happening in particular educational settings, it must evolve to align itself with those settings. Other evolutions occur when the conditions of test administration are modified. Movement to computer-based testing is an obvious example.

One of the ironies of educational measurement is that such changes in a testing program—even when they are widely viewed as improvements— might jeopardize score comparability to some extent, which is usually viewed as anything but an improvement! One route around this problem is to adopt a new scale, but for numerous reasons rescaling is often viewed as an unacceptable alternative.[2] So, frequently, it is decided to make certain adjustments to the testing program and/or psychometric "fixes" with the goal of keeping the score scale as unaltered as possible. Then the overarching question becomes, "Has the score scale been maintained adequately enough?" Psychometric evidence to address this question is primarily the focus of the chapters by Liu and Walker (Chapter 7) and by Eignor (Chapter 8).

Such psychometric evidence is generally viewed in terms of criteria for linking, for which there are many lists in the literature. For example, the list given by Liu and Walker (Chapter 7, Section 7.2.2) is as follows:

---

[1] Robert L. Brennan is E. F. Lindquist Chair in Measurement and Testing, and Director, Center for Advanced Studies in Measurement and Assessment, University of Iowa. The opinions expressed in this chapter are those of the author and not necessarily of the University of Iowa.
[2] Rescaling is considered in more detail in the last section of this discussion.

1. Same construct
2. Equity
3. Symmetry
4. Subpopulation invariance
5. Equal reliability
6. Same inferences
7. Same target population
8. Same measurement characteristics/conditions

The extent to which equity and subpopulation invariance are satisfied is largely a consequence of test-developer decisions that relate to the other six criteria. Both the Liu and Walker chapter and the Eignor chapter in this volume consider aspects of these other six criteria, but interestingly, Liu and Walker focus primarily on subpopulation invariance without much direct consideration of equity, whereas Eignor focuses more on equity issues without much consideration of subpopulation invariance.

In the next two sections, I provide a summary of these two chapters that is interspersed with my own comments. The final section provides a brief consideration of the need for an integration of equity and subpopulation invariance, followed by a consideration of linking versus rescaling.

9.1. The Liu and Walker Chapter on Test Content Changes

Liu and Walker discussed score linking issues related to test content changes, using the new SAT® to illustrate their points. Actually, in many respects, the new SAT plays such a central role in their chapter that the chapter itself might be viewed largely as a review of rationale, studies, and methodology used to support various decisions made about the new SAT.

Liu and Walker provide the following insightful focus for their chapter on score linking issues:

> At some point early in the redesign process, before we begin to investigate issues of score comparability, the testing organization must make a conscious decision about what is most important in the test revision. ... The determination of this most important factor will have strong implications for the rest of the redesign process. ... We need to ask ourselves: What do we want to achieve with the new test? What are the constraints? All the revisions and data collections should be guided by this redesign principle.

As Liu and Walker noted, in the context of the new SAT, the College Board stated a priori that they wanted the new critical reading (CR) test and old verbal (OV) test to be "equatable," as well as the new math (NM) test and the old math (OM) test. This a priori constraint influenced many aspects of the work done by the Educational Testing Service (ETS). Note that the new SAT also consists of a new writing (NW) test, for which a score scale had to be established, but that is not the focus of the Liu and Walker chapter.

To examine "equatability" Liu and Walker considered the following:

- Test specifications
- Item characteristics
- Empirical relationships between old and new tests
- Reliability for old and new tests
- Conditional standard errors of measurement (CSEMs) for old and new tests, and
- Subpopulation invariance for males and females.

To provide data for various empirical analyses, ETS conducted an extensive, well-designed, and well-executed field trial. The basic structure was as follows:

- Design 1: *Equivalent groups*. Each student took either a complete old SAT (OV + OM) or a complete new SAT (CR + NM + NW).
- Design 2: *Counterbalanced single group*. Each student took an old and a new component (OV and CR, or OM and NM).

The field trial, however, had one important limitation: Sample sizes were not sufficient for separate linkings for subgroups other than males and females.

9.1.1. Content Specifications and Item Characteristics

Liu and Walker provided a concise and excellent summary of content differences between the old and new SATs. Among the differences they cite between CR and OV are the following:

- Analogy items in OV were replaced by short reading passages in CR.
- There is a larger number of reading comprehension items in CR than in OV.
- Test length was reduced from 78 items in OV to 67 items in CR.

Among the differences that Liu and Walker cited between NM and OM are the following:

- There are no quantitative comparison items in NM.
- The content in NM was expanded to cover third-year college-preparatory math.
- Test length was reduced from 60 items in OM to 54 items in NM.

Additional differences between the old and new SATs incude the following:

- The introduction of NW that consists of both multiple-choice questions and a single essay prompt

- Section timing changes

- An increase in total testing time from three hours to 3 hours and 45 minutes

Liu and Walker concluded that "the content specifications on the new test do not suggest dramatic changes from the old test." With respect to item characteristics (deltas and biserials), OV and CR are very similar, as are OM and NM.

On balance, it appears that item statistics are more similar than are content specifications for the old and new SATs. This is not too surprising given the "redesign" context mentioned previously. Basically, most of the content changes were determined (tentatively) before the new SAT items were selected for the field trial; thus, it was possible to some extent to pick new SAT items that would likely perform similarly as a set to items in the old SAT.

9.1.2. Empirical Relationships

Liu and Walker used Pearson product-moment correlations (r) and reductions in uncertainty $\left(\mathrm{RiU} = 1 - \sqrt{1 - r^2}\right)$ to quantify certain empirical relations between the old and new SAT. Dorans (2000, 2004d) argued that it is reasonable to require at least 50% reduction in uncertainty for test score linkage in high-stakes settings. This criterion requires that $r \geq .866$. Liu and Walker report that

$$r(\mathrm{CR,OV}) = .912 \rightarrow \mathrm{RiU} = .59 \text{ (i.e., 59%)}$$

and

$$r(\mathrm{NM,OM}) = .922 \rightarrow \mathrm{RiU} = .61 \text{ (i.e., 61%)}.$$

Clearly, the two RiU values exceed the 50% threshold, although this threshold is somewhat arbitrary. Another benchmark that can be considered is the old and new cross-test correlations

$$r(\mathrm{OV,OM}) = r(\mathrm{CR,NM}) = .79,$$

which are notably lower than $r(CR,OV) = .912$ and $r(NM,OM) = .922$, as one would hope and suspect.

Observed-score correlations can be informative for judging the adequacy of linking, but true-score correlations (ρ) that approach unity are essential for an argument that a linking deserves to be characterized as equating. True-score correlations depend, of course, on reliabilities.

9.1.3. Reliability and CSEMs

With respect to reliability (Rel), Liu and Walker stated that "high reliability on both tests is needed to ensure that the equated scores are informative enough to be accepted by test users (Dorans, 2004d)." They go on to report that

$$Rel(OV) \doteq Rel(CR) = (.91 - .93)$$

and

$$Rel(OM) \doteq Rel(NM) = (.91 - .93)$$

These results are encouraging in two respects. First, letting ρ designate true-score correlation, these results mean that

$$\rho(CR,OV) \doteq \rho(NM,OM) \doteq 1,$$

suggesting that the old and new tests are measuring similar constructs in an overall sense. Second, because the reliabilities are approximately equal, as are the standard deviations, the CSEMs are also about equal (in the low 30s on the SAT scale.) These are important results in supporting the view that the score scale is maintained reasonably well, although these results do not guarantee that scores for all examinees are interchangeable.

9.1.4. Subpopulation Invariance for Males and Females

Liu and Walker pointed out that "when population invariance does not hold, it tells us that the differential difficulty of the two tests to be equated is not consistent across different subgroups." Methodology for examining subpopulation invariance is evolving at a rapid rate. Perhaps the most salient initial discussion was by Dorans and Holland (2000); additional perspectives are provided by Kolen and Brennan (2004), among others.

For the new SAT, sample sizes from the field trial were adequate for examining subpopulation invariance for males and females, only. Liu and Walker provide results for OV and CR in great detail; they state that stronger results (i.e., less subpopulation sensitivity) hold for OM and NM. Two types of statistics are reported by Liu and Walker:

1. The Dorans and Holland (2000) root mean square difference (RMSD) and root expected mean square difference (REMSD) statistics, which Liu and Walker usually evaluated relative to a "difference that matters" DTM of 5.
2. Percentage indexes:
   - Percent of formula scores for which the absolute value of the total and subgroup conversions differ by more than 5 points, which will be abbreviated PS (i.e., percent of scores), and
   - Percent of examinees for whom the absolute value of the total and subgroup conversions differ by more than 5 points, which will be abbreviated PE (i.e., percent of examinees).

An excellent feature of the Liu and Walker discussion of subpopulation invariance is that they first provide results for two parallel OV forms; these results serve as an informative baseline for subsequent results based on CR and OV. Stated briefly, the subpopulation invariance study of the two OV forms resulted in RMSD < 5 at all scale score levels, and for both males and females PS = 0 and PE = 0. These results strongly suggest that the linking of two OV forms deserves to be called an equating. Ideally, it would be desirable to have similar analyses for two CR forms, but two such forms were not available for the field trial.

The linking of OV and CR for males and females resulted in RMSD < 5 for all but very low scale scores: for males, PS = 3.5 and PE = 0.7, and for females, PS = 1.2 and PE = 0.4. These results suggest minor evidence of subpopulation sensitivity with respect to gender. Liu and Walker summarize these results in the following terms: "... based on the equatability analyses discussed above, we think that the term *equating* might be defended for the linkage from new critical reading to the old verbal, and for the linkage from new math to the old math."

There is a somewhat different perspective on these analyses, however, that might lead to a slightly more tentative conclusion. The RMSD and REMSD statistics compare the male (M) and female (F) linkings to the total-group (T) linking; these statistics do not compare the male and female linkings directly. When there are more than two subgroups, comparing each of them to the total group using RMSD and/or REMSD is convenient because it gives a single result regardless of how many subgroups are involved. When there are only two subgroups, however, a direct comparison of the two linkings seems to me to be an obvious comparison to consider. (Kolen & Brennan, 2004, provide statistics for pairwise linkings.)

Figure 7.2 in Liu and Walker plots scaled-score differences for M-T and F-T when two OV forms are linked. The difference between these two plots gives the M-F scaled-score differences. It appears from Figure 7.2 that even when two OV forms are linked, the M-F differences suggest a hint of subpopulation sensitivity around scale scores of 500 and near 800, using DTM = 5 as a benchmark. Using the same benchmark, when OV and CR are linked and the M-F differences are examined, Figure 7.3 suggests that there is some evidence of subpopulation sensitivity throughout much of the scale score range.

I would argue that when we consider subpopulation sensitivity there are two questions that are typically of interest. First, how large are the differences between the linkings for the various subpopulations? In the context of the Liu and Walker chapter, this question is answered by examining directly the M-F scaled-score differences. Second, when a decision is made to use the total-group linking operationally, by how much are examinees in the various subpopulations advantaged/disadvantaged? In the context of the Liu and Walker chapter, this question is answered by examining the M-T and F-T differences. In most cases, both questions are relevant, but the answers will not be the same. There is no unqualified "correct" perspective; these are simply two different perspectives that answer different questions.

9.1.5. Other Comments

The Liu and Walker chapter provided an excellent discussion of numerous issues that relate to linking, and an excellent review of the linking conducted for the new SAT. For this linking, the field-test design and data collection were superb, but it is important to keep in mind the practical constraints involved in the field test. One such constraint was that the data were not collected in an operational setting. For this reason and others, conclusions about subpopulation invariance for the new SAT are necessarily somewhat tentative. Firmer conclusions will be possible when a substantial body of operational data for the new SAT is available.

In their discussion of empirical relationships, reliability, and subpopulation invariance, Liu and Walker employed numerous statistics and often drew conclusions based in part on the magnitude of such statistics compared to some benchmark. Two obvious examples are the 50% RiU criterion, which requires that $r \geq .866$ for test score linkage in high-stakes settings, and DTM = 5 for the SAT. Although I believe that a DTM standard provides a useful benchmark, I do not think that conclusions about subpopulation invariance should be based exclusively on a DTM standard (see Brennan, 2006). Population sensitivity, like most other psychometric issues, is a matter of degree. Exclusive use of any single benchmark can obscure this basic fact and lead to unwarranted or too firm conclusions. I am not quarrelling with the Liu and Walker discussion of these matters, but a word of caution seems in order.

9.2. Eignor Chapter on Mode of Administration

Eignor discussed "linking scores derived under different modes of test administration," with almost exclusive attention given to paper-and-pencil (P&P) testing and two varieties of computerized testing: computer-adaptive testing (CAT) and other nonadaptive forms of computer-based testing (CBT). Eignor discussed these different modes of administration in the context of three types of linking (equating, calibration, and concordance) and three designs (random groups, single group counterbalanced design, and nonequivalent groups anchor-test design). See Holland (Chapter 2) and Kolen (Chapter 3) for detailed treatments of types of linking and data collection designs, respectively.

9.2.1. Types of Linking

In the terminology used by Eignor:

- Equating requires that the two tests (or forms) measure the same construct at approximately the same level of difficulty and with the same reliability. Eignor noted that equity is satisfied for equated scores, and it is a matter of indifference to any examinee as to which form she or he takes. In this sense, scores that deserve to be called "equated" are "truly interchangeable," to quote Eignor. As an example, Eignor cited linking a linear CBT version of an extant P&P test built to the same specifications.

- Calibration also requires that the two tests measure the same construct at approximately the same level of difficulty, but reliabilities could differ. As an example, Eignor cited linking a CAT version of an extant P&P test. Eignor argued persuasively that in this case second-order equity will not be satisfied because conditional standard errors of measurement will differ for the CAT and P&P tests.

- Concordance requires that the two tests measure similar constructs, with somewhat similar levels of difficulty and reliability. Eignor argued that "scores that have been concorded cannot be treated as being interchangeable." As an example, Eignor cited a CBT test and a P&P

test constructed to somewhat different specifications (e.g., the use of innovative item types and/or updated test content for the CBT).

It seems that the above taxonomic terms and the examples might be misaligned sometimes. For example, it is not clear that linking scores for a P&P test and a linear CBT version of it will always result in "equated" scores in the sense used by Holland (Chapter 2, Section 2.4.1) and most recent treatments of equating and linking (e.g., Kolen & Brennan, 2004). CBT constrains certain types of behavior in ways that some examinees might consider frustrating or confusing, with a potential negative impact on at least some scores. Furthermore, some examinees' scores might be influenced by differences in clarity between the presentation of items (particularly figures) in the two administrative modes. Kolen (Chapter 3, Section 3.2) explicitly included the conditions of administration as a formal component in his treatment of linking relationships. As a consequence, his treatment has direct relevance for mode of administration studies.

When Eignor argued that "scores that have been concorded cannot be treated as being interchangeable," he could mean two things. First, such scores are *not* interchangeable; second, such scores should not be used interchangeably. The first statement is unarguable in the sense that such scores are not "equated." The second statement, however, focuses on "use" of scores, which immediately engages a number of practical issues. For example, the quintessential example of concordance is the linking of ACT® and SAT scores, which traditionally results in a single table of "equivalent" scores that *are* indeed used as if they were interchangeable. In my experience, arguing against such use is a lost cause, but cautioning users about potential errors in such use is both necessary and possible.

In my opinion, Eignor's discussion of equating, calibration, and concordance is primarily in the context of equity issues (what might be called the "matter of indifference" criterion), but his chapter does not get into technical details about equity. It is difficult to treat equity in a manner that is both practically useful and technically defensible. Although much work in this area remains to be done, a particularly useful article is provided by Hanson, Harris, Pommerich, Sconing, and Yi (2001). They introduced the terms "closely equatable scores" (equating), "weakly equatable scores" (calibration), and "nonequatable" scores (concordance). They focused on construct dis/similarity, first-order equity, and second-order equity, and they considered linkage at the level of individual scores and at the level of score distributions.

9.2.2. Designs

The majority of the Eignor chapter focuses on three designs and examples of them that have been discussed in the literature on linking computerized and P&P tests. This is an excellent discussion that is noteworthy for its comprehensiveness and clarity, and I make no attempt to summarize it. Rather, I focus here primarily on a few issues that I think might be somewhat arguable or merit more consideration. My concerns are very minor, however, compared to the quality of Eignor's discussion of designs.

Random groups design. For establishing a linkage between a computerized and P&P test, often a random groups design is preferable to other designs provided, as Eignor noted that differential dropout is not a significant problem and sample sizes are sufficient. Relative to a single group design, sample size requirements for a random groups design are larger. However, relatively small sample sizes are adequate using linear linking with a random groups design.

Single group counterbalanced design. A distinct advantage of the random groups design is that each examinee takes only one test or test form, which means that administration conditions in the study mirror those that will be used operationally. By contrast, for the single group counterbalanced design, each examinee takes two tests or test forms, which raises the distinct possibility of contamination due to practice and/or fatigue effects. Eignor provided an excellent discussion of these effects in the context of the single group counterbalanced design.

Nonequivalent groups anchor test design.[3] A crucial aspect of the nonequivalent groups anchor-test design is that, for this design to work well, the anchor test needs to mirror the full-length test in all respects (see Kolen & Brennan, 2004), including mode of administration. Also, in considering this design, it is helpful to consider the location of the anchor (before, after, or embedded) and whether the anchor is part of the score (interval or external). It appears that Eignor's discussion usually makes an implicit assumption that the anchor is external.

Eignor correctly noted that

> Both groups would need to take exactly the same anchor test in exactly the same position and in exactly the same mode. (The) same mode for the anchor test across tests ... makes it difficult to conduct linkings with this design when the test and the anchor are to be given consecutively in one testing session.

---

[3] This design is sometimes called the common-item nonequivalent groups design (see Kolen & Brennan, 2004). See Kolen (Chapter 3) for further discussion of these designs.

There is one additional and potentially insurmountable problem when computerized and P&P tests are linked using the nonequivalent groups anchor test design. The crux of the matter is that the items in an anchor-test administered via computer will not necessarily function the same way in the P&P mode, and there is no way to circumvent this potential problem using the nonequivalent groups anchor-test design. See Kolen (Chapter 3, Section 3.2) for more on the role of mode of administration.

9.2.3. Other Comments

In at least two places Eignor noted that "estimated true scores on the reference form (for a CAT) can ... be linked or calibrated with observed scores on the test given in the paper-and-pencil mode." It is rather natural to do this because observed scores (rather than true scores) are usually reported for a P&P test, whereas for a CAT often item response theory (IRT) theta estimates are transformed to IRT estimated true scores. Logically, however, it seems rather inconsistent to link observed scores (on a P&P test) with true scores (on a CAT) when both tests are presumably measuring the same construct. Note that there is no reason to believe that this linkage would be the same as a true-score to true-score linking or an observed-score to observed-score linking.

Eignor noted that "samples used in the linking should be representative of the population," which is clearly desirable. However, very often, linking is conducted using data outside an operational administration, and in such cases, practical data collection issues often render the data quite unrepresentative of the population that will take the new CBT. When this occurs, results need to be interpreted with caution.[4]

9.3. Additional Perspectives

The two preceding chapters in this part are very well written and well reasoned. They are truly state-of-the-art considerations of linking scores for tests that are undergoing changes in content specifications and/or

---

[4] Perhaps the quintessential example of unrepresentativeness is data typically used to create ACT–SAT concordances. By definition, the self-selected group of examinees who choose to take both tests is not the group for which the concordance will be used. There is no practical way to avoid this problem, but it does limit the scope of legitimate inferences. These concerns were discussed directly in the chapters by Dorans and Walker (Chapter 10), Pommerich (Chapter 11), and Sawyer (Chapter 12) in the section on concordance.

administrative conditions. However, the state of the art is not as far advanced as we might like in all respects. In particular, it seems that we need more integration of equity and subpopulation invariance in both theory and practice. Also, the two chapters discussed here only hint at one important question that almost always arises when tests undergo transitions—namely should scores be linked or should a rescaling be undertaken?

9.3.1. Equity and Subpopulation Invariance

As noted previously, the Liu and Walker chapter gives considerable attention to subpopulation invariance, whereas the Eignor chapter focuses more on equity issues in a general sense. Eignor, however, did make the insightful statement that "it would be particularly interesting to see whether linkings between CATs and paper-and-pencil tests, which have been shown not to satisfy the equity requirement, also do not satisfy the population invariance property."

Stated more broadly, I suggest that a deep understanding of linking requires an integrated treatment of both subpopulation invariance and equity (as well as other criteria, of course). Such a treatment remains to be developed. In my opinion, subpopulation invariance is the simpler matter. We have more statistical and psychometric tools to quantify it and more consensus about how to study it. By contrast, it does not seem that the field of psychometrics has achieved any consensus about how to study equity, although I believe that Hanson et al. (2001) provides some useful perspectives, as does Kim, Brennan, and Kolen (2005).

A theoretically coherent and practically useful integration of equity and subpopulation invariance would be a tremendous contribution to the field of linking. In the meantime, I suggest that any linking of tests in transition should give at least some consideration to both subpopulation invariance and equity (as well as other criteria, of course), even if the treatment is not as integrated as we might like, given current limitations of the field.

9.3.2. Linking Versus Rescaling

One of the most sensitive and potentially volatile issues often encountered when tests undergo transition is whether scores should be linked or rescaled. The comments I offer here are intended as a brief, general consideration of this matter, not evaluative comments specifically directed at the chapters discussed here or any particular testing program.

Actually, it is not quite accurate to characterize the situation considered here simply as linking versus rescaling. Consider, for example, the rescaling of the "new" ACT first administered in 1989 (see Brennan, 1989). Separate studies were conducted that led to a rescaling for each of the four tests in the ACT. In addition, for two of the tests, there were old-scale to new-scale linkings in the sense of concordances that were made available to users to facilitate transition from the old score scale to the new score scale.[5] In addition, of course, new forms of the tests in the new ACT were linked in the sense of equated. For the purposes of this discussion, the important point is that the new scales were indeed a break with the past in the sense that particular scores on the old scales did not have the same meaning on the new scales. So, in that sense, scores were rescaled rather than linked.

As noted previously, in educational settings that focus primarily on student achievement, testing programs are almost always in a state of transition, or they should be. Sometimes the transitions are abrupt; sometimes they are more gradual. For example, the introduction of the "new" ACT in 1989 and the recentering of the SAT (Dorans, 2002) were rather abrupt changes that involved a rescaling of scores for these programs. For less abrupt changes, a central concern is often whether the linking can be defended as an "equating."

In the usual course of events, from one year to the next, changes in testing programs are typically not dramatic, and seldom does anyone quarrel with calling the linking of scores from year to year an "equating." I suggest, however, that this common view might merit some qualification from at least two (somewhat related) perspectives. First, for almost all testing programs, when any given form is equated, the links to past years are seldom older than 3–4 years, if that. So, there is only indirect evidence about the maintenance of the score scale for a longer period of time.[6] Second, over an extended period of time, even small year-to-year changes could add up to substantial differences between old and new forms.

The *Standards for Educational and Psychological Testing* (American Educational Research Association, American Psychological Association, & National Council on Measurement in Education [AERA, APA, & NCME], 1999) addressed the matter of rescaling as follows:

> Standard 4.16: If test specifications are changed from one version of a test to a subsequent version, such changes should be identified in the test manual, and an indication should be given

---

[5] These concordances were used only for a limited period of time.

[6] The indirect evidence is based on transitivity assumptions. For example, if Form G administered in 2005 is equated to Form D administered in 2000, and Form D was previously equated to Form A administered in 1997, then we claim that Form G has been equated to Form A—but only if all relevant assumptions are fulfilled.

that converted scores for the two versions may not be strictly equivalent. When substantial changes in test specifications occur, either scores should be reported on a new scale or a clear statement should be provided to alert users that the scores are not directly comparable with those on earlier versions of the test.

On the surface, this standard might seem unambiguously clear. In my opinion, however, this standard provides relatively little practical guidance for determining when a rescaling should be undertaken. For the reasons discussed next, I am not at all sure that this standard could be written in a manner that would provide practical guidance applicable to all testing programs.

Most of the problem is how to interpret the two key phrases: "substantial changes in test specifications" and "directly comparable." A related problem involves the inferences drawn with test scores. For example, if comparisons are typically made among examinees within a 4-year window, it might not matter much if test specifications change substantially only over a 10-year window. On the other hand, even relatively small changes in test specifications might influence a 20-year trend line.

The phrase "directly comparable" is also problematic. A strict interpretation of that phrase would seem to be that, for each and every examinee, it is a matter of indifference which form she or he takes. In this sense, "directly comparable" means that scores are "strictly interchangeable" (a phrase used in the comment to Standard 4.16) or, stated differently, the criterion of score equity is achieved in its fullest sense. As Lord (1980) noted decades ago, however, under this criterion, equating is either impossible or unnecessary! No one would argue about the ideal being equated scores in the strict sense of "directly comparable," but this unachievable goal does not provide practical guidance with respect to when a linking can be justified as an "equating" or when changes in a testing program are so substantial that a rescaling should be undertaken. It is also worth noting that most of the literature on linking (except for equating) has been generated since the 1999 Standards (AERA, APA, & NCME, 1999) was published. It is not clear, of course, whether this new linking literature would cause the authors of the Standards to modify Standard 4.16.

Rescaling might be a psychometric issue, but decisions about whether to rescale are seldom made by psychometricians. In my career, on several occasions I have suggested that rescaling be undertaken for particular testing programs. Usually that advice has been rejected outright or postponed, sometimes indefinitely. Resistance to rescaling is often visceral. Some reasons for this resistance are quite understandable (e.g., time, cost, analysis difficulties, communication complexities); other reasons are more subtle or even misguided. For example, some view rescaling as an implied admission of mistakes in the previous scale. Others honestly believe that a test can be improved without in any way altering the meaning of the scores.

In the future, my guess is that rescaling will continue to be a relatively rare undertaking, and arguments about the merits of linking versus rescaling will continue. Whether scores are equated, linked in some weaker sense, or rescaled, however, the overarching consideration in my opinion is that users be given appropriate guidance about score interpretation and use. Part of that guidance ought to be explicit indications of the amount of error in scores and in the likely uses made of scores, as well as admonitions about likely misinterpretations of scores.

Acknowledgments

The author gratefully acknowledges helpful comments by Michael J. Kolen on a previous version of the manuscript.

Part 4: Concordance

How do we know whether we can achieve the interchangeability of scores associated with equating, the meaningful comparability of scales suggested by a concordance, or simply have to settle for the expected scores provided by prediction?

Neil Dorans and Michael Walker in *Sizing up Linkages*, answer this question by contrasting equating, concordance, and prediction. Data about the size and shape of professional athletes are used to illustrate how measures of uncertainty reduction and population invariance can help us distinguish among settings in which it is better to equate, concord, or predict.

Mary Pommerich in *Concordance: The Good, the Bad, and the Ugly* makes it clear that concordance is a weaker form of linking than equating. Concordance tables are often created as a convenience to test users, allowing them to link scores across tests that were never intended to be linked. Her chapter discusses a variety of practical issues that should be considered throughout the concordance process. She uses a linkage between ACT® and SAT® scores for use in undergraduate college admissions to illustrate her points.

In *Some Further Thoughts on Concordance*, Richard Sawyer discusses some general ideas on the uses of concordance tables. He relates them to points made in the two preceding chapters. He illustrates his ideas with the same example that Pommerich used. He ends his chapter with his own unique contribution to the mix of levity and serious scholarship that characterizes this part.

10   Sizing Up Linkages

Neil J. Dorans and Michael E. Walker[1]

Educational Testing Service

10.1. Introduction

A link between scores on two tests is a transformation from a score on one to a score on the other. Transformations that link the scores on two tests can be of different types. For example, any score can be predicted from any other score(s) via an asymmetric regression equation. Alternatively, symmetric relationships can be established between pairs of scores, given the correct data collection designs. Whether these symmetric relationships possess any interpretative value can be determined with the help of statistical indexes used in conjunction with reasoned thresholds.

A variety of frameworks have been proposed for categories of score linking (Angoff, 1971; Dorans, 2000, 2004d; Feuer, Holland, Green, Bertenthal, & Hemphill, 1999; Flanagan, 1951; Kolen, 2004a; Linn. 1993; Mislevy, 1992). Holland and Dorans (2006) divided linking methods into three basic categories: *predicting, scale aligning,* and *equating.* In the Holland and Dorans framework, which is described in Holland (Chapter 2), equating represents the end point of a continuum that begins with methods that make no assumptions about the relationship between the tests being linked (prediction and battery scaling) and proceeds to methods that are appropriate for linking tests that measure similar constructs and could be built to the same set of specifications (concordances and equating).

All linking frameworks define equating as the strongest form of linking between the scores on two tests. The goal of equating is to establish an effective equivalence between scores on two test forms such that the scores

---

[1] The opinions expressed in this chapter are those of the authors and not necessarily of Educational Testing Service.

from each test can be used as if they had come from the same test. To achieve this goal of interchangeable scores, strong requirements must be put on the blueprints for the two tests and on the method used for linking scores. Among other things, the two tests must measure the same construct at about the same level of difficulty and with nearly the same reliability.

Predicting is the oldest form of score linking. The goal of predicting is to estimate an examinee's score on a test from other information about that examinee. The predictor is often multivariate in nature. It might include scores from several other tests, demographic information, and other types of information. When the predictor is multivariate and the model is compensatory, as is often the case, there is an asymmetry between the predictor and the predicted score, in that the predicted score can come from many combinations of the multivariate predictor. In the case of univariate and multivariate predictors, there is also an asymmetry that results from the loss function used to predict the criterion. Asymmetry prevents prediction from meeting one of the fundamental prerequisites of equating, the goal of which is to produce scores that can be used interchangeably. All the same, predicting has been confused with equating since the earliest days of psychometrics, and continues to be confused with it.

The goal of scale aligning is to transform the scores from two different tests onto a common scale. The statistical procedures used for scale alignment can also be used to equate tests. Holland (Chapter 2, Section 2.3) reported that scale aligning has many subcategories, including activities such as battery scaling (Kolen, 2004a), anchor scaling (Holland & Dorans, 2006), vertical scaling (Kolen & Brennan, 2004), calibration (Holland & Dorans, 2006), and concordance (Pommerich & Dorans, 2004a). Concordances represent scalings of tests that are very similar but that were not created with the idea that their scores would be used interchangeably.

In this chapter, we present criteria and procedures that can be used to distinguish among equating, predicting, and concordance (the form of scale alignment that is closest to equating). We argue that scale alignment is the default linkage. We also maintain that prediction might be the preferred form of linkage among unreliable tests.

A critical question that we address in this chapter is: How do we know whether we can achieve the interchangeability of scores associated with equating or the meaningful comparability of scales suggested by a concordance, or do we have to settle for the expected scores provided by prediction?

In Section 10.2 we review the five critical requirements for equating and indicate which requirements are not met by predicting and scaling for concordance. In Section 10.3 we discuss the important role of reliability. In Section 10.4 we describe measures of uncertainty that can be used to evaluate whether the interchangeability of scores sought through equating is within reach or whether the scale alignment provided by a concordance can be sensibly interpreted. In Section 10.5 indexes of population invariance are introduced that help separate equating from scaling for concordance. In Section 10.6 data about size and shape are used to illustrate how measures of uncertainty reduction and population invariance can help us distinguish among settings in which it is better to equate, concord, or predict. Finally, in Section 10.7 we summarize key points that help in making distinctions among equating, concording, and predicting.

10.2. What Makes a Linking an Equating?

What distinguishes test equating from other forms of linking is its goal. The goal of equating two tests is to allow the scores from both to be used interchangeably, for any purpose. This is a very demanding goal, and experience has shown that to achieve it, the two tests and the methods used to link them must satisfy very strong requirements.

Dorans and Holland (2000) listed five requirements that are widely viewed as necessary for test equating to be successful: (a) The tests should measure the *same constructs*; (b) the tests should have the *same reliability*; (c) the equating function for equating the scores of test Y to those of test X should be the *inverse* of the equating function for equating the scores of X to those of Y; (d) it should be a *matter of indifference* to an examinee to be tested by either one of two tests that have been equated; and (e) the choice of (sub)population used to estimate the equating function between the scores of tests X and Y should not matter; that is, the equating function used to link the scores of X and Y should be *population invariant*. For more details about these requirements, see Holland (Chapter 2, Section 2.4.1).

If we examine the five requirements, we can see why concordance and prediction will not meet the criteria for equating. Concordances are used with tests that measure similar things according to different blueprints. Although the tests might have similar difficulty and reliability, they will satisfy requirement (a) only approximately: a limitation that might be reflected in the failure of requirement (e) and possibly requirement (d).

Prediction methods need not satisfy any of the five requirements. The asymmetry between predictors and outcomes violates requirement (c). Furthermore, requirements (a) and (b) of measuring the same construct and being equally reliable play no role in prediction. Requirement (d) is irrelevant in this context. Finally, it often makes sense to include subgroup membership as predictors to improve prediction. This incorporates population sensitivity directly into the prediction, whereas equating functions should not depend on subpopulations, according to requirement (e).

To achieve the interchangeability of scores, two tests must measure the same construct, should have equal reliability, and their linkage must be invariant across populations. Dorans and Holland (2000) showed that the correlation between the two tests sets an upper bound on the population dependence of the linking. Thus, when the correlation between the two tests is high, which implies high test score reliability, then the linkage between the tests will be minimally variant across important subgroups.

To assess whether two scores measure the same construct, we can evaluate the similarities of the processes that produced the scores to see if the constructs measured are similar. A careful content evaluation is needed to establish similarity. At the very least, a logical evaluation of test specifications can be done. Although this approach is a good first step, one should avoid the pitfall of assuming construct similarity based solely on a description of test content. English is a living language that has been fed by many sources (Winchester, 1998). Many words have multiple meanings. Our use of language is elastic. We see similarities among words that have little in common. For example, assuming that a verbal reasoning test measures the same thing as a test of English simply because the test titles make them sound like similar constructs is a mistake (Dorans, 2004d). Distinctions that are made between measures of the same construct on the basis of differences in test specifications might not be reflected in empirical results when examinee performance is studied.

Examining the similarity of examinee performance on two measures rather than relying solely on the apparent similarity or dissimilarity of the test specifications provides the best evaluation of the similarity of the two measures. The ambiguity of language makes it all the more important to assess the strength of the empirical relationship between the scores to be linked. Ideally, an empirical evaluation will use procedures such as factor analysis or other variants of structural equation modeling. At the very least, correlations should be computed from a joint distribution of scores on the tests to be linked.

Requirement (e), which is easy to test in practice, also can be used to explain why requirements (a) and (b) are needed. If two tests measure different things or are not equally reliable, then the standard linking methods will not produce results that are invariant across certain subpopulations of examinees. Dorans and Holland (2000) used requirement (e), rather than requirement (d), to develop quantitative measures of equatability. Their measures indicate the degree to which equating functions depend on the subpopulations used to estimate them. von Davier, Holland, and Thayer (2004a) extended the Dorans and Holland work to the multiple population case. Yin, Brennan, and Kolen

(2004) also extended the Dorans and Holland work. A special issue of *Journal of Educational Measurement* (Dorans, 2004a) contains further extensions of population sensitivity assessment.

This section briefly outlined some ways to distinguish among equating, concordance, and prediction. Now that we know these distinctions, we can turn to statistics that can help determine which type of link is most appropriate given the data.

10.3. Why Is Reliability Important?

Adequate reliability is needed to ensure that the results associated with an equating are informative enough to be acceptable for practical use with individuals. Strictly speaking, equating only requires scores that are equally reliable. Hence, sets of random numbers generated by the same process and assigned to individuals are "equatable" in this formal sense of equating. The utility of these scores as "measures" of individual attributes is nonexistent, however.

Support for the importance of reliability can be extracted from the Holland and Hoskens (2003) treatment of classical test theory as a first-order item response theory. They looked at predicting a true score on a test from an observed score on that test and another nonparallel test that measures a different construct. They noted that in both these cases it is necessary to condition on nontest information such as group membership whenever the reliability of the observed score is low and the nontest information is related to the observed score. In others words, to the extent that the reliability departs from unity, the estimate of the true score is subpopulation dependent. By implication, when the reliability is high, there is less opportunity for differences to exist between the observed score and the nontest information that is independent of the true score.

Reliability is the squared correlation between an observed score and its expectation. The correlation between sets of scores can be used to distinguish formally equivalent but mostly meaningless scores from scores that are formally equivalent and potentially useful. Two measures with low and equal reliability and a true-score correlation close to unity might possess high levels of potential linkability, but it will take some effort to convert that potential linkability into actual linkability that can be used in practice. The degree of relationship needed will depend on the use of the scores. Randomly generated scores are fine if we only want to use the scores to estimate a score distribution. High correlations between measures and, consequently, high reliability are needed for settings in which scores are used to make significant decisions that affect the course of an individual's life. Note that as the correlation between two measures approaches unity, population invariance will be achieved and the predicted, concordant, and equated scores will converge (Dorans & Holland, 2000). Thus, high correlations, and hence high reliabilities, are good and cause distinctions among classes of linkages to vanish. Unfortunately, these correlations are directly computable only in the single group design, which is rarely used for data collection (see Kolen, Chapter 3, Section 3.5).

10.4. Uncertainty Reduction

Dorans (2004d) used the concept of uncertainty reduction to assess the degree of alignment between two linked scores, **X** and **Y**. Reduction in uncertainty (RiU) is defined as

$$\text{RiU} = 1 - \sqrt{1 - \rho_{xy}^2},$$

where ρ_{xy}^2 is the squared correlation between scores on **X** and **Y**, Alternatively, we can write

$$100 \times \text{RiU} = 100 \times \left[\frac{\sigma_{YP} - \sigma_{YP}\sqrt{(1 - \rho_{xy}^2)}}{\sigma_{YP}} \right],$$

where σ_{YP} is the standard deviation of **Y** in population **P**. This standard deviation represents the total uncertainty associated with predicting a score on **Y** given no other information. The right-hand term in the numerator is the familiar standard error of prediction (SEP), which indicates the amount of uncertainty in **Y** that remains after **X** is used to predict **Y**. The difference between the two terms gives the amount by which uncertainty in predicting **Y** has been reduced by using **X** as a predictor. In this form, RiU is seen to be the percentage of uncertainty in **Y** that is eliminated with knowledge of **X**.

Related to the SEP is the standard error of measurement (SEM):

$$\text{SEM} = \sigma_{YP}\sqrt{1 - \rho_{yy'}}.$$

Here $\rho_{yy'}$ is the reliability of score on **Y**. The SEM of **Y** is less than or equal to the SEP. (The equality occurs when $\rho_{xy}^2 = \rho_{yy'}$, in which case the true-score correlation between **X** and **Y** must be unity and **X** must be perfectly reliable.) This fact is hardly surprising. Recall that the reliability coefficient $\rho_{yy'}$ is properly interpreted as the correlation between scores on a measure **Y** and scores on a parallel measure **Y'**. The reliability coefficient can also be interpreted as the squared correlation between observed scores on **Y** and the true scores that **Y** estimates. Interpreting the SEM in terms of reduction of uncertainty, we see that the true scores for measure **Y** (we can think of these as scores from a perfectly reliable measure of the construct that **Y** measures) are as good or better predictors of **Y** than any other possible predictor **X**.

Note that when $\rho_{xy} = 0$, there is a zero reduction in uncertainty about scores on the measure to be predicted. For example, if the information in the predictor variable (say, a randomly selected student number) has no relationship with variation in scores on the variable to be predicted (e.g., high-school grade-point average [GPA]), then the predictor does nothing to reduce uncertainty about performance on the variable to be predicted (high-school GPA). In contrast, 100% reduction of uncertainty is achieved when $\rho_{xy} = 1$.

A 50% reduction in uncertainty is halfway between 100% reduction ($\rho_{xy} = 1$) and 0% reduction ($\rho_{xy} = 0$). A correlation coefficient of at least .866 between the predictor and the score to be predicted is needed to reduce the uncertainty of knowing a person's score by at least 50%. If a predictor cannot reduce uncertainty by at least 50%, it is unlikely that the predictor can serve as a valid surrogate, via concordance or equating, for the score being predicted.

The above is a strong statement that might engender dissent. It implies that two scores with a correlation of .866 are needed before useful equating or concordance can be obtained. Others might argue that this implied criterion is unnecessarily strict. Note, however, that whereas the number .866 in correlation units is 86.6% of the way to a perfect correlation, the corresponding number of .50 in RiU units is only halfway to zero uncertainty.

Comparison of the RiU to other measures might help to place the above suggestion into context. Table 10.1 provides such a comparison. It shows how RiU relates to the reliability of a measure **Y** (in the case of equating), the correlation between **Y** and a predictor **X** (in the case of concordance), and the SEM (or SEP) as a percent of standard deviation on **Y**. Table 10.1 shows that an RiU of .50 corresponds to a reliability of .75 and an SEM of one-half the standard deviation. These reliability and SEM measures represent a test with fairly low precision. In a sense, scores from the same form of the test are not highly comparable to each other. It only stands to reason that any attempt to link such a test to another test of comparable reliability is bound to end in disappointment. As mentioned earlier, low reliability is likely to result in subpopulation dependence of the equating functions (Dorans & Holland, 2000; Holland & Hoskens, 2003).

Table 10.1 also shows the signal-to-noise ratio (SNR). The SNR is the ratio of explained variance to unexplained variance in a measure **Y**. In the context of reliability, SNR is the ratio of true-score variance to error variance; more generally, in the context of prediction, SNR is the ratio of predicted score variance to residual variance. Consider the true score, error score case first. When the correlation of an observed score with its true score is .87, the reliability is .75. If we knew the true score and used it to predict an observed score, the SNR associated with this correlation of .87 and reliability of .75 would be 3:1.[2] The same reasoning leads to a SNR of 3:1 for a correlation of .87 in the context of prediction.

Perhaps the most provocative relationship in Table 10.1 involves the decibel (dB), which is a logarithmic translation of the SNR. This measure is quite familiar to physical scientists and engineers. The psychometric analogue is computed for the prediction case using

$$dB = 10\log_{10}\left(\frac{\rho_{xy}^2 \sigma_{YP}^2}{\left(1 - \rho_{xy}^2\right)\sigma_{YP}^2}\right).$$

Table 10.1 includes some common sounds, along with estimates of their decibel levels. According to the table, a reliability (or squared correlation) of .5, a correlation of .71, and an RiU of .29 correspond to 0 dB, the threshold of human hearing. A reliability of .91, a correlation of .95, and an RiU of .70 are equivelant to 10 dB, which corresponds to an auditory stimulus with the intensity of gently rustling leaves. A reliability of .99 and an RiU of .90 correspond to 20 dB, the intensity of a whisper. Not until an RiU of .99 and a reliability close to 1.0 do we reach the intensity of normal human speech.

If we push the auditory analogy, we would reach the conclusion that we should not even bother with a test with a reliability less than .50, that the reliability of .91 that people in the education field usually consider quite high results in measures that are soothing but far from informative, and

---

[2] Recall that reliability is defined as $\rho_{yy'} = \sigma_T^2 / \sigma_{YP}^2$, where σ_{YP}^2 is the total score variance and σ_T^2 is the true-score variance. Because by definition $\sigma_{YP}^2 = \sigma_T^2 + \sigma_E^2$, where σ_E^2 is the error variance, the SNR (the ratio of true score to error variance) can be computed as $\rho_{yy'} / \left(1 - \rho_{yy'}\right)$.

Table 10.1. Comparison of several measures of signal strength: RiU, correlation, reliability, SEM or SEP, SNR, and decibels

RiU	ρ_{xy}	ρ_{xx}	SEM, SEP (as % of SD)	SNR	dB	Reference sound
0.999	1.000	1.000	0.1	999999:1	60.000	Normal speech
0.997	1.000	1.000	0.3	99999:1	50.000	
0.990	1.000	1.000	1.0	9999:1	40.000	
0.968	0.999	0.999	3.2	999:1	29.996	
0.929	0.997	0.995	7.1	199:1	22.989	
0.900	0.995	0.990	10.0	99:1	19.956	Whisper
0.859	0.990	0.980	14.1	49:1	16.902	
0.827	0.985	0.970	17.3	32.3:1	15.097	
0.800	0.980	0.960	20.0	24.0:1	13.802	
0.776	0.975	0.950	22.4	19.0:1	12.788	
0.755	0.970	0.940	24.5	15.7:1	11.950	
0.735	0.964	0.930	26.5	13.3:1	11.234	
0.717	0.959	0.920	28.3	11.5:1	10.607	
0.700	0.954	0.910	30.0	10.1:1	10.048	Rustling leaves
0.684	0.949	0.900	31.6	9.0:1	9.542	
0.613	0.922	0.850	38.7	5.7:1	7.533	
0.553	0.894	0.800	44.7	4.0:1	6.021	
0.500	0.866	0.750	50.0	3.0:1	4.771	
0.452	0.837	0.700	54.8	2.3:1	3.680	
0.408	0.806	0.650	59.2	1.9:1	2.688	
0.368	0.775	0.600	63.2	1.5:1	1.761	
0.329	0.742	0.550	67.1	1.2:1	0.872	
0.293	0.707	0.500	70.7	1.0:1	0.000	Threshold of hearing

that only with reliability of .99 can our test convey information with any degree of certainty. It is a safe guess that few experts in the field would take so extreme a position as the above. Placed in this context, however, an RiU of 50% (and its correlation of .87, reliability of .75, and 4.77 dB) appears neither stringent nor unreasonable.

Another measure of uncertainty is the Holland-Hoskens prediction inflation factor, which measures the increase in prediction error when the true score for one construct is predicted using the observed measure of a separate construct, rather than using an observed score for the construct being predicted (Holland & Hoskens, 2003). A simplified approximation is Assuming unit variance for **Y**, the denominator is the squared SEM of **Y**,

$$H = \sqrt{\frac{1 - \rho_{xy}^2 / \rho_{yy'}}{1 - \rho_{yy'}}}.$$

or the error variance associated with predicting the true scores on **Y** from the observed scores on **Y**. The denominator is also the proportion of total variance in **Y** that cannot be predicted by any means. The numerator is equal to 1 minus the ratio of the proportion of variance in **Y** that **X** can predict to the proportion of variance in **Y** that is predictable. Note that the right-hand term of the numerator is the correlation between scores on **X** and **Y** corrected for the unreliability of **Y**; so that the right-hand term gives the squared correlation between scores on **X** and the true scores on **Y**. Thus, the numerator gives the error variance associated with predicting the true scores on **Y** from the observed scores on **X**. The entire ratio gives an index of the increased error of prediction associated with relating measures of two different constructs.

It might be difficult to develop useful criteria for H; nonetheless, the index can be useful as a diagnostic tool. The prediction inflation factor H is generally greater than 1. For equating situations, H should be very close to 1. For larger values of H, equating is less appropriate, but concordance might still be possible. As mentioned earlier, the magnitude of the correlation also plays a role. Lower values of H associated with low correlations suggest that the reliabilities of the measures stand in the way of a meaningful equating or concordance. Low values of H for high correlations suggest that equating might be possible. High values of H associated with lower correlations suggest that prediction is the only option. High values of H for high correlations indicate highly reliable criterion variables.

10.5. Population Invariance of Linking Functions

Linking is a relationship that is defined in a population. The degree to which two scores can be linked depends on the properties that the scores have in the population in which they are linked. Population-free linking, although of interest in a theoretical sense, is in practice unattainable. What is of interest is the degree to which a linking is population sensitive. Checking the equivalence of equating relationships across subpopulations is a sure way of assessing the population invariance requirement. The absence or presence of population invariance distinguishes a concordance (absence of invariance) from an equating (presence of invariance). Equatings are essentially invariant across subpopulations from the population of interest. Concordances are expected to be sensitive to choice of population, as are predictions.

Since the publication of Dorans and Holland (2000), there has been a surge of interest in examining the sensitivity of linking functions to choice of population (Dorans, 2004e; Kolen, 2004b; von Davier & Liu, 2006; Yang, 2004; Yin et al., 2004, to cite a few). Population invariance is one of the requirements for equating. It is a necessary condition, but by itself, it is not sufficient to demonstrate that a linking is an equating. After all, the identity function, which is population invariant, is rarely useful as an equating. In the full application of the approach, equatings are performed at the total-group level, as is normally the case, and at subgroup levels. Typically, level is defined by gender or race/ethnicity.

Dorans and Holland (2000) provided an extensive treatment of population invariance. They start from a system of subpopulations of $\mathbf{P}$ that partitions $\mathbf{P}$ into $\{\mathbf{P}_j: j = 1, 2, \ldots\}$. They let w_j denote the relative proportion of examinees from $\mathbf{P}$ that are in $\mathbf{P}_j$, so that, $\sum_j w_j = 1$, and they let G denote a variable that indicates to which subpopulation a given unit belongs, so that $G = j$ denotes membership in population $\mathbf{P}_j$. Thus, $w_j = P\{G = j\}$. Let $e_{P_j}(y)$ denote the linking function for $\mathbf{Y}$ to $\mathbf{X}$ on $\mathbf{P}_j$ and let $e_P(y)$ denote the linking function for score $\mathbf{Y}$ to score $\mathbf{X}$ on the "whole" population, $\mathbf{P}$. The authors emphasized that they intended this notation to apply to any linking function including two general measures of the population dependence of linking functions.

The first measure of population dependence is defined for each $\mathbf{Y}$ score, y. It is the standardized root mean square difference (RMSD) of the subpopulation linking functions from the overall population linking function for a given y value:

$$\mathrm{RMSD}(y) = \frac{\sqrt{\sum_j w_j [e_{P_j}(y) - e_P(y)]^2}}{\sigma_{XP}}.$$

This measure is sensitive to the amount of the difference between each of the separate linking functions, $e_{P_j}(y)$, and the overall linking function, $e_P(y)$. The measure is computed at each y value, and the contribution of each subpopulation is weighted by its proportional representation in the overall population, $\mathbf{P}$. The square root is used to bring the measure back to the scale of **X** score points.[3] The divisor, σ_{XP}, is used to make the units of this measure the "proportion of the standard deviation of **X** scores in **P**." For example, a value of 0.1 for RMSD*(y)* is interpreted as a RMSD of 10% of the standard deviation of **X** scores in **P** in the linking functions at score *y* of **Y**. Thus, RMSD*(y)* is a type of *effect size* for each *y* value.

To obtain a single number summarizing the values of RMSD*(y)*, Dorans and Holland (2000) introduced a related measure by averaging over the distribution of **Y** in **P** before taking the square root in RMSD*(y)*. This is the root expected mean square difference (REMSD):

$$\text{REMSD} = \frac{\sqrt{E_P\left\{\sum_j w_j\ e_{P_j}(y) - e_P(y)\ ^2\right\}}}{\sigma_{XP}} = \frac{\sqrt{\sum_j w_j E_P\left\{\ e_{P_j}(y) - e_P(y)\ ^2\right\}}}{\sigma_{XP}},$$

where *y* denotes a random **Y** score sampled from the base population, **P**, and $E_P\{\cdot\}$ denotes averaging over this distribution. The distribution used to compute this average is the discrete distribution of **Y** over **P**.

Dorans and Holland (2000) provided a special version of this general REMSD index for the special case in which there are two subpopulations (e.g., female and male), and the linkings across these two subpopulations and the total population are linear and share a common slope;

$$\text{RMSD}(y) = \text{REMSD} = \sqrt{w_1 w_2}\left(\left|\frac{\mu_{XP_1} - \mu_{XP_2}}{\sigma_{XP}} - \frac{\mu_{YP_1} - \mu_{YP_2}}{\sigma_{YP}}\right|\right)$$

So for this special case of two groups and parallel-linear linking functions (i.e., where the linkings for the two groups are linear with the same slope), the REMSD is equal to the difference in standard score means between the two groups, multiplied by the square root of the relative sizes of the two

---

[3] Earlier, we used a prediction equation to represent scores on test **X** in terms of scores on test **Y**. Now we use equating to represent scores on test **Y** in terms of scores on test **X**. To some readers, this change might appear inconsistent; however, it is not. We always consider **Y** to be the newer test and **X** to be the older test. Typically in a prediction setting, we progress in a forward direction, estimating scores on a new test **Y** from scores on an old test **X**. In equating, we transform scores on the new test **Y** to a scale that has properties similar to scores on the old test **X**. In other words, our notation has not changed; our focus has. Consequently, whereas in the prediction case the standard deviation of **Y** mattered more, in the case of equating the standard deviation of **X** in population **P** plays a prominent role.

groups. If the two groups are of equal size, such that $w_1 = w_2$, then the REMSD is half the difference in standardized means.

One of the criticisms of the Dorans-Holland approach to measuring population invariance is the number of equatings involved. For number of groups G, each measure must be equated $G + 1$ times. One way to avoid an excessive amounts of equating is to equate in the total group, as is the usual practice, and to examine the distributions of the equated score **Y** in each subgroup to see if they match the distribution of scores on the reference test **X** across all relevant subgroups. If the equatings are in fact population invariant, then the equating that worked in the total group should hold in each subgroup. Measures of agreement such as percent relative error (von Davier et al., 2004b) can be used to see how well the equated score distributions match the distributions of a measure to which they were equated across various subgroups. If the population invariance requirement is met, then the match should be very good.

A second approach entails performing several simple linear equatings. If the linkings of the tests are actually *parallel linear* in both populations and the differences in standardized means among subgroups (e.g., males and females) are equal on both tests, then population invariance would hold. To the extent that the linking relationships within each group are not well approximated by a parallel-linear form, this simple difference in standardized means will be misleading. However, it can be a quick and easy check on whether a serious linking problem exists by computing differences in standardized mean differences (Dorans, 2004d).

Earlier, a case was made for high correlations between the tests to be linked. Greater reductions in uncertainty are associated with higher correlations. Additionally, Dorans and Holland (2000) showed the correlation between the two scores places an upper bound on the RMSD:

$$\text{RMSD} \le \sqrt{2\left(1 - \rho_{xy}\right)}$$

where ρ_{xy} is the correlation between the scores to be linked. This bound agrees with the intuition that the higher the correlation between the two tests, the harder it is to violate the population invariance requirement. Also, as the correlation drops, the possibilities for divergence from equating grow.

10.6. Sizing Up Linkages

To size up whether a linking would best be served by concording, equating, or predicting, we could have used test data from the educational assessment arena, most notably the ACT® and SAT®. Plenty has been written about relating these two measures (see Dorans, Lyu, Pommerich, & Houston, 1997; Pommerich & Dorans, 2004a). We prefer, however, to avoid the sensitive political and policy issues associated with linking scores from these two approaches to assessing collegiate academic preparedness. The construct of collegiate academic preparedness is too intangible for us.

10.6.1. Coastal Aspirations and Midland Acquisitions

{This section is fictional. Any resemblance to anything that this might resemble is just that— a resemblance.}

Instead, we will use a construct that is tangible—a construct we know something about or at least know more about than most experts in education might know about the construct of academic preparedness. We choose to use the construct of "size and shape." We think we know what this size and shape measure is. It is not complicated. We can see it directly. We must infer academic preparedness from indirect measures, such as numbers-based machine-scoring of answers to multiple-choice questions, or numbers based on human-scoring of examinee-produced responses to written prompts. In contrast, we can directly access size and shape through our senses. We can measure this construct reliably. Thus, we can ignore measurement precision considerations in this domain.

Even given the advantages of physical versus psychological measurement, the construct of size and shape might be less accessible than it appears at first glance, as we will see. Consider a society in which the greatest opportunities presented themselves to individuals who had attained the greatest size and shape. Naturally, many institutions clamored for a quick and effective measure of size and shape.

Two alternative approaches to size assessment emerged, each championed by a corporate giant in the size assessment industry. One company, Coastal Aspirations (CA), believed that stature determined the individual's merit and that stature was best expressed in inches or centimeters. CA manufactured rulers and other measures of length for the expressed purpose of assessing an individual's stature. To emphasize the importance of stature (CA's motto was "Why settle for the moon when you can reach for the stars?"), CA squared the length measure when reporting a person's size.

In contrast, Midland Acquisitions (MA) built their company on the principle that it is what you have acquired over years of digestion that determines your size. MA, like others in the size assessment community, argued that stature measures like those produced by CA made size appear more determined by nature than by nourishment. Consequently, MA focused on weight and manufactured scales for measuring weight in pounds or grams. The company also provided test preparation regimens of beer and pasta, touting guaranteed weight gains. Mocking their competitor, MA proclaimed "Why chase the Ethereal when you can have The Real?"

For a while, things were rather peaceful, as different institutions of higher size began using the AREA (Aspired Rectangularity Assessment) and the MASS (Midland Acquisitions Size Survey) to screen applicants. Some institutions (e.g., the NBA) favored the AREA; others (e.g., the NFL) preferred the MASS; whereas others (e.g., the MLB) accepted both measures without hesitation.[4] As the applicant pool began to expand (no pun intended), the institutions realized that it might be useful to have some sort of concordance between the AREA and the MASS, so as to be able to compare applicants presenting either one or the other of the two measures. Section 10.6.2 reports on research conducted by the authors to assess the feasibility of constructing such a concordance.

10.6.2. Data Description, Analyses, and Digestion

The data consisted of 648 nonrandomly selected individuals who were currently enrolled in each of the three major institutions using the AREA and the MASS: the NFL, the NBA, and the MLB. Approximately equal numbers from each institution were included. Table 10.2 gives summary information from the AREA and the MASS for each institution.

Table 10.2 indicates immediately that the AREA and the MASS do not align the groups in the same order. For example, the NBA has the highest mean scores on the AREA, whereas the other two groups do not differ much from each other. On the other hand, the NFL has the highest scores on the MASS, followed by the NBA, and, finally, the MLB. This reordering of the groups across the two measures gives initial evidence that they are measuring different constructs.

The correlation between AREA and MASS for the total group is .44, considerably less than the correlations between AREA and MASS in the subgroups. The RiU for the total group is .10, indicating that a linkage

---

[4] The NBA as an institution appeared to favor tall, lean individuals; the NFL favored fairly heavy, shorter people; and the MLB appeared to have a greater mix of stature and weight. Any similarity of the names of the organizations or of the summary statistics to the National Basketball Association, the National Football League, or Major League Baseball is purely intentional.

Table 10.2. Summary information for total group and for subgroups on AREA and MASS

	Group[c]			
	MLB	NBA	NFL	Total
AREA[a]				
N	220	212	216	648
Mean	108.1	125.5	109.0	114.1
SD	6.9	11.4	7.4	11.8
Min	89.8	84.5	89.8	84.5
Max	134.5	162.0	128.0	162.0
MASS[b]				
N	220	212	216	648
Mean	202.6	223.3	248.9	224.8
SD	19.4	29.9	47.6	39.2
Min	160.0	133.0	174.0	133.0
Max	250.0	335.0	370.0	370.0
AREA-MASS correlation	0.63	0.84	0.70	0.44
Reduction in Uncertainty	0.22	0.45	0.29	0.10

[a]The AREA measure is a function of height in inches: AREA   .02 * 50.
[b]The MASS measure is equal to weight in pounds.
[c]The groups correspond to professional sport played by the candidate: MLB = baseball, NBA = basketball, NFL = football.

between AREA and MASS in the total group will not be very successful. The conclusions drawn from these indexes are reinforced by Figure 10.1, which shows the linear concordance line superimposed on the scatterplot for the three groups. The large degree of spread around the concordance line indicates a very weak relationship.

As a next step, concordances between the two measures were computed in each group separately. Figure 10.2 shows the difference plots for the three subgroup concordance functions, with the total-group concordance as the criterion. We see the total-group concordance most closely matches the MLB concordance. The total-group concordance is less similar to the NBA concordance and quite dissimilar from the NFL concordance. The subgroup concordances differ quite a bit from each other.

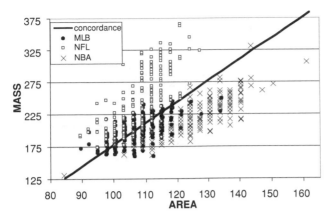

Figure 10.1. Scatterplot of the MASS with AREA scores for three subgroups. The solid line represents the total group concordance between MASS and AREA.

The RMSD and REMSD indexes formalize the dissimilarities among the group concordances. Figure 10.3 plots the RMSD and REMSD measures as a function of AREA score. The two indexes are shown on the MASS scale. Both indexes are compared to the difference that matters (DTM; Dorans & Feigenbaum, 1994), operationalized here as a difference of 5 pounds on the MASS scale.[5] The RMSD exceeds the DTM across the range of the AREA score scale, indicating that the differences among the group concordance functions are not trivial. This demonstrated lack of invariance presents a final piece of convincing evidence of the inappropriateness of using a common concordance for all groups.

Table 10.3 gives information on the total-group and subgroup concordances. In addition to the slope and intercept parameters for each concordance, Table 10.3 shows the standard error of the estimate of MASS score from AREA score. As can be seen, the error associated with estimating MASS score from AREA score with the total-group concordance is much smaller for the MLB group than for the other two groups. The individual concordance computed in the MLB group produces

---

[5] The difference that matters, as explained by Dorans & Feigenbaum, refers to half a reporting score unit on a test. The authors reasoned that any two unrounded scores that were within one-half unit of each other would round to the same reported score. Thus, any difference less than one-half unit could be treated as unimportant. In this chapter, the meaning of the DTM was altered slightly to accommodate the somewhat different data. We chose 5 pounds as the DTM, believing that any difference in people's weights of less than 5 pounds could reasonably be treated as irrelevant.

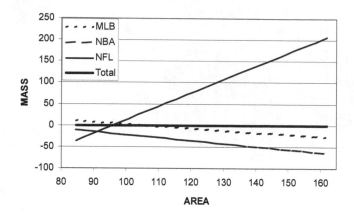

Figure 10.2. Difference plots of the concordance of MASS and AREA computed in three subgroups separately. The criterion is the total-group concordance.

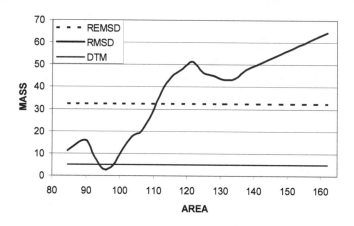

Figure 10.3. RMSD as a function of AREA score. The DTM of 5 score points on the MASS scale is shown for reference.

only a slight improvement in the error of estimate. The NBA concordance fares much better than the total-group concordance in the NBA group. The NFL concordance shows an improvement over the total-group concordance for that group as well. However, the improvement is not as great for the NFL as for the NBA. The RiU values in Table 10.2 indicate that a concordance would be the most useful for relating MASS to AREA scores for the NBA group, as the correlation between the two scores is highest for this group.

Table 10.3. Results of concording AREA to MASS in the total sample versus in each subgroup separately

	Group			
	MLB	NBA	NFL	Total
Concordance parameters				
Slope	2.8	2.6	6.4	3.3
Intercept	−102.8	−106.5	−453.8	−153.3
Standard error of estimate				
Total-group concordance	18.6	44.5	53.9	41.7
Individual concordance	16.8	17.2	36.7	—

10.7. Summary

The fictional example presented in this chapter illuminates some important points made earlier in the chapter. First, the equal construct requirement is key to equating. Without it, it is doubtful that the invariance requirement can be met. Care must be taken in assessing whether the two tests to be equated measure the same construct. We can have more confidence that they do if they are built to the same set of specifications. Claims that the two tests measure the same construct are generally not sufficient. In our example, both "tests" purportedly measure size. However, the MASS is really weight in pounds, whereas the AREA is a function of squared height. Given that the two tests measure different constructs, they cannot be equated.

When two tests measure similar but not identical constructs, concordance is still a possibility. Often, there is a desire to produce a single concordance that can be applied to all populations. As noted earlier, population dependence of the linking function often results when the two tests do not measure the same construct. A natural consequence of this lack of invariance is the need to produce different concordance functions for each group. We saw that our total-group concordance performed poorly in two out of the three groups studied. The concordance functions for each group separately generally fared better. Separate concordances, however unpalatable, can result in more equitable treatment of test-takers.

Even in the case of concordances, some minimum level of relationship between the tests to be concorded is needed. We have recommended an RiU of .50, corresponding to a correlation of .866, as the minimum requirement for equating or concording two tests. In many respects, the correlation is more crucial than the reliability. In our example, both measures had perfect reliability. However, this fact alone did not ensure a successful linking. The strength of the relationship between the two measures determines whether we can successfully estimate the score on one test using the score on another.

The ability to link two tests successfully via concordance does not mean that the scores on the two tests can therefore be used interchangeably. Our example makes this point very salient. The NBA group in particular exhibited a strong relationship between AREA (squared height) and MASS (weight). Few people, however, would make the mistake of considering weight and height equivalent. If the two measures were equivalent, then an NFL offensive lineman (generally a fairly heavy individual) would be an apt substitute for an NBA center (usually quite tall but not necessarily heavy). This lack of equivalence might not be so obvious with educational tests, but the point is just as valid. For this reason, caution should always be exercised in using and interpreting the results from concordances.

10.8. Postscript

We fully recognize that measuring size and shape is more than a matter of height or weight. Science fiction writers presume that sophisticated measures of size and shape exist. H. G. Wells (1895) needed this information to allow his Time Machine to traverse the dimension of time. Michael Crichton (1999) required similar precise knowledge of size and shape and molecule structure to allow his archaeologists to flit back and forth to medieval times in *Timeline*. Finally, Gene Roddenberry presumed precise measurement of size and shape. Otherwise, the transporter would not be able to move molecules from one set of coordinates to another in every episode of *Star Trek*. Our assessment of size and shape was admittedly primitive, but appropriate for our purposes.

11 Concordance: The Good, the Bad, and the Ugly

Mary Pommerich[1]

Defense Manpower Data Center

11.1 Background

A long, long time ago, a group of people known as "equaters" ruled the earth. The equaters were so named because they were proponents of the practice of equating—the linking of scores across (nearly) parallel test forms, namely forms built to the same specifications. The equaters were a powerful group of people. They made the rules, and through the use of theory and assumptions, they intimidated nonequaters to ensure that score linkages would be conducted only between alternate forms of the same test.

As happens so often throughout history, power struggles ensued. Test users rebelled against the limitations that were invoked by the restrictive rules of the equaters. The public thirsted for more diverse types of linkage, and rogue measurement practitioners known as "linkers" began to advocate linking scores across tests built to different specifications that did not meet the (nearly) parallel forms assumption. The movement snowballed, and suddenly everyone except the equaters wanted to link scores across tests that were never intended to be linked!

Now let us fast forward to the early 1960s to see what is happening in the equater camp. We find two influential measurement experts, William Angoff from the Educational Testing Service (ETS) and E. F. Lindquist from the American College Testing Program (now known as ACT, Inc.)

---

[1] The views expressed are those of the author and not necessarily those of the Department of Defense or the United States Government.

addressing the issue of "equating" nonparallel tests. From Angoff (1962) we learn that "complaints have been heard from various sources that the amount of testing that is going on these days is excessive and burdensome to the schools" (p. 1). He proceeded to critique the proposed solutions of (a) creating equivalency tables between scores from tests by different publishers and (b) converting scores on tests produced by all publishers to a single, common score scale, and he presented a litany of problems inherent with these approaches.

From Lindquist (1964) we hear arguments against creating tables of comparable scores across the SAT® and ACT® test batteries. He takes a pessimistic stance, stating that "if the two agencies were jointly to provide an approved conversion table, no matter what precautions were taken to guard against misuses and misinterpretations, the total effect would probably be increased misuses of the test results, or a more widespread failure to use the test results in the best way possible" (p. 1). Lindquist presented a litany of reasons for why scores should not be linked across the ACT and SAT batteries.

Let us fast forward again, this time to the late 1990s and early 2000s. Here we see that history both repeats itself and contradicts itself. A national committee studies the feasibility of developing a scale to link scores from commercial and state assessments to each other and to the National Assessment of Educational Progress (NAEP) and determines that it is not plausible (Feuer, Holland, Green, Bertenthal, & Hemphill, 1999). Various sources are complaining that the amount of testing is excessive and burdensome to the schools. The Student Testing Flexibility Act of 2003 (S. 956, 2003) is introduced to Congress in April of 2003 in order to "give schools that are making the grade some relief from the burdensome testing requirements of No Child Left Behind" (Leahy, n.d.). Meanwhile, ACT, the College Board, and ETS have collaborated to produce a table of comparable scores between ACT composite and SAT I verbal + math scores (Dorans, Lyu, Pommerich, & Houston, 1997). Although the litany of problems associated with tables of comparable scores outlined by Angoff (1962) and Lindquist (1964) in the 1960s have not changed, societal expectations have, necessitating changes in the practices of test developers.

Today we find ourselves in a period of transition as demand for linkages between nonparallel tests increases. The linkers and equaters live together in an uneasy peace. Still somewhat of the underdog, the linkers continue to strive for acceptance, whereas the equaters remain smug in the knowledge that they have left the linkers quite a legacy to follow. That legacy includes the following:

1. Very high standards that are maintained across forms to be linked and across linkage results
2. A rigorous and well-designed process for building forms, collecting data, and linking scores
3. Scores that are interchangeable (i.e., have the same meaning) across different forms

In an ideal world, this legacy would be upheld when linking scores across nonparallel tests. In the real world, this cannot happen. Thus, linkers run the risk of alienating either measurement practitioners (if they opt to conduct a linkage between distinct tests) or test users (if they opt not to conduct the linkage). A happy medium would be to conduct a linkage in such a way as to achieve a healthy balance between fulfilling the needs of test users and maintaining the standards that measurement practitioners have come to expect. This is the challenge for linkers.

11.2. Definitions

What is this term "concordance" and where does it fall in this new world order that is developing in the testing milieu? Let us start by first defining linking as the process of relating scores across different forms or tests. This is an umbrella term, under which both equating and concordance fall. Equating occurs when scores are linked across tests built to the *same* specifications, whereas concordance occurs when scores are linked across tests built to *different* specifications. Equating and concordance are related in that methods used to equate parallel forms of a test (such as equipercentile linking) are commonly used to conduct concordances. Because nonparallel forms are linked in a concordance, corresponding scores are not viewed as interchangeable, as are scores linked via an equating. This is a somewhat simplistic representation of the relationship between equating and concordance, but it is sufficient for our needs. The reader is referred to Holland (Chapter 2) and Holland and Dorans (2006) for a more detailed delineation of categories of score linking methods.

An example of a concordance is provided by the table of comparable scores between ACT composite and SAT I verbal + math scores referred to earlier. To create this concordance, ACT and SAT I scores were obtained from 14 institutions and two states for students taking both tests. After screening on a variety of factors, the final concordance sample size was 103,525. Equipercentile methods were used to link scores across the two tests. Results were published in Dorans et al. (1997) and made available nationwide by the test developers. This concordance will be used as an example to discuss relevant issues throughout this chapter. We often see ACT–SAT concordances utilized as an example when concordances are discussed. This is likely because the ACT and SAT tests are well known, the linkage is widely used, and it is one of the best examples of a concordance out there.

11.3. The Concordance Process

Now that we have given a definition for concordance, let us expand upon that definition to more clearly elaborate our vision of concordance. We prefer to think of concordance as an entire process rather than just a type of linkage or an outcome. In our conception, the actual linking of scores is but one component of the concordance process. Pommerich, Hanson, Harris, and Sconing (2004) proposed a four-stage process for conducting linkages that consists of the following:

1. Choosing an appropriate linkage type and methodology
2. Linking scores and computing summary measures
3. Evaluating the quality of the linkage and determining what to report
4. Making recommendations for the interpretation and use of the linkage results

Let us review these stages from the perspective of concordance to develop an understanding of the concordance process.

11.3.1. Choosing an Appropriate Linkage Type and Methodology

The natural first step in any linkage is to choose an appropriate linkage type for the problem at hand. We do not just say "we shall conduct a concordance" and forge ahead. Clearly, there are situations in which the assumptions of equating do not hold. It might be less obvious to us that sometimes concordance is not appropriate either. How exactly can we evaluate whether concordance is appropriate? Dorans (2004d) provided a nice example. He demonstrated a number of tools that practitioners can use to evaluate the feasibility of concordance. He advocated extensive evaluation of factors such as (a) content similarity across the tests being linked, (b) the strength of the relationship between scores on the tests, and (c) the similarity of performance across demographic groups within each test. Using these criteria, he made recommendations for when concordance is not appropriate and suggests prediction as an alternative in such cases.

The linkage types addressed in Dorans (2004d) are limited to equating, concordance, and prediction. A wider variety of linkage types have been defined in an assortment of sources, including Flanagan (1951), Angoff

(1971), Mislevy (1992), Linn (1993), Feuer et al. (1999), and Kolen and Brennan (2004). Kolen (2004a) compared and contrasted the linking frameworks that are defined in each of these articles and provided an historical perspective for concordance. Holland (Chapter 2) and Holland and Dorans (2006) presented a linking framework that builds on these preceding frameworks and provided a more detailed assessment of the factors that define a concordance situation.

Once we have selected concordance as the appropriate linkage type for our situation at hand, the next step is to choose an appropriate methodology with which to conduct the linkage. There might be multiple methods for linking the scores that should be considered. For example, a variety of ACT–SAT concordances were conducted between 1966 and 1980 using both linear and nonlinear linking methods. The results from these studies suggested that nonlinear linking methods were often needed to represent the relationship between scores on these two tests (Marco, Abdel-fattah, & Baron, 1992). In another example, Yin, Brennan, and Kolen (2004) conducted concordances between scores on the ACT and the Iowa Tests of Educational Development using linear, parallel-linear, and equipercentile methods. They compared the invariance of the results in order to evaluate the different linkage methods.

11.3.2. Linking Scores and Computing Summary Measures

Once a linkage type and methodology have been selected, the process of linking scores can begin. Again, we probably should not just forge ahead and conduct the linkage. Instead, we should first give some attention to our data. One of the reasons that equating is considered to be the most rigorous form of linkage is that studies are carefully designed and implemented to collect appropriate data. In a concordance, on the other hand, the sample is most likely to be a convenience sample of examinees that have taken both tests (a single group design). Some factors of concern in a single group design are the amount of time that occurs between the two tests, the order of administration of the two tests, and repeat testing on either test. In an equating with a single group design, these factors can be controlled in advance by the study design. In a concordance with a single group design, these factors are not typically controlled in advance. (See Kolen, Chapter 3, for a further discussion of commonly used data collection designs and issues associated with the different designs.)

Thus, a concordance sample should be carefully screened so that the concordance results are not distorted by practice effects or learning that might occur between the administration of the two tests. In collecting a concordance sample, it is also important to note that linking relationships can be affected by group characteristics. For example, males might display a different relationship between scores on the two tests than females. Likewise, examinees that choose to take both tests might not be typical of the population to which the concordance results will likely be applied— namely, those who take only one of the tests. For these reasons, every attempt should be made to collect a concordance sample that is as similar as possible to the population to whom the results will be applied.

Once the data collection and screening has been adequately addressed, the linking can proceed. For every linking method used (and for every concordance sample), there are likely to be unique methodological issues that will arise and should be considered. In the ACT–SAT concordance that we are using as our example (Dorans et al., 1997), equipercentile methods were used to link scores across the two tests. The equipercentile procedure matches scores on Test A and Test B that have the same percentile rank across the two tests. Thus, if concordant score points are used for selection, the same percentages of examinees will be selected using either test. (More detailed information on the method is available in Kolen, Chapter 3, and Kolen & Brennan, 2004.) Two methodological issues that were considered in conducting this concordance were whether to smooth the results of the equipercentile linkings and how to best compute the concordance standard errors.

It is a common practice to smooth the results from equipercentile equatings in order to reduce the effect of sampling error on the results. This does not mean, however, that the results of an equipercentile concordance should automatically be smoothed, as smoothing can induce bias. In the case of the 1997 ACT–SAT concordance, the convenience sample was substantially larger ($N = 103,525$) than what you would see in a typical equating. As a result, evaluations of smoothed and unsmoothed results showed little difference, and smoothing was deemed unnecessary.

Pommerich et al. (2004) provided an in-depth discussion of the issue of smoothing for the 1997 ACT–SAT concordance, along with a discussion of the issue of computing concordance standard errors. Standard errors are a summary measure that can be used to evaluate the quality of the linkage at individual score points. Pommerich et al. discussed the computation of both analytic and bootstrap standard errors and proposed a criterion that standard errors at each concordant score point should be no greater than the average standard error typically observed in a well-maintained equating. This criterion will be discussed more in Section 11.3.3.

11.3.3. Evaluating the Quality of the Linkage and Determining What to Report

Once we have conducted our linkage and computed summary measures, what do we do next? This is where the issue of balance comes into play. Let us reiterate our earlier contention that the challenge for linkers is to achieve a healthy balance between fulfilling the needs of test users and maintaining the standards that measurement practitioners have come to expect. Lindquist's (1964) concerns about the misuse and misinterpretation of ACT–SAT concordance results are no less pertinent today than they were when he raised them.

One means of achieving the desired balance is to restrict the results that are given to users, so as to minimize the possibility for misuse or misinterpretation. Two areas of evaluation can help determine whether such a step is warranted. The first is to evaluate the stability of the concordances at individual scores points. The second is to evaluate the generalizability of the concordance to other samples. These two types of evaluation are demonstrated in detail in Pommerich et al. (2004) and will be summarized more succinctly here.

11.3.3.1. Evaluating the Stability of Concordances

In evaluating the results of an equipercentile concordance, it is vital to note that the equipercentile function does not directly take into account the number of observations at individual score points. It operates on percentile ranks, which are aggregated over score points. Ideally, we would have sufficient observations at all scores points to obtain stable results throughout the entire score scale. Rarely is this the case in practice. Consequently, concordance results might be unstable at score points where very few examinees score, even though we might have a very large sample size overall. The smaller the concordance sample sizes, the more likely sparse data at individual score points are to be a concern. Although the equipercentile procedure identifies a corresponding score point on Test B for each score point on Test A, it does not mean that the correspondence is equally good across all score points on Test A.

The proposed standard error criterion, mentioned earlier, comes into play here. We can evaluate the standard error for the concordance at each score point on Test A to see how stable the results are. If the standard error is not acceptable at a given score point, then we might choose not to report results for that score point. The practice of restricting the reporting of results might seem harsh, but this choice will be driven by the data; namely, the standard error criterion will be met at score points where there are sufficient observations to yield stable results.

Let us demonstrate with an example. Table 11.1 shows the average ACT and SAT scores for the national concordance sample and for an institution with 868 ACT–SAT examinees. The test scores suggest that the sample for this institution is quite a bit more academically able than the national concordance sample. Because of this performance difference, the institution might well be concerned about whether the national concordance adequately represents their examinee population. An institution-specific concordance might be warranted in this case.

Figure 11.1 plots concordant SAT I V+M scores that correspond to ACT composite scores for the national concordance sample and for the institution. Note that the institution results are smoothed because of the small sample size, whereas the national results are unsmoothed. Note also that results are not reported for ACT composite scores below 11. This is because less than .05% of the national concordance sample scored below 11 and because ACT composite scores of 10 or less are typically chance-level scores.

The concordant score points for the institution are similar to those of the national concordance throughout much of the ACT composite score scale, with the results diverging at scores of 11–14. These are the score points for which it would seem to be most beneficial for the institution to use the institution-specific concordance rather than the national concordance. However, if we look carefully at our data and standard errors for this institution, we see evidence that the concordance results are not stable at these score points. The N-counts show 0–1 examinees at each ACT score point of 11–17. Overall, less than 2% of the sample scored below 21. The standard error criterion that we have devised is met only for scores of 21 or higher. These findings indicate that it is not warranted to report results based on this sample for scores below 21. If the institution would like to have institution-specific concordances for scores below 21, then it would be necessary to obtain more data at the lower score points, so that those score points would be better represented and the concordance results more stable.

Table 11.1. Average ACT and SAT scores for the national concordance sample versus an institution with 868 examinees

Sample	N	Average scores	
		ACT	SAT
National	103,525	23.2	1071.4
Institution	868	29.2	1230.4

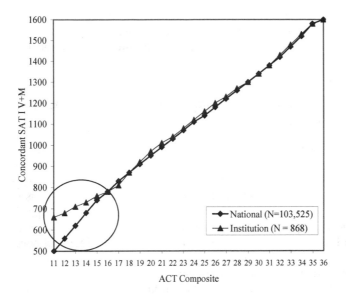

Figure 11.1. Concordance between ACT composite and SAT I V+M scores for an institution sample versus the national sample.

11.3.3.2. Evaluating the Generalizability of a Concordance

Ideally, concordances would be conducted using a random sample from the population(s) of interest, rather than a self-selected sample of examinees that choose to take both tests. Unfortunately, this is just not practical. As a result, concordance results will likely be applied to samples that differ on some characteristics from the concordance sample. Thus, it is important to consider how well the results will generalize to other samples and whether it is suitable to use the concordances with a particular group of interest.

One way to evaluate the generalizability of a concordance is to cross-validate the concordance (i.e., use two separate samples or bootstrap sampling methods to see how much results differ across samples). Another way is to compare the concordance sample relative to national test populations (i.e., evaluate whether the dual-testing sample is representative of the single-testing sample). A third way is to assess the invariance of the concordance results across different subgroups such as males or females. In general, invariance is expected to hold in an equating but not in a concordance. However, if concordance results are widely variable across subgroups, then a concordance based on a pooled sample might not well represent the subgroups. If any of the above evaluations suggest that the concordance results might not generalize well beyond the concordance sample, then the potential for misuse or misinterpretation of results is increased.

11.3.4. Making Recommendations for the Interpretation and Use of Linkage Results

Once a linkage is publicly released, there is little control over how results are used. We can write extensive guidelines identifying proper and improper uses and interpretations, but we cannot ensure that all users will read them or even understand them. After all, how many of us thoroughly read and understand the manuals that come with the appliances and technological gadgets that we purchase? Developers of concordance tables must admit that some (if not many) users might misinterpret concordances, particularly concordances based on equipercentile methods. It might be a natural tendency to use equipercentile concordance results as a prediction of an individual's score on the test not taken, although this is not a proper interpretation of the results.

As defined earlier, the equipercentile method identifies corresponding score points on Test A and Test B that result in the same percentages being selected using either test. This allows students to submit a score from either Test A or Test B. However, if an equipercentile-derived concordance table is used to establish comparable cut-scores on Test A and Test B, the same individuals would not necessarily be selected using scores on Test A versus scores on Test B (assuming the examinees took both tests). Hanson, Harris, Pommerich, Sconing, and Yi (2001) warned that "it is always possible to develop a link function that results in almost perfect comparability of distributions in one population, no matter how incomparable the two scores are for individuals" (p. 2). For these reasons, it is helpful to evaluate the consequences of using equipercentile concordance results at an individual level. Some ways to do so are to evaluate departure from equity and evaluate the consequences of misclassification. These types of evaluation will be briefly discussed here; the reader is referred to Pommerich et al. (2004) for a more detailed discussion.

11.3.4.1. Evaluating the Consequences for Individuals

Let us start by assuming that the equipercentile method has been used to identify score points on Test B that are concordant with score points on Test A. Equity holds if the distributions of concordant and actual scores for

Test B are equal. This is a somewhat looser definition of equity than originally defined by Lord (1980) because it does not take into account true scores. However, our definition is suitable for our purpose of demonstration.

The degree of departure from equity indicates the consequences of using equipercentile concordances at an individual level. There are no known means of measuring departure from equity directly, but it can be measured indirectly via observed score measures (Hanson et al., 2001). One means of doing so is to evaluate the consistency of classifications at concordant score points. For example, suppose an ACT composite score of X has a concordant SAT I V+M score of Y. At those two cut-scores, X on the ACT and Y on the SAT, evaluate what percent of decisions would be the same using individuals' actual SAT scores versus using their ACT scores. Another means of measuring departure from equity is to evaluate the variability of observed scores on Test Y, given each score point on Test X (i.e., compute the mean, standard deviation, minimum, and maximum of observed SAT I scores for examinees at each given ACT score point). More variable results indicate a greater departure from equity. Equipercentile results can also be compared to results from regression, which is specifically designed for the purpose of predicting an individual's score.

If any of the above evaluations suggest there would be too much departure from equity if a concordant score point was used as a substitute for an individual's actual score, you might want to recommend some alternatives to the concordance user. Alternatives could include the following:

- Using score ranges rather than a single concordant score point
- Using decision zones (i.e., identifying scores for which additional information or testing would be required)
- Placing less weight on test scores and more weight on other measures in making decisions
- Reporting regression results (prediction) rather than equipercentile results (concordance)

Consideration should also be given to the consequences of misclassification. Classification error based on an ACT–SAT concordance could result in a qualified student not being admitted to an institution, placed in a course that is too easy, denied a scholarship, or declared ineligible to play sports. Likewise, a classification error could result in an unqualified student being admitted to an institution, placed in a course that is too difficult, given a scholarship, or declared eligible to play sports. As the likelihood of misclassification increases, or as the consequences of classification error grow more severe, dependence on the concordance should be lessened accordingly.

11.3.4.2. Contrasting Concordance with Prediction

A few comments on concordance versus prediction seem in order here before continuing with our discussion of concordance. Again, the linkage of ACT and SAT scores will serve as our example. Holland (Chapter 2) distinguished between three basic categories of linking methods: predicting, scale aligning, and equating. A prediction is obtained when linear regression methods are used to predict ACT scores from SAT scores and vice versa. A concordance is obtained when scale-aligning methods such as equipercentile linking are used to identify comparable distributions of scores across the ACT and SAT tests. Application of the equipercentile method would not be considered an equating in the ACT–SAT case because the equal construct requirement (Holland, Chapter 2, Section 2.4.1; Holland & Dorans, 2006) is not upheld across the two tests.

Regression methods and equipercentile methods serve very different purposes. Hence, the predictions that are yielded by regression differ from the concordances that are yielded by equipercentile linking. An important difference is that concordances are symmetric, whereas predictions are not. Table 11.2 demonstrates this point. In the 1997 national ACT–SAT concordance (derived by equipercentile methods), an ACT composite of 33 has a concordant SAT I V+M score of 1470. Likewise, a SAT I V+M score of 1470 has a concordant ACT composite score of 33. However, when regression is applied to the same data, an ACT composite of 33 has a predicted SAT I V+M score of 1430, whereas an SAT I V+M score of 1430 has a predicted ACT composite score of 31.

Table 11.2. Demonstration of symmetry issue for equipercentile-defined concordances and regression-defined predictions

Method/outcome	ACT C[a]		SAT I V+M
Equipercentile/concordance	33	⇔	1470
Regression/prediction	33	⇒	1430
	31	⇐	1430

[a]ACT C=ACT composite.

Regression-defined predictions also exhibit regression toward the mean, which is particularly noticeable in the tails of the score distribution. Equipercentile-defined concordances have essentially the same percentile rank; regression-defined predictions do not. Table 11.3 shows SAT I V+M scores that correspond to ACT composite scores of 11 and 36, for the case of concordance versus prediction. The prediction results are very close to the average SAT I V+M score observed in the sample (which can be thought of as the target prediction); the concordance results are not. The maximum possible ACT composite score (36) corresponds to the maximum possible SAT I V+M score (1600) in the case of concordance, but not prediction. Likewise, results for an ACT composite score of 11 are very different across the concordance and prediction cases. Clearly, using equipercentile concordances or regression predictions for purposes other than which they are intended could give very misleading results. A more detailed discussion of this issue is presented in Pommerich et al. (2004).

Table 11.3. Corresponding SAT I V+M scores for ACT composite scores of 11 and 36, by linkage type

ACT C [a]	Corresponding SAT I V+M		Average observed SAT I V+M
	Concordance	Prediction	
11	500	630	633.08
36	1600	1540	1540.00

[a] ACT C=ACT composite.

11.4. The Concordance Dilemma

The discussion of the concordance process emphasizes the complexity of concordances and highlights some of the concerns with using concordances to make important decisions. Simply by virtue of making such linkages available, we create the potential for misuse and misinterpretation of the results. Clearly, conducting a concordance is not a task that one should undertake lightly.

One might well ask what has shifted since the 1960s, when Lindquist (1964) took his wary stance against ACT–SAT concordances and Angoff (1962) wrote at length of the limitations of concordances. From the measurement practitioner's perspective, not much has changed. Influential measurement experts continue to urge caution in conducting linkages between scores on nonparallel tests (e.g., Kolen, 2001). However, the balance of power seems to be shifting from the practitioners to the users. A psychologist might argue that the desire for instant gratification that prevails in today's society is causing the balance to shift in favor of the consumer—in this case, the concordance user. Likewise, as many consumer goods are increasingly being viewed as a necessity rather than a luxury, so too are concordances (at least in the eyes of users).

Let us attempt to make a distinction between necessity and luxury concordances from the perspective of a measurement practitioner. A concordance might be considered a necessity in cases in which there is a clear psychometric rationale for providing the concordance, such as providing continuity for users between scores across previous and new versions of a test. However, even in such cases, the concordance must be justifiable (i.e., upheld by an evaluation in the manner advocated by Dorans, 2004d). In cases in which the psychometric rationale for the concordance is fuzzy and/or the concordance appears more influenced by user demand than by psychometric need, a concordance is more likely to be a luxury than a necessity. A worst-case example might be a concordance conducted in the hopes of increasing the marketability of one or both tests. This would seem to clearly fall in the category of a luxury concordance. If the balance of power is indeed shifting from practitioners to users, practitioners might find themselves increasingly fighting against conducting luxury concordances.

A user's perspective on necessity versus luxury concordances is likely to differ from a practitioner's perspective. A user might well hold the belief that if a concordance is useful, then how can it *not* be viewed as a necessity? The concept of a luxury concordance might be incomprehensible to some users. On the other hand, some practitioners might argue that all concordances are a luxury. This perspective is likely to be driven by concerns about the limitations of concordances and the lack of awareness of those limitations on the part of users. The contrast in perspective between users and practitioners creates a concordance dilemma that is not easily resolved. How do we reconcile the benefits that users can gain from a concordance with the limitations of the linkage and the potential for misuse and misinterpretation of results? A review of the good, bad, and just plain ugly aspects of concordance might help illuminate the dilemma.

11.4.1. Concordance: The Good

First and foremost, it cannot be denied that concordances can be extremely beneficial to users. Consider the case of ACT–SAT concordances. They can give students and schools more flexibility in their testing options. They can reduce testing costs for students and allow students more choices in applying to college. They can reduce testing time for schools. They can allow students and schools to get a relative comparison of performance across the two tests. The extensive use of ACT–SAT concordances by schools, counselors, students, and parents speaks volumes of the actual benefit of the concordances to users.

Because the ACT–SAT concordances are so widely used, it is encouraging to see that there is increasing collaboration among the major test developers in creating the concordances. In 1991, ACT, Inc., the College Board, and ETS collaborated to collect data for a concordance. ACT, Inc. and ETS each then produced separate concordance tables (Marco & Abdel-fattah, 1991; Houston & Sawyer, 1991). The collaboration on data collection was unprecedented at the time; however, imagine the confusion on the part of the users who contacted both ACT and ETS and received different tables containing different results based on slightly different samples and different methods. In the 1997 ACT–SAT concordance (Dorans et al., 1997), not only did ACT, Inc., the College Board, and ETS collaborate to collect data for the concordance, but they also collaborated to produce a national concordance table. The scope of the data collection, along with the degree of collaboration, set a new precedent for developers of concordance tables.

It is our belief that the collaboration among the test developers to conduct ACT–SAT concordances is setting the bar higher for concordances between other pairs of tests. The large-scale collaborations in 1991 and 1997 made results available to a larger audience, promoted greater awareness of appropriate uses and limitations of concordances through explicit documentation, and stimulated additional, important research and commentary on concordance (e.g., Dorans, 1999, 2000, 2004d; Dorans & Walker, Chapter 10; Hanson et al., 2001; Marco et al., 1992; Pommerich & Dorans, 2004a; Pommerich, Hanson, Harris, & Sconing, 2000, 2004; Sawyer, Chapter 12). Because of research conducted on ACT–SAT concordances and other types of linkage, the emphasis in the measurement field is shifting from an equating-only perspective to a more inclusive linking perspective. Researchers are not just writing about equating any more, instead they are writing about equating *and* linking (e.g., Holland & Dorans, 2006; Kolen & Brennan, 2004). This more inclusive perspective fits better with the reality of what is happening in the measurement field than does a rigid focus on equating.

11.4.2. Concordance: The Bad

Our earlier discussion of the concordance process gives an idea of some of the limitations and concerns associated with concordance. There are many practical issues in conducting concordances that will need to be addressed for each unique concordance. Aside from technical issues, a critical operational concern with concordances might be that once you get started with reporting a concordance, you can never really stop. Every time a scoring change is made to one of the tests, the concordances need to be updated. In the case of the ACT–SAT concordances, the 1997 concordance is probably not valid for use with the revised version of the SAT that was introduced in March 2005, given the content changes that were made. It is likely that the test developers are working together to produce an updated concordance table, but in the meantime, what do users do before the table is completed?

In a similar vein, the act of making one concordance available is likely to trigger additional requests for concordances between other pairs of tests. After all, once users see what is possible, why should they settle for anything less? Unfortunately, some requested concordances might not be warranted by the characteristics of the tests asked to be linked (recall our earlier discussion on choosing an appropriate linkage type). This could set up a conflict between the users and the test developers. Because user understanding of concordances varies widely, it is a risky business for test developers to go down that path of creating more and more concordances. The potential for misuse and misinterpretation of concordance results increases as the relationship decreases between the tests that are linked.

Regardless of the quality of a concordance, it seems that we will never be able to squash the fallacy that concordant scores are "equivalent." A good case in point is a *New York Times* article about the revised SAT (Lewin, 2005) that discusses a student who received "an ACT score equivalent to 1520" on the SAT without identifying the source for this assertion. Concordance developers can say that concordant scores are not interchangeable or equivalent until they are blue in the face, but the prevailing interpretation by users appears to be one of equivalence.

Another important concern with developers providing concordances between tests is that schools might defer to the developer-provided concordances rather than conducting their own research to link scores for their student population. This might be particularly pertinent in cases where the school population differs from the concordance sample, and the developer-provided concordance does not well represent the relationship between scores at that school. Conversely, in a bit of a catch-22, schools might develop their own linkages that have more limitations than developer-provided concordances. As highlighted earlier, there are likely to be more limitations in concordances associated with smaller sample sizes. Also, some schools might have less expertise in developing linkages than the test developers.

11.4.3. Concordance: The Ugly

The distinction between bad and ugly is a fine line; however, there are a couple of aspects of concordance that stand out as being particularly problematic. Unexpectedly, these problems are created and/or exacerbated by the prevalence of technology in our society. To demonstrate, let us present our contention that

Concordances + the Internet = Mass Confusion!

A recent Internet search for "ACT–SAT concordance" led to some very interesting concordance tables on a variety of different Web sites. Some of these tables were outdated, contained incorrect linkages, did not identify the source of the table, or lacked any documentation beyond the table itself. There are a variety of interesting variations on the national concordance from who knows where floating about in the vast Internet space, available for anyone with access to a computer to find. Few Web sites (except for those sponsored by the test developers) list any information on how to use or interpret the results. All of the cautions taken by the test developer to develop explicit documentation against the misuse and misinterpretation of the concordance results might be gone by the wayside, lost to the whims of the user who developed the Web site.

The Internet can be quite a boon for test developers, because it allows for the vast proliferation of concordance information to be disseminated to the public. Unfortunately, the Internet also allows for the vast proliferation of incorrect, undocumented, outdated, and incomplete concordance information. Closely related is the fact that there is no established means with which to get rid of outdated concordances that have been superseded by more recent concordances. Old concordances are a bit like hazardous waste. We must safely dispose of them when we no longer need them. Unfortunately, the proliferation of potential misinformation due to the availability of outdated and/or incorrect concordances is a problem that we might not be able to explicitly control, except through the passage of time.

11.5. Conclusions

The elucidation of the good, bad, and ugly aspects of concordance does not resolve our concordance dilemma, but, rather, serves to further identify factors that contribute to the dilemma. At a glance, the weaknesses of concordances appear to outnumber their strengths. However, the usefulness of a concordance is a powerful inducement, particularly if it creates a high demand for the concordance from users. Even knowing what we now know about the concordance process and the limitations inherent with concordances, it is difficult to ignore user demands, particularly if they are made by powerful clientele.

When considering whether to conduct a concordance, we would be well served to evaluate whether the concordance fits more into the necessity or luxury category. We would also be well served to evaluate whether a concordance is actually warranted by our data. If these evaluations suggest that a concordance might be in order, then our best counsel is to exert caution throughout the entire concordance process. As such, we propose five goals for developers of concordance tables to strive for when conducting concordances:

1. Flexibility in linking practices
2. Responsibility in creating and disseminating concordance tables
3. Awareness of the limitations of concordances
4. Notification as to proper interpretation and use of results
5. Knowledge of users and their practices

Henceforth, these goals will be known as the FRANK goals of concordance. It is our hope that realization of these goals will allow concordance developers to maintain a healthy balance between meeting user needs and upholding measurement standards.

We would be remiss if we ended our discourse here, without any consideration for what the future might hold for concordance. Let us fast forward to the year 2050. We envision that that various sources will still be complaining that the amount of testing is excessive and burdensome to the schools. We envision that the feasibility of developing a common score scale for all tests will be revisited. We envision that measurement practitioners will continue to urge caution in conducting linkages between distinct tests because of potential for misuse and misinterpretation of results. Although history is certainly cyclical, it also evolves, so the outcome of these future complaints, considerations, and cautions remains to be seen.

12   Some Further Thoughts on Concordance

Richard Sawyer[1]

ACT, Inc.

Both preceding chapters in this part treat the limitations of concordance tables (tables that relate scores on tests that measure similar, but not identical, constructs). Dorans and Walker (Chapter 10) discussed requirements for equating and statistical indicators of concordance quality. The statistical indicators are based on correlation coefficients and on the root mean square difference between linking functions. Pommerich (Chapter 11) also addressed the quality of concordance, but emphasized how to do a good concordance study.

In this chapter, I discuss some general ideas on the *uses* of concordance tables. In presenting the ideas, I comment on how they relate to points made in the two preceding chapters on concordance. I illustrate the ideas with the example that Pommerich used: linkage between the ACT® and the SAT® in undergraduate college admission.

12.1. Four Common Score Uses in College Admission

The effectiveness of a procedure is best evaluated in the context of a particular use: A procedure or tool that is adequate for one use might not be suitable for another use. For ACT–SAT concordance, therefore, we need to identify common uses. The uses should drive both the statistical procedure used to develop a table and the statistical criteria against which the quality of the table will be evaluated.

With regard to uses, I am referring specifically to decisions based on test scores, rather than to inferences about an examinee's knowledge and skills. The problem of making inferences about an examinee's standing with respect to the content domain of Test Y, given a score on Test X, is an

---

[1] The opinions expressed in this chapter are those of the author and not necessarily of ACT, Inc.

interesting one, but I do not consider it here. It could be addressed by investigating the overlap and differences in the dimensional structures of Test *X* and Test *Y*.

One way to describe uses of concordance tables is according to who the user is. In using ACT–SAT concordance tables in college admission, two important groups of users are the following:

- Postsecondary institutions that use concordance tables in making admission selection decisions
- Students who are applying for admission to college, and the students' parents and counselors who are advising them

Table 12.1 shows four common uses of ACT–SAT concordance tables. I discuss each of them in turn.

Table 12.1. Four common uses of ACT–SAT concordance tables

User	
Postsecondary Institutions	Students, parents, and counselors
Use 1: Use scores on different tests in making selection decisions based in part on probability of future academic success.	*Use 3*: Compare scores on different tests for jointly tested students.
Example: We use either ACT scores or SAT scores in making admission decisions. What scores on the ACT and the SAT result in acceptable probabilities of future success?	*Example*: I've taken both the ACT and the SAT. Which of my scores is "better"?
Use 2: Use scores on different tests interchangeably in an administrative system.	*Use 4*: Estimate a score for a single tested student.
Example: We accept both ACT scores and SAT scores in our admission system, and we want to use them interchangeably. (The key word here is *interchangeably*.)	*Example*: I took the ACT, and don't want to have to take another test. The college to which I am applying uses mostly SAT scores. What is the SAT score that corresponds to my ACT score?

There are, of course, other uses of concordance tables for other tests and in other contexts. For example, an institution that currently uses a Test *X* for course placement might want to use another Test *Y* in place of, or in addition to, Test *X*. The institution has a validated cutoff score on *X*, but does not yet have a cutoff score on *Y*. The institution applies a concordance table, along with other information, to determine a temporary cutoff score on Y. The institution later adjusts the temporary cutoff score given the results of a validity study.

Another common use of concordance tables is to simplify covariates in statistical studies. A test score might be a covariate in some model; the majority of students have data on test Y, but a minority has data on X. Rather than trying to include both X and Y in the model, people will convert X to Y. I will not speak to either of these uses, but will confine my remarks to the college admission testing examples.

12.1.1. Use 1: Making Selection Decisions Based on Estimated Probability of Success

This is the scenario for Use 1: Test scores are one component of a system for making admission decisions. The scores are used to identify students who are likely to be successful in the first year of college. The institution accepts scores on both Test X and Test Y.

If you follow the *Standards for Educational and Psychological Testing* (American Educational Research Association, American Psychological Association, & National Council on Measurement in Education, 1999), and if you have sufficient data, then you do not need a concordance table: Instead, you can do predictive validity studies for X and Y and use the results to develop separate decision rules for X and Y, each in the context of all other information that you use in making admission decisions. The University of Texas at Austin is an example of an institution that does this (Lavergne & Walker, 2001). By doing so, you improve on the accuracy of selection decisions: Predictions based on X and Y separately will likely be more accurate than predictions based on a mixture of actual scores and concordant scores. (An exception to this would occur if there were insufficient data to estimate separate predictions for X and Y, but X and Y were highly correlated.)

Another advantage is that the institution can also study the effectiveness of X and Y separately in making admission decisions. A key question is this: Does using X by itself increase the proportion of enrolled students who are academically successful over that which would occur if the institution used all other relevant variables, but not X? The same question could be asked about Y. Moreover, one could, with sufficient data, compare the effectiveness of X and Y.

Although standard statistics, such as regression coefficients and the change in squared multiple correlation, are related to this question, I believe it is preferable to calculate statistics that more directly address institutions' reasons for using test scores. A principal reason that institutions use scores on college admission tests in making admission decisions is their belief that by doing so, they will improve the academic success rate of admitted students. Given this goal, it makes sense for institutions to estimate a success rate (the proportion of applicants who, if admitted and enrolled, would succeed). An indicator of the effectiveness of a college admission test for achieving this goal would be the difference between the success rate associated with using the test and the success rate associated with not using the test (Sawyer, 2007).

12.1.2. Use 2: Using Scores on Different Tests Interchangeably in an Administrative System

In Use 2, scores on different tests are treated interchangeably in an administrative system. Here, the key word is *interchangeably*: Institutions often use concordance tables to convert scores on Test X to the scale on Test Y and then process all scores in a single system.

This use is based mainly on practicality and convenience. An institution might not have the data or other resources to do separate validity studies for X and Y. Even if an institution has done validity studies for both X and Y, it might prefer the convenience of working with a single metric. Such institutions want to process all applications, regardless of which scores they contain, in the same way. They cannot or do not want to maintain separate admission decision rules and procedures.

These institutions also want to make the same admission decision for an applicant, regardless of which test the applicant submits scores on. In practice, of course, this is not possible. Measurement error alone guarantees that taking the same test twice could yield test scores that would result in different admission decisions. Moreover, differences in the constructs measured by X and Y will add to the inconsistency.

Most institutions understand that although they might like to make the same decision for each individual applicant, regardless of test score submitted, they cannot do so. Instead, institutions are satisfied if they can make the same decisions for a very large proportion of their total group of applicants. The consistency rate, described in the Pommerich chapter, speaks to this goal.

One factor that affects the consistency rate is the proportion of applicants selected. If an institution selects a very high or a very low proportion of applicants, then it will obtain a high proportion of consistent decisions regardless of how well the equating requirements are satisfied. I return to this point later in the chapter.

The practical importance of the concept of consistency itself depends on the proportion of applicants for which an institution applies a concordance table. If nearly all applicants submit scores on Test X (and just a few submit scores on Test Y), then few applicants would be affected by inconsistency.

Institutions' interest in making consistent decisions is related to the symmetry property of equating functions, which Dorans and Walker (Chapter 10, Section 10.2) discussed. On examining a concordance table, an institution can see immediately whether the symmetry property is preserved. Evaluating the other properties (equal constructs, equal reliability, equity, and population invariance) requires examining other kinds of evidence, not as readily accessible to institutions. The equipercentile linking function preserves symmetry, and because it preserves percentile ranks, it satisfies a notion of equity. For this reason, institutions demand equipercentile concordance.

12.1.2.1. Evaluating the Effectiveness of Concordance Tables for Use 2

Dorans and Walker (Chapter 10, Section 10.4) discussed several indicators, based on the correlation ρ_{XY} between X and Y, to describe the degree of alignment between linked scores on X and Y:

Reduction in uncertainty: $\text{RiU} = 1 - \sqrt{1 - \rho_{XY}^2}$

Signal-to-noise ratio: $\text{SNR} = \rho_{XY}^2 / \left(1 - \rho_{XY}^2\right)$

Decibel: $\text{dB} = 10 \log_{10}(\text{SNR})$

Their recommended standard for concordance is $\rho_{XY} = \sqrt{3}/2$ (about .87), or RiU = .50, or SNR = 3.0, or dB = 4.77.

This proposed standard does not seem unreasonable, given the results that have been obtained in large-scale ACT–SAT concordance studies. The proposed standard might be too strict in some contexts, however. Depending on the use being made of the tests and depending on other contextual factors, a lower correlation might be sufficient. As stated earlier, my inclination is to evaluate statistical results in the context of particular uses and goals. In the case of undergraduate college admission testing, some issues that could be considered by an institution are the following: How much of a role do test scores have in making admission decisions? What proportion of applicants does the institution admit?

Moreover, the correlation between X and Y (and the associated indicators RiU, SNR, and dB) addresses the issue of prediction accuracy in terms of reducing prediction error variance. I believe that for Use 2, consistency of decisions is a more important goal of users than is prediction accuracy, per se. As is discussed below, prediction accuracy and consistency of decisions are related, but they are not the same.

For a group of examinees who have taken both Test X and Test Y, we can define a consistency rate as the proportion of examinees who would be selected on either test, or who would not be selected on either test:

$$CR(p) = P[X \geq x_p, Y \geq y_p] + P[X < x_p, Y < y_p], \qquad (12.1)$$

where $P[X \geq x_p] = P[Y \geq y_p] = 1 - p$. In this scenario, x_p and y_p are cutoff scores on X and Y, and $1 - p$ is the proportion of examinees selected. A consistency rate can be interpreted as a proportion of examinees, which I believe is easier than interpreting correlations or transformations of correlations.

The use of strict cutoffs on test scores is a mathematical idealization and simplification. In practice, institutions also typically use other quantitative variables (such as high school grades), other objective qualitative variables (e.g., extracurricular activities), as well as subjective criteria in making admission decisions. In principle, if one had data on all of the important components of admission decisions, one could estimate how concordance tables affect the consistency of the decisions, given all of the other components. It is unlikely, however, that institutions would be willing to invest their resources to assemble and analyze the required data.

Note that we can obtain a high consistency rate simply by selecting nearly all (or almost none) of the examinees. One can show, by a differentiation argument, that for continuous random variables, CR(p) is minimized when $p = 1/2$. In general, the required strength of the statistical relationship between X and Y needed to achieve an acceptable consistency rate depends on the selection rate.

If we assume that X and Y have a bivariate normal distribution, then CR(p) is also a function of ρ_{XY}:

$$CR(p; \rho_{XY}) = \Phi[-z_p, -z_p ; \rho_{XY}] + \Phi[z_p, z_p ; \rho_{XY}] \qquad (12.2)$$

In this equation, Φ is the bivariate normal distribution function for two variables with correlation ρ_{XY} and z_p is the pth percentile of a normal distribution. Note that consistency rates could also be calculated for repeat administrations of the same test, given an assumed reliability. Brennan (1981) applied this procedure to coefficients of agreement in criterion-referenced testing.

I will now show an example of consistency rates[2] for concordance between the ACT sum score (on the English, mathematics, reading, and science tests) and the SAT verbal plus mathematics (V + M) sum score. The concordant scores were calculated from all students who took both the ACT and the SAT I and who graduated from high school in 1999. The data were assembled by Michael Nettles and his colleagues when he was at the University of Michigan. There are 260,899 records in this dataset. The correlation between the ACT sum score and the SAT V + M sum score was 0.90. The results are shown in Figure 12.1.

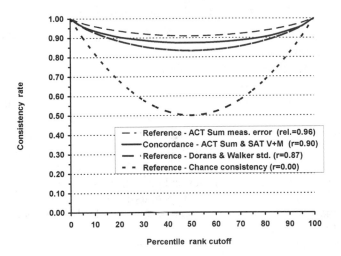

Figure 12.1. Consistency rates between concordant ACT sum score and SAT V + M score.

The curve on top corresponds to a reference consistency rate for the ACT sum score, assuming a reliability of .96:

$$CR(p; 0.96) = \Phi[-z_p, -z_p; 0.96] + \Phi[z_p, z_p; 0.96].$$

The second (solid) curve shows the consistency rate between classifications based on ACT and SAT scores calculated from the concordance data. The third curve shows the consistency rate referenced to

---

[2] Consistency rates are also sometimes reported in terms of Kappa (κ): $\kappa = [CR(p; \rho) - CR(p; 0)] / [1 - CR(p; 0)]$. Kappa is a consistency rate normalized with respect to chance agreement: From the observed consistency rate, first subtract off the consistency of decisions resulting from hypothetical test scores that are statistically independent; then divide by the difference between 1.0 (perfect consistency) and chance consistency. Rather than report normalized consistencies, I just show the bottom curve in Figure 12.1 for reference. For a summary and criticism of Kappa, see Uebersax (2006).

the standard of .87 proposed in the Dorans and Walker chapter. The bottom curve shows the consistency rate for two variables that are statistically independent:

$$CR(p; 0) = (1 - p)^2 + p^2.$$

There are several points worth noting about Figure 12.1:

- As we would expect, the least consistency occurs when the selection cutoff is near the median.
- The top reference curve, corresponding to the effects of measurement error, bottoms out at about 0.92.
- The observed concordance curve (solid line) bottoms out at about .88. Thus, a decrease of .04 in minimum consistency is the penalty an institution would incur in using concordant ACT and SAT scores.
- The consistency rate corresponding to Dorans and Walker's (Chapter 10, Section 10.4) proposed standard of $\rho_{XY} = 0.87$ bottoms out at about 0.83. Stated another way, if the correlation between ACT and SAT scores had been 0.87, rather than 0.90, then the penalty in consistency an institution would incur for using concordant scores would be .09 below the reliability standard.
- Finally, for high or low selection cutoffs, you will get high consistency, no matter what the correlation is. Thus, a correlation less than 0.87 could be acceptable in certain situations.

12.1.2.2. Institutional Variation in Concordance Relationships

We know from the discussion in Dorans and Walker (Chapter 10) that concordance relationships might differ from group to group. The relationships might vary by demographic group (as Dorans & Holland, 2000, and others have noted) and by other characteristics, such as previous educational preparation. Because different institutions can have markedly different applicant populations, background and educational differences among the applicant populations could show up as variation in concordance relationships among the institutions.

The following example is based on data collected for an ACT–SAT concordance study (Dorans et al., 1997) following the recentering of SAT I scores in 1995. Figure 12.2 shows the concordance relationship between ACT sum scores and SAT V + M sum scores. Curves are given for the relationship estimated from the entire concordance sample of over 103,000 records and for two particular institutions whose concordance relationships differed from each other more than from the other institutions. The sample size for each institution was approximately 2,300 records.

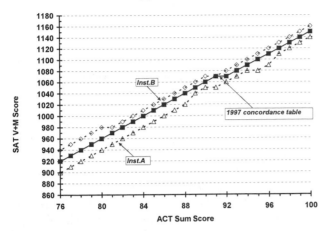

Figure 12.2. Concordant ACT sum and SAT V + M scores for two institutions.

Note that for ACT sum scores between 76 and 80, the two institutions' concordant SAT V + M sum scores differ from each other by 40 score units and from the total group concordant scores by 20 score units. Differences this large and larger also occurred for ACT sum scores below 76; I truncated the range of ACT sum scores in Figure 12.2 to display the differences more clearly. If either of these two institutions used the total-group concordance table for applicants with ACT sum scores below 80, it would misrepresent the concordant SAT V + M scores for its applicants by 20 units. The estimated conditional standard errors for the concordant SAT V + M scores within institution were uniformly less than 3 SAT score units; therefore, differences among the three curves are very unlikely to have arisen by chance.

One way to determine the practical significance of the differences is to calculate consistency rates near the admission cutoff scores separately using the national table and the institution-specific table. For either institution, the maximum decrease in consistency rate associated with using the general concordance table, rather than a local table, was 0.01. The maximum decrease in consistency occurred for ACT sum scores of 78 to 90 (approximately the 35th to the 65th percentiles at this institution).

A maximum decrease in consistency of only .01 is reassuring to institutions that want to use a generic concordance table, rather than to construct their own tables. This reassurance should be tempered, however, by the likelihood that the result was driven by the use of data only from jointly tested examinees. Examinees who have taken only the ACT, or only the SAT, could differ from each other, and from jointly tested examinees, in the constructs measured by the two tests. These differences could then propagate to differences among institutions in concordance relationships for single-tested examinees. For further discussion of this issue, see Section 12.1.4.

12.1.3. Use 3: Comparing Scores on Different Tests for Jointly Tested Students

Now let us turn to a common use by students. The scenario for Use 3 is this: I have taken both the ACT (X) and the SAT (Y). Which of my scores is "better"? I want to submit the "better" score. We get this question very frequently from students, parents, and counselors.

An exaggeration of this question is: "I have taken the SAT I. Did I do better on verbal (X) or on mathematics (Y)?" A greater exaggeration is, "Am I taller than I am heavier?" This relates to the playful example in Dorans and Walker (Chapter 10, Section 10.6), to which I will return later.

Note that comparing an actual score to a regression-based predicted score could return an ambiguous answer to this question: The regression line of Y on X does not yield the same prediction as the regression line of X on Y. For the region between the two regression lines, the answer would be "Y is better than X, and X is better than Y." In terms of the five requirements for equating that Dorans and Walker discussed, regression-based predictions violate the symmetry requirement.

One way to compare X and Y unambiguously is to say, "Your score on X is above those of P_x % of the members of a given reference group. Your score on Y is above those of P_y % of the members of the same reference group." This is an equipercentile comparison. A more informative answer would be: "Given the measurement accuracy of X, your likely range of scores on X if you took a different form of X is x_1 to x_2. The range of Y scores with similar percentile ranks among jointly tested students is y_1 to y_2."

In general, examinees are not aware that if a different reference group (e.g., defined by gender, ethnicity, or region) were used to make the comparisons, one might get a different answer. But then, they do not care, either: The reference group that they are concerned about is the total group of applicants among whom they are competing for admission.

I have previously mentioned Dorans and Walker's discussion of the equity requirement: It should be a matter of indifference to an examinee to be tested by either one of two tests that have been equated. The particular use of concordance tables that I am discussing now could be said to have an "anti-equity requirement": Examinees are *not* indifferent to which test scores they report. Examinees might not be well trained in the formal aspects of measurement theory, but they have a keen appreciation for its practical implications. In contrast to a college, which wants a high consistency rate, if you are an examinee who can choose which test score to submit, and if your scores are near the cutoff, you would want a low consistency rate.

The practical advice ACT, Inc. gives is that students interested in the concordance table it constructed in cooperation with the College Board and ETS need to ask each institution they apply to what concordance table it uses. As Pommerich points out in her chapter, there are many tables floating around on the Internet.

12.1.4. Use 4: Estimating a Score for Single-Tested Students

Another common use of concordance tables is by students who have taken only one test (such as the ACT) and who want to estimate the score they would have received if they had taken another test (such as the SAT). The advice we give is the same as in Use 3, where students have taken both tests: ask the institution to which they arc applying what table it uses. Although a regression-based estimate would seem to be appropriate here, students and institutions typically use equipercentile tables.

What is interesting and problematic about this particular use is the typical design of concordance studies. As Pommerich noted in her chapter, concordance tables are based on available data from students who chose to take both tests. It would be risky, for example, to base an equipercentile concordance on the entire user group for each test, because the two user groups could differ on many characteristics that affect concordance.

I believe that significant variation in concordant scores could exist according to whether a student elects to take only one test or to take both tests: My personal experience in talking with test users suggests that students are more likely to take the test on which they think (or that their advisors think) the students will do better. In Use 4 (estimating a score on Test Y from a student who takes only Test X), therefore, there is a possibility that the concordance table (based on data from self-selected jointly tested examinees) is not appropriate for an important group to which it is applied (examinees who choose to take only one exam.)

We also know that jointly tested examinees perform differently than the general group of examinees on either test. In the 1997 concordance study, the mean ACT composite score of jointly tested students was approximately 4/10 of a standard deviation higher than those of all ACT-tested students (ACT, 1997b), and about 3/10 of a standard deviation lower than those of all SAT-tested students (The College Board, 1997).

This at least raises the possibility of variation in concordance relationships among students according to the test(s) they decide to take. Concordance tables are developed using data from jointly tested students. They are applied, however, to students who might have taken only one test. It is possible that the characteristics of the groups differ in significant ways and are related to the constructs measured by the ACT and the SAT. Unfortunately, we do not have the data required to study this.

One way to overcome this potential limitation (and to determine whether it is practically important) would be to administer the ACT (or the SAT) to samples of students who have previously taken only the other test and to collect information from all students on their use of concordance tables. The complexity and cost of such a study makes it unlikely that it will be done.

Another, more feasible, approach is similar to the projection method that Holland (Chapter 2, Section 2.2.2) described previously: Model the joint distribution of X and Y, given covariates. The covariates would consist of demographic variables, high school grades, and other variables that are collected on both X and Y and that are related to their test scores. Then weight the modeled joint distribution of X and Y by a specified distribution of the covariates in a population of interest.

12.2. Other Thoughts on Concordance Tables

Pommerich (Chapter 11, Section 11.4) mentioned that test publishers create concordance tables in response to user demand. This is certainly true. Satisfying users' demands in the best way we can technically, but advising them of the limitations of what we do, is a requirement of doing business responsibly.

The test publishing companies do alert users to the limitations of ACT–SAT concordance tables. My subjective interpretation of conversations with students, parents, teachers, and institution officials is that they believe that in the big scheme of things, the ACT–SAT concordance tables are good enough for their uses. In the big scheme of things, they are probably right.

The greater concern is that users might think that concordance between *any* two tests is unproblematic. In part, this occurs from what Braun and Mislevy (2005) called the widely assumed truth that a test is a test is a test. For example, I have seen requests for concordances between a reading test designed for adults who dropped out of high school (many of whom can barely read and write) and a reading test designed for placing students in first-year courses in college.

Another potentially problematic practice is chaining concordances. Suppose that you do not have (and cannot feasibly obtain) data on students who have taken both X and Y. You do, however, have data on students who have taken both X and Z and (separately) on students who have taken both Y and Z. So, you relate X and Y through Z. This can produce misleading results, particularly when either sublink is weak or if the two tables are developed from different groups.

12.3. Coastal Aspirations and Midland Acquisitions

Dorans and Walker (Chapter 10, Section 10.6) concluded their chapter with an example of a test developed by two competing companies, Coastal Aspirations and Midland Acquisitions. These two companies develop assessments for professional athletes. Coastal Aspirations believes in measuring height, whereas Midland Acquisitions believes in measuring mass.

They show that the concordances for three groups of athletes (baseball players, basketball players, and football players) differed drastically, especially for large scores. One reason for the discrepancies is that the correlation between the two measures was only .44. I think another factor that drove these results is that there was extreme prior selection on the two measures. This extreme degree of prior selection would not occur in the ACT–SAT example.

12.4. Conclusions

Evaluating the adequacy of concordance tables depends on the particular use being made of them. Even in the general context of college admission, there are distinct uses of ACT–SAT concordance tables. If an institution is using a concordance table merely as an intermediate step in predicting academic success and if it has sufficient outcome data from students who have taken either test, then it would do better just to develop separate predictions for each test and to avoid concordance altogether. For institutions that want to use ACT and SAT scores interchangeably in an administrative system, the consistency rate is an informative indicator of the effectiveness of the table. Consistency rates estimated from past ACT–SAT concordance data are high.

Projection methods are a promising tool for estimating variation in concordance relationships over population subgroups.

12.5. Postscript

Given the potential problems that we have identified with concordance, I would like to conclude my remarks on a note of optimism. Although I do not follow professional athletics closely, I do know that both Coastal Aspirations and Midland Acquisitions are fine companies. I am thoroughly convinced that the cause of the disappointing results presented in the Dorans and Walker chapter is not due to gross unreliability in either of the tests.

I did read in the newspaper that one of Coastal Aspirations' principal customers pressured it to change the height construct of its test to something closer to the mass construct favored by Midland Acquisitions. As a result, Coastal Aspirations developed a new version of its test.

Moreover, in response to user demand, both companies also developed new direct measures of sports performance. In contrast to the traditional height and mass measures, the direct measures ask examinees to shoot baskets, hit baseballs, and tackle opponents for approximately 30 min.

I also have heard that Coastal Aspirations and Midland Acquisitions are apparently planning a new concordance study. If the reports about Coastal Aspirations' new constructs are true, the new concordance study will likely yield better results than those reported by Dorans and Walker. I look forward to seeing them.

Part 5: Vertical Scaling

Vertical scaling used to be practiced by a small group of psychometricians responsible for a few nationally standardized primary and secondary school achievement test batteries. It has received a great deal of attention since states have begun creating their own assessments.

Deborah Harris in *Practical Issues in Vertical Scaling* examines issues that a practitioner would encounter when developing a vertical scale for an operational testing program. She presents a framework of issues to consider when creating a vertical scale and demonstrates that practical and theoretical issues interact in context-specific ways. An example involving the scaling of two math tests provides an illustration of some of the issues.

Richard Patz and Lihua Yao examine item response theory (IRT) methods for vertically scaling educational assessments in *Methods and Models for Vertical Scaling*. They compare "divide and conquer" and unified approaches to models and data analyses in this context. They introduce a unified multidimensional, multigroup IRT model that captures differences in dimensionality and scale definition across grade levels. They explore properties of this model using data from a cross-grade writing assessment and discuss limitations and alternatives to vertical scaling for assessment programs.

Wendy Yen in *Vertical Scaling and No Child Left Behind* discusses concepts raised by the previous two chapters while she examines the role of vertical scaling in the pre-No Child Left Behind (NCLB) era and the NCLB era. An example is given of an alternative type of analysis that can provide answers to user questions about student growth over grades, without requiring the assumptions or expense of a vertical scale.

13 Practical Issues in Vertical Scaling

Deborah J. Harris[1]

ACT, Inc.

13.1. Introduction

The capability to measure students along a continuum, such as measuring growth in mathematics from grade 3 to grade 6, has become more and more important, especially with the recent federal legislation No Child Left Behind Act of 2001 (NCLB) and the concept of adequate yearly progress, by which it is to be determined if students are making sufficient gains as they advance through the education system. An assessment with a vertical scale is the most common way of evaluating growth from one grade level to another.

Vertical scaling refers to the process of linking different levels of an assessment, which measure the same construct, onto a common score scale (see Holland, Chapter 2, for placement of vertical scaling into a linking framework). Many elementary and secondary test batteries report scores on a vertical scale, such as the Iowa Tests of Basic Skills (ITBS; Hoover, Dunbar, & Frisbie, 2001) and ACT, Inc.'s Educational Planning and Assessment System (EPAS; ACT, 2000).

Why is there a need for a chapter addressing practical issues? Because when one constructs a vertical scale, decisions have to be made with respect to the definition of growth, scaling design, statistical methods, type of scales, and so forth (see Harris, Hendrickson, Tong, Shin, & Shyu, 2004; Kolen, 2003). Different decisions can lead to different vertical scales, which in turn can lead to different reported scores and different decisions. The literature shows that vertical scaling is design dependent

---

[1] The opinions expressed in this chapter are those of the author and not necessarily of ACT, Inc.

(Harris, 1991), group dependent (Harris & Hoover, 1987; Skaggs & Lissitz, 1988; Slinde & Linn, 1979), and method dependent (Kolen, 1981; Skaggs & Lissitz, 1986).

This chapter examines issues that a practitioner would encounter when developing a vertical scale for an operational testing program. Although there is no single right way to develop a score scale, there are many options available, and the practitioner who chooses a method with a careful eye to both the purpose of the scale (i.e., how the resulting scores are intended to be used) and to the literature is more likely to create a scale that will facilitate appropriate decision-making. The chapter considers five sets of issues: conceptual, technical, implementation, maintenance, and other. An example involving the vertical scaling of two math tests is given throughout the chapter to provide an illustration of some of the issues that are discussed. The example uses data from the PLAN and ACT mathematics tests. However, the reader interested in a more complete summary should consult the PLAN and ACT technical manuals (ACT, 1997a, 1999).

The literature cited in this chapter, as well as on Web sites and in technical manuals and in other documentation relating to operational verticals scales (although the latter are often scant on details), should be consulted for additional information. Specific papers are helpful to address specific issues; four sources are recommended for general treatments and overviews on vertical scaling: Kolen and Brennan (2004), a book on equating and scaling that covers many issues related to vertical scaling, Kolen (2003) a conference presentation that discusses several topics in vertical scaling that need to be addressed, Petersen, Kolen, and Hoover (1989), a chapter that covers basic scaling and linking information, and Harris et al. (2004), a conference presentation that discusses practical issues related to vertical scaling. Literature not specific to vertical scaling, such as equating literature, item parameter calibration literature, computer estimation program manuals, and score reporting literature, should also be consulted, as vertical scaling covers a wide range of issues. The companion chapters by Patz and Yao (Chapter 14) and Yen (Chapter 15) should also be consulted.

It is also recommended that the reader consult multiple sources, because inconsistencies abound: for example, the Rasch model was found to be both acceptable (e.g., Schulz, Perlman, Rice, & Wright, 1992) and unacceptable (e.g., Phillips, 1983) for vertical scaling applications. Similarly, grade-to-grade variability in ability was shown to increase (Andrews, 1995; Yen, 1986), decrease (Hoover, 1984a), or remain stable across grade levels (Bock, 1983). Harris et al. (2004) contained the beginning of a comprehensive review of the literature related to vertical scaling, which might be useful to those readers who either have difficulty gaining access to the original source material or who prefer to read a summarized version. In addition to providing information as to where various methods yield consistent, or inconsistent, results, a comprehensive summary of the literature also helps identify issues requiring further investigation.

As mentioned earlier, valuable information regarding vertical scaling is also found by examining current practice. Vertical scales continue to be built and used by test publishers, despite the lack of a commonly accepted set of procedures. Although research done using simulated conditions can be very informative, what is actually done in practice might be of most interest to potential practitioners. Harris et al. (2004) provided an appendix with an initial attempt to document how vertical scales were operationally implemented by various publishers for their testing programs.

13.2. Conceptual Issues

The tendency is to jump into methodology immediately, but the conceptual issues really need to be considered first, both to ensure that there really is a need for a vertical scale and because the decisions made up front have tremendous impact on the resulting scales.

13.2.1. Do You Really Need a Vertical Scale?

The first issue to resolve is the actual need for a vertical scale. For example, if one is a grade-school administrator who wants to ensure that all graduating sixth graders know the capitols of all 50 states, there is no need for a vertical scale. All students can be given the same test, and raw scores can be used to monitor progress over time. However, for subjects where knowledge acquisition is gradual, or follows a sequence, moving students to where one wants them to end up is more of a process. For example, if one wants students to be able to multiply three-digit numbers, repeatedly testing on multiplying three-digit numbers is not really effective. Instead, one wants to monitor (know) if they know their basic multiplication facts, if they can multiply and carry, and so on. Administering the "final" test content at an earlier grade will not really enable one to target effective instruction. However, having a scale, or sequence, that follows the process from, say, numeral recognition through three-digit multiplication would allow one to monitor progress and provide intervention where needed. A vertical scale could be helpful for the later situation.

A vertical scale, therefore, is not the only option. A scale might not be needed (i.e., the raw score scale might be sufficient) or other options might be preferable to a vertical scale. For example, Lissitz and Huynh (2003) advocated vertically moderated standards as being more useful than vertical scales in assessing adequate yearly progress.

However, as mentioned earlier, a vertical scale is often helpful in guiding students along a continuum. As an example that will be followed throughout this chapter, consider the mathematics tests in the ACT and PLAN programs. They have a common philosophical basis in measuring students' knowledge and skills typically attained during a student's secondary school experience. The ACT is intended primarily for 11th and 12th graders; PLAN is primarily intended for 10th graders. It was determined that placing the two tests on the same scale would facilitate the goal of providing a longitudinal approach to educational planning, assessment, instructional support, and evaluation. See the PLAN and ACT technical manuals (ACT, 1997a, 1999) for details regarding the use of the PLAN/ACT scale.

13.2.2. Developing Test Specifications

Issues such as what grades to include in the assessment, what content to cover, what item types to use, what time limits, who is writing the items, and so on can have a large impact on the resulting scale. How content is defined across the grades (i.e., the amount of overlapping content in, say, the third and fourth grades) has a major impact on the resulting score scale.

Issues such as how to model grade-to-grade overlap depends, in part, on how the assessment structures content across grades. Kolen (2003) listed "Over what test content should grade-to-grade growth be defined?" (p. 6) as an issue in need of further study, illustrating the relationship between test content and the nature of growth.

Issues such as balancing completeness of coverage with motivation and frustration issues of administering too many items of inappropriate difficulty or interest to examinees in a given grade, deciding how many grade levels should receive particular items, the number of concepts that overlap, and so on are philosophical as well as practical or measurement issues. Construct dimensionality issues are also partially embedded in the nature of growth. The importance of content dimensionality in establishing vertical scales continues to be an issue.

The content specifications for the ACT and PLAN mathematics tests, taken from ACT (1999) are shown in Tables 13.1 and 13.2.

The test specifications make concrete some of the assumptions regarding growth concrete. For example, the inclusion of plane geometry in both PLAN and ACT specifications indicates this is a topic that one expects to be covered at both levels, whereas trigonometry is not. The more detailed specifications that are actually used for forms construction (sublevels of topics within the broader area of plane geometry), as well as statistical specifications, such as average or target p-values, would indicate how the progression of plane geometry across levels is thought to occur. For example, topics intended for the PLAN assessment might be more difficult for 10th graders than for 12th graders, and more advanced topics might be included on the ACT and not included on the PLAN.

Table 13.1. Specifications for the ACT mathematics test

Content area	Proportion of test	No. of items
Pre-Algebra[a]	.23	14
Elementary Algebra[b]	.17	10
Intermediate Algebra[c]	.15	9
Coordinate Geometry[d]	.15	9
Plane Geometry[e]	.23	14
Trigonometry[f]	.07	4
Total	1.00	60

[a]Pre-Algebra. Items in this content area are based on operations using whole numbers, decimals, fractions, and integers; place value; square roots and approximations; the concept of exponents; scientific notation; factors; ratio, proportion, and percent; linear equations in one variable; absolute value and ordering numbers by value; elementary counting techniques and simple probability; data collection, representation, and interpretation; and understanding simple descriptive statistics.

[b]Elementary Algebra. Items in this content area are based on properties of exponents and square roots, evaluation of algebraic expressions through substitution, using variables to express functional relationships, understanding algebraic operations, and the solution of quadratic equations by factoring.

[c]Intermediate Algebra. Items in this content area are based on an understanding of the quadratic formula, rational and radical expressions, absolute value equations and inequalities, sequences and patterns, systems of equations, quadratic inequalities, functions, modeling, matrices, roots of polynomials, and complex numbers.

[d]Coordinate Geometry. Items in this content area are based on graphing and the relations between equations and graphs, including points, lines, polynomials, circles, and other curves; graphing inequalities; slope; parallel and perpendicular lines; distance; midpoints; and conics.

[e]Plane Geometry. Items in this content area are based on the properties and relations of plane figures, including angles and relations among perpendicular and parallel lines; properties of circles, triangles, rectangles, parallelograms, and trapezoids, transformations, the concept of proof and proof techniques volume; and applications of geometry to three dimensions.

[f]Trigonometry. Items in this content area are based on understanding trigonometric relations in right triangles; values and properties of trigonometric functions; graphing trigonometric functions; modeling using trigonometric functions; use of trigonometric identities; and solving trigonometric equations.

Table 13.2. Specifications for the PLAN mathematics test

Content area	Proportion of test	No. of items
Pre-Algebra[a]	.35	14
Elementary Algebra[b]	.20	8
Coordinate Geometry[c]	.18	7
Plane Geometry[d]	.27	11
Total	1.00	40

[a]Pre-Algebra. Items in this category are based on operations with whole numbers, integers, decimals, and fractions. The topics covered include prime factorization, comparison of fractions, conversions, scientific notation, square roots, percent, absolute probability, mean, median, and mode.

[b]Elementary Algebra. The items in this category are based on operations with algebraic expressions. The operations include evaluation of algebraic expressions by substitution; simplification of algebraic expressions, additions, subtraction and multiplication of polynomials; factorization of polynomials; and solution of quadratic equations by factoring.

[c]Coordinate Geometry. Items in this category cover topics on graphing in the standard coordinate plane. The topics include graphs of linear equations, measurement of lines, and determination of the slope of a line.

[d]Plane Geometry. Items in this category cover such topics as measurement of plane surfaces, properties of polygons, properties of triangles, the Pythagorean Theorem, and relationships involving circles.

Vertical scales are often created after test forms for different levels are created. It should be understood that the nature of the forms themselves—in particular, their content and statistical specifications in relation to each other—has a large impact on any resulting vertical scale, including ceiling and floor effects, and the amount of overlap between different levels.

13.2.3. How Is Growth Defined?

Perhaps the most publicized debate in the vertical scaling literature is in relation to using item response theory (IRT) as a scaling method. A key issue in the debate over scale shrinkage was the nature of growth and whether within-grade variance should increase, decrease, or remain constant as the grade increased. Camilli (1988) stated.

> The scale shrinkage controversy has opened up an important debate in educational measurement. It is not a debate between IRT methods and traditional scaling methods. In fact, it was shown in this paper that the two types of methods (IRT and percentage correct scores) could lead to similar conclusions about shrinkage within grades. The more interesting issue raised is how children learn, and this question goes far beyond measurement technology. (pp. 239–240).

The primary reason for creating vertical scales is to measure learning across time. Without an understanding of the nature of growth, it is not possible to clearly evaluate whether a vertical scale is functioning as it should. For example, if the true nature of growth shows increasing variability over time, then a vertical scale that shows constant variability over time would not be judged as adequate. These issues are philosophical and deal with child development, psychology, and how the educational curriculum is implemented. The pattern of growth might vary across grades (i.e., increase from, say, first to fourth grade, then remain constant) and across academic subjects (the nature of mathematics might yield a different growth pattern than, say, English; punctuation might be different from comprehension). Different ways of constructing and implementing a curriculum might also impact growth across time. A spiral curriculum (where a concept is covered at multiple points in time, at increasing depth) might yield gradual growth, whereas a different implementation might yield a more stair-step pattern of growth. Additionally, how one chooses to assess growth will have an impact, as growth is generally operationally defined by some assessment tool.

In addition, there is the interaction with test construction/design. Should specifications be developed to meet a preexisting growth model or should the model of growth be developed based on empirical information obtained from an assessment built to a philosophy of curriculum? Given that results will differ depending on choice of particular practices, scaling methods, assessment forms, and so forth, how does one decide what to do? For example, Harris and Hoover (1987) found that examinees received higher ability estimates if the test level they were administered was calibrated on less able examinees. How should this information be used in selecting procedures? Could findings like this be manipulated for advantage? Or, are aspects of these issues somewhat irrelevant to most practitioners, as Yen and Burket (1997) suggested, as long as most comparisons tend to be within a grade, using the same instrument (e.g., fourth graders administered the ITBS are compared to other fourth graders administered the ITBS)?

One problem in trying to address the issue of defining growth is that test publishers rarely make the information explicit. It seems likely that most definitions are determined operationally, based on a combination of empirical data, the test development process, and preconceptions regarding the nature of growth. For example, a practitioner who believes within-grade variance should remain constant over grades might not develop test specifications or a data collection design with this in mind, but might reject scaling methods that resulted in large changes in within-grade variance over grades.

In our example, the nature of growth for the PLAN and ACT mathematics scale was determined using two main sources of information: curriculum surveys, content experts, and educators, and empirical data. The former were used to develop the test specifications, which included the content covered on both assessments and the targeted difficulty and complexity of the content. Empirical data were then used to operationally define, for example, within-grade variability.

13.3. Technical Issues

The separation of technical and implementation issues followed here is admittedly arbitrary. The intent is to separate the decision to use, say, the three-parameter logistic model in scaling from the particular choice of estimation program used to estimate item parameters.

When initially developing a score scale, decisions need to be made as to the number of score points, how the scale will be anchored, how vertically scaled levels are mapped into the score scale, how equated raw scores or thetas are mapped onto the scale (linearly? normalized? arcsine transformation?), and how, where, or if gaps or clumping (multiple raw scores mapping into a single reported score) occur. Is the scale to have a target mean and standard deviation for a particular population or sample? Are the scale values integers? Two digits? Are the values chosen likely to be confused with some other scale? Does the scale aid in score interpretation or detract from it? Most scales are not equal interval, despite some claims to the contrary. Is this clear to users? What is the best scale to measure growth?

Yen and Burket (1997) discussed the need for criteria regarding what makes for a desirable scale. Even if we could define the gold standard in terms of what characteristics a good scale should have, we are still left with the problem of how to obtain these properties. How do we manipulate the results obtained from some objective set of procedures and software? Do we smooth? If so, how much and with what method? What are the ideal characteristics that a scale should possess? Tomkowicz and Schaeffer (2002) provided a case study into manipulating results to obtain a final scale with what they viewed as desirable scale characteristics. How much subjective manipulation is acceptable? And as there really is little that is objective about the choice of software to use, the methods to use, the data to use, and so forth, does it really matter?

13.3.1. Data Collection Design

One of the most obvious choices in collecting data to scale a test is the data collection design (see Kolen, Chapter 3). According to Kolen and Brennan (2004), "It needs to be made explicit that the differences between the grade-equivalent scales of test publishers lie mainly in the method of data collection (e.g., scaling test versus anchor test), not in the statistical method used to link the test levels" (p. 235).

Different data collection designs can be used to create vertical scales, such as scaling test, common items, or single group to scaling test (a separate test containing, for example, both third and fourth-grade items, which is administered to both third- and fourth-grade students in addition to the regular third- or fourth-grade test, respectively), common items (a set of anchor items appearing, e.g., in both the third- and the fourth-grade tests), or single group (where one group of students is administered, e.g., both a third-grade test and a fourth-grade test). Common items can be internal or external, they can span the entire range of content and difficulty, or any subset of the range. The number of items required to provide adequate linking using common items has not been determined. What characteristics the sample of examinees need to display has not been determined, nor has the number of examinees required for vertical scaling been agreed upon. No general rules exist in terms of how to edit items or data; there is no consensus on how to use goodness-of-fit indexes in determining whether to retain items or examinees in establishing vertical scales. No single combination of methodology, data collection design, and sample has been found to be superior to others to a generalizable extent, and most designs seem to work well in at least some of the settings studied.

It should be noted that the way a design is implemented also can vary. For example, a scaling test can cover the full range of, say, grade 3 to grade 8, or there can be two scaling tests that cover, say, grades 3 to 6 and 5 to 8, and so on. In addition, some common-item designs are implemented with overlap to both a higher and lower level (e.g., grade 5 overlaps with both grade 6 and grade 4) or to only a lower level (e.g., grade 5 only overlaps with grade 4). At times, two distinct designs (e.g., scaling test and common item) on a particular battery might have more in common than the same method (e.g., common item, across two batteries). For example, the common-item design used in Boughton, Lorie, and Yao (2005), where the common items are scattered throughout a test form and the linking is one-directional in that a grade 5 test also includes grade 4 items, but a grade 4 test does not include grade 5 items, is very different from the common-item design used in Tong (2005) and Hendrickson, Wei, Kolen, and Tong (2005) where the common items are concentrated at the ends of the test forms, and tests overlap with both the next higher and the next lower grade (i.e., a grade 5 test has both grade 4 and grade 6 items). (It should be noted that the determination of the common item pattern is not just a data collection issue, it is also impacted by the test specifications and the nature of growth.)

Practical issues such as testing time and the nature of the items (it is difficult to have common-item designs with some types of passage-based item or constructed response item) as well as the nature and number of examinees available for scaling also impact how data are collected. Crocker and Algina (1986) stated that the these sorts of practical issue are often the "prime criterion" in selecting a data collection design for equating, but that the main criteria should be the tenability of the design assumptions, practicality, and accuracy. This is likely to also hold for vertical scaling.

Hendrickson, Kolen, and Tong (2004) found an interaction between scaling design (common item vs. scaling test) and calibration procedure; Loyd and Plake (1987) also found that design can have a substantial influence on the results. Andrews (1995) found that score scales developed with different methods and different designs differed enough to consider scaling design as an "important factor" when creating a vertical scale.

Raju, Edwards, and Osberg (1983) examined the effect of anchor-test size in vertical scaling with Rasch and 3PL and found that shorter anchors (as few as six items) could be as effective as longer ones. Barron and Hoover (2001) found context effects to be problematic in using common items to create a vertical scale. Harris (1991) found that although both designs appeared adequate, Angoff's Design 2 (counterbalanced, single group design) exhibited more stability than Angoff's Design 1 (random groups design). Kolen (Chapter 3) provided a current updated description of Angoff's designs. Holmes (1982) compared a single group method and two external anchor common-item methods and found that the single group method consistently produced the most accurate results, although the advantage was small.

Various operational vertical scales have been established using different data collection designs. The Stanford Achievement Test Series (Harcourt Educational Measurement; 1985) and Metropolitan Achievement Tests (The Psychological Corporation, 1988) used a single group design variant: Each student was administered two adjacent levels. The Mississippi Curriculum Test (Tomkowicz & Schaeffer, 2002) used internal anchor items to link to the TerraNova K-12 assessment system. The Iowa Tests of Basic Skills (Iowa Tests of Basic Skills, 2003) used a scaling test design.

In our example, the goal of the scaling was to place PLAN scores on the existing ACT score scale. Data from a random groups design were used as the primary data (12th graders were randomly administered the ACT or the

PLAN), with data from a random groups design (10th graders were randomly administered the ACT or the PLAN) and two single group designs (11th graders and 12th graders administered both ACT and PLAN, in a counterbalanced order) used to evaluate potential scales and to check assumptions of the scaling.

13.3.2. Scaling Methods

Different methods of developing scores include normatively, Guttman scaling (which might be unrealistic in practice; see Kolen & Brennan, 2004, who suggested that the probabilistic approach is more likely to be appropriate in practice than the deterministic approach), Thurstone scaling, Hieronymus scaling, and IRT scaling. Kolen and Brennan, and Petersen et al. (1989) discussed these methods, and scale construction in general, including linear and nonlinear transformations, creating scales that incorporate content meaning, or normative meaning, or score precision information, as well as developmental score scales such as grade equivalents. The PLAN and ACT mathematics tests were scaled using an equal-standard-error-of-measurement property (see ACT, 1989).

13.3.3. Reported Scale

Reported scores are generally integer scores or decimal scores rounded to a preset number of decimal places. When using IRT methodology, it would be possible to report ability estimates such as thetas or logits, rather than scores, although it generally is not done. It is assumed that examinees and general users of test results would have difficulty interpreting estimated theta or logit values. Commonly, some underlying scale is developed as a result of the scaling method, which is then transformed in some way to a reported scale. This can involve linear or nonlinear transformations, truncation, extrapolation, and rounding.

Numerous examples of different types of scales exist. For example, Angoff (1971) listed percent mastery, standard scores, percentile ranks, normalized standard scores, age-equivalent scores, grade-equivalent scores, and IQ scores. Petersen et al. (1989) discussed having primary and secondary scales. They advocated creating reported scales that facilitate score meaning and minimize likely score misinterpretations, such as being confused with another score scale that already exists.

Kolen and Brennan (2004) provided additional examples of scales based on psychometric models, including Thurstone and Rasch; domain scores are also discussed. Additional issues include how to compute raw scores on a test (e.g., number correct, pattern scoring, corrected for guessing) and how to scale tests within a test battery. (Should all tests be scaled the same way and/or have the same range of score values, even if the range is not optimal for all tests within the battery?) Should estimated true scores be used? For multiple-choice tests, should scores below the "chance" level be truncated? If you use normative information in creating a scale, on what group should the norms be based? If you use an equal standard error of measurement (SEM) method, what reliability values should be used? For example, if the number of achievable scores differs for math and language arts, do we want the same number of reported scale score points? (Kolen & Brennan, p. 345, suggested some ways to determine a reasonable number of score points.)

One important issue with some constructed response items is that raw scores for a prompt generally have meaning based on the scoring rubric. Depending on how those scores are combined with other items and then transformed into a reported score, this direct meaning might be lost.

In our example, the reported scale for PLAN is 1-32 on the 1–36 ACT scale. Because the PLAN assessment does not contain the more difficult items that the ACT assessment does, it was determined that the maximum scale score achievable for PLAN should be less than the maximum score achievable for ACT. A top of 32 was arrived at empirically, from examining data, test specifications, and scale characteristics.

13.3.4. Criteria

What are meaningful ways to compare different vertical scales resulting from different methodologies? What criteria do we use? Effect sizes? Heuristics/common sense? Is there some objective measure that could be applied, such as the reliability of gain scores on the scale, or empirical studies involving multiple test forms and multiple occasions? How do we determine if one scale is better than another or if a particular scale is acceptable? One very important and neglected area is how to evaluate if a scaling is acceptable or best.

Harris and Crouse (1993) summarized the various criteria that have been applied in equating studies and gave an example of how different criteria change the resulting decision on what is best equating; something similar should be done for vertical scaling.

Arce-Ferrer, Frisbie, and Kolen (2002) used the standard error of proportions in reporting changes in school performance with achievement levels. Holland (2002) proposed two measures of distance to examine the difference between two cumulative distribution functions: the vertical (difference in percent at the same score) and horizontal (difference in percentiles for the same percentage) distances. Tong and Kolen (2005) used effect sizes. Other studies have used cross-validation (e.g., Holmes, 1982), "reasonableness," such as grade-to-grade growth (e.g., Karkee, Lewis, Hoskens, Yao, & Haug, 2003), and first-order equity (e.g., Harris, 1991). Simulations have been used, but as the data are simulated to fit a particular model, recovery of "truth" might be a more useful criterion for examining issues such as the effect of concurrent or separate calibrations than in evaluating the resulting scales themselves. Yen (1986) argued that "clearer criteria are needed for judging the appropriateness and usefulness of alternative scaling procedures and more information is needed about the qualities of the different scales that are available" (p. 299).

Criteria need to be determined that will be generally accepted as a way to evaluate the acceptability of a vertical scale. Two primary criteria were used in evaluating placing PLAN on the existing ACT scale: how closely the same-scale property was met (meaning an obtained PLAN scale score can be interpreted as approximately the ACT scale score that an examinee would have obtained if he/she has taken the ACT at the same time that the PLAN was taken) and how equal the conditional SEM was across the score scale range. Other factors, such as gaps in the reported scale, were also considered.

13.4. Implementation Issues

Many issues arise in the construction of vertical scales, which might be loosely grouped under the umbrella of "technical issues." These include scale indeterminacy, calibration method (concurrent, separate, etc.), choice of item parameter linking (mean-sigma, a curvilinear method, etc.) for placing separate item parameter calibrations on the same scale, choice of model (classical, IRT, testlet, polytomous, number of parameters, etc.), choice of item parameter estimation procedure, and so on. Much of the vertical scaling literature that does exist compares and contrasts scales created using different technical methods. However, there is no definitive comparison study (it is unlikely that there could be), and the practitioner does not have any unequivocal guidelines to follow.

There are a multitude of methodologies and variations on these methodologies that can be used to create vertical scales. If an assessment includes both constructed response and multiple-choice types of items, they might be scaled in a single calibration run, or scaled separately and combined later. Examinee raw scores might be computed by using a number correct score, a corrected-for-guessing score, or an IRT-based score (typically, theta). Different items or contents or sections can be weighted differentially, and combined in various ways, to form raw scores.

Item calibrations can be conducted concurrently, or separately. Fixed item parameters can be used, or various item parameter linking procedures, such as item characteristic curve methods or mean-sigma, have been used to place item parameter estimates from separate calibrations on a common scale. Different approaches exist to chain different calibration runs together. Different "bases" can be used, such as scaling through a calibrated item pool or a base form approach. For, say, a K-8 battery, any grade test from K to 8 could be used as the base form to create the scale. No single combination of methodology, data collection design, and sample has been found to be superior to others to a generalizable extent; most designs seem to work well in at least some of the settings studied.

New, innovative methods are also being explored, such as the hierarchical and multivariate modeling approaches discussed in Patz, Yao, Chi, Lewis, and Hoskens (2003) and Patz and Yao (Chapter 14). The hierarchical multigroup method allows the functional form of growth to be explicitly estimated, whereas the multidimensional multigroup model can consider the dimensionality differences that occur at different levels. Although the authors presented these models as exploratory, it is clear that they address some additional issues related to vertical scaling that bear further research.

Research summaries should be created (along the lines of meta-analyses?) to summarize when particular methods appear to work well. Research comparing the results of applying different combinations of methods should be continued. One of the best exchanges I am aware of were the IRT versus classical scaling exchanges: There were IRT advocates implementing classical methods and classical advocates implementing IRT methods, different data, different implementation decisions, inconsistent results, and so on. It was a relatively open exchange of impact (results of the two approaches) and we all benefited from it. For the PLAN–ACT example, details, including the strong true-score model used, specifics regarding the examinee samples, the formulas used in computing the SEM and the same-scale property are provided in ACT (1999). Note that not all operational vertical scalings are this well documented in the public domain.

One implementation issue that is especially important is the choice of software. Although some vertical scaling can be done by hand, virtually all research and operational scaling makes use of computer programs. Most software programs make numerous options available, although many users likely implement only default settings. Although programs certainly differ in the extent of documentation and the ease of implementing alternatives, users frequently lack the knowledge to make an informed decision. For example, a smoothing program might offer degrees of .05 and .10, as defaults, yet provide no guidance to the user for determining which of these would be a better alternative. Some programs provide limited information as to what algorithms are used, how to interpret output, and how truncation, interpolation, extrapolation, smoothing, and so on are handled, which can impact the final reported scale values.

Perhaps one of the less considered decisions is that of which IRT calibration program to use. Several authors found the particular software used for IRT parameter estimation could have an impact. In addition to the more obvious estimation method differences, (e.g., Hendrickson et al., 2004, looked at three IRT proficiency estimation procedures: expected a posteriori [EAP], maximum a posteriori [MAP], and maximum likelihood estimate [MLE], even issues as subtle as the number of EM cycles in BilogMG or whether to use default settings might have an impact.

Programs are complex and the manuals are often obscure about what computations are actually being done, and for proprietary reasons, source code is generally not available. When a publisher uses a program developed in-house, there is generally even less information about the program made available, making it difficult to know the effect of the program (what options were used, how calculations were done, etc.) on the final scale. One solution is for the test developer to do comparison studies, although, admittedly, a case could be made that a disinterested party would be preferred. Fitzpatrick (1994), for example, compared parameter estimates produced by PARDUX and BIGSTEPS.

Way, Twing, and Ansley (1988) compared Bilog and Logist using two different calibration procedures, as did Omar and Hoover (1997). Omar (1997) followed up on the previous study, examining BilogMG. Childs and Chen (1999) described obtaining comparable item parameter estimates from MULTILOG and PARSCALE. Pomplun, Omar, and Custer (2004) compared WINSTEPS and BilogMG, finding that WINSTEPS tended to result in more accurate individual and mean measurement, whereas BilogMG resulted in more accurate standard deviations. Hendrickson et al. (2004) compared MULTILOG and ICL and found that the computer program/estimation method used impacted the resulting vertical scale.

Limitations, such as the number of categories allowed for polytomous items, or the size of a data matrix that can be input, might also affect the final vertical scales, as they require collapsing of data categories or the winnowing of data. Bishop and Omar (2002) mentioned that in their study, a number of decisions had to be made, such as collapsing categories of data, because of limitations in the software used. Writing one's own programs might eliminate this problem, but this leads to the issue of potential lack of comparability with other investigators, making consistencies and inconsistencies in different methods of scaling, and so forth more difficult to discern.

Most of the studies reported in the literature do not provide much detail on how computer runs were conducted, although some exceptions exist (e.g., Jodoin, Keller, & Swaminathan, 2003, provided information on the optional commands they used). Proprietary software was used in the scaling of PLAN and ACT; information on the algorithms used is provided in ACT (1999).

To summarize, there is no clear guidance to a practitioner on what software to use in vertical scaling. When new versions of software appear, it is up to the practitioner to determine, for example, if parameter estimates calculated under the new and old versions are comparable. It is suggested that more use be made of open-source software, where, for good and bad, how calculations are done is publicly available.

13.5. Scale Maintenance Issues

One issue that has not been addressed much in the literature is that of maintaining vertical scales over time and over new forms. For example, should new grade 3 forms be equated to the original grade 3 form or should there be an attempt to link the entire range of, say, grade K to grade 8 forms to the original set of forms on which the scale was set? What types of drift, or error, are we apt to see over time? How often should a vertical scale be monitored? Reevaluated? Reconstructed? Because of the different results that different procedures have lead to, what are the dangers of "mixing and matching" procedures over time? Also, what is the trade-off between what is practically possible and what is best from a consistency standpoint?

Issues such as data collection designs, equating methodologies, and examinee sample characteristics need to be considered in equating new forms to a vertical scale (see Kolen, Chapter 3 for additional discussion of these issues). How equating is defined, whether by Lord's (1980) equity definition, Angoff's (1971) equipercentile definition, Divgi's (1981) two approaches, Morris' (1982) method including conditional variance, an IRT true-score definition, or some other definition, should guide the equating of new forms (see Harris & Crouse, 1993). A choice of equating methodology needs to be made, which might or might not correspond to the methodology used to scale. For example, IRT could be used to create the vertical scale, but classical methods, such as equipercentile methods, could be used to equate new forms. However, if the assessment is constructed using IRT procedures, equating (and scaling) the test using IRT could take advantage of the test development procedures.

An equating is always referenced to a particular population of examinees (Flanagan, 1964). The data collection design/samples combination is the most important part of any equating study (assuming, of course, that the characteristics of the instruments make equating defensible). No equating methodology exists that can counteract bad data. One of the most important sample characteristics (in addition to size of the sample, motivation, and appropriateness for the test being equated) is that the sample be representative of the population in which one is interested.

There is no easy mechanism to apply to determine which equating method is preferable in any given situation. Additionally, there is no universally accepted criterion to know if an equating is best or even acceptable. When the new forms are part of a vertical scale, the issues are much more complex. Also, whether, say, new forms at one level are equated separately from new forms at a different level depends in part on how new forms are introduced. For example, if a new battery is introduced at a single point in time, and not very frequently, equating the new forms to the previous scale simultaneously might be done. However, if new forms are introduced frequently, and at different times, equating the forms separately is more practical.

Hoskens, Lewis, and Patz (2003) looked at maintaining a vertical scale over time, examining several approaches, including equating within each grade, an augmented approach that used both vertical and horizontal anchors, and a concurrent and a separate method of setting a new vertical scale for all grades concurrently and linking it to the previous vertical scale. They found that the method chosen had an impact, with the horizontal and augmented methods indicating grade-to-grade variability was relatively flat, and the other methods indicating an increase in variability.

There are additional practical issues that might also affect the stability of scales, such as changes in software used to calibrate items (e.g., a change from Bilog to BilogMG) or a change in a vendor (e.g., when a state department moves its test development from one testing company to another).

In our example, new forms of the PLAN and ACT mathematics assessments are equated. The stability of the PLAN-ACT scale over time was checked in 1995, using a scaling test design. Both the original methodology (equal SEM method) and IRT methodology were used to create PLAN scores, which were then compared to the existing PLAN scores. The resulting scales were somewhat different, which was expected because of the different design (there was a test length adjustment used in the 1988 scaling, as well as a difference from a random groups to a scaling test design) and a slight change in the test specifications for PLAN between the form used for the 1988 scaling and the form used in the 1995 scale. It was determined, however, that the differences were not compelling. It should be noted this was not a traditional examination of scale drift, but a comparison of an entirely new scale created under different circumstances, to the original scale. A change in administration policy to allow the use of calculators on the mathematics assessments in 1996 also led to a reexamination of the PLAN-ACT scale.

13.6. Other Issues

Issues that arise in other contexts (e.g., single-grade-level testing) might be magnified in a vertical scaling context. Some of these issues were mentioned earlier, such as content dimensionality issues, but other issues, such as moving a paper-and-pencil test to a computer-based test, were not. (See Eignor, Chapter 8, for a discussion of issues related to moving from a paper mode to a computer mode.) The fact that multiple levels need to be considered simultaneously increases the complexity of dealing with issues such as these. Issues arise when not all examinees answer all items, whether from a matrix sampling design or from an examinee choice model, where an examinee chooses, for example, which two questions to answer of the five questions available. These issues become more complex when the consistency of scores needs to be maintained vertically (across grades) as well as horizontally (within a grade). This is also true for issues such as modifications in test specifications, conducting standard settings (assuming there is a desire for continuity across grades), translating the test into other languages, preequating test forms, pretesting items, and dealing with test speededness and guessing issues. Technical issues, such as establishing validity for score use or computing reliability coefficients, as well as operational issues such as training raters to grade essay responses are more problematic in a vertical scaling context. Although it is possible to establish a scale initially and then subsequently treat each grade separately, there still needs to be monitoring across the entire range of grades to ensure reasonableness (e.g., that a cutoff for adequate performance is not set at a score of 130 for grade 3 and at 120 for grade 4).

Although these issues might (e.g., dimensionality) or might not (e.g., translation issues) directly impact the setting of the vertical scale, they all might impact the usefulness of the scale as it is put into operational use.

13.7. Summary

This chapter presents issues that a practitioner would encounter when developing a vertical scale for an operational testing program: using a framework of conceptual issues, technical issues, implementation issues, maintenance issues, and other issues. The scaling of the PLAN and ACT mathematics tests is used as an example to demonstrate some of the issues underlying vertical scales. The practitioner who chooses methods with careful attention to his/her purpose of the scale (i.e., how the resulting scores are intended to be used) and to the literature and current practices of other test publishers is more likely to create a scale that will lead to scores on which appropriate decisions can be made.

Vertical scaling is a complex process, involving philosophical, technical, and practical issues. Although it can be disconcerting that there is no consensus on the best way to create a scale, it is also comforting. Many assessments, such as ITBS (Iowa Test of Basic Skills, 2003), Stanford Achievement Test (Harcourt Educational Measurement, 1985), and EPAS (ACT, 2000), state-specific tests, and so on, have created vertical scales in different ways, yet all of those scales appear to be functioning adequately for some of the same purposes. Perhaps there are many roads to Rome. However, that does not mean that all roads lead to Rome, or that all implementations of vertical scaling lead to acceptable scales for all purposes. Instead of arguing which single scaling method is the best, we might do better to see which slate of options work for which purposes, under which conditions.

14 Methods and Models for Vertical Scaling

Richard J. Patz and Lihua Yao[1]

CTB/McGraw-Hill

14.1. Introduction

When one test form is significantly and intentionally more difficult than another, a link that places scores from these test forms on a common scale might be called a "vertical" link, and the scale on which the scores are reported will commonly be called a "vertical scale." Tests might be scaled so that they support interpretations that are not available by examining or summarizing only the items answered correctly or incorrectly. Scaling allows one to compare scores from different test forms, and vertical scaling is intended to support the comparison of scores obtained at each of a number of test forms (or "levels") of systematically different difficulty. When differences in population proficiency at adjacent levels are modest in comparison to differences between examinees within levels and when the expectations or standards against which examinees are to be measured overlap extensively, then linking the adjacent test levels to a common scale will generally make sense and provide meaningful information. These conditions are satisfied in the case of achievement test batteries that measure development of proficiency in broad domains such as reading and mathematics. For a more formal way of examining content overlap that might support meaningful vertical scaling, see Wise and Alt (2006). Tests that are vertically scaled are intended to support valid inferences regarding growth over time, and they also support the use of "out-of-level" testing, which can be a prescribed accommodation for some students.

---

[1] The opinions expressed in this chapter are those of the authors and not necessarily of CTB/McGraw-Hill.

There are significant limitations to the inferences supported by vertical scaling of test forms. Because adjacent test levels are not parallel forms, vertical scaling does not constitute an equating of forms in the sense defined in Holland (Chapter 2, Section 2.4.1). Rather, it represents a form of test linking. Furthermore, the validity of inferences based on such linkages will depend on the strength of the link. Under most vertical scaling research designs, the strength of the link will generally diminish as the distance between test levels increases; that is, although an achievement test battery might measure achievement in mathematics on a scale that spans grades 2 to 10, comparisons between scores based on the 2nd- and 10th-grade forms will typically not be well supported, although comparisons based on adjacent forms (e.g., grades 2 to 3) might be very well supported.

In this chapter we examine the statistical modeling issues in analyzing and reporting information from vertically linked test forms. In Section 14.2 we discuss general modeling issues that one must consider when evaluating approaches to vertical scaling. In Section 14.3 we develop and implement a multigroup multidimensional item response theory (IRT) model for vertical scaling. We conclude with a general discussion of the standard and emerging modeling approaches.

14.2. General Modeling Issues in Vertical Scaling Contexts

We will focus on IRT scales in this chapter, but it is worth noting at the start that assessments that measure growth over large grade spans on a common scale predate modern advances in item IRT. For example, editions of the *California Achievement Tests* published before 1980 (e.g., CTB/McGraw-Hill, 1979) used Thurstone scaling (Thurstone, 1928), as described in Gulliksen (1950, pp. 284–286). Under this version of Thurstone scaling, raw scores (i.e., number correct scores) for equivalent groups of examinees are normalized and linearly equated.

Testing a nationally representative sample of students at a range of grade levels via common or linked test forms allows one to derive grade-equivalent scales. A student's grade-equivalent score is defined as the grade level for which the student's performance is the national median. A special 1984 edition of *Educational Measurement: Issues and Practice* (Hoover, 1984a, 1984b; Burket, 1984) presents a discussion of historical approaches to the development of vertical scales for achievement test batteries, with an emphasis on the advantages and disadvantages of grade-equivalent scores.

The IRT scales are based on probabilistic models for examinee responses to individual items (Lord, 1980). Comparisons of IRT and Thurstone scales in a variety of contexts can be found in Yen (1986), Yen and Burket (1997), and Williams, Pommerich, and Thissen (1998).

Item response models describe the probability with which an examinee, with proficiency described by a score on a continuous scale, responds correctly (or provides a partially correct response) to each of a set of items. Examples include the one-parameter (Rasch, 1960), two-parameter, or three-parameter logistic models (Birnbaum, 1968) that one typically uses for dichotomously scored multiple-choice items, as well as (generalized) partial credit models (e.g., Fischer, 1995; Muraki, 1992; Yen, 1993) for polytomously scored constructed-response items.

When one fits any of these IRT models to examinee response data, the resulting "latent variable" proficiency estimate for any examinee is statistically identified as that variable that explains the statistical dependence of responses to multiple items by individual examinees. Conditional independence of item responses given proficiency is a fundamental IRT modeling assumption, and it has direct implications not only for model building and estimation but also for interpretation of reported scale scores. Scale scores have an immediate interpretation, not only as the general proficiency on the domain defined by the items on the exam but also in terms of the probability with which an examinee correctly responds to particular items. This observation is exploited, for example, in standard setting procedures that elicit judgments regarding required levels of mastery on a set of items that are ordered by difficulty (e.g., Bookmark standard setting as introduced by Lewis, Mitzel, & Green, 1995; see also Mitzel, Lewis, Patz, & Green, 2001).

Properly developed vertical scales add several compelling features to achievement tests. They facilitate the estimation and tracking of growth over time. For instance, we might obtain repeated measures on individual students using different age- and grade-appropriate test forms. These measures would help us determine how much growth has occurred at different intervals. Second, it would appear that vertically scaled achievement tests would allow more robust comparisons, relative to single, cross-grade administrations. In particular, vertical scales allow comparisons of one grade level to another and of one cohort to another.

Less obvious, but perhaps equally important, is the fact that vertical scaling allows additional comparisons between test items. Vertical scaling can lead to more efficient field testing of new content, as items targeted for one grade might be found to be of more appropriate difficulty for an adjacent grade. Final form selection for a target grade can then identify appropriate items from a larger pool. In addition, standard setting can be made more reliable, because a richer set of items (from adjacent levels of the test) might be ordered and the scale more finely segmented as the density of items increases.

All of these advantages that vertical scaling promise to deliver rest on the accuracy of the information provided by the vertical scaling analysis. In the case of IRT models, this information comes in the form of model parameters, the appropriateness and fit of the model, and the reliability with which model parameters can be estimated. For these reasons, we encourage extensive examination of modeling approaches that support vertical scaling.

14.2.1. Unified Versus Divide-and-Conquer Statistical Modeling and Analysis in Educational Assessment

Complex inference problems lend themselves to "divide-and-conquer" analysis strategies, where one breaks the problem down into a series of simpler problems that are tackled in sequence. Educational assessment programs regularly employ this strategy.

The National Assessment of Educational Progress (NAEP), for example, has the complicated task of measuring and tracking, over time, the achievement of students in the nation as a whole as well as in selected subgroups of the nation. Divide-and-conquer features of the NAEP analyses include the following: (a) Errors in the rating process for constructed-response items are monitored during the scoring, but then assumed to not exist in subsequent analyses; (b) IRT item parameters are estimated using a simple $N(0,1)$ model for proficiency and then assumed to be fixed and known at their estimated values in subsequent analyses (Patz & Junker, 1999b).

Similarly, operational scoring of standardized tests typically proceeds under an assumption that the test's characteristics (e.g., item parameters, raw-score to scale-score conversions) are known and fixed at values based on an earlier analysis. Although it would be possible to reestimate test characteristics for the population being scored, that would not be feasible in practice for many applications. Furthermore, for certain inferences regarding test scores (e.g., comparisons with a norm group), it would not be desirable to reestimate the item and test characteristics.

Divide-and-conquer analyses have advantages that extend beyond their ability to work where more unified or integrated approaches might fail. The results of each subanalysis will generally be easy to interpret, and this might be especially important for validity in assessment contexts. Furthermore, sources of uncertainty or model misspecification might be easier to identify and easier to isolate from other analyses. For example, if an IRT model does not fit response data well, this fact might be easier to identify in an analysis that focuses on the IRT model and does not include parameters for rater accuracy or parameters for subpopulation effects. A clear disadvantage of a divide-and-conquer analysis, however, is the difficulty associated with propagating errors or uncertainty from one part of the analysis to another. For example, standard errors associated with mean achievement levels in NAEP do not reflect any uncertainty attributable to errors in the human rating process.

Vertical scaling data (i.e., data from tests administered at an ordered set of grade levels) lends itself to both divide-and-conquer and unified analyses. Unified analysis might take the form of the concurrent estimation of a single unidimensional IRT model that spans the grade levels and models the population proficiency distribution for each grade. Divide-and-conquer approaches might involve separate unidimensional analysis of data from each grade level (or possibly pairs of levels), followed by an analysis focused on the relationships between the grade-by-grade results.

There has been some study of the relative performance of divide-and-conquer versus unified analysis (i.e., separate vs. concurrent IRT estimation) in the case of equating (Hanson & Béguin, 2002; Kim & Cohen, 1998; Petersen, Cook, & Stocking, 1983). There is some evidence that when the model is correctly specified, concurrent calibration produces more accurate results than separate calibration. Hanson and Béguin provided some evidence to indicate that this is at least partly due to the fact that there is one set of parameter estimates for the common items, which is based on more data than the two separate sets of parameter estimates for the common items in separate calibration.

Several variations of divide-and-conquer are currently in use for vertical scaling. Karkee, Lewis, Hoskens, and Yao (2003) and Hoskens, Lewis, and Patz (2003) compared these methods to a unified (i.e., concurrent calibration) approach. These extensive analyses using real assessment data fail to indicate any advantage to the unified approach, but, instead, suggest that separate calibration by grade level might be superior. Patz and Hanson (2002) conjectured that whereas a concurrent calibration might produce more accurate results when the model is correctly specified, it might be that separate estimation or fixed estimation is more robust than concurrent estimation to model misspecification.

We next examine an extension of the concurrent calibration model in an effort to identify a modeling approach that will bring the advantages of unified analysis without the liability of model misfit. To do this and to aid in the comparisons, we next introduce a general model framework.

14.2.2. A General Hierarchical IRT Model Framework for Vertical Scaling

It is helpful to introduce a formal statistical model for examining general statistical issues in vertical scaling. We find Patz and Junker's (1999b) description useful here. Item response data consists of a set $\{X_{ij} : i = 1, 2, ..., N; j = 1, 2, ..., J\}$ of J discrete observations (or measures) on each of N individual examinees or subjects. IRT models quantify examinee i's propensity to answer item j correctly based on the examinee's location θ_i on a latent scale and on characteristics of the items captured by parameters β_j. We allow covariates $Y = (Y_1, Y_2, ..., Y_N)$ on subjects (e.g., demographic or grade-level information) and covariates $Z = (Z_1, Z_2, ..., Z_J)$ on items (perhaps conditions under which the items were administered). Finally, we will let $\lambda = (\lambda_1, \lambda_2, ..., \lambda_L)$ represent the parameters of the distribution of θ in the population; for example, if θ is assumed to be Normally distributed, then perhaps $\lambda = (\mu, \sigma)$, the usual normal mean and standard deviation parameters. We also assume independence of item responses within examinees given proficiency (i.e., local independence), and independence of item responses across subjects given θ and the relevant covariates. These assumptions imply that

$$p(X \mid \beta, \lambda, Y, Z) = \int p(X \mid \theta, \beta, \lambda, Y, Z) p(\theta \mid \beta, \lambda, Y, Z) d\theta$$

$$= \int p(X \mid \theta, \beta, Y, Z) p(\theta \mid \lambda, Y, Z) d\theta$$

$$= \int p(X \mid \theta, \beta, Z) p(\theta \mid \lambda, Y) d\theta \tag{14.1}$$

$$= \prod_{i=1}^{N} \int \prod_{j=1}^{J} p(X_{ij} \mid \theta_i, \beta_j, Z_j) p(\theta_i \mid \lambda, Y_i) d\theta_i,$$

where X_{ij} is the response of examinee i to item j. The second equality in Equation 14.1 embodies the assumptions stated earlier that (a) λ contains parameters of the θ distribution and not the item response functions (IRFs) and (b) β contains parameters of the item IRFs and not of the θ distribution. Similarly, the third equality states that Y contains covariates that can only affect X through their effect on the θ distribution, and Z contains covariates that affect X directly, not through the θ distribution. In general, any of the parameters, latent variables, or covariates in this setup can be multidimensional. Furthermore, all standard IRT models and estimation methods can be characterized in relation to this general framework.

In a fully Bayesian analysis, a prior distribution $p(\beta, \lambda \mid Y, Z)$ for the parameters λ and β is specified. It is usually most convenient to also assume that all parameters are a priori independent, so that for J items and L parameters characterizing the population distribution of θ,

$$p(\beta, \lambda \mid Y, Z) = p(\beta \mid Z) p(\lambda \mid Y) = \prod_1^J p_j(\beta_j \mid Z) \prod_1^L p_\ell(\lambda_\ell \mid Y).$$

Usually in IRT our interest is in features of the joint posterior $p(\theta, \beta, \lambda \mid X, Y, Z)$, which under the above assumptions we can write as

$$p(\theta, \beta, \lambda \mid X, Y, Z) \propto p(X \mid \theta, \beta, \lambda, Y, Z) p(\theta \mid \beta, \lambda, Y, Z) p(\beta \mid \lambda, Y, Z) p(\lambda \mid Y, Z) \quad (14.2)$$
$$= p(X \mid \theta, \beta, Z) p(\theta \mid \lambda, Y) p(\beta \mid Z) p(\lambda \mid Y),$$

where the constant of proportionality is allowed to depend on X, Y, and Z but not θ, β, or λ. For example, we might be interested in the expected a posteriori (EAP) and maximum a posteriori (MAP) values of parameters, posterior standard errors, and so forth, all of which can be calculated from Equation 14.2 (Patz & Junker, 1999b).

All unknown quantities of interest in the model, including the expected or most probable values of parameters, their statistical dependence on one another, and the degree of precision with which they can be characterized, are captured in this posterior distribution. Estimation and examination of this distribution will support unified analyses as generally described earlier. If the joint posterior distribution $p(\theta, \beta, \lambda \mid X, Y, Z)$ could not be estimated easily, we might resort to a divide-and-conquer approach involving a sequence of analyses, each of which focuses on one part of the model and makes simplifying assumptions regarding others.

Item response theory models commonly estimated using marginal maximum likelihood via the E-M algorithm might be seen as a special case of the general model described earlier. In this case, $p(X \mid \theta, \beta)$ is a standard unidimensional IRT model (e.g., 3PL), and characteristics λ of the proficiency distribution are fixed so that $p(\theta \mid \lambda) = N(0, 1)$. Separate calibration approaches to the vertical scaling problem might be viewed as repeated estimation of the simple IRT model (once for each grade), followed by a linear transformation of results based on a separate analysis of parameters of items common to two or more grades. (See, e.g., Hanson & Béguin, 2002)

Concurrent estimation of a unidimensional, multigroup, IRT model, which is the standard unified analysis of vertical scaling data, might also be seen as a special case of the general framework. Here again, $p(X \mid \theta, \beta)$

is a unidimensional IRT model, the covariate Y of interest is the grade level of the student, and features of the proficiency distribution λ are $\{\mu_g, \sigma_g\}_{g=1}^{G}$, the mean and standard deviation of the population at each grade g.

In the remainder of this chapter we will investigate a model in which θ is multidimensional. For an alternative treatment in which the proficiency distribution is treated hierarchically with a parameterized, cross-grade growth trajectory, see Patz and Yao (2007).

In order to implement the multidimensional modeling approach and to retain flexibility to easily examine modeling alternatives, we develop Markov chain Monte Carlo (MCMC) algorithms. MCMC can be implemented in a straightforward manner for fitting item response models (Patz & Junker, 1999a), and variations of standard IRT models can be developed and examined with relative ease using MCMC method (Béguin & Glas, 2001; Patz & Junker, 1999b).

14.3. A Multidimensional, Multigroup IRT Model for Vertical Scaling

We now examine an extension of unidimensional, multigroup IRT models for use in vertical scaling. We allow the ability distribution to be multidimensional and we estimate multidimensional item parameters.

An IRT assumption of unidimensionality is a convenient assumption with powerful implications. Measurement specialists generally recognize that unidimensionality will not hold exactly in real testing data and that violations of unidimensionality might be attributable to any number of factors: variations (or similarities) in content objectives, item formats, and response modes. One must consider carefully the threat that multidimensionality poses to the validity of unidimensional scores.

When calibrating items from a single test form, on which it has been determined that each student will receive a single score, the IRT assumption of unidimensionality must be viewed, not in relation to multidimensionality in general, but in relation to alternative ways of deriving a single score from analyzing responses to test content (e.g., creating an arithmetic average of several subscores). Mild deviations from unidimensionality might have only a very modest impact on the accuracy of scores.

When calibrating items from multiple test forms for the purpose of measuring students across a range of grade levels, the IRT assumption of unidimensionality would appear implausible. This is recognized implicitly by test publishers, who warn against making comparisons of scores arising from nonadjacent test scores. It is clear that tests measuring seventh-grade mathematics achievement are measuring different constructs than tests measuring fourth-grade mathematics achievement.

Developing a unified approach to modeling growth across grades in a domain of knowledge must take some account of these large differences in test content and examinee skills. Failure to account for this complexity, in general, and multidimensionality, in particular, is very possibly the reason that concurrent calibration of a unidimensional IRT model fails to perform well in practice (Hoskens et al., 2003; Karkee et al., 2003).

In this section we develop and implement a multidimensional multigroup IRT model, and we explore the model characteristics and estimation properties by fitting the model to data from a state writing assessment program. This work builds on the work of Reckase (1985, 1997), Reckase and McKinley (1991), and Bèguin and Glas (2001), but extends the multidimensional approach to the multigroup case for application to vertical scaling problems. We completely specify the model in Section 14.3.1, and we describe the estimation approach in Section 14.3.2. In Section 14.3.3 we describe the dataset to which we fit the model, and in Section 14.3.4 we examine selected results. The data analyses are intended to assist in evaluating the modeling approach and estimation strategy. A thorough examination and discussion of the multidimensional properties of the dataset is not within the scope of this chapter.

14.3.1. Model Specification and Estimation

Let D be the number of subscales or the number of dimensions that need to be measured; then θ_i is a vector of dimension D for each examinee i.

For dichotomous item j, the probability of a correct response for an examinee with ability θ_i for the multidimensional three-parameter logistic (3PL; Reckase, 1997) model is

$$P_{i,j} = P(x_{i,j} = 1 \mid \theta_i, \beta_j) = \beta_{3,j} + \frac{1-\beta_{3,j}}{1+e^{(-\beta_{2,j} \odot \theta_i^T + \beta_{1,j})}}, \qquad (14.3)$$

where for each j,

- $x_{ij} = 0$ or 1 is the response of examinee i to item j.
- $\vec{\beta}_{2,j} \odot \vec{\theta}_i^T = \sum_{l=1}^{D} \beta_{2jl}\theta_{il}$ is a dot product.
- $\vec{\beta}_{2,j} = (\beta_{2j1},...,\beta_{2jD})$ is a vector of dimension D of item discrimination parameters.

- $\beta_{1,j}$ is the scale difficulty parameter.
- $\beta_{3,j}$ is the scale guessing parameter.

For polytomous item j, the probability of a response $k-1$ for an examinee with ability θ_i is given by the multidimensional two-parameter partial credit model (2PPC) as

$$P_{i,j,k} = P(x_{i,j} = k-1 \mid \theta_i, \beta_j) = \frac{e^{(k-1)\beta_{2,j}\odot\theta_i^T - \sum_{t=1}^{k}\beta_{\delta_t,j}}}{\sum_{m=1}^{K_j} e^{[(m-1)\beta_{2,j}\odot\theta_i^T - \sum_{t=1}^{m}\beta_{\delta_t,j}]}}, \tag{14.4}$$

where

- $x_{ij} = 0,..., K_j - 1$ is the response of examinee i to item j.
- $\beta_{2,j} = (\beta_{2j1},..., \beta_{2jD})$ is a vector of dimension D for the item discrimination parameters.
- $\beta_{\delta_k j}$ for $k = 1,2,...,K_j$ are the threshold or alpha parameters, $\beta_{\delta_1 j} = 0$, and K_j is the number of response categories for the jth item.

A related multidimensional modeling approach for dichotomous and polytomous items, multidimensional random coefficients multinomial logit (MRCML) models, was developed by Adams, Wilson, and Wang (1997). These models are generalizations in the Rasch family of models, with slope parameters that are not estimated but can be specified. Comparisons between our approach and that of MRCML models would be possible in confirmatory applications.

Note that the multidimensional model we have specified is *compensatory* in nature, so that higher ability on one dimension might compensate for lower ability on another dimension; that is, the same dot product and success probability might be achieved with different profiles of abilities.

14.3.2. The Estimation Method

We estimate the model using MCMC methods. The item and ability parameters are estimated using the Metropolis-Hasting algorithm that samples from the joint posterior distribution (Patz & Junker, 1999a, 1999b). The estimation algorithms were implemented in the computer program BMIRT (Bayesian Multivariate Item Response Theory; Yao, 2003).

14.3.3. Data

The data for this study were extracted from responses to the 2002 Colorado Student Assessment Program (CSAP) writing assessments in grades 3 through 10. Illustrative results are presented here for grades 3 though 7 only. Each assessment is composed of both multiple-choice and constructed-response items. Between 24% and 25%t of the items are constructed-response items in grades 4 through 7; constructed-response items composed 34% of the grade 3 assessment. The configurations of the 2002 CSAP writing assessments for grades 3 through 7 are shown in Table 14.1.

Table 14.1. Configuration item types for 2002 Colorado Student Assessment Program

Grade	Maximum possible points	Total no. of items		Frequency of CR items with the given number of obtainable scores			
		MC	CR	1	2	3	4
3	56	35	18	15	3	0	0
4	69	40	13	7	1	0	5
5	70	41	13	7	1	0	5
6	71	42	13	7	1	0	5
7	67	38	13	7	1	0	5

Note. MC: multiple choice; CR: constructed response.

Writing is measured by two standards on the CSAP assessment:

- Standard 1. "Write for a Variety of Purposes." Students write and speak for a variety of purposes and audiences.
- Standard 2. "Write Using Conventions." Students write and speak using conventional grammar, usage, sentence structure, punctuation, capitalization, and spelling.

As indicated in Table 14.2, the proportion of items measuring Standard 1 and Standard 2 tends to change with grade. In grade 3, nearly two-thirds of the score points measure the use of writing conventions; the proportions of score points measuring Standards 1 and 2 are 34% and 66%, respectively. The relative contribution of each standard to the total score changes nearly uniformly; by grade 7, the proportions of score points measuring Standards 1 and 2 are 54% and 46%, respectively.

14.3.3.1. Common-Item Design

The assessments were constructed with common items between adjacent grades to support the establishment of a vertical scale. This was accomplished by (a) constructing a "core" test at each grade based on the test frameworks, (b) selecting items from each core test that were appropriate in terms of standards coverage, curriculum, and range of difficulty for the grade above (except in grade 10, for which there is no tested grade above), and (c) similarly selecting items appropriate for the grade below (except in grade 3, for which there is no tested grade below). The target of 10 items from the core test appropriate for the adjacent grade above and 10 items appropriate for the grade below was set to provide a target of 20 items in common between grades. In order to maintain the test framework at each grade, the set of common items was specified to be representative of the overall test in terms of standards representation, range of difficulty, and, when possible, item format. However, due to content constraints, this target was not always met.

Table 14.2. Number of obtainable score points and percent of total score by item type and standard for the CSAP assessments and common items

| Test items | Grade | Standard 1[a] | | | Standard 2[b] | | | Grand total | Percent of total score by standard | |
		MC	CR	Total	MC	CR	Total		St. 1 total	St. 2 total
Total	3	7	12	19	28	9	37	56	34	66
Common	3–4	5		5	13		13	18	36	64
Total	4	12	21	33	28	8	36	69	48	52
Common	4–5	7	4	11	11		11	22	50	50
Total	5	18	21	39	23	8	31	70	56	44
Common	5–6	8		8	10		10	18	44	56
Total	6	16	21	37	26	8	34	71	52	48
Common	6–7	5	4	9	14		14	23	39	61
Test	7	15	21	36	23	8	31	67	54	46

Note. MC: multiple choice; CR: constructed response; St.: standard.
[a]Standard 1 requires students to "Write for a Variety of Purposes."
[b]Standard 2 requires students to "Write Using Conventions."

As indicated in Table 14.2, there are an average of 20 obtainable score points from common items between grades, with a range from 18 to 23. Both multiple-choice and constructed-response items were used as common items between grade levels 4–5 and 6–7, whereas adjacent grade levels 3–4, and 5–6 had only multiple-choice items in common. The common items appeared in approximately the same location in each test in which the item appeared.

14.3.3.2. Sample

A data sample of 2,500 cases per grade selected for preliminary calibration analyses was used in the current study. The sample was drawn to be representative of the state in terms of gender, ethnicity, and distribution of students across Colorado's four performance levels.

14.3.4. Results of Model Fitting

We fit the multidimensional model to a number of subsets of the full CSAP writing dataset in order to examine the model behavior. The dimensional structure observable within each grade was examined using both the BMIRT software written to fit the model in this chapter as well as the item factor analysis program TestFact (Wilson, Wood, & Gibbons, 1987). TestFact can only be used for a test of multiple-choice items with specified (not estimated) guessing parameters, but TestFact analyses provide some independent results that shed some light on the BMIRT analyses.   In addition, we examined the dimensional structure of the combined, multigrade dataset.   We review selected results that illustrate the types of analysis that the modeling approach supports. A complete examination of dimensionality issues in this CSAP data is beyond the scope of this chapter.

14.3.4.1. Grade 3 Students on Multiple-Choice Items Common to Grades 3 and 4

We fit a two-dimensional model to the dataset consisting of responses by 2,500 grade 3 examinees to the items in common between the grade 3 and grade 4 forms. Parameter estimates are given in Table 14.3. Also presented is the angle of the item in relation to the axes for the two dimensions. The angles are computed from the slope parameters according to

$$\alpha_j = \arcsin(\frac{\beta_{2,j}}{(\sum_{l=1}^{D}\beta_{2,jl}^2)^{1/2}}) \tag{14.5}$$

for item j.

Because this dataset consists of multiple-choice items only from a single population of examinees, it is also possible to fit a similar two-dimensional IRT model using TestFact. TestFact uses an ogive rather than logistic function, and TestFact takes guessing parameters as input but does not estimate them. A reasonable comparison between the two fits might be the correlation between slope parameter estimated for each item on each dimension from BMIRT and the slope parameter estimated by TestFact. Table 14.4 presents those correlations. The TestFact fit was obtained by specifying a guessing parameter of 0.2 for each item. The fact that the correlation is so high suggests that TestFact and BMIRT are identifying and associating items with similar dimensions for this dataset.

Table 14.3. Parameter estimates (posterior means) from a two-dimensional fit of grade 3 examinees on items in common between grade 3 and grade 4 forms

Item	Slope Dim 1	Dim 2	Angle	Location	Guessing
1	2.933	0.000	0	-0.176	0.304
2	0.559	0.556	43	-1.140	0.289
3	1.062	1.453	53	-2.563	0.230
4	0.833	1.309	56	-2.244	0.224
5	0.825	1.459	59	-3.076	0.211
6	0.855	1.224	53	-2.327	0.212
7	0.985	1.711	60	-0.058	0.206
8	2.013	0.364	10	-0.827	0.267
9	2.945	0.576	11	0.922	0.263
10	1.361	1.028	36	-2.072	0.270
11	1.043	1.428	53	-2.929	0.286
12	0.815	1.663	64	-0.389	0.200
13	1.102	0.809	36	-0.812	0.249
14	1.062	1.287	51	-3.090	0.289
15	0.850	1.926	65	-0.767	0.211
16	0.938	1.378	55	-2.156	0.184
17	0.874	0.586	33	-1.978	0.239
18	1.015	0.724	35	-1.780	0.281

Table 14.4. Correlation of BMIRT and TestFact slope parameters from two-dimensional fit of grade 3 examinees on items in common between grade 3 and grade 4 forms

	TestFact Slope 1	TestFact Slope 2
BMIRT Slope 1	.95	-.70
BMIRT Slope 2	-.76	.98

14.3.4.2. Multidimensionality Within Level for Multiple-Choice Items Only and Multiple-Choice and Constructed-Response Combined

We examined data separately by grade, fitting one-, two-, and three-dimensional models. We fit these models to data using (a) multiple-choice items alone and (b) the complete test with multiple-choice and constructed response items. To examine the degree of multidimensionality, we used Akaike's (1987) information criterion (AIC). The AIC is a model selection statistic that rewards model-data fit but imposes a penalty for adding additional parameters to the model. The results, shown in Tables 14.5 and 14.6, suggest that the addition of constructed-response items yields a distinct second dimension to otherwise unidimensional grade-by-grade calibrations. For example, for grade 4, first column AIC_1 (the AIC statistic for the one-dimensional fit) in Table 14.5 is smaller (i.e., better) than AICs from two- and three- dimensional fits. We indicate that the one-dimensional fit is preferred in the last column of Table 14.5. By contrast, Table 14.6 indicates that the AIC_2 (AIC statistic for the two-dimensional fit) is smaller than AICs from one- and three-dimensional fit for grades 4–7, and preference for a two-dimensional model at these grades is reflected in Table 14.6.

Table 14.5. AIC model selection criteria based on only the multiple-choice item data for the one-, two-, and three-dimensional IRT models (number of dimensions for best-fitting model according to AIC is noted)

Grade	AIC_1	AIC_2	AIC_3	Number of Dimensions
3	65604	68914	72279	1
4	85638	89353	94521	1
5	97902	101497	106569	1
6	107841	111716	116733	1
7	94886	98871	104288	1

Table 14.6. AIC model selection criteria based on only the total test with multiple-choice and constructed-response items, for the one-, two-, and three-dimensional IRT models (number of dimensions for the best-fitting model is noted)

Grade	AIC_1	AIC_2	AIC_3	Number of Dimensions
3	93395	95006	97429	1
4	128205	125156	126203	2
5	139091	137230	139170	2
6	145260	144122	145008	2
7	140045	138994	140080	2

Also of interest is the question of how dimensionality differs for a set of items that is common to adjacent grade-level forms. We examine this by fitting and comparing two-dimensional models for these common items estimated using first the lower-grade students and then the upper-grade students. In particular, we estimate 90% posterior credible intervals for item angle, and we flag those items (0 indicates no overlapping; 1 indicates overlapping) for which intervals derived using adjacent grade-level data do not overlap. For example, we do a two-dimensional fit for items common to grades 3 and 4 using grade 3 data only and compare it to the same model fit using the grade 4 data only. We further examine this aspect of multidimensionality by making this same comparison regarding common items when they are calibrated with all of the items in each form. These comparisons are presented in Tables 14.7 and 14.8 for grades 3–4. The results suggest that some items do have different dimensional characteristics when calibrated in one grade versus another and that the number of such items differs across commonitem sets.

Table 14.7. Comparison of item angles for items in common between Grades 3 and 4, based on calibration using data from each grade separately, and using the full set of multiple-choice and constructed-response items in each grade level

	Grade 3 Calibrating with all grade 3 items				Grade 4 Calibrating with all grade 4 items				Intervals overlap
Items	Mean	SD	5%	95%	Mean	SD	5%	95%	
1	0	0	0	0	0	0	0	0	1
2	29	7	17	41	16	5	8	24	1
3	30	5	22	38	18	4	11	25	1
4	25	5	17	33	19	5	11	27	1
5	25	6	15	35	20	5	12	28	1
6	30	5	22	38	25	6	15	35	1
7	32	5	24	40	11	4	4	18	0
8	5	3	0	10	10	3	5	15	1
9	5	2	2	8	9	4	2	16	1
10	20	4	13	27	15	3	10	20	1
11	31	5	23	39	12	4	5	19	0
12	31	5	23	39	13	3	8	18	0
13	38	5	30	46	18	4	11	25	0
14	24	6	14	34	12	4	5	19	1
15	35	5	27	43	9	3	4	14	0
16	33	5	25	41	12	4	5	19	0
17	37	6	27	47	19	6	9	29	1
18	33	5	25	41	14	5	6	22	0

Table 14.8. Comparison of item angles for items in common between grades 3 and 4, based on calibration using data from each grade separately, and using *common-items only*

Items	Grade 3 Calibrating with common items only				Grade 4 Calibrating with common items only				Intervals overlap
	Mean	SD	5%	95%	Mean	SD	5%	95%	
1	0	0	0	0	0	0	0	0	1
2	43	8	30	56	54	6	44	64	1
3	53	6	43	63	56	5	48	64	1
4	56	6	46	66	55	7	43	67	1
5	59	7	47	71	48	6	38	58	1
6	53	6	43	63	54	7	42	66	1
7	60	4	53	67	44	4	37	51	0
8	10	4	3	17	8	3	3	13	1
9	11	4	4	18	5	2	2	8	1
10	36	5	28	44	30	4	23	37	1
11	53	6	43	63	48	6	38	58	1
12	64	5	56	72	40	3	35	45	0
13	36	6	26	46	30	5	22	38	1
14	51	7	39	63	34	6	24	44	1
15	65	4	58	72	51	4	44	58	1
16	55	5	47	63	55	5	47	63	1
17	33	8	20	46	35	8	22	48	1
18	35	8	22	48	23	7	11	35	1

It is also clear from Tables 14.7 and 14.8 that the definition and affiliation of items with dimensions does depend on whether the common (multiple-choice only) items are used or if the complete set of (multiple-choice and constructed-response) items are used in the calibrations. For example, item 18 in Table 14.7, one can see that the estimate of the angle is 33°, and the 90% credible interval ranges from 25 to 41 when estimated using grade 3 data only. This same item has an angle estimates of 14° and a credible interval ranging from 6 to 22 using grade 4 data only. The fact that these credible intervals do not overlap suggests that the relationship of the item to the dimensions identified by responses to on-grade test forms does in fact differ across the grades. It is noteworthy, however, that the two credible intervals for the same item 18 do overlap if all the items (including constructed response items) in the test were used to do the estimation. A cursory review by content experts of the items demonstrating variable multidimensional characteristics across grades did not reveal a substantive explanation for the observed patterns.

14.3.4.3. A Five-Dimensional Fit Across Grades 3–7 CSAP Writing

We fit a multigroup five-dimensional model to the combined data from grades 3–7, with the population distribution for grade 3 fixed as a standard multivariate Normal distribution of dimension 5. Visual inspection of the item angles suggests that some dimensions are associated with items from most of the grades, whereas other dimensions seem to associate with items clustered in a single grade. Table 14.9 summarizes the dimensions that appear to be relevant for the items in each grade-level test. A more complete set of model comparisons would elaborate on these observations and would be necessary to draw any strong conclusions about the dimensionality characteristics of the CSAP data.

Table 14.9. Primary dimensions for each grade indicated by inspection of the loading patterns resulting from the five-dimensional concurrent estimation of grades 3–7

Grade	Dimension 1	Dimension 2	Dimension 3	Dimension 4	Dimension 5
3	*		*	*	*
4	*			*	*
5	*			*	
6	*				*
7					*

Finally, we note that we were able to use this multidimensional model-fitting methodology to conduct additional exploratory analyses. For example, we fit a number of multidimensional models to the full Colorado grade 3–10 writing data, including models with ability dimensions numbering from 1 to 8. We also fit, for example, an eight-dimensional model in which the association of items with dimensions was constrained so that each grade had an associated dimension. Items unique to a grade level identified an on-grade dimension, and items common to adjacent grades were two dimensional. Fitting this last model is conceptually close to the standard "divide-and-conquer" approach of fitting a series of one-dimensional models and then using common items in a separate linking procedure. Although a number of noteworthy patterns emerged, the specific nature of this dataset limits the generalizability and relevance of the findings. We have identified what we believe to be a useful tool for examining multidimensionality in vertical scaling (and other) contexts, and we have demonstrated its application to the analysis of practical assessment data.

14.4. Discussion

In this chapter we have introduced vertical scaling methods and we have examined general issues in modeling educational assessment data for which vertical scaling might be appropriate. We have described the divide-and-conquer and unified approaches currently in practice and we have developed and explored a unified multidimensional, multigroup IRT approach that might overcome significant limitations of existing approaches.

We developed MCMC fitting algorithms for the model and demonstrated that model fitting yields results consistent with those of TestFact when applied to multiple-choice items. We extended the model to allow simultaneous multidimensional scaling of multiple-choice and constructed-response items, an advance not seen elsewhere in the literature. We also explored multidimensionality features of writing assessment data from a multiple-grade administration using forms with items in common at adjacent grades.

These analyses suggest that multidimensionality exists in the assessment data and that a larger degree of multidimensionality might exist when: (a) multiple-choice and constructed-response items are scaled together and (b) when more grade levels are calibrated simultaneously.

Current divide-and-conquer approaches might provide a way of dealing constructively with multidimensionality by separately calibrating more nearly unidimensional models and linking the results in a separate linking step.

The results of these analyses suggest that (a) comprehensive modeling approaches are possible, (b) modeling multidimensionality will be important, and (c) we have considerable work ahead of us before we are able to supplant existing divide-and-conquer approaches and reap the benefits that unified modeling might bring. It might well be that what is needed is a sufficiently multidimensional model with a layer for parameterizing growth by dimension.

Finally, we note that the real data that we have analyzed here come from a single administration of a cross-grade assessment. This type of data is of significant interest, and it is generally the only type of data that might be available when a vertical scale must be established. The growth that is modeled and analyzed captures changes in the distribution of proficiency from one grade level to the next. Perhaps the most powerful information available to inform us about growth over grade levels, however, will come from longitudinal data collected as students progress over years of schooling. Such data have just become more readily available as states in the United States increasingly establish assessment programs that annually test all students in a range of grades (e.g., 3–8, as required by *No Child*

Left Behind). These data will allow us to examine individual growth trajectories, as advocated by Willet (1994), Singer (1998), and Singer and Willet (2003). Such considerations will allow us to reexamine the definition of vertical scales for achievement tests. We expect the tools that we have developed here for multidimensional analysis to facilitate this promising area of study.

15 Vertical Scaling and No Child Left Behind

Wendy M. Yen[1]

Educational Testing Service

The chapters by Harris (Chapter 13) and by Patz and Yao (Chapter 14) are quite different examinations of vertical scaling issues. The Harris chapter surveys practical issues related to implementing vertical scales, and the Patz and Yao chapter primarily studies the complex technical issue of using multidimensional item response theory models with vertical scaling. Given the great differences between these chapters, it is difficult to provide an integrated discussion of them. Thus, although this chapter contains some brief comments on the Harris, and Patz and Yao chapters, most of this chapter contains general observations on vertical scaling, observations harvested from vertically scaling K-12 achievement tests for over 25 years. Over those years, interest in vertical scales has changed. In particular, the No Child Left Behind Act of 2001 (NCLB) has led to changes in both who is interested in developing vertical scales and why they want to develop them. These changes have produced differences in expectations, evaluations, and issues related to implementing vertical scales.

15.1. Comments on the Other Vertical Scaling Chapters

15.1.1. The Harris Chapter

The Harris (Chapter 13) chapter is an excellent survey of the conceptual, technical, implementation, and maintenance issues related to the development and use of vertical scales, and the chapter provides a particularly valuable reference list. The Harris chapter should be read by

---

[1] The opinions expressed in this chapter are those of the author and not necessarily of Educational Testing Service.

anyone interested in general issues of vertical scaling. One particularly useful aspect of the Harris chapter is that she raises questions that need to be answered by those creating vertical scales. Perhaps the most telling of these questions is, Do you really need a vertical scale? I will address that question in relation to NCLB requirements.

15.1.2. The Patz and Yao Chapter

The Patz and Yao (Chapter 14) chapter contrasts vertical scaling based on a "divide-and-conquer" approach with vertical scaling within a unified item response theory (IRT) model. In the divide-and-conquer approach, test levels are scaled independently. Then a procedure such as that of Stocking and Lord (1983) is employed to link the results of adjacent levels. In a unified approach, the test levels are scaled simultaneously. Patz and Yao discussed limitations of a common unified approach (concurrent, multigroup, unidimensional IRT calibration of test levels), and they examined a unified model alternative. A multidimensional multigroup model was employed, allowing scores to be weighted averages of underlying dimensions, with the weights varying by test level. Such a model permits the explanation, based on empirical results, of complex shifts in what tests are measuring grade by grade.

Multidimensional modeling holds promise for K-12 assessment, although, as the authors noted, more work is required on the models before they are ready for operational implementation. One caution that I would note is that K-12 test users are understandably very focused on NCLB accountability. For that reason, they have great interest in the scores and state standards against which they are being evaluated. They want to know how their students are doing relative to those standards and what they need to do to improve performance relative to those standards. They have minimal interest in any score or subscore that is empirically identified that they cannot directly relate to the state standards. Thus, to be useful to K-12 educators, any dimensions empirically determined from a complex scaling model need to be related to state standards.

15.2. Vertical Scales: An Historical Perspective

15.2.1. A Folding Ruler: An Aside

I have been interested in vertical scales for a bit more than 25 years. When I was about 5 years old, I used to follow my father around as he did home improvements. He had a folding ruler with which I would play. It was yellow, with hinged 1-foot lengths that would unfold (making a nice thwacking sound) to 6 feet. If I held the extended ruler at one end, it would curve gracefully through space. To my disappointment, if I leaned it too much to the side, one of the looser hinges would suddenly bend sharply.

A vertical scale is akin to a folding ruler. Although educational achievement tests tend to have very strong first factors, they are multidimensional, paralleling changes in the curriculum. This dimensionality changes both within and across test levels. The direction of the scale (i.e., the relative importance of the different dimensions) changes as the test levels become more difficult. Thus, the scale bends or curves through space. Connections between some levels are stronger (i.e., have tighter hinges) than others, and sometimes the links between levels are too loose to maintain a sturdy connection between the test levels.

15.2.2. Pre-NCLB Interest in Vertical Scales

Before NCLB, the K-12 norm-referenced test (NRT) test publishers (such as CTB/McGraw-Hill, Harcourt Educational Measurement, and Riverside Publishing) conducted the vast majority of the vertical scaling. They produced these scales to satisfy users and to facilitate internal business systems. The primary uses of vertical scales were grade equivalents, functional level testing, scale scores for growth analyses, and computer-adaptive testing.

A large-scale K-12 test publisher cannot stay competitive without grade equivalents, which are demanded by customers. Grade equivalents are developed through the combination of a vertical scale and norms (Petersen, Kolen, & Hoover, 1989). The development of grade equivalents requires that normative scale score averages increase by grade. The vast majority of uses of grade equivalents are low stakes; they basically are a means of communicating the main idea of test results to those with minimal testing background, such as students, parents, and some teachers.

In functional level testing, a short locator test is used to identify the (vertically scaled) test level that is best matched to a student's current achievement. That level is then administered to the student. Scores obtained on different test levels that are linked via the vertical scale (e.g., scale scores, normative results) can be pooled for group reporting. Results that are not vertically linked—such as number-correct scores on the full test or on its subscores—cannot be pooled for group reporting. The promise of functional level testing is to obtain the most accurate measure of a student's performance, given the multiple test levels that are available. The problem with functional level testing is that it is operationally cumbersome to administer different test levels to different students in the same classroom. The fact that raw scores cannot be pooled across test levels is also awkward. Despite its promise, users today rarely choose to use functional level testing in operational K-12 testing programs.

When K-12 test levels are vertically scaled, these scale scores can be used to longitudinally track academic growth of individual students or cohorts. Before NCLB, there were a few sophisticated school districts that chose to conduct such growth analyses; however, the vast majority of users depended on cross-sectional results, for example, comparing this year's fourth-grade students to last year's. Some large-scale research studies on hierarchical modeling conducted by university researchers used vertical scales, and at least one state (Tennessee) used vertical scales, in combination with national norms, to conduct value-added evaluations of teacher effects on growth in student achievement test scores (Braun, 2005; Sanders, Saxton, & Horn, 1997).

Vertical scales based on K-12 achievement tests or items can also be used in computer-adaptive testing (CAT). As with functional level testing, the goal is to get the most accurate measure of a student's achievement as efficiently as possible. Use of CAT algorithms for item selection and terminating testing virtually require use of IRT to calibrate the items on one scale. Whereas in the late 1970s and early 1980s CAT appeared to hold tremendous promise for K-12 testing, as well as for testing in many other settings (Weiss, 1983), to date only a small minority of school systems have used CAT in K-12 (e.g., Northwest Evaluation Association; Kingsbury & Hauser, 2004).

K-12 publishers rely on vertical scales to organize their internal psychometric analysis systems. Publishers have very large numbers of items whose psychometric qualities need to be stored, accessed, and used. There might be items for 13 grades for 10 or so content areas (e.g., word analysis, reading vocabulary, reading comprehension, language expression, language mechanics, mathematics computation, mathematics problem solving, science, social studies.). In those systems that employ IRT, the items' parameter(s) are stored in scale score units (i.e., based on the cross-grade vertical scaling). This greatly facilitates the selection of items to create test forms at a variety of appropriate difficulty levels for either shelf or custom assessments.

In addition, scoring systems are arranged using the (vertical) scale score system. For example, to score a particular test form/level, the item parameters or raw score-to-scale score conversion table is stored in scale score units. When a student's test form/level is identified, the appropriate scoring table or algorithm translates the student's responses into a scale score. The normative tables contain scale score-to-norm conversions (e.g., scale score-to-grade equivalent, scale score-to-percentile). The norm tables are organized by grade/testing date (e.g., grade 3 fall, grade 3 spring) and are independent of the test form/level that the student took. Thus, the vertical scale provides an efficient backbone for the organization and access of items, test forms, and normative derived scores.

How successful were the pre-NCLB vertical scales in meeting the user and publisher needs?

As described earlier, to develop grade equivalents, it is necessary that the vertical scales show increasing average performance over grades. In the development of test blueprints, the K-12 publishers carefully map content strands to provide overlap and connections between the measurements at different grades and test levels. To demonstrate between-grade growth, this design must be accurately connected to typical or modal curricula across the nation. In the vast majority of cases, K-12 test publishers have been successful in producing measures that showed grade-to-grade growth. This growth is not necessarily smooth, but smoothness is not expected when there can be variations over grades in the strength of the connection between tests and curricula. The last 2–3 years of high school typically show minimal growth between grades, perhaps due to a looser connection of norm-referenced tests to high-school curricula than elementary curricula. Lower motivation for older high-school students could also play an important role. Despite these difficulties, K-12 publishers produced measures with vertical scales that demonstrated normative growth over grades.

The vast majority of uses of NRT results are horizontal: to compare this year's results (a) to a national norm at the same grade level or (b) to last year's results for that grade for the same school/district/state. Other uses that rely on the vertical scale (e.g., grade equivalents) tend to be low stakes. Publishers do provide cautions about using results from different parts of a vertical scale (e.g., a student at a lower grade getting a high scale score is probably thinking about content differently than a higher grade student getting that same scale score). It is also generally acknowledged and accepted that cross-grade correlations of scores are lower than within-grade (between parallel form) correlations of scores.

It is worth mentioning that in the 1980s, a brouhaha arose about scale shrinkage that occurred with some IRT vertical scales (Camilli, 1988; Clemans, 1993; Yen, 1986; Yen & Burket, 1997; Yen, Burket, & Fitzpatrick, 1996). In scale shrinkage, scale score standard deviations and IRT item difficulty parameter standard deviations decrease over grades, and IRT item discrimination parameter means increase over grades. Many hypotheses were generated to explain this phenomenon and there was much discussion about the implications of scale shrinkage. In actuality, because the vast majority of uses of NRT scores are horizontal, few test users were aware of the issue or cared about it, and scale shrinkage remained an issue primarily of academic interest. With the evolution of test design and IRT parameter estimation software, scale shrinkage disappeared.

Overall, the vertical scales developed by K-12 NRT publishers successfully addressed the needs of users and publishers.

15.3. The NCLB Era

Under NCLB, it is the responsibility of each state to develop its own challenging content standards and assessments to measure progress in achieving those standards. With the advent of NCLB, interest in NRTs has greatly declined, although some states do take an NRT core set of items (and vertical scale) and augment it to improve the coverage of unique state standards. There is interest in vertical scaling for Titles III and I of NCLB and for evaluation of growth.

15.3.1. Title III

Title III of NCLB states, "A State shall approve evaluation measures…that are designed to assess…the progress of children in attaining English proficiency, including a child's level of comprehension, speaking, listening, reading, and writing skills in English." Title III generates interest in vertical scales, both explicitly and implicitly. Nonnative English-speaking children enter our schools with a wide range of English skills, so in assessing these skills accurately, functional level testing (which assumes the existence of a vertical scale) can be particularly important. Behavioral scale anchoring (i.e., examples of what students know and can do at different scale scores) is of interest to those trying to attach meaning to the student scores. On these vertical scales of English proficiency, setting performance standards related to exiting English learner programs is of particular importance.

At Educational Testing Service (ETS), we have recently developed vertically scaled assessments of English acquisition skills for two different clients   (Comprehensive   English   Language   Learning   Assessment

[Educational Testing Service, 2005] and the New York State English as a Second Language Achievement Test [Wang & Smith, 2003]). These assessments display properties different from traditional measures of achievement. For example, the lowest test level, measuring introductory skills, can include a wide range of content (letters of the alphabet, words, sentences, paragraphs) and show much greater units of growth that those seen at higher test levels. These differences reinforce the advice given by Braun (1988) that growth is most accurately evaluated by comparing students who start at the same place; when students start at different places on a scale, differences in scale units can greatly complicate interpretations. At the group level, cross-sectional results show much different growth patterns over the grades for listening and speaking than for reading and writing. listening/speaking skills rise rapidly in the early grades and then top out. reading/writing, which are academic skills, continue to rise throughout the grades. For traditional achievement measures, "grade" is the most relevant time measure; however, for English acquisition skills, both "number of years in the United States" and "grade" are relevant time measures. In interpreting cross-sectional growth over grades for English acquisition tests, immigration patterns also need to be considered. For example, whereas for traditional achievement measures, growth is expected across virtually all grades, for English acquisition tests, performance can dip at grades where a large influx of students new to the United States can occur (e.g., grade 9, where students are coming to the United States for high school). Thus, growth expectations for vertically scaled English acquisition tests can differ from the expectations for traditional educational achievement tests.

15.3.2. Title I

Title I of NCLB focuses on the adequate yearly progress in the percents of students reaching the Proficient performance standard established in each state. Thus, comparisons are made from year to year in the percents of Proficient students at a given grade and no statistical connection is required between the tests at different grades.

Typically, the NCLB assessments and their performance standards have been developed in a piecemeal fashion, because the legislation eased in the assessment requirements over the years. For example, NCLB legislation started with a requirement (in reading and mathematics) of one assessment in each of three grade ranges (grades 3 to 5, 6 to 9, and 10 to 12). Later, states were required to have assessments in each of grades 3 to 8. Also in the Title I legislation there is no requirement for longitudinal or growth measures. For these reasons, few states have vertical scales for their NCLB assessments. Vertical scales that demonstrate cross-sectional growth over grades can be more difficult to develop if the content standards/curricula/test blueprints have not been designed from their inception to have hierarchical content strands with substantial between-grade overlap. Furthermore, performance standards that are set independently by grade might not "grow" on a vertical scale (e.g., Proficient for grade 7 might not be at a higher scale score than Proficient for grade 8). Thus, it might be more difficult to develop vertical scales that produce expected progressions over grades for NCLB state assessments than it was for NRTs.

Although the Title I legislation does not require it, there has been increasing interest in vertical scales among NCLB practitioners.[2] Why is that? I can speculate on several reasons. First, there might be a mistaken impression among some practitioners that a vertical scale is required. Second, there are those who want to use NCLB assessment results within evaluation and accountability systems. Within such systems, being able to distinguish input (i.e., performance before a particular instructional treatment) from output is particularly helpful. Some of those interested in accountability are specifically interested in value-added models, and some of these models require the use of vertical scales. Finally, I believe that most educators care dearly about student growth, and vertical scale is a catch-all phrase that, for many people, includes any type of growth measure.

15.3.3. Educators' Interest in Growth Measures

It became important to us to understand what educators wanted in terms of a growth measure in the NCLB era. Toward that end, we gathered in-depth information from educators in one state via phone interviews, large-group meetings, and a small working group (Smith & Yen, 2006). We discussed with them the pros and cons of three types of growth measure (vertical scales, state norms, and cross-grade regressions [expectations]) and listened to the issues that they were trying to address. Their interests seemed to center around answering the following questions:

---

[2] In November 2005, the U.S. Department of Education invited states to submit proposals for developing growth models for adequate yearly progress consistent with the principles of *No Child Left Behind*. In May 2006, the Department approved two programs as part of this pilot (U.S. Department of Education, 2006).

Parents:
- Did my child make a year's worth of progress in a year?
- Is my child growing appropriately toward meeting state standards?
- Is my child growing as much in Math as Reading?
- Did my child grow as much this year as last year?

Teachers:
- Did my students make a year's worth of progress in a year?
- Did my students grow appropriately toward meeting state standards?
- How close are my students to becoming Proficient?
- Are there students with unusually low growth who need special attention?

Administrators:
- Did the students in our district/school make a year's worth of progress in all content areas?
- Are our students growing appropriately toward meeting state standards?
- Does this school/program show as much growth as that one?
- Can I measure student growth even for students who do not change proficiency categories?
- Can I pool together results from different grades to draw summary conclusions?

Most of these questions are variations on one underlying question: Is the amount of growth observed reasonable or appropriate? There are two aspects inherent in answering such a question: the absolute and the normative. The absolute aspect compares a measurement to a fixed criterion, such as the score needed to be called Proficient. The normative aspect arises from interest in how the growth of this particular student (or group of students) compares with that of other students. A vertical scale by itself does not address either the absolute or normative aspect of growth questions.

Cross-grade growth expectations, which are connected to proficiency levels, answer these questions without the assumptions or development costs of a vertical scale. Such cross-grade growth expectations are obtained from longitudinal data, say from grade 3 to grade 4, that are analyzed using regression techniques; scores at a subsequent grade level are regressed onto scores at a previous grade level. Figure 15.1 provides one example of a report that could display the growth results for one district relative to the regression and the absolute performance criterion (Proficiency) established by the state. In this example, grade 3 and grade 4 have independent scales, with no vertical scale connecting them. The state regression line shows the relationship of the scores for the two grades when students are tracked from grade 3 to grade 4. Results for one district can be compared to the state results. In this particular example, the district showed above-average growth (relative to the state) for low-scoring students and below-average growth for high-scoring students. It is also possible, using graphs such as this, to separate out results for different programs within a district and compare their relative amounts of growth. Examples of individual student score reports based on longitudinal regressions are presented in Smith and Yen (2006).

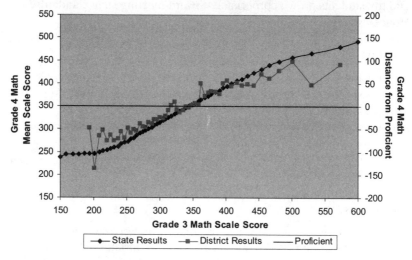

Figure 15.1. Sample longitudinal regressions of grade 4 Math on grade 3 Math at a state level and a district level.

15.4. Summary

Pre-NCLB, vertical scales were ubiquitous in K-12 assessment. The vertical scales developed by K-12 publishers satisfied general criteria for a usable scale; that is, their average scores increased by grade. The most common uses of vertical scales were embedded within grade equivalents, which were used in low-stakes settings. High-stakes usages that relied heavily on the vertical scale properties were fairly rare. Publishers did provide cautions about use of the vertical scale results.

Under NCLB, Title III requires "evaluation measures...that are designed to assess...the progress of children in attaining English proficiency...." Vertical scales are an obvious means of satisfying this requirement. In evaluating the properties of vertical scales for English language attainment, such as expectations of increasing scores by grade, special care is needed to consider the properties of the different scales (such as academic vs. nonacademic skills) and the special characteristics of this student population. Particular care is needed in comparing amounts of growth in different parts of these scales.

In satisfying Title I of NCLB, vertical scales are not required. Vertical scales might not demonstrate grade-to-grade growth as clearly for state assessments developed under NCLB if the content of those tests, and the related curricula, have not been developed to be hierarchical. Under NCLB, users of the test scores are interested in evaluating academic growth in aspects that are both absolute (e.g., compared to a proficient cut-score) and relative (e.g., relative to how much other students grow). A vertical scale by itself does not address either of these aspects, and alternative analysis procedures can be used. For example, cross-grade longitudinal growth expectations (regressions) based on nonvertically scaled tests can address most of the growth questions being asked without the assumptions or expense involved in the development of vertical scales.

Part 6: Linking Group Assessments to Individual Assessments

Over the past two decades, the use of standardized tests in the nation's schools has increased sharply. This has led to increased interest in results obtained by surveys of educational achievement that provide aggregate results; chief among those are the National Assessment of Educational Progress (NAEP). There have been a number of attempts to link other assessments to the NAEP scale.

David Thissen reviews several studies involving linkages with NAEP in *Linking Assessments Based on Aggregate Reporting: Background and Issues*. He examines the procedures used and then gives consideration to some questions that have arisen about the validity of the results. He concludes that statistical procedures for accomplishing such linkages have advanced considerably in the past decade, but our understanding of nonrandom sources of variation lags behind.

In *An Enhanced Method for Mapping State Standards onto the NAEP Scale*, Henry Braun and Jiahe Qian modify and evaluate a procedure developed to link state standards to the NAEP scale. The modification makes more efficient use of the available data and provides more comprehensive estimates of the variances to be attached to the NAEP scale score equivalents of the state standards. The method is applied to data from mathematics assessments.

Daniel Koretz discusses the two preceding chapters briefly in *Using Aggregate-Level Linkages for Estimation and Validation: Comments on Thissen and Braun & Qian*. He comments on the linkage-based inferences they address, the evaluative evidence they bring to bear, and their conclusions. He also elaborates on the instability of aggregate linkages over time. He comments briefly on the extent of this instability problem, its causes, and its implications for validity.

16 Linking Assessments Based on Aggregate Reporting: Background and Issues

David Thissen[1]

L.L. Thurstone Psychometric Laboratory, University of North Carolina at Chapel Hill

Over the past two decades, the use of standardized tests in the nation's schools has increased sharply. According to a report prepared for Congress more than 10 years ago by the Office of Technology Assessment, "The rise in testing reflects a heightened demand from legislators at all levels—and their constituents—for evidence that education dollars are spent effectively. Holding schools and teachers accountable has increasingly become synonymous with increased standardized testing" (U.S. Congress, Office of Technology Assessment [OTA], 1992, pp. 3–4). This trend culminated with the passage of the No Child Left Behind Act of 2001 (NCLB) in 2002; that law requires that each state administer census assessments of reading and mathematics proficiency in grades 3–8, and at least once during grades 10–12, beginning with the 2005–2006 academic year. Additional assessments of science are required by academic year 2007–2008.

This increase in emphasis on the use of standardized tests to assess achievement in the schools has led to a corresponding increase in interest in the results obtained by national and international surveys of educational achievement that provide aggregate results for the nation and internationally. Chief among those are the National Assessment of Educational Progress (NAEP) and the Third International Mathematics and Science Study (TIMSS).

The NAEP is a widely respected indicator of educational performance (Beaton & Zwick, 1992), with a scale that offers national comparability and information on change over time.

---

[1] The opinions expressed in this chapter are those of the author and not necessarily of the University of North Carolina at Chapel Hill.

NAEP has proven to be a valuable tool to track and understand educational progress in the United States. It was created in 1969 and is the only regularly conducted national survey of educational achievement at the elementary, middle, and high school levels. It was designed to be an educational indicator, a barometer of the Nation's elementary and secondary educational condition. NAEP reports group data only, not individual scores. (U.S. Congress, Office of Technology Assessment, 1992, pp. 30–31)

Jones (1996) offered a capsule summary of the evolution of NAEP, and Jones and Olkin (2004) provided a book-length treatment of its 40-year history.

The administration of NAEP and the presentation of its results are unusual in that no scores are assigned to individual examinees. Instead, a complex sampling design is coupled with the models and methods of item response theory (IRT) to yield estimates of statistics that describe the population distribution of proficiency: the mean, various quantiles, and the percentages with proficiency in regions on the scale known as achievement levels.

TIMSS is the current incarnation of a series of international comparative studies conducted by the International Association for the Evaluation of Educational Achievement (IEA) since its inception in 1959 (Mullis et al., 1997). Whereas TIMSS releases scores on several scales, its primary reporting, like that of NAEP, is for large demographic groups—in the case of TIMSS, nations.

For a number of reasons and purposes to be discussed in subsequent sections, there have been several attempts to link the results and scales of NAEP and TIMSS (and other international assessments) to each other (Beaton & Gonzalez, 1993; Johnson, 1998; Johnson & Siegendorf, 1998; Pashley & Phillips, 1993) and to statewide assessments (Ercikan, 1997; Linn & Kiplinger, 1994; McLaughlin, 1998a, 1998b; Waltman, 1997; Williams, Rosa, McLeod, Thissen, & Sanford, 1998). These linkages differ from many other more common applications of equating and from the construction of concordance tables, in that for NAEP (and TIMSS, for the most part) there are no individual scores to put in a concordance or "crosswalk" table. Instead, the goal is to use the results from the administration of some other assessment to make estimates of the aggregate results that an assessment like NAEP might produce. The idea that statistical linking might be used to accomplish that goal is relatively new, having its genesis in systematizations of test linking by Mislevy (1992) and Linn (1993); those descriptions of alternate forms of test linking are described in Section 16.1.

16.1. Linking Methods

Test linkage provides a mechanism to obtain from the results of one test, by statistical inference, the results that would have been obtained if a second test had been given. In the context of aggregate reporting, *results* usually refers to the distribution of scores, although whether the scores might be treated as interchangeable is never far from consideration. Applications of this idea use the results from regularly administered tests, like those from a statewide testing program, to infer the results that would have been obtained had, say, NAEP measured that subject-matter area that year in that state. The idea is that if a test measuring mathematics proficiency is given, then one should be able to produce a reasonably good estimate of what would have happened had another test of mathematics proficiency been given, even if the second test is scored on a different scale. However, if the tests were constructed using different specifications and might not measure exactly the same aspects of mathematics proficiency, a number of technical problems arise when the tests are to be linked. Different linking methods might solve some of those technical problems.

Using slightly different terms, Mislevy (1992) and Linn (1993) described three levels of test linking that could be useful for different purposes; Holland and Dorans' (2006) more recent codification used the terms *equating*, *scale aligning*, and *predicting* to describe essentially the same classes of statistical activities. See Holland (Chapter 2) for explicit definitions of these classes of linkage.

Equating is the term used to describe the strongest form of test linking. If two test forms are equated, scores on the two forms are interchangeable for any use; in equipercentile equating, probably the most common form, tables are constructed setting equal scores on the two test forms that correspond to the same percentiles in a common population. In practice, valid equating, in the sense of producing interchangeable scores, is limited to alternate forms of tests constructed from the same test specifications (Mislevy, 1992). Holland and Dorans (2006) and Dorans and Holland (2000) listed five requirements widely viewed as necessary for test equating to be successful. These requirements are as follows: (a) The tests should measure the same constructs; (b) the tests should have the same reliability; (c) the equating function should be symmetrical; (d) it should be a matter of indifference to an examinee to be tested by either test; (e) the equating function should be population invariant. Holland (Chapter 2) discussed each of these requirements in detail.

Essentially none of those five requirements are met in any of the examples (to be described below) that link other assessments to the scales of NAEP or TIMSS. Nevertheless, some studies have used the statistical mechanics of equipercentile equating to construct linkages; this kind of activity was called *statistical moderation* by Mislevy (1992). Holland (Chapter 2, Section 2.3.2) referred to this as anchor scaling.

Holland (Chapter 2, Section 2.3) and Holland and Dorans (2006) described a large family of linkage activities under the superordinate term *scale aligning*; however, of the various contexts for linkage and statistical procedures included in that family such as *concordance* and *vertical scaling, calibration* has been most often considered (and, as we will see in subsequent sections, equally often rejected) as a mechanism to link other scales to that of NAEP. Calibration is used to provide comparable scores on tests that "measure the same thing" (Mislevy, 1992, p. 22), but with different degrees of precision, as might be the case with short and long forms of the same test. Calibration is usually based on IRT, which requires item-level data from one of the linking designs described by Holland and Dorans (2006). Revised forms of NAEP are calibrated with respect to each other (Yamamoto & Mazzeo, 1992). It is conceivable that another test could be calibrated to the scale of an aggregate-reporting measure like NAEP, but for such a linkage to be accurate, the two tests would have to match content specifications closely. We are not aware of any calibration of any other test to an aggregate-reporting measure.

In the taxonomy of Holland and Dorans (2006), described by Holland (Chapter 2, Section 2.2.2), *projection* is a specific form of *prediction* that makes use of an empirical relation between scores on tests that do not measure the same thing in order to predict the distribution of one test (e.g., NAEP) from the distribution of scores on another test (e.g., a state assessment). Mislevy (1992) described projection without attention to other, simpler prediction systems, and Linn (1993) discussed prediction without so much attention to the *distributions* of predicted scores that Holland and Dorans marked as the distinction between prediction and projection.

If two tests are constructed to measure mathematics proficiency, they usually exhibit a strong positive relation between the scores, even if the test specifications and administration procedures are sufficiently different that they do not measure exactly the same thing. An empirically estimated bivariate relation between the test scores, and the known marginal distribution of the scores on the first test, both within subpopulations, if necessary, can be used to infer the marginal distribution for the second test. The projected marginal distribution can then be used to compute statistics.

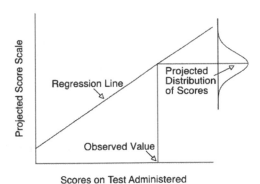

Figure 16.1. A schematized view of projection. The important feature of projection is that each score on the *X*-axis test is projected as a distribution of scores on the *Y*-axis test.

Figure 16.1 shows a schematized view of projection, modeled after Figure 4 of Pashley and Phillips (1993). The important feature of projection is that each score on the *X*-axis test is transformed into a distribution of scores on the *Y*-axis test; those distributions are then totaled to provide the basis for the computation of aggregate results. The representation of the projected distributions might have some functional form (like the curve shown in Figure 16.1) or it might be a series of random draws (multiple random imputations, called *plausible values* in the nomenclature of NAEP [Mislevy, Johnson, & Muraki, 1992]) from that distribution. Many of the examples in the following sections involve projection.

16.2. The Seeds Are Sown: Linkages of NAEP with IAEP and the ASVAB

16.2.1. The Linkage of 1992 NAEP with 1991 IAEP

One of the first studies to use projection to link assessments characterized by aggregate reporting was the linkage of the 1991 International Assessment of Educational Progress (IAEP) and the 1992 NAEP mathematics assessment by Pashley and Phillips (1993). At the time, NAEP was just beginning to use achievement levels established by the National Assessment Governing Board (NAGB) as a primary reporting scale. The goal of the study was to "predict the percentages of 13-year-olds in each of the 20 countries that participated in the 1991 IAEP in mathematics who would have performed at or above each of the three achievement levels established by NAGB for U.S. students" (Pashley & Phillips, p. 5). This study was regarded as a particularly opportune trial for test linking, because the IAEP had been constructed largely following NAEP blueprints, so the assessments themselves were very similar.

A special sample of 1,609 U.S. grade 8 students (a subset of the 1992 NAEP operational sample) was assessed with both instruments in early 1992. After determining that IRT analysis of this special 1992 IAEP data produced results very similar to those obtained in the main analysis of the 1991 IAEP data, Pashley and Phillips (1993) used the original 1991 IAEP item parameters to compute plausible values of proficiency for the IAEP data in the special sample. In parallel, the analysis of the national 1992 NAEP data produced plausible values for NAEP proficiency for the same students. Similar conditioning variables were used in the computation of both sets of plausible values.

The plausible values for proficiency from NAEP were regressed on the plausible values for proficiency from IAEP five times, once for each pairing of five plausible values on each test. Then, using one of each student's plausible values for IAEP proficiency with the corresponding regression line, a predicted distribution of NAEP proficiency was computed using a Normal distribution and the assumption of homogeneous error variance; the predicted distributions were like that in Figure 16.1. Five such distributions were computed for each student, and the area above each achievement-level cut-score was computed; the average of those areas was taken as the probability that the student falls in each achievement level. The average of those probabilities across students gives the desired result: an estimate of the proportion in each NAEP achievement level, predicted from the results obtained from an administration of IAEP.

Pashley and Phillips (1993) checked the consistency of the results across plausible value replications and found little variation. They used split-sample techniques to estimate standard errors and confidence intervals for the aggregate statistics and obtained suitably narrow confidence intervals. (They also carefully concatenated several sources of random variation into their confidence intervals.) As another empirical check on the results, they used the entire linking sample to estimate the 1992 national U.S. proportions and found the actual percentages to be within the confidence intervals.

They then computed confidence intervals for the percentages in NAGB's basic, proficient, and advanced achievement levels for each of the 20 other countries that had participated in IAEP in 1991. Pashley and

Phillips (1993) noted that some caveats should be kept in mind when considering the results: The first of these is that they "assumed that the relationship between the IAEP and NAEP assessments observed in the 1992 U.S. linking sample also holds for other countries that were assessed in 1991" (p. 33); that is, relatively extreme population invariance of the linking function was assumed—between countries! That assumption would have been very difficult to check. The inference is basically, in some sense, about what would have happened had NAEP been administered in other countries. However, it is not exactly clear what that means. NAEP does not exist in other languages and has never been administered in other countries, so this is a very strong assumption about relatively unlikely population invariance. Further, Pashley and Phillips noted that "there were differences in IAEP and NAEP sample definitions, such as type of schools surveyed and age or grade of students" (p. 33).

The study by Pashley and Phillips (1993) foreshadowed several subsequent studies in both their goal, to estimate the proportions of students in NAEP's achievement levels, without administering NAEP and in the questions that haunt the results: Is it reasonable to assume that the regression of NAEP mathematics proficiency on IAEP mathematics proficiency would be the same in all countries? What are the effects of the fact that different countries actually define the population of students differently and/or administer the assessments under somewhat different conditions?

16.2.2. The Linkage of the ASVAB with NAEP

The Armed Services Vocational Aptitude Battery (ASVAB) includes several tests that are administered to all applicants for military service in the United States. Because of the self-selected nature of this population, in the past, special surveys with nationally representative samples have been conducted to develop norms for the ASVAB and to submit the required report to Congress on the proficiency of the population of military recruits (U.S. Department of Defense, 1982). As part of an effort to obviate these special surveys by linking the ASVAB to the NAEP scale, Bloxom, Pashley, Nicewander, and Yan (1995) used projection technology to link the ASVAB to the NAEP mathematics scale for 12th-grade students.

Data collection for this study took place in May 1992, only a few weeks after that for the NAEP-IAEP study; early reports of its results made it the second of the pair of path-breaking projects that were to set the stage, along with the Mislevy (1992) and Linn (1993) theoretical work, for the decade of linkages to NAEP.

Data for the Bloxom et al. (1995) ASVAB-NAEP linkage were extensive. The examinees, all applicants for military service, responded to the entire ASVAB, comprising 10 tests as well as the entire NAEP background-variable questionnaire and three blocks of NAEP items. The ASVAB was an operational test with very real consequences for the military applicants in the sample; the administration of the NAEP materials was presented as nonoperational but for research purposes. Although NAEP data collection also includes other questionnaires from which background demographic data are derived, ASVAB background data were merged from Department of Defense data files. After all of the records were matched, the total sample size was 8,239.

The projection of NAEP results from the ASVAB used the same IRT technology that is used to compute the NAEP results (Johnson & Allen, 1992). The statistical results of NAEP are computed by combining the item responses with the data from the demographic background questionnaire to infer the posterior distribution for proficiency for each examinee. Plausible values are drawn from those posterior distributions; with the sampling weights, those plausible values are used to compute the reported statistics and their standard errors.

To understand the projection technique employed by Bloxom et al. (1995), it is useful to list in more detail some of the stages of data analysis for NAEP. The parameters for IRT models are estimated for each item for the entire national NAEP sample (including linking data from the previous administration of NAEP). Those item parameters yield curves that represent the probability of each item response as a function of proficiency—for NAEP mathematics, on five dimensions. Then, given those curves and the item response data, optimal linear combinations for the background variables are formed for the regression of proficiency on the background variables, using theory developed by Mislevy (1984, 1985, 1990) and Thomas (1993a) and computer software called MGROUP (Rogers, 1991; Sheehan, 1985, Thomas, 1993b). The regression of proficiency on the background variables, with an assumption of Gaussian error, is used to produce a distribution over proficiency for each combination of background-variable values. Finally, for each person, the (IRT) curves associated with their item responses are multiplied by the proficiency distribution associated with their background-variable values. That product represents the distribution of proficiency for persons with those item responses and those values of the background variables; plausible values are drawn from the product distribution, and subsequent statistics are computed as though the plausible values represented observations on the unobserved proficiency dimensions.

An interesting feature of the NAEP scoring system is that after estimation of the parameters of the regression equations that relate the background variables to underlying proficiency, it is not actually necessary to have item response data from the examinees to compute the proficiency distributions and all of the subsequent results. Bloxom et al. (1995) used this feature of the NAEP scoring system to project results from ASVAB data: In the projection system, they used ASVAB background variables and reliability-scaled ASVAB standard scores in place of the usual NAEP background variables and then computed projected NAEP results, omitting the NAEP item responses. Because the ASVAB data included scores on tests of various aspects of mathematics, regression of the NAEP mathematics dimensions on the ASVAB data in combination with the more usual background variables produced predictions of the NAEP results very nearly as accurate as those obtained when the NAEP item responses were included in the computation.

The ASVAB projection used 46 variables (precluding any simple graphical presentation like Figure 16.1). The ASVAB projection used plausible values from the conditional distributions as data in the computation of the results. Bloxom et al. (1995) evaluated the ASVAB projection system in several ways. They split the sample and examined the cross-validation of the results from one-half the sample to the other. Additionally, they conducted an extensive simulation study that assumed that a model very much like the one that they fitted was true and they repeatedly generated data from that model to determine if the analysis would recover the true values of the parameters. In general, the results were favorable toward the accuracy of the projection.

However, Bloxom et al. (1995) found that, although their sample performed at an above-average level for the mathematics items on the ASVAB with respect to the most recent ASVAB national norms, that same sample performed well below the national average on the NAEP items. The implication is that motivation might have been substantially reduced for these examinees for the NAEP items, relative to the ASVAB items or possibly relative to national samples administered NAEP items in other contexts. This problem leaves an open question on the actual relation between ASVAB scores obtained in the regular administration of that test and NAEP data obtained in their usual context.

16.3. State Linkages with NAEP

Even before No Child Left Behind (NCLB), statewide achievement testing programs were common. However, due to different responses to the spirit of reform in education and educational measurement in the 1980s and 1990s, many of these statewide testing programs were unique. The motivation for the differences among the testing programs arose from the fact that each state had increasingly well-specified curricular goals and there was a desire to measure progress toward those goals. This uniqueness has now been codified into law with the provisions and interpretations of NCLB. A penalty for the differences among local testing programs is that efforts to compare performance to any national standards have been frustrated by the lack of comparability of the results from different tests.

The development of unique testing programs for purposes of accountability has led critics to suggest that a state had "developed its own tests so it could duck national comparison" (Simmons, 1995). One possible response to this criticism is to use nationally normed tests in addition to the tests already mandated—then one set of tests can be used to assess progress toward the state's curricular goals, whereas another set of tests provide data that can be compared to other states and the nation. However, the U.S. Congress Office of Technology Assessment (1992) report correctly emphasized that large-scale testing is very costly, both in dollars and in opportunity cost; testing requires student and teacher time that could better be spent on other educational activities. The administration of more tests to serve the increasing demands for various kinds of accountability might in itself be detrimental to the performance of the educational system. Linkage of statewide tests to the NAEP scale was seen as a way to obtain national comparative data without additional testing.

Additionally, since the expansion of NAEP in 1990 to provide state-level data in the voluntary Trial State Assessment (TSA),[2] there has been increasing pressure on NAEP to provide data for even smaller geographical units, including local school districts or even schools. In addition to the problems associated with ever-increasing amounts of testing, Jones (1997) noted that employing NAEP to produce state-, district-, or school-level results might threaten the integrity of NAEP for its primary purpose: "to monitor progress in educational attainment, nationally, by region, and for certain demographic subgroups" (p. 17). Jones suggested that linking procedures, whereby NAEP results could be estimated from findings from state testing programs, might serve as an alternative to any increased testing, including expansion of NAEP.

16.3.1. The Linkage of the KIRIS with NAEP

Among the earliest attempts to link a statewide assessment to NAEP was one that involved the Kentucky Instructional Results Information System

---

[2] The expansion of NAEP to provide results for each state was originally designated the "Trial State Assessment" when Congress removed the previously existing prohibition of NAEP reports of results disaggregated below the national level.

(KIRIS; Kentucky Department of Education, 1993), the statewide testing program in Kentucky from 1991–1992 until 1997–1998. KIRIS included tests of reading, mathematics, science, social studies, and writing, using multiple-choice items, open-ended items, performance assessments, and portfolio components. Tests were administered on a census basis in the accountability years (grades 4, 8, and 12) and on an optional basis in grades 2–3, 5–7, and 9–11. KIRIS was a high-stakes accountability system at the school level: Schools and teachers were rewarded financially for improvement in performance from year to year, and sanctions were imposed on schools and the staff within schools where test scores showed decreased performance.

The primary reporting scale for KIRIS was a four-category system, dividing students into proficiency levels labeled *distinguished*, *proficient*, *apprentice*, and *novice*. The percentage of "successful" students (the sum of those scoring in the distinguished and proficient categories) in each of the subject-matter areas was used as the primary statistic for score reporting and to implement accountability contingencies. The goal of the linkage of KIRIS with NAEP was to use NAEP data collected within and outside of Kentucky to estimate the corresponding percentage of "successful" students (by KIRIS criteria) in the nation as a whole, without administration of KIRIS outside of Kentucky.

An equipercentile process was used to link the KIRIS categories to the NAEP score scale.[3] The analysis was used to conclude that although 3.2% of Kentucky fourth-grade students were *successful* (distinguished or proficient) in 1992, 5.4% of the students in the nation would have been so classified had KIRIS been administered nationally.

At the request of the Kentucky Department of Education, the 1992 administration of NAEP–TSA included more subject-matter areas and grades in Kentucky than were scheduled nationally; similar linkages were developed for reading in grades 8 and 12 and mathematics in grades 4, 8, and 12. The NAEP data were collected and scored in the course of the scheduled administration of NAEP–TSA by the NAEP contractors, whereas the KIRIS data were derived from the scheduled census administration of that battery. Because the NAEP data collection did not include identifying information for individual students, it was not possible to match individual examinees' results for NAEP and KIRIS. As a result, only limited analysis is possible to investigate the extent to which the NAEP and KIRIS tests with the same names measure the same aspects of proficiency. The correlations between the average scores for schools on the

---

[3] No published description of the KIRIS–NAEP linkage has been provided. This description is based on information kindly provided by Earl Ogata of the Kentucky Department of Education (personal communication, July 1995).

NAEP and KIRIS scales for mathematics were 0.74, 0.78, and 0.79 for grades 4, 8, and 12, respectively. Those correlations are not as high as would usually be obtained between two tests that are to be equated or concorded. Dorans (2004d) maintained that correlations of .87 or higher or *reductions in uncertainties* of 50% or higher are desirable for scores that are to be equated or concorded.

Subsequent KIRIS results indicate that, for fourth-grade reading, the percentage of students in Kentucky scoring in the proficient and distinguished categories increased from 3% in 1992 to 8% in 1993 and 13% in 1994. If the concordance performed as desired, that should imply that 13% would score above the concorded score of 273 on NAEP reading in 1994, but the fact is that only 6% scored at the advanced level on NAEP in 1994.[4] There were no statistically significant changes between Kentucky's 1992 and 1994 NAEP reading scores. Ignoring the issue of statistical significance, Kentucky's average decreased from 213 to 212 on the NAEP scale. Examining more subject areas and grade levels, Hambleton et al. (1995) and Koretz and Barron (1998) found that gains in scores on the KIRIS consistently exceeded Kentucky's score gains on NAEP.

Before these results were available, the Kentucky Department of Education noted that gains in KIRIS scores relative to the 1992 national baseline could be due to any of three causes:

- Increased student learning that would be reflected in future administrations of NAEP
- Increased student learning to which NAEP is not sensitive because it might not measure higher order skills or ability to represent information as well as KIRIS
- Increased motivation to do well on KIRIS tests in subsequent years compared to 1991–1992

The data suggest that the first scenario is unlikely, leaving the second two possibilities, neither of which is entirely compatible with strong conclusions about national comparisons based on the linkage of KIRIS and NAEP.

---

[4]The tabulations of NAEP results include the percentage of students who score in the category labeled *advanced*; for fourth-grade reading, that is the percentage of students whose scores are 275 or higher, which is very near the cut-score of 273 obtained in the KIRIS equating.

16.3.2. Equipercentile Linkages of Statewide Assessment Scales with NAEP

Using data from the 1990 NAEP–TSA that measured mathematics achievement in 38 states (and 2 territories), and statewide results in 4 of those states that used assessments provided by CTB, Ercikan (1997) examined equipercentile linking functions between the statewide assessments and NAEP. Three of the states used different versions of the Comprehensive Tests of Basic Skills, Fourth Edition (CTBS/4; CTB/McGraw-Hill, 1993c), and the fourth used the California Achievement Test, Form E (CAT/E; CTB/McGraw-Hill, 1993b). In order to obtain comparable linking functions, Ercikan used a preexisting equating study among versions of the CAT and CTBS to convert all four states' scores onto the CAT/5 scale (CTB/Macmillan/McGraw-Hill, 1993a). Then equipercentile linking procedures were used to link the CAT/5 statewide mathematics scores (on the NCE scale) with the NAEP scale, matching the distribution of the approximately 2,500 students in the NAEP–TSA sample with the statewide population results (for populations that ranged from approximately 8,000 to 50,000).

Ercikan (1997) found that the linking results differed substantially among the four states. She noted that these differences might be due to any or all of several differences between the two sets of tests. "These differences include different testing dates, motivational differences between students taking statewide tests and the NAEP test, and content differences that result in different abilities being assessed by each test" (p. 156). Kolen (Chapter 3, Section 3.2) discussed the critical importance of test administration conditions to the process of achieving equated scores.

Linn and Kiplinger (1994) conducted a more elaborate investigation of the adequacy of linking statewide standardized test results to NAEP using equipercentile methods. They obtained statewide assessment data and NAEP–TSA results for four states for both 1990 and 1992. Two of the states used different forms of the Stanford Achievement Test, one state used the Iowa Tests of Basic Skills (ITBS), and one used the California Achievement Test (CAT). Linn and Kiplinger used the 1990 data to establish the linking functions and the 1992 data to evaluate the accuracy of those linking functions as "predictions" of the 1992 NAEP results from 1992 statewide assessment results.

Lacking a common metric for the four states' tests, Linn and Kiplinger (1994) did not attempt to compare the linking functions across states. However, they did examine the invariance of the linkings between male and female examinees for two states for which gender identification was available for the statewide test data, and they found that the linking functions differed between the sexes. When the 1990 linking functions were used to predict the 1992 NAEP results from 1992 statewide assessment scores, Linn and Kiplinger found differences substantially larger than could be expected from sampling error in one or both tails of the distributions in all four states. This led Linn and Kiplinger to the conclusion that linking relations between statewide assessment scores and NAEP are neither invariant across subgroups in the population nor stable across time. Describing the Linn and Kiplinger results, Glaser and Linn (1993) wrote, "In general, the equating did not hold, and analyses showed differences larger than chance along most parts of the achievement distribution" (p. 127).

Waltman (1997) examined results obtained with an equipercentile linking of the 1992 administration of the ITBS in Iowa with the 1992 NAEP–TSA mathematics assessments. The goal of Waltman's study was to "investigate the extent to which performance regions on the ITBS and NAEP mathematics score scales could be identified that would classify students in a similar manner." To this end, Waltman replicated NAGB's standard-setting process with ITBS items in an attempt to obtain cut-scores on the ITBS scale that would correspond to NAGB's basic, proficient, and advanced categories. She compared the results obtained from that standard-setting activity to those obtained using equipercentile linking of the ITBS to the NAEP scale and found that the results differed substantially. In contrast to the results obtained by Ercikan (1997) and Linn and Kiplinger (1994), Waltman did not find subgroup differences in the linking function. However, she did not examine either gender or between-state differences; the only subgroups considered were defined by the "type of community (TOC)" classification into "advantaged urban, disadvantaged urban, extremely rural, and other nonextreme" students. In addition, Waltman noted that both the ITBS and NAEP were tests with low-stakes outcomes in Iowa at that time, which might have increased the stability of the results.

16.3.3. The Linkage of the NC EOG with NAEP

The first edition of the North Carolina End-of-Grade (NC EOG) tests for grades 3–8 assessed the achievement of public school students in mathematics and reading. A special data collection effort was mounted in February 1994 to provide a linkage between the NC EOG and NAEP scales for eighth-grade mathematics (Williams, Rosa, McLeod, Thissen, & Sanford, 1998). The original goal of the linkage was to provide estimates of North Carolina statewide achievement results on the NAEP scale in years when NAEP was not administered; subsequently, the linkage was briefly used to report estimates of results on the NAEP scale for individual school districts in North Carolina.

There had been a planned 1994 administration of the NAEP–TSA in mathematics; however, that was subsequently canceled due to budgetary constraints. To develop a linkage between NC EOG and the NAEP scale and to partially replace the "lost" 1994 NAEP results, a special administration in 1994 involved a test comprising 78 items, including a short form of the NC EOG mathematics test for grade 8 (40 multiple-choice items) and two blocks of released 1992 NAEP mathematics items (38 items: 29 multiple choice and 9 constructed response). Examinees were selected in a two-stage sampling design formulated by Westat, Inc., the sampling subcontractor for the NAEP–TSA, for what would have been the 1994 administration of NAEP–TSA had it been funded. A total of 2,824 students were tested.

This was the first of the state-NAEP linkage studies that provided matched individual-level scores on the statewide assessment and NAEP, permitting examination of the relation between the two. The correlation between the NC EOG and NAEP scores was .73, compared to internal consistency reliability coefficients of .82 for the NC EOG items and .88 for the NAEP items; if the two tests measured the same thing, the correlation between them would more closely approach their reliability. In addition, the differences (in standard deviation units) between the average scores for students in two ethnic classifications (BHN [Black, Hispanic, and Native American examinees] and WA [White, Asian/Pacific Islander, and Other examinees]) differed between the two tests; that difference was substantially larger for the NAEP scores than for the NC EOG scores. These two pieces of evidence suggested that the two tests do not measure exactly the same aspects of mathematics proficiency, and so neither concordance nor calibration were considered viable alternatives for the linking. Therefore, the NC EOG–NAEP linkage was done using projection.

Two projections were made of the NAEP results from NC EOG scores. The first used the scores on the short version of the NC EOG mathematics test that was included in the February special linkage study, and the second predicted the February NAEP results from the May 1994 operational administration of the NC EOG tests (individual student responses were matched for the students in the special study). The average of the NC EOG scores from the February special administration of the NC EOG mathematics test was about 0.4 standard units lower than observed in the regular May administration. Because subsequent predictions of NAEP performance would be based on May operational testing, the results of the projection from the May administration of the NC EOG test to a putative February administration of NAEP were used.

The NC EOG–NAEP linkage analyses proceeded through two phases: (a) selection of a model for NAEP averages and standard deviations, conditional on EOG scores and the ethnic classification, and (b) bootstrap computation of standard errors for the regression coefficients.

For the projection, students were categorized into groups based on ethnic classification and EOG scaled score. The projection equations fitted the NAEP posterior mean of each Ethnic classification × EOG score. The standard deviations of the posteriors were predicted from the EOG scores. After the regression equations were developed to predict the means and standard deviations for NAEP proficiency for each Ethnic classification × EOG score category, Gaussian distributions with these means and standard deviations were used in the projection system as estimates of the conditional distribution of proficiency. When the projection was done for new observations on the NC EOG test, those distributions were weighted by the number of observations in each category and summed, to yield the projected NAEP distribution.

Standard errors for the regression coefficients were computed using a bootstrap procedure described by Sitter (1992a, 1992b). The bootstrap plan included finite population corrections at the first and second sampling stages, for schools and for students within schools. Subsequently, simulation was used to estimate the precision of statistics computed from the projected distribution.

In addition to its planned use to provide off-year estimates of mathematics proficiency on the NAEP scale for North Carolina, the NC EOG–NAEP projection was used for a short time to provide results on the NAEP scale for each of the school districts in the state (Triplett, 1995). However, both of those uses received mixed reviews from both the professional community and the public.

Subsequent use of the projection system to predict the 1996 NAEP–TSA results gave results that were relatively close to the mark, but erred in the direction that suggested that scores were increasing faster over time on the NC EOG than on NAEP, echoing what had been found earlier in Kentucky with KIRIS (Williams et al., 1998). After 1996, the NC EOG program came to have increasingly high stakes, which would have been expected to have an increasing differential effect on the NC EOG scores relative to NAEP.

Presentation of projected NAEP-scale results at the district level was not an unambiguous public relations success. A story in the Raleigh (NC) *News & Observer* (Simmons, 1995) quoted one school district testing specialist as saying, "The way they went about building these comparisons is so complex that I just don't see the value in it. They built this Rube Goldberg machine of equations and then said, 'Trust us. The numbers will work out in the end.'" Another official from a school district that scored particularly low said, "Is it helpful for us to know this? No, I can't say we really needed this information."

Additionally, more sophisticated statistically inclined reviewers of the system privately raised serious concerns: Given the clear lack of population invariance in the linking across the ethnic classification, one could question whether there were other, unmodeled, failures of population invariance that could have rendered the system inaccurate when applied to smaller groups, such as school districts. These concerns, coupled with accumulating evidence that such linkages would not be stable over time, and the extravagant cost of studies sufficiently large and detailed to check on potential problems led to the abandonment of the use of the linkage after reports were issued for only 2 years.

16.3.4. The "Four-State Study"

With the background of the several linkage studies with NAEP heretofore mentioned and the idea that states might want to translate their statewide assessment results onto the NAEP scale in years in which NAEP is not administered, the National Center for Education Statistics (NCES) called on the Educational Statistics Services to investigate the feasibility of linkage between four states' mathematics assessments and NAEP (McLaughlin 1998a, 1998b). Because data from four states were involved, this has come to be known as the "four-state study" even though the studies by Linn and Kiplinger (1994) and Ercikan (1997) also involved data from two other sets of four states.

McLaughlin's (1998a, 1998b) study made use of more complex data and models than any previous linkage to NAEP, except, perhaps, the ASVAB linkage. With the cooperation of state education agencies in the four states, individual state assessment results were located and linked for most of the students in the 1996 NAEP mathematics samples in those states. The linkages used projection involving multilevel regression models that included both student-level and school-level terms. Although McLaughlin did not find significant school-level effects on the slope parameters relating the NAEP scores with the state assessment scores, there were effects on the school intercepts such that students in schools with higher average state scores were projected to have higher average NAEP scores.

McLaughlin's (1998a, 1998b) projections also included significant effects for minority status (in all states and both grades) and gender (in one state at grade 4 and three states at grade 8); school locale was considered but not found significant. McLaughlin found that differences between groups on NAEP's results could be substantially underestimated using the linkages, probably due at least in part to other, unmodeled effects such as parental educational level.

In three of the four states, McLaughlin (1998a, 1998b) was able to use the linkage developed on the 1996 data to postdict NAEP school means in 1992, using 1992 state assessment data. In two states, gains from 1992 to 1996 were substantially larger on the state assessment than they were on NAEP, and in a third state, NAEP showed a gain while the state assessment showed a drop.

Thus, this far more extensive study came to approximately the same conclusions that had been accumulating throughout the 1990s: Although it is possible to construct linkages of statewide assessments to the NAEP scale, the linkages are usually not invariant over subpopulations and not particularly stable over time and might require data components, such as school-level information or data on an extensive background variables, which complicate the usage of linkage as a replacement for administration of the "real assessment."

16.5. More Recent Linkages with NAEP

16.5.1. The Linkage of the TIMSS with NAEP

The Third International Mathematics and Science Study (TIMSS) conducted in 1995, and the administration of NAEP in 1996, provided an opportunity to compare the mathematics and science performance of states (based on their NAEP results) with countries (based on their TIMSS results) using a linkage between the scales of the two assessments. Johnson (1998) described the technical details of that linkage, and Johnson and Siegendorf (1998) provided an extensive set of tables comparing the performance of each state to 41 nations, with the tables answering the question "If the public schools in _____ participated in TIMSS, how would their average performance in mathematics [or science] compare to that of students in the 41 nations that took TIMSS at grade 8?"

Only aggregate data were available to construct and evaluate the linkage of TIMSS as administered in 1995 with NAEP from 1996. The linkage was "statistical moderation" (Mislevy, 1992), a form of what Holland (Chapter 2, Section 2.3.2) called anchor scaling, making use of linear linking between the grade 8 NAEP distributions of mathematics and science proficiency for the United States and the U.S. distribution of mathematics and science proficiency from TIMSS. Johnson (1998, pp. 4-1–4-2) showed that the two pairs of distributions had very similar shapes.

Linear linking was used to transform scores on the 500-point across-grade NAEP scale to the 300-point within-grade metric used by TIMSS.

Johnson (1998) described the exhaustive estimation of the variance of the linking function (and, hence, of the linked results), including components of variance for sampling, measurement error, model misspecification (as determined from the variation in the linking functions across subgroups), and an estimate of the temporal shift (because TIMSS was conduced in 1995 and NAEP was conducted in 1996). It also happened that Minnesota had actually participated in TIMSS (as a countrylike state) in 1995. As validation, the linkage was used to postdict Minnesota's 1995 TIMSS results from that state's 1996 NAEP results, and the actual results were well within the confidence intervals around the prediction. Further, Missouri and Oregon participated in a state-level administration of TIMSS in 1998; Johnson (1998) reported that predicted TIMSS results for those states using the 1995 TIMSS/1996 NAEP linking functions were consistent with their actual TIMSS results.

Johnson (1998) and Johnson and Siegendorf (1998) presented the results of the NAEP–TIMSS link with a number of cautions. Johnson (1998) wrote that "the linking was evaluated for a variety of demographic subgroups. While the predicted values from the various subgroup-based linkings were not significantly different from each other, there was still enough difference to suggest that caution be used in applying the links to subpopulations" (p. 11-1). Johnson and Siegendorf (1998) wrote that "the SOLE purpose of these profiles is to allow the comparison of the predicted TIMSS performance for individual states with the actual TIMSS performance of individual countries. It is NOT appropriate to use these profiles to compare performance between states or between countries" (p. 7). Johnson (1998) noted that "the link ... assumes that the relationship between NAEP and TIMSS is the same within the states as it is in the country as a whole" and that "there is no guarantee that the link established in this report would hold in subsequent years" (p. 11-3).

Johnson (1998) also noted that a parallel linkage was attempted for grade 4 mathematics, but that its results have not been released. One possible reason is that the results of that linkage might not have passed the very careful checks that were put in place to evaluate the grade 8 linkage. The linkage of disparate assessments remains a fragile enterprise. Another attempt to link the scales of NAEP and TIMSS is expected with the next nearly simultaneous administrations of the two assessments (E.G. Johnson, personal communication, March 22, 2005); it will be interesting indeed to compare that linkage with the results from 1995–1996, to examine the stability of such linkages over time.

16.5.2. Linkage to Compare States' Standards

In an extraordinarily influential unpublished paper, Musick (1996) compared the proportions labeled *proficient* (or some approximately equivalent term) in a number of statewide assessment systems and those estimated to be proficient by NAEP and found wide variation. That comparison suggested that some more formal linkage of state achievement-level standards with the scale and achievement-level standards of NAEP could be informative about the relative difficulty of the state standards.

McLaughlin and Bandeira de Mello (2002, 2003) used school-level results from the NAEP samples for 2000 and 2002 and the proportion of students labeled proficient by their state in each of the NAEP-sampled schools to estimate cut-scores on the NAEP scale that were, in the equipercentile sense, equivalent to the state standards. As expected, they found wide variation across states in the linked NAEP-scale cut-scores for categories that were considered approximately equivalent to proficient.

Braun and Qian (2006) offered a number of technical modifications to McLaughlin and Bandeira de Mello's (2002, 2003) procedures, largely involving the more extensive use of NAEP's sampling weights in the computation of the proportions "proficient" within schools. Braun and Qian also used the NAEP jackknife procedure to estimate the contribution of the sampling of schools and students to the variance of the estimates of the cut-scores, and they combine that variation with measurement error variance to obtain improved confidence intervals for the NAEP-scale cut-scores corresponding to the state's achievement levels. Braun and Qian (Chapter 17) discussed these contributions in more detail.

16.6. Problems Requiring Further Research

16.6.1. Motivational Effects

Among the measurement problems that Wainer (1993) posed as pressing needs for research were the questions: "How can we separate demonstrated proficiency from motivation?" and "Are examinees poorly taught or just not trying?" (p. 12). Motivational differences that lead to differences in performance on two tests being linked might invalidate the attempt to infer what would have happened had one test been given from the results of another. If the data for two assessments in a linkage study arise from circumstances under which the examinees are more motivated on one than the other, the average level of the projection might be too high or too low relative to that which would be obtained if the second test had actually been administered.

Bloxom et al. (1995) attributed the substantial difference they found between ASVAB and NAEP scores, relative to national norms for both tests, to motivational differences; this was suggested by the fact that the ASVAB scores had personal consequences for the participants in their research, whereas the NAEP results did not. A substantial difference, about 0.4 standard units, was observed between average scores on the low-stakes special administration of the NC EOG mathematics test for the NAEP linkage described earlier and the operational administration (Williams et al., 1998).

In a study of the effect of motivation on test scores, Wolf and Smith (1995) administered alternate forms of a college-level introductory psychology test under conditions that suggested that the score on the test would count toward the test-taker's grade, or that it would not count. (The entire testing situation was within an experimental setting, with informed consent, so the extent of the motivational manipulation is not entirely clear.) Wolf and Smith found that scores were about 0.25 standard units higher for their more motivated group. Although Wolf and Smith considered that motivational effect on the outcome relatively small, we note that 0.25 standard units on the NAEP scale for eighth-grade mathematics is about 9 points, which is more than enough to represent a reliable difference between state averages, for instance.

From a less experimental, but more realistic, context, Figure 16.2 shows the differences (for grades 3–8) between average scores from a low-stakes item tryout administration and a high-stakes operational administration on North Carolina's statewide reading test. In the spring of 2002, one form of the first edition of the NC EOG reading test was administered to representative sample of North Carolina students as part of the item tryout for the second edition of the test. Very shortly thereafter, other forms of the first edition were administered operationally. Figure 16.2 shows the difference between average scores on the operational administration and those from the item tryout, plotted as a function of grade with a regression line superimposed to clarify the trend. The results in Figure 16.2 illustrate average score differences on the order of 0.2–0.4 standard units—as large as those found by Wolf and Smith (1995), or larger.

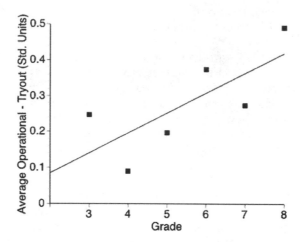

Figure 16.2. Differences (for grades 3–8) between average scores from a low-stakes item tryout administration and a high-stakes operational administration on North Carolina's statewide reading test, plotted as a function of grade.

A rhetorical question that could haunt attempts to estimate proportions scoring in NAEP's low-stakes achievement levels from a high-stakes statewide assessment is how many students would be classified as "proficient" by NAEP if they thought, when NAEP was administered, that it was their statewide assessment and that they might be retained in grade if they did not answer enough questions correctly? As the stakes surrounding statewide assessments escalate, one could argue that students become increasingly testwise, learning to expend effort only when it counts.

16.6.2. The Stability of Linking

In the 1990s, one of the reasons for linking regularly administered tests to the NAEP scale was that linkages offered the opportunity to fill in the gaps between administrations of NAEP that cover a particular subject area at a particular grade level. To be valid for this purpose, the relation between proficiency as measured by NAEP and the test scores and background variables that are used in the linkage must remain constant over time. After a presentation on the NC EOG–NAEP linkage, Paul Williams (personal communication, January 1995) asked if we knew anything about the period of time over which such linkages might wisely continue to be used. We did not.

Accumulated evidence now suggests that the answer is "not for very long." As previously mentioned, Hambleton et al. (1995) and Koretz and Barron (1998) found that gains in scores on the KIRIS in the 1990s consistently exceeded Kentucky's score gains on NAEP. Linn and Kiplinger (1994) reported that linkages of statewide tests to NAEP based on 1990 data did not predict 1992 results very well (in the tails of the distributions).

In addition to the NC EOG–NAEP linkage, we also linked reading and mathematics scores for the NC EOG reading and mathematics tests for grades 5 and 8 to the scale of the Iowa Tests of Basic Skills (ITBS), using sets of data collected in 1993 and 1994.[5] The results for the 1993 and 1994 datasets differed significantly in level, with the ITBS scores showing less improvement between 1993 and 1994 than did the NC EOG scores. The differences were sufficiently large that we judged the 1993 linkage not to be adequate to project the 1994 data.

Why might scale linkages be so unstable over time? Instability over time is a kind of lack of invariance, specifically from one time to another. Green (2003) stated that "the most obvious explanation of the failure of invariance in equating is that the different test forms" (in our context, different assessments) "place different emphasis on different parts of content, and that test takers have had differential exposure to, or differential interest in, various aspects of test content" (quoted by Kolen, 2004b, pp. 11–12). Curricular emphases in, say, a state, can change very fast.

As an illustration, consider the data presented in Figure 16.3, which is a plot of the differences in average scores on the NC EOG (second edition) mathematics scale between 2000 and 2001, plotted as a function of grade, with a regression line superimposed to clarify the absence of any trend. In the spring of 2000, the items that were to comprise the second edition of the NC EOG mathematics tests were embedded in the operational administration of the first edition tests, whereas in 2001, the second edition was operational. Figure 16.3 shows the difference between the average scores obtained across grades for the two administrations. Unlike Figure 16.2, Figure. 16.3 does *not* show a putative motivational effect; the students thought that both the item tryout second edition items and the operational first edition items were all part of a high-stakes test in 2000.

---

[5] The NC EOG-ITBS linkages were done by Kathleen Rosa and Lori McLeod, in collaboration with the author.

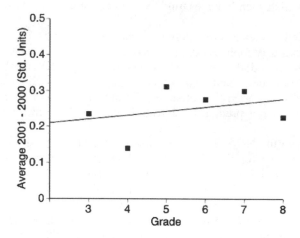

Figure 16.3. Differences in average scores on the NC EOG (second edition) mathematics scale between 2000 (when the second edition's curriculum had not been fully implemented) and 2001 (the first year of full implementation of the new curriculum), plotted as a function of grade.

However, Figure 16.3 does show a likely curricular effect: The new edition of the test was required because the statewide curriculum changed. The curricular change was substantial, including increased emphasis on computation, and there were corresponding changes in the content balance of the assessment. (Koretz, Bertenthal, & Green [1999, p. 32] included as their Figure 2-5 a graphic showing a sharp decrease on the computational subset of items of the ITBS during the 1990s, as mathematics curricula shifted away from emphasis on context-free computation. Results such as those have led to reemphasis on computation in some more recent mathematics curricula.) Students in 2000, who had probably followed the old curriculum, scored substantially lower than did students in 2001, who had followed the new curriculum for a year. As was the case with motivational differences, there is evidence that curricular differences can account for changes in averages of as much as 0.25 standard units or more.

16.7. Conclusions

Although fraught with difficulty, the linkage of disparate assessments characterized by aggregate reporting continues. As noted previously, although earlier attempts to link NAEP with international assessments have not been unambiguously successful, further linkages between NAEP and TIMSS are planned. The use of NAEP's scale to compare the meaning of different states' achievement-level standards has high salience for the educational community, as shown by the fact that it was featured in Linn's (2003) presidential address to the American Educational Research Association. Further use of school-level linkage of the scales of statewide assessments and NAEP is planned, to use such a linkage to create a hybrid across-state database placing the results of various statewide assessments on a common scale for the purpose of research on the relationships between school factors and school achievement (D. McLaughlin, personal communication, January 7, 2005).

The continuing use of linkage between disparate assessments is not making the results easier to rely upon or even to interpret. The most difficult problem to solve might be variation in the unknown level of motivation with which students approach any large-scale standardized test that lacks direct personal consequences. (The fact is, we do not know very much about the effects of the level of motivation with which students approach tests with important personal consequences; we simply assume that it is high and hope that it is not so high as to create anxiety and reduce performance.) This problem has not newly arisen with linkage; linkage studies merely provide the opportunity to observe variation that might be due to differential motivation. We have never known the level of motivation for students responding to NAEP, or whether differences in that level of motivation, as opposed to differences in knowledge and skills, might account for observed differences in test scores. The data collected for purposes of test linkage serve as a reminder that it would be useful to obtain some measure of motivation, on some scale, in any large-scale testing program, as an index of validity; or that we at least attempt to convince ourselves that the level of motivation, whatever it is, does not covary with other aspects of the data that we might interpret.

Where possible, it might be best to avoid special administrations of either test for purposes of linkage construction. If the motivational level of the examinees is unknown during the regular administration of a test like NAEP, it is doubly unknown when that test is administered in a different context. Planned database management could permit linkages to be developed from the regular administration of tests, by matching data after the fact. That has been done in most recent linkage attempts.

The question of the stability of test linkage over time or populations is entirely empirical. We need to observe the extent to which the conditional relations between scores on the two tests being linked are constant or variable over time, or between groups. In principle, a partial answer to this question could be obtained retrospectively—with respect to NAEP, the students who have participated in NAEP over the past few years have also likely taken other tests, and those historical data could be used to produce multiple linkages that could be compared. In practice, such retrospective analysis is unlikely to be possible because the data required to match observations on one test with those of the other (i.e., student identification of some sort) have not been readily available. Thus, this question must be left to future research, as time passes and multiple linkages are done. It would be wise if future administrations of NAEP recorded and incorporated in the dataset suitable individual identification for matching with data from other testing programs, using adequate safeguards for privacy.

Many of the issues that this chapter has raised with respect to linkage have been discussed in more detail in two National Research Council (NRC) reports, *Uncommon Measures: Equivalence and Linking among Educational Tests* (Feuer, Holland, Green, Bertenthal, & Hemphill, 1998) and *Embedding Questions: The Pursuit of a Common Measure in Uncommon Tests* (Koretz et al., 1999). Readers seeking an expanded treatment of these topics, as well as consideration of the issues as they apply to individual test scores, are encouraged to peruse those volumes.

Acknowledgments. I am grateful to Lyle V. Jones, Neil Dorans, and Mary Pommerich for advice on earlier drafts of this chapter. However, the opinions expressed and any errors that remain are of course my own.

17 An Enhanced Method for Mapping State Standards onto the NAEP Scale

Henry I. Braun and Jiahe Qian[1]

Boston College and Educational Testing Service

17.1. Introduction

During the 1990s, under the impetus of standards-based reform, many states established performance standards for their students in selected grades and subjects. Under the most recent reauthorization of the Elementary and Secondary Education Act (ESEA), the No Child Left Behind Act of 2001 (NCLB), all states are required to set such standards in reading and mathematics for grades 3–8 as well as in at least one grade in high school. NCLB, however, leaves to the states the responsibility of determining the curriculum, selecting the assessments, and setting challenging academic standards. Not surprisingly, the result has been substantial heterogeneity in both the quality and apparent stringency of the standards set by the states (Lane, 2004; Linn, 2003). One consequence is that in a particular grade, very different proportions of students in the various states have been declared to have met a standard with the same label (e.g., proficient). These differences have occasioned much confusion and concern among stakeholders.

A moment's reflection shows that unambiguous comparisons of standards among states are problematic in view of the flexibility accorded to the states under NCLB; that is, were states using the same test, then determining the relative stringency of the standards could be accomplished by simply comparing the cut-points established by each state. In the present

---

[1] The opinions expressed in this chapter are those of the authors and not necessarily of Boston College or Educational Testing Service.

context, such direct comparisons are impossible. It is evident that there would be value in somehow placing all state standards on a common basis to facilitate approximate but credible comparisons in student test performance. As will be made clear below, any such effort cannot eliminate an essential indeterminacy that must be taken into account in the interpretation of the results. Nonetheless, given the both the importance and visibility of the issue, it seems appropriate to address it as responsibly as one can.

In the past, there have been a number of calls to somehow link all of the states' test score scales directly or, failing that, to map them all on to the NAEP scale, inasmuch as the National Assessment of Educational Progress (NAEP) is the only test that is administered in a uniform manner across states. (Moreover, NAEP is generally regarded as meeting high standards with respect to test design, test content, and psychometric quality.[2]) If such linkages were possible, then comparisons among state standards would be relatively straightforward. Unfortunately, the literature is replete with arguments against the appropriateness of such mappings (e.g. Linn, 1993). More recently, two studies carried out under the auspices of the National Research Council (Feuer, Holland, Green, Bertenthal, & Hemphill, 1998; Koretz, Bertenthal, & Green, 1999) concluded that, for a number of reasons, mappings at the student level could not be validly constructed.

McLaughlin and his associates (McLaughlin & Bandeira de Mello, 2002, 2003) made an innovative attempt to circumvent some of the difficulties cited in the NRC studies. Their approach was to carry out the mapping to the NAEP scale only at the school level (at a single point) and then, by aggregation, to the state level. Specifically, they employed equipercentile linking (Braun & Holland, 1982; Kolen, Chapter 3) in each school to find a point on the NAEP score scale that best corresponds to the state standard. That point represents the local estimate of the state standard on the NAEP scale. A simple average of these local estimates across all the schools in the NAEP sample (approximately 80–100 schools) yields the final estimate of the NAEP scale score equivalent to the state standard. It should be noted that in their computations, they used the so-called full population estimates (FPE) of NAEP score distributions (McLaughlin, 2000; Pitoniak & Mead, 2003), rather than the reported NAEP distributions. Evidence for the plausibility of most of these mappings of the state standards to the NAEP scale can be found in McLaughlin and Bandeira de Mello (2002).

This chapter presents an alternative approach, albeit one that also relies on equipercentile linking. This method takes into account NAEP's complex sample design both in obtaining an estimate of the NAEP equivalent

---

[2] For a general introduction to NAEP, see Jones & Olkin (2004).

of a state standard and in deriving an estimated variance of the NAEP equivalent. The method was applied to data from states' 2000 mathematics assessment and the NAEP 2000 mathematics assessment, as well as to data from states' 2002 reading assessment and the NAEP 2002 reading assessment.[3] Aside from our use of the reported NAEP distributions, the main difference between the approach adopted in this study and that of McLaughlin and his associates is that we obtain what might be termed a direct estimate of the NAEP equivalent by using appropriately weighted estimates of the state's NAEP distribution and of the proportion of students meeting the state's achievement standard(s). The rationale is that such a direct estimate should be more precise than one that relies on a simple average of a large number of less precise estimates from a probability sample of schools.

We conduct a number of data analyses that support, on methodological grounds, a preference for this approach to that of McLaughlin and Bandeira de Mello (2003). We then assert that most of the observed differences among states in the proportions of students meeting states' proficiency standards are the result of differences in the stringency of their standards. This is followed by an examination of the evidence for the assertion. If it is essentially correct, then it has important implications for education policy. In particular, it begs the question of whether all students deemed proficient are actually prepared to succeed once they leave the public school system.

Underlying both the approach described here and McLaughlin's approach is the assumption that, for a particular subject and grade, the state tests and NAEP are similar in content and structure. This is necessary so that the linking is not simply a meaningless exercise in numerology. It is also worth noting that both approaches treat as equivalent the proportions meeting a standard defined in terms of an estimate of the state score distribution and a cut-point defined in terms of an estimate of a NAEP score distribution. These two estimates are based on data at different levels of analysis: the former on cumulating scores of individual students and the latter on obtaining a direct estimate of the underlying true-score distribution. Of course, there are also differences in the use of a census rather than a sample, in exclusion rules, in the kinds of instruments used, and so on. However, inasmuch as state test forms are usually fairly long and have reasonably high reliabilities, we believe that for our purposes that we can ignore these differences.

In the next two sections we provide a brief outline and a more detailed description of the proposed method. Section 17.4 describes the derivation

---

[3] Data from both grades 4 and 8 were analyzed. Because of space limitations, only the results from grade 4 are presented here. The technical report by Braun and Qian (2006) contains the full set of results.

of the variance estimates and Section 17.5 presents results for grade 4 in both mathematics and reading. Specifically, state-by-state results are presented for standards labeled proficient or its equivalent. Section 17.6 describes mapping NAEP standards into a state scale and Section 17.7 offers conclusions and recommendations.

17.2. Outline of the Methodology

The procedure is carried out separately for each state. In the description that follows, we refer to the mathematics data. An identical procedure was used for the reading data. Let P, which is formally defined in Section 17.3.2, denote the statewide proportion of students meeting a particular standard. To emphasize the differences in the two approaches, we will refer to our method as weighted aggregate mapping (WAM) and that of McLaughlin and associates as unweighted local mapping (ULM).

1. Based on the proportions of students who meet a state's performance standard on that state's own assessment in NAEP-sampled schools, estimate the proportion of students in the state as a whole who meet the state's standard. First, we identify the schools in the state NAEP sample and match them with their records in the National Longitudinal School-Level State Assessment Score Database.[4] For each school, we obtain the proportion of students meeting the state standard. Using the school weights from the NAEP design, we obtain an estimate of P using a ratio estimator, $\bar{p}_w$, which is a weighted average estimate of the number of students meeting the standard over a weighted average estimate of the number of eligible students. (See Section 17.3.1 for more detail.)

2. Based on the NAEP sample of schools and students within schools, estimate the distribution of scores on the NAEP assessment for the state as a whole. This is the procedure that is carried out to generate the results contained in the NCES report that follows each NAEP assessment. Let $\hat{F}$ denote the estimated distribution.

3. Find the point on the NAEP score scale at which the estimated proportion of students in the state scoring above that point equals the

---

[4] The National Longitudinal School-Level State Assessment Score Database (NLSLSASD; www.schooldata.org) is constructed and maintained by the American Institutes for Research (AIR) for NCES. Its purpose is to collect and validate data from state testing programs across the country. It contains assessment data for approximately 80,000 public schools in the United States and is updated annually.

proportion of students in the state meeting the state's own performance standard. Using the results of 1 and 2, we map the performance
standard to the NAEP scale, by finding the point y_{WAM} on the NAEP
scale that is the $(1 - \bar{p}_w)$th quantile:

$$y_{\text{WAM}} = \hat{F}^{-1}(1 - \bar{p}_w).$$

We take y_{WAM} to be *the estimated NAEP equivalent score to the
state standard*. If the state employs more than one standard, the above
procedure can be repeated for each one.

4. Compute the variance of the estimated NAEP equivalent score. Using
the jackknife procedure, we estimate the contribution of the sampling
of schools and students to the variance of the estimator and combine
it with an estimate of the contribution of measurement error to obtain
a total variance estimate.

Figure 17.1 illustrates the mapping procedure. The dashed curve on the
left-hand side represents an estimate of the state distribution of scores on
the state test, based on all students in the schools selected for the state's
NAEP sample. The area in the upper tail of this distribution above the state
standard is an estimate of the proportion of students in the state meeting or
exceeding that standard, and is denoted by $\hat{p}_w$. In practice, only $\hat{p}_w$ need
to be obtained from the data. The curve on the right-hand side represents the
estimated distribution of NAEP scores for the state. This is the usual reported NAEP distribution based on students in the state's NAEP sample
who took the NAEP assessment. The estimated NAEP equivalent to the
state standard, y_{WAM}, is the point on the NAEP scale, such that the corresponding upper tail area of the NAEP distribution also equals $\hat{p}_w$.

The estimate y_{WAM} is derived from a single composite distribution of
the scores of all assessed students in all NAEP selected schools in a state.
The estimate proposed by McLaughlin and associates is the average of the
mapped standards obtained from each of the schools in the NAEP sample.
We denote this estimate by $\bar{z}_{\text{ULM}}$. (More detail can be found in Appendix
A of Braun & Qian, 2006.) Although the empirical results generally show
small differences between y_{WAM} and $\bar{z}_{\text{ULM}}$, there are important conceptual
differences. Appendix B of Braun and Qian (2006) provided an analysis of
these differences. In particular, the assumption underlying the calculation
of $\bar{z}_{\text{ULM}}$ (namely that the estimates of the NAEP equivalent from the
schools in a state participating in NAEP can be treated as a simple random
sample) is not supported by the data.

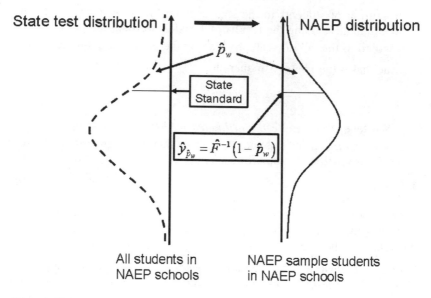

Figure 17.1. The schematic of the mapping procedure.

17.3. Details of the Methodology

17.3.1. The Weights for NAEP Schools

State NAEP samples are obtained through a two-stage probability sampling design. The first stage constitutes a probability sample of schools containing the relevant grade. The second stage involves the selection of a random sample of students within each school.

To account for the unequal probabilities of selection and to allow for adjustments for nonresponse, each school and each student were assigned separate sampling weights. If these weights are not employed in the computation of the statistics of interest, the resulting estimates can be biased. With this caution in mind, we applied appropriate weights in the estimation of the proportion of students in the state above the standard. In general, the student weight is inversely proportional to the product of the school selection probability and the student selection probability.

Formally, let N be the total number of schools in a state and M_k be the number of students who were grade-eligible at school k. Therefore, the total number of eligible students in the state is $\sum_{l=1}^{N} M_l$. Let n be the number of schools in the state NAEP sample. Let π_k be the school selection probability, which is proportional to its size M_k, and let $\pi_{i|k}$ be the conditional probability of selection for student i in school k. Suppose that b students are randomly selected from school k. Then the unconditional selection probability of student i in school k is

$$\pi_{ki} = \pi_k \cdot \pi_{i|k} = \frac{a \cdot M_k}{\sum_{l=1}^{N} M_l} \cdot \frac{b}{M_k},$$

where a is a constant of normalization. Then the weight of student i in school k is

$$w_{ki} = w_k \cdot w_{i|k} = \frac{1}{a \cdot M_k / \sum_{l-1}^{N} M_l} \cdot \frac{1}{b / M_k}.$$

This formula is only an approximation because students are selected without replacement and the vicissitudes of field work necessitate modifications to the ideal weights. For example, nonresponse adjustments to the weights are employed in NAEP to account for effects of schools and students who were selected but did not participate. In any case, the weight of school k in a state NAEP sample is approximately

$$w_k = \frac{1}{a \cdot M_k / \sum_{l=1}^{N} M_l},$$

which equals the inverse of the approximate school selection probability. Because school weights are not retained in the NAEP database, for this study the estimates of school weights were computed in two steps. First, the sum of the student design weights for each school was calculated and then this sum was divided by the number of eligible students. Details of the creation of school design weights for NAEP can be found in *NAEP 1998 Technical Report* (Qian, Kaplan, Johnson, Krenzke, & Rust, 2001, Chap. 11).

17.3.2. The Ratio Estimator for the Target Proportion

Let P_k be the proportion of students achieving the standard at school k. The total number of students meeting the standard is $\sum_{l=1}^{N} P_l \cdot M_l$. The state-wide target proportion of students meeting the standard is approximately

$$P = \frac{\sum_{l=1}^{N} P_l \cdot M_l}{\sum_{l=1}^{N} M_l}.$$

Using Horvitz–Thompson estimators, the numerator and denominator of P are estimated separately from the state's NAEP school sample. For example, $\sum_{l=1}^{n} w_l M_l$ estimates the total number of eligible students in the state and $\sum_{l=1}^{n} w_l (P_l \cdot M_l)$ estimates the total number of students meeting the standard. The target proportion, P, of students meeting the standard can be estimated by a ratio estimator:

$$\overline{p}_w = \frac{\sum_{l=1}^{n} w_l (P_l \cdot M_l)}{\sum_{l=1}^{n} w_l M_l}.$$

The Horvitz–Thompson estimators $\sum_{l=1}^{n} w_l M_l$ and $\sum_{l=1}^{n} w_l (P_l \cdot M_l)$, are unbiased estimators of the corresponding population totals. Nevertheless, the ratio estimator $\overline{p}_w$ is biased with an order of $O(1/n)$ (Cochran, 1977).

An interesting result can be derived by substituting for the school weight w_l in $\overline{p}_w$ the inverse of the school selection probability. Simple algebra shows that the corresponding estimate reduces to $(1/n) \sum_{l=1}^{n} P_l$, which is denoted by $\overline{p}$. Thus, with this simplification, the ratio estimator equals the simple average of P_l in the sample. Because the weights in NAEP samples reflect the effects of oversampling, nonresponse adjustments, and trimming, the actual school weight, w_l, will differ somewhat from

$\sum\limits_{l=1}^{N} M_l /(a \cdot M_l)$ and, therefore, $\overline{p}_w$ will also differ slightly from $\overline{p}$. However, since the school size data are not available for all schools in the states
in the study, we have chosen to replace P by $\overline{P}$, the population analog of
$\overline{p}$; that is $\overline{P} = (1/N)\sum\limits_{l=1}^{N} P_l$.

We have chosen to use the ratio estimator $\overline{p}_w$ in our analysis. A plausible alternative would be to employ $\overline{P}$, which is based on data from all the
schools in the state containing the relevant grade. With our choice, the
same schools contribute to the estimation of the relevant parameters of the
state test score distribution and the NAEP score distribution. We believe
that this match is more consistent with the logic underlying McLaughlin's
method and should yield results with smaller mean squared error. As we
see below, the differences between $\overline{p}_w$ and $\overline{P}$ are typically very small.

17.3.3. Empirical Evaluation of the Estimates

17.3.3.1. Data Resources

The data analyzed in this study consisted of the NAEP 2000 mathematics proficiency distributions for grade 4 students in the R3[5] sample. We
also employed the 2000 state grade 4 mathematics tests. The state data
were obtained from the NLSLSASD database. This database contains the
proportions of students, by school, meeting each of the state's standards,
for nearly all states, beginning as early as the academic year 1994. However, it does not contain scores for individual students.

17.3.3.2. Evaluation of the Bias of the Estimates of the Target Proportions

We evaluate the approximate bias of the sample estimates of the proportion proficient by analyzing the grade 4 (G4) 2000 mathematics standards.
We compare the ratio estimator, $\overline{p}_w$, and the ordinary simple average of
school proportions, $\overline{p}$, to $\overline{P}$, the statewide target proportion of students
meeting the standard, which was defined in the previous section. For pre-
sent purposes, $\overline{P}$ is treated as the true state percentage.

---

[5] For reporting purposes, two sample types, R2 and R3, were formed in the 2000
operational NAEP assessment. The sample type R2 provides inferences for a less
inclusive population where accommodations were not permitted; the sample type
R3 provides inferences for a more inclusive population where accommodations
were permitted. Since 2002, only the R3 sample type has been employed.

Table 17.1 summarizes, for each state standard of proficiency,[6] the key statistics of the 2000 state mathematics test score distribution. The first and second columns of the tables contain the total number of (grade-relevant) schools in the state population and the number of NAEP schools in the sample for each state. The third column is the statewide target proportion of students meeting the standard. The fourth and fifth columns are the estimates denoted by $\bar{p}_w$ and $\bar{p}$.

We now define the bias of the estimators $\bar{p}_w$ and $\bar{p}$ as $\bar{p}_w - \bar{P}$ and $\bar{p} - \bar{P}$, respectively. The biases of both estimators are small: For G4 of 2000 math, the bias of $\bar{p}$ is larger than the bias of $\bar{p}_w$ for 11 out of 17 state proficient standards. The averages of the absolute biases for $\bar{p}$ and $\bar{p}_w$ are 1.2% and 1.5% and the maxima of the absolute biases are 6.7% and 6.0%, respectively. The average of the differences between two estimators is just 1.1%.

17.3.3.3. Evaluation of the Estimates of the NAEP Equivalent to the State Standard

Because the target quantity, the NAEP scale score equivalent to the state standard, is not known, it is difficult to determine the bias of an estimate. However, both sampling theory and general NAEP empirical results indicate that estimates using design weights provide superior results to those that do not. The estimate y_{WAM} defined in Section 17.2 does employ these design weights.

In McLaughlin's analysis, FPEs of the NAEP scale score distribution were used. A FPE adjusts the estimated NAEP score distribution to account for the exclusion of some students with disabilities (SD) or limited English proficiency (LEP) in the NAEP assessments. The FPE approach requires the imputation of the performance of those excluded students (McLaughlin, 2000). Because the imputed scale scores for excluded SD/LEP students usually fall at the low end of the distribution, the FPE of the NAEP distribution is stochastically smaller than the reported NAEP distribution. To study the impact of the FPE adjustment, we also applied McLaughlin's procedure to the reported NAEP distribution. We use $\bar{z}'_{\text{ULM}}$ to denote the latter results.

---

[6] Some of the state standards for proficiency were selected by their names and others were inferred by the authors.

Table 17.1. G4 2000 math: The unweighted and weighted proportions of tested students with scores at or above the state standards of proficient

State and standard	No. of schools in state	No. of schools in NAEP sample	State school population Proportion of students meeting the standard, P	NAEP school sample Weighted average proportion meeting the standard, $\bar{p}_w$	Unweighted average proportion meeting the standard, $\bar{p}$
	(1)	(2)	(3)	(4)	(5)
CA PR50	4,827	77	0.50	0.53	0.51
GA Meets	999	98	0.62	0.62	0.61
KS Proficient	741	75	0.37	0.36	0.34
LA Proficient	787	106	0.11	0.11	0.11
MA Proficient	1,020	105	0.40	0.42	0.40
ME Meets	343	105	0.23	0.24	0.23
MI Satisfactory	1,910	84	0.75	0.77	0.76
MO Proficient	1,097	99	0.37	0.36	0.36
NC Consist Mastery	1,229	107	0.84	0.85	0.84
NE Proficient	161	17	0.64	0.60	0.62
NY Meets	1,476	40	0.67	0.68	0.67
OH Pass	1,990	84	0.49	0.43	0.42
RI Proficient	188	108	0.20	0.21	0.20
SC Proficient	549	101	0.24	0.23	0.23
TX Pass	3,417	99	0.87	0.89	0.88
VT Meets	213	60	0.69	0.69	0.68
WY Proficient	162	83	0.27	0.26	0.27

Table 17.2 presents three estimates of the NAEP equivalents to the state standards for G4 of the 2000 state mathematics tests, for state standards of proficient. Columns (1) and (2) contain the results for $\bar{z}_{ULM}$ and $\bar{z}'_{ULM}$, and column (3) presents those for y_{WAM}. For G4 of 2000 math, on average, y_{WAM} is about 0.7 points higher than $\bar{z}_{ULM}$, but about 2.1 points lower than the mean of $\bar{z}'_{ULM}$, which is 229.8. Overall, of the 17 state proficient standards, for 10, $\bar{z}_{ULM}$ is lower than y_{WAM}, and for 14, y_{WAM} is lower than $\bar{z}'_{ULM}$. Although y_{WAM} is usually larger than $\bar{z}_{ULM}$, in some cases $\bar{z}_{ULM}$ is higher. For example, for G4 of 2000 math in California (CA PR50), $\bar{z}_{ULM}$

is about 1.8 points higher than y_{WAM}. This is the largest positive discrepancy among all jurisdictions. It appears that the patterns in the mapped equivalents from the two methods are qualitatively similar. There are systematic differences, however, that are due to our use of school weights and of NAEP reported distributions (see Braun & Qian, 2006).

17.4. Estimation of Variances

17.4.1. Variance Estimation for a Simple Average of School Statistics

Inasmuch as NAEP estimates are based on a sample from a finite population, they are subject to uncertainty due to sampling. Schools are selected with probability proportional to size. Furthermore, because of the effects of clustering of students within schools and of nonresponse and poststratification adjustments, observations made on different students cannot be assumed to be independent of each other. To account for the differential probabilities of selection, each student has an associated sampling weight, which should be used in the computation of any statistic and which is itself subject to sampling variability.

Ignoring the effects of a complex sample design usually results in underestimating the true sampling variability. If the statistic does not use sampling weights (e.g., the simple average $\overline{z}_{\mathrm{ULM}}$), it implicitly treats schools as if they were collected by simple random sampling. Following this logic, an estimate of the variance of $\overline{z}_{\mathrm{ULM}}$, including a finite population correction, yields the following variance estimate:

$$v_{\mathrm{SRS}}\left(\overline{z}_{\mathrm{ULM}}\right) = \frac{1-f}{n(n-1)} \sum_{l=1}^{n} \left(z_l - \overline{z}_{\mathrm{ULM}}\right)^2,$$

where n is the number of schools in a sample, f is the fraction of schools selected, and z_l is the NAEP equivalent score for school l. Note that McLaughlin (2000) neither employed the finite population correction nor accounted for measurement error.

17.4.2. The Variances of Estimated NAEP Scale Score Equivalents

Our approach to variance estimation is consistent with the procedures developed by NAEP for the estimation of the variances of reporting statistics (Allen, Donoghue, & Schoeps, 2001). The total variance of the estimate of

Table 17.2 G4 2000 math: The unweighted and weighted NAEP equivalents to the state standards of proficient

State & standard	Scale scores $\overline{z}_{ULM}$ [a] (1)	Scale scores (ULM w/o FPE) $\overline{z}'_{ULM}$ (2)	Scale scores y_{WAM} (3)	(1)–(3) (4)	SD of $\{z_i\}$ (5)	Variance of (1) by $v_{SRS}(\overline{z}_{ULM})$ (6)	Jackknifed variance of (3) $v_J(y_{WAM})$ (7)	Measurement error of (3) $(1+M^{-1})B$ (8)	Total variance of (3) $v_T(y_{WAM})$ (9)
CA PR50	213.8	217.9	212.0	1.8	11.1	1.6	2.6	0.2	2.8
GA Meets	209.4	210.4	209.0	0.4	9.8	0.9	1.7	0.1	1.8
KS Proficient	244.3	245.2	244.4	−0.1	8.2	0.8	1.2	0.2	1.4
LA Proficient	249.9	250.3	250.8	−0.9	9.8	0.8	0.7	0.9	1.6
MA Proficient	242.2	243.1	241.9	0.3	8.3	0.6	0.8	0.0	0.8
ME Meets	248.6	249.8	248.2	0.4	9.1	0.5	0.9	0.5	1.3
MI Satisfactory	205.4	211.9	207.4	−2.0	19.6	4.4	5.3	0.2	5.6
MO Proficient	237.0	237.9	238.5	−1.5	12.8	1.5	1.2	0.3	1.5
NC Consist Mastery	203.1	203.2	202.7	0.4	10.7	1.0	2.2	1.0	3.1
NE Proficient	216.7	217.6	215.8	0.9	15.4	12.5	33.4	3.6	37.0[b]
NY Meets	214.8	217.4	216.3	−1.5	9.8	2.3	8.8	0.0	8.8
OH Pass	234.6	237.1	236.3	−1.7	9.6	1.1	2.1	0.2	2.3
RI Proficient	250.5	250.0	250.6	−0.1	11.0	0.5	1.0	0.1	1.0
SC Proficient	243.4	244.6	243.9	−0.5	9.4	0.7	1.4	0.4	1.8
TX Pass	194.8	203.0	200.6	−5.8	23.7	5.5	1.5	1.0	2.5
VT Meets	216.4	219.4	218.4	−2.0	15.6	2.9	4.1	0.4	4.5
WY Proficient	246.9	248.0	246.8	0.1	9.7	0.6	1.8	0.5	2.3

[a] The abbreviations ULM and WAM are defined in Sec. 17.2. [b] Note that the variance estimates for Nebraska are disturbingly large. Checking the analysis revealed that the data set employed was a 20% subset of the full data set. The reduced sample size accounts for the tabled results.

the NAEP equivalent of a state standard consists of two components: (a) the error due to sampling schools and students and (b) the error of measurement that reflects the uncertainty in an assessed student's performance. The sampling error is estimated by the jackknife replicate resampling procedure (JRR) applied both to schools (for the state data) and to students (for the NAEP data). The measurement error is estimated by utilizing the variability among the plausible values generated for each assessed student.

17.4.2.1. The NAEP Jackknife Replicate Resampling Approach

The JRR procedure for NAEP involves the formation of a large number of strata, typically consisting of pairs of schools. In NAEP, there are usually 62 strata. For the jth replicate, one school in the jth stratum is randomly deleted and an appropriate set of weights is computed. The calculation of the 62 jackknife replicate weights for NAEP state samples can be found in the *NAEP 1998 Technical Report* (Allen et al., 2001) and in Wolter (1985).

To implement the JRR for this study, we not only need the jackknife replicate weights for students but also the jackknife replicate weights for schools. These are formed by the same procedure described in Section 17.3.1. For the jth replicate, we apply the jth jackknife replicate weights for schools to estimate the corresponding proportion of students meeting the standard, $\bar{P}_{w,(j)}$. Then we map $\bar{P}_{w,(j)}$ to the NAEP scale and find the point $y_{\text{WAM},(j)}$, the $\left(1 - \bar{P}_{w,(j)}\right)$th quantile of the distribution of NAEP scores based on that same replicate and employing the corresponding replicate weights for students. Finally, the variance of the estimate y_{WAM} that is due to sampling is estimated by

$$v_J\left(y_{\text{WAM}}\right) = \sum_{j=1}^{62}\left(y_{\text{WAM},(j)} - y_{\text{WAM}}\right)^2.$$

17.4.2.2. Estimation of the Measurement Errors and Total Variances

The measurement error component is estimated by carrying out the estimation procedure outlined in Section 17.2 for each of the $M = 5$ sets of plausible values. Let the NAEP equivalent of a state standard estimated by the mth set of plausible values be $y_{\text{WAM},m}$, $m = 1,\ldots, M$, and denote the mean of $y_{\text{WAM},m}$ by $\bar{y}_{\text{WAM},\cdot}$. Finally, let

$$B = \sum_{m=1}^{M} \frac{\left(y_{\text{WAM},m} - \bar{y}_{\text{WAM},\cdot}\right)^2}{M-1}.$$

Then the total variance is estimated by

$$v_T\left(y_{\text{WAM}}\right) = v_J\left(y_{\text{WAM}}\right) + \left(1 + M^{-1}\right)B,$$

where $\left(1 + M^{-1}\right)$ is a finite population correction factor. The estimation process mimics that of operational NAEP: The calculation of $v_J\left(y_{\text{WAM}}\right)$ is based on the first plausible value, and the estimation of B is based on all five plausible values. For details, see Allen et al., 2001.

17.4.3. Evaluation of the Variance Estimates

In Table 17.2, for G4 2000 math, column (6) displays the variance of $\bar{z}_{\text{ULM}}$, obtained by application of the formula $v_{\text{SRS}}\left(\bar{z}_{\text{ULM}}\right)$ in Section 17.4.1, and columns (7), (8), and (9) display the variance due to sampling, the variance due to measurement uncertainty and the total variance of y_{WAM}, respectively. We first compare the jackknifed variances, $v_J\left(y_{\text{WAM}}\right)$, of column (7) with the variances in column (6). On average, for G4 2000 math, the jackknifed variance is 4.2, and the corresponding average of $v_{\text{SRS}}\left(\bar{z}_{\text{ULM}}\right)$ is 2.2. Clearly, the effect of complex sampling on the variance of estimates is substantial and $v_{\text{SRS}}\left(\bar{z}_{\text{ULM}}\right)$ underestimates the true sampling variability. The average measurement error is 0.56 for G4 2000 math (representing 12% of the total variance). Although measurement error is only a small fraction of the total variance, ignoring measurement error would further underestimate the true variance of the estimators.

Kish (1965) defined the design effect (DEFF) as the ratio of the variance of a statistic from a complex sample to the variance of the statistic from a simple random sample of the same size. If $v_{\text{SRS}}\left(\bar{z}_{\text{ULM}}\right)$ is treated as a variance estimate based on simple random sampling, the DEFF for the NAEP equivalent of the 2000 state mathematics standard ranges from 2.0 to 2.5. This is consistent with the DEFFs for reported NAEP statistics. It shows that the complex sampling effects cannot be ignored in the calculation of variances.

The differences in the estimated variances for $\bar{z}_{ULM}$ and y_{WAM} are illustrated in Figure 17.2, which contains two sets of plots for G4 2000 math: (a) a plot of y_{WAM} against an estimate of its total variance and (b) a plot of $\bar{z}_{ULM}$ against its estimated variance, using the formula $v_{SRS}\left(\bar{z}_{ULM}\right)$.

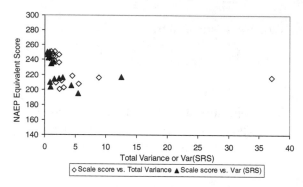

Figure 17.2 G4 2000 math (proficient): NAEP equivalent scores (WAM or ULM) versus variance [Total variance or Var(SRS)].

Nearly all of the rhombus icons, representing the total variances of y_{WAM}, are located to the right of the triangle icons representing the variances of $\bar{z}_{ULM}$. Even with the larger estimated variances, for most states the magnitudes of the estimated standard deviations of the mapped equivalents are modest in comparison to the differences among the equivalents. Note that these variances address only one aspect of the stability of the estimated equivalents. Other relevant evidence would be obtained by carrying out the linkage separately for different subgroups of the student population. Unfortunately, the requisite data are generally not available.

17.5. Results

17.5.1. The State Standards for Grade 4 2000 Mathematics

Based on the analysis of the 2000 mathematics data, the results obtained through WAM show the same patterns as the results obtained through ULM. For WAM, these findings are illustrated in Figure 17.3. For example, Louisiana has the highest mapped NAEP scale score. This state has 11.4% at or above the proficiency standard and its NAEP equivalent is 250.8. The second most stringent standard is Rhode Island's proficient, with 21.9% at or above this standard and a NAEP equivalent of 250.6. The next most stringent is Maine's meets, with 23.9% at or above this standard and a mapped standard of 248.2. The least stringent is Texas' standard of pass, with 88.8% of the students meeting the standard and a mapped standard of 200.6. These results are consistent with those obtained by ULM.

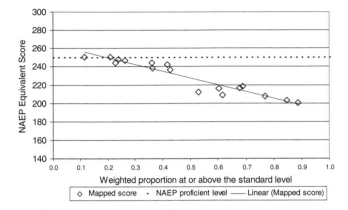

Figure 17.3. G4 2000 math: NAEP equivalent scores to state proficient standards versus proportions at or above state proficient standards.

An ordinary least squares regression line has been superimposed on Figure 17.3. There is relatively little scatter about the line, even at extreme values of percent above the standard. The pattern is clear: States with higher percentages above their standard tend to have a lower NAEP equivalent to that standard. The correlation in Figure 17.3 is –0.96. It is important to recognize that the observed pattern is not a logical consequence of the methodology. Now, if one constructed a comparable figure based on the quantiles of a single, approximately normal distribution (e.g., the national NAEP distribution for G4 2000 math), then one would obtain a straight-line relationship, particularly for percents between 20 and 80. However, the data points in Figure 17.3 are drawn from many different states, each with its own test and distribution of test scores.

The availability of estimated variances for mapped standards makes possible the construction of confidence intervals. The confidence intervals are relatively wide because, on average, the total variance is 4.72 for the proficient standards of G4 2000 math. Typically, the bands cover the regression line, supporting the inverse relationship between the percentages meeting the standard and the mapped standards. Although there are some reversals, they are usually within the margin of error indicated by the estimated variances. For example, Vermont has 68.8% of students above its standard of meets, which is higher than the 67.8% of New York's meets. However, the mapped standard for Vermont is 218.4, which is also higher than the 216.3 of New York's. The standard errors of the NAEP equivalent scores are 2.1 and 3.0 for Vermont and New York. Therefore, the difference between 218.4 and 216.3 is not significant. At the same time, we should recognize that such reversals might be due, at least in part, to real differences in distributions of achievement between states.

We note that most of the NAEP equivalents in Figure 17.3 are lower than the NAEP standards for proficiency, which is 249 (Braswell et al., 2001) and that the range of NAEP equivalent scores is about 50 points. Such differences are certainly very large in the context of NAEP scores. Thus, there appears to be a wide range of expectations for student achievement at the proficient level. Of course, such an inference requires that the pattern of differences among the mapped equivalents on the common scale (here, the NAEP scale) can be reasonably interpreted as reflecting real differences in stringency.

To the extent that interpretation is correct, one can draw useful conclusions from Figure 17.3. Consider data points lying on a vertical line. These correspond to states with the same value of $\bar{p}_w$; that is, they each have the same proportion of students above their respective standard. The higher a state's point, the higher its corresponding NAEP equivalent and we infer that it has set a more stringent standard and, therefore, that its students have demonstrated superior achievement. Now consider data points lying on a horizontal line. These correspond to states with the same NAEP equivalent. The further to the right a state's point falls, the greater its value of $\bar{p}_w$, and we infer that its students have demonstrated superior achievement. Note that in Figure 17.3 there is minimal vertical scatter but somewhat greater horizontal scatter (taking into account the different scales on the two axes). (To some degree, this is expected because the least squares line minimizes a function of the vertical scatter.) That there is a modest amount of horizontal scatter suggests that the high negative correlation observed is not simply an artifact of the methodology.

Results for grade 8 mathematics (Braun & Qian, 2006) are very similar to those for grade 4. There is a strong negative linear relationship between the NAEP equivalents to the state standards and the percents above the standards. This holds true when only standards for proficiency are considered. In this case, the range of NAEP equivalent scores is about 70 points.

17.5.2. The State Standards for Grade 4 2002 Reading

It is possible that the regularity apparent in the results for mathematics is due, in part, to the nature of the subject matter. Consequently, Braun and Qian (2006) carried out a parallel analysis for the G4 2002 reading data and obtained similar results. They reported a strong negative linear relationship with a correlation of -0.87. The range of NAEP equivalent scores for G4 was about 64 points and there was a very substantial range of states' standards.

Results for grade 8 reading (Braun & Qian, 2006) were very similar to those for grade 4 reading. There was a strong negative linear relationship between the NAEP equivalents to the state standards and the percents above the standard. This held true when only standards for proficiency were considered. In this case, the range of NAEP equivalent scores was about 80 points.

17.6. Mapping the NAEP Achievement Standards onto a State Test Scale

When state standards are mapped onto the NAEP scale, we can compare and evaluate the different standards despite the differences in tests and standard-setting procedures. The application described in this section is a reverse mapping procedure—that is, finding a point on the state test score scale that best corresponds to the NAEP achievement cut-point. These *state equivalents to the NAEP achievement levels* could provide state educators and policy makers with useful information to directly compare their standards to national benchmarks.

Figure 17.4 illustrates the reverse mapping procedure, which, as earlier, is based on the principle of equipercentile linking. Although the figure is analogous to that of Figure 17.1, the direction of the mapping is reversed: going from right to left. The curve on the right-hand side represents the estimated distribution of NAEP scores for the students sampled in the state. The point on the NAEP scale is the cut-point of a NAEP achievement level, which represents one of the NAEP standards: basic, proficient, or advanced. Let the upper tail area be equal to $\hat{p}_w$. The curve on the left-hand side represents the distribution of scores on the state test of all students in all schools in the state. The estimated state equivalent standard of the NAEP achievement level is the point on the state scale above which the tail area is also equal to $\hat{p}_w$.

To accomplish the reverse mapping, the actual distribution of state test scores is required. (That is why the distribution is represented by a solid rather than a dashed line as in Figure 17.1.) Unfortunately, actual student scores for most states are not in the NLSLSASD database. Accordingly, we were only able to conduct a case study for the G4 2000 Michigan state mathematics test, for which the appropriate data were available.[7]

The reverse mapping procedure also employs the JRR approach to estimate the variances for the sampling and measurement errors, as described

---

[7] The 2000–2001 Michigan student-level data was publicly available (http://www.schooldata.org).

in Section 17.4. The procedure uses the distribution of student scores to calculate $\hat{p}_w$, rather than the proportions of students in each school meeting the standard. Therefore, the reverse procedure employs student design weights to estimate the distribution, and the replicate weights for the JRR procedure are also computed from student design weights. Again, measurement error is estimated from repeating the procedure for each set of plausible values.

Table 17.3 presents the state equivalents to the NAEP mathematics achievement levels and their standard errors (SE). The mapped NAEP achievement levels on the Michigan state test scale are 518, 554, and 595 for basic, proficient, and advanced levels,[8] respectively. The corresponding percentages of students meeting these levels are about 70.2, 27.5, and 2.8, respectively.

Table 17.3. The state equivalents to the NAEP mathematics achievement levels and their SEs for the 2000 Michigan state mathematics test, grade 4

	Basic	Proficient	Advanced
NAEP achievement level	214	249	282
State equivalent standard	518	554	595
SE due to sampling error	1.21	3.14	0.98 [a]
SE due to measurement error	0.79	0.30	0.14
Total SE	1.45	3.16	0.99

[a]On average, only 2.8% of Michigan students meet the mapped standard for advanced. Therefore, the number of students at each school meeting the standard is small and results in a jackknifed variance that is very large: 51.39. In particular, the 41st replicate contributes about 98% of the total sampling variation. Evidently, this is a very problematic estimate. After considering several approaches, we decided to use the Winsorized variance estimate, which is listed in Table 17.3. In the calculation of the Winsorized estimate, the largest and smallest of the squared deviations are replaced by their nearest-neighbor values.

The Michigan state test score distribution indicates that the percentages of students meeting state standards, moderate and satisfactory, are 91.3 and 75.1, respectively. It appears that the standard of satisfactory is set at a level lower than the basic standard of the NAEP mathematics assessment.

---

[8] The three cut-points of NAEP achievement levels, basic, proficient, and advanced, are 214, 249, and 282, respectively (Braswell et al., 2001).

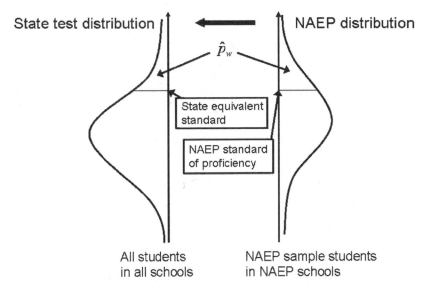

Figure 17.4. Schematic of the reverse mapping.

17.7. Conclusions and Recommendations

The purpose of this study was to continue methodological development of an approach originally proposed by McLaughlin and associates for making useful comparisons among state standards. (We again emphasize that this mapping procedure should NOT be used to make high-stakes decisions about schools or districts.) It is assumed that the state assessment and the NAEP assessment reflect similar content and have comparable structures, although they differ in test and item formats as well as standard setting procedures. This development consisted of two modifications: (a) a shift from a school-based to a student-based strategy for estimating the NAEP equivalent to a state standard and (b) the derivation of a more refined estimate of the variance of the NAEP equivalent by taking into account the NAEP design in the calculation of sampling error and by obtaining an estimate of the contribution of measurement error.

The new methodology was applied to four sets of data: (a) year 2000 state mathematics tests and the NAEP 2000 mathematics assessments for grades 4 and 8 and (b) year 2002 state reading tests and the NAEP 2002 reading assessments for grades 4 and 8. For the first dataset, we also applied the method due to McLaughlin and associates.[9] We find that for both mathematics and reading, there is a strong negative linear relationship across states between the proportions meeting the standard and the apparent stringency of the standard as indicated by its NAEP equivalent.

Comparable results can be found in a recent report by Kingsbury, Olson, Cronin, Hauser, and Houser (2003) describing an effort to map proficiency standards for 12 states onto a common scale, which is used to report test scores for the Northwest Evaluation Association (NWEA) assessment battery. This exercise was carried out in both reading and mathematics for grades 3–10, employing data collected between 1999 and 2003. In contrast to the present case, NWEA has available individual student scores on both the state test and the (common) NWEA scale. They found substantial heterogeneity among the NWEA equivalents of the state proficiency standards and a strong negative correlation between the percent proficient and the NWEA equivalent to the state's proficiency standard.

Although their linking methods as well as their data have both strengths and weaknesses in comparison to the exercise described in this chapter, it is instructive to compare the results of the two approaches. We did so for 2000 mathematics in grades 4 and 8 and for 2002 reading in grades 4 and 8.[10] There is good agreement between the rankings of the states on the apparent stringency of their proficiency standards, adding to the credibility of our findings.

Recall that the motivation for attempting to map state standards onto a common scale was to account for the observed differences among states in the proportions of students declared proficient. The credibility and utility of the results depend on making two arguments: first, that the estimated NAEP equivalents are both well estimated and stable; second, that one can interpret the results as indicating that the most important factor in explaining why two states have substantially different proportions of students meeting the proficiency standard is where they have set the standards, rather than substantial differences in the relevant skills in their student populations or the tests used.

---

[9] The results of the McLaughlin method are more fully presented in the report by Braun and Qian (2006). The results of the two methods are qualitatively similar, although they did differ substantially in some cases.

[10] Unfortunately the overlap among states for which data is available is not as great as one would hope, being greater in grade 8 than in grade 4.

With respect to the first argument, the estimated standard deviations of the NAEP equivalents, taking into account both sampling and measurement errors, are generally small in comparison to the range of the NAEP equivalents. Stability is best addressed by implementing the linkage for different subgroups. As we have already indicated, that is possible only for a few states. An alternative is to examine, for each state, the correlation between performance on the state test and on NAEP. This can be done at the school level. For example, using the NLSLSASD files, for each state one can compute the raw Spearman correlation across schools between the percent proficient on the state test and the estimated NAEP mean. For grade 4 math, the median correlation is about 0.7. Ideally, one would like to supplement the quantitative analysis with an intensive examination of the degree of alignment between the state test frameworks and the NAEP frameworks. This has not been done.

With respect to the second argument, the essential difficulty is that one must reason from the observed results (e.g. Figure 17.3) back to the true state of nature. It is possible to construct alternative scenarios that are consistent with Figure 17.3 but lead to different inferences about the relative stringency of states' standards. Although some of these alternative scenarios can be ruled out by appeal to additional data at our disposal, others can only be addressed indirectly.

Our preferred interpretation, that the variation in NAEP equivalents largely reflects differences in the stringency of states' proficiency standards, is certainly consistent with Figure 17.3. It is also supported by the fact that there is no or, at best, a very weak relationship between states' percent proficient and states' performance on NAEP. Figure 17.5 displays the relevant scatter-plot for grade 4 math. Moreover, the heterogeneity among the NAEP equivalents is much greater than among NAEP means.[11] These two features certainly contribute to the strong negative correlations evident in Figure 17.3 and its analogues.

What might be a possible alternative scenario? Suppose that two states (denoted A and B) employ the same test for accountability, which differs from NAEP in the relative emphasis placed on the different content strands. In particular, imagine that there is one strand that is strongly repre-

---

[11] For grade 4 math, the coefficient of variation of the NAEP equivalents is about 19 times larger than that for the NAEP means. For grade 4 reading, the ratio is about 9. For grade 8 math, the ratio is about 18, and for grade 8 reading, it is about 16.

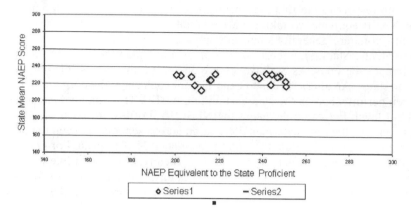

Figure 17.5. G4 2000 math: NAEP equivalent scores to state proficient standards versus state mean NAEP scores.

sented on the state test but hardly at all on the NAEP assessment. Suppose further that the states set their proficiency thresholds at the same point on the scale. Thus, by construction, their standards are of equal stringency. Now if the students in State A are better prepared for the state test (with special attention to that one strand) than students in State B, then the distribution of scores in State A will be stochastically larger than that in State B and, perforce, the percent proficient in State A will be greater than the percent proficient in State B. However, State A's advantage is not reflected in the NAEP distributions of the two states. Consequently, the NAEP equivalent for State A will be lower than that for State B—and one would conclude (incorrectly) that State A's proficiency standard is less stringent than State B's.

Could an approximation to such a scenario, aggregated over a number of pairs of states, have plausibly generated Figure 17.3? We argue in the negative: first, because assessment frameworks do not differ substantially in (say) grade 4 math. Consequently, differences in emphasis are not likely to lead to substantial differences in percent proficient that are not accompanied by corresponding differences in NAEP distributions; that is, observing the range in the percent proficient similar to that in Figure 17.3 is implausible under this scenario. Moreover, under this scenario, if it were the case that states with the higher values of the percent proficient were being penalized by the linking method for their superior performance on the state tests that is not reflected in NAEP, then one might expect that those states would display lower within-state correlations between an indicator of state test performance and NAEP scores. We carried out this computation for the states in Figure 17.3, after dividing them into two groups based on a median split on the percent proficient. For each state, we calculated the Spearman correlation across schools between the percent proficient on the state test and the estimated mean on NAEP. The mean correlations in the two groups were nearly identical.[12]

Clearly, one can posit different scenarios that offer alternative explanations for the wide range in percent proficient that has been observed. We believe we are on safe ground with the assertion that our results support the contention that differences across states in performance expectations, as manifested in the apparent stringency of the proficiency standards, remain the most plausible explanation of the heterogeneity in percent proficient. At the same time, we recognize that the issue cannot be settled directly unless states adopt a common content framework and implement a common examination based on that framework. Because that is unlikely, we must accommodate to the inherent ambiguity in the situation. Thus, we should certainly refrain from making fine distinctions among NAEP equivalents. At the very least, confidence bands, based on the estimated standard errors, should be used for all comparisons, with the recognition that they do not capture all of the uncertainty that attaches to the NAEP equivalents for the intended inferences.

That state standards for proficiency can apparently differ by 50 or more points on the NAEP scale should give pause both to policy makers and educators. What, indeed, is expected of students in states with the lowest NAEP equivalents? How do these expectations differ from states with the highest NAEP equivalents? What does the achievement of proficiency signify in terms of what students know and can do? In our view, mapping state standards to the NAEP scale makes possible conversations that could be more constructive than simple comparisons of percent above standard. In particular, it should provide greater impetus to carry out an intensive cross-state analysis of content and performance standards.

Finally, we note that under NCLB, a state's NAEP results are to be used to confirm its success in achieving adequate yearly progress. Currently, such a confirmation is based on observing changes at the mean of the distribution of state test and changes at the mean of the state's NAEP distribution. It is possible to use changes in the estimated NAEP equivalent over time in a similar manner. For example, if the proportion above the proficient standard on a state's test increases over time while the NAEP distribution remains constant, then the estimated NAEP equivalent would correspondingly decrease. It is possible, but not obvious, that tracking changes

---

[12] The Spearman correlations for two groups are 0.69 and 0.73 separately. For this calculation, Nebraska was set aside as an outlier.

in the NAEP equivalent is to be preferred to tracking changes in the mean for the purpose of monitoring state outcomes. At the same time, interpreting trends in state test scores is problematic in view of the many factors that can impact score levels. Attempting to do so in terms of linkages to another test (e.g., NAEP) is more problematic still because of the many ways in which the invariance of the linkage over time might fail. This is likely to be the case no matter which feature of the distributions is selected. For more on these issues, consult Thissen (Chapter 16) and Koretz (Chapter 18).

18 Using Aggregate-Level Linkages for Estimation and Validation: Comments on Thissen and Braun & Qian

Daniel Koretz[1]

Harvard Graduate School of Education

Both of the preceding chapters (Thissen, Chapter 16, and Braun & Qian, Chapter 17) addressed the practicalities of linking aggregate-level results, but they are very different in tone and focus. The Thissen chapter carefully considered a variety of actual linkages and is pessimistic about the support that they offer for their intended inferences. The Braun and Qian chapter, by contrast, considered in greater depth only two variants of one type of link and is quite positive about the utility of the results. The two chapters also differ in the nature of the inferences that they address and the types of evidence that they put forward to evaluate them.

I will discuss each chapter briefly, commenting on the linkage-based inferences that they address, the evaluative evidence that they bring to bear, and their conclusions. In a final section, I will elaborate on one of the threats discussed by Thissen (Chapter 16): the instability of aggregate linkages over time. I will comment briefly on the extent of this problem, its causes, and, more importantly, its implications for validity. The characteristics and severity of the instability of aggregate linkages over time are not only important for evaluating the traditional product of linkages (i.e., estimates of performance on an unadministered test) but they are also a key to validating certain inferences based on the administered test, including some of the most important inferences currently based on scores from large-scale assessments.

---

[1] The opinions expressed in this chapter are those of the author and not necessarily of the Harvard Graduate School of Education.

18.1. Comments on the Thissen Chapter

Thissen's chapter is broad in scope, referencing nearly a dozen different uses of aggregate linkages. Although he classified them somewhat differently, the intended uses of the links he examined can be placed into three broad categories:

Estimating a concurrent aggregate score on an unadministered test. In current practice, the aggregate score estimated is most often a percentage above a cut (PAC). In Thissen's examples, and in current policy, this is most often done to gain normative information that that cannot be provided by the administered test alone—for example, to allow a state to obtain nationally normative information while administering a test tailored to its own standards. This category of inferences includes not only the estimation of state-level aggregate statistics but also the efforts to extend inferences from an assessment such as the National Assessment of Educational Progress (NAEP) to lower levels of aggregation.

Providing off-year estimates of performance on an infrequent assessment, such as NAEP. Despite the substantial efforts that have been put into it in the past, this function of linking no longer seems particularly valuable, given that NAEP is now scheduled biannually and state-level change in NAEP scores is typically very slow. However, these efforts, such as the one that Thissen discussed, remain relevant because they spurred substantial evaluative work, and the factors that could undermine these inferences are germane to other linkage-based inferences as well.

Evaluating either the level of scores or score gains. Thissen discussed both: the evaluation of the level of ASVAB scores via a linkage to NAEP and the evaluation of gains on state tests in Kentucky and North Carolina, which, in both cases, were much steeper than those on NAEP. These inferences do not fit with Thissen's general definition of aggregate linkage—that is, "a mechanism to obtain from the results of one test, by statistical inference, the results that would have been obtained if a second test had been given" (p. 289). Rather, in these cases, one does have in hand observed performance on the second measure, and a question of interest (although not the one that motivated the linkage in at least two of Thissen's three examples) is the consistency of observed performance on the first test with performance on the second estimated from the first by means of a link. Nonetheless, the methodological issues are for the most part the same.

The primary evaluative evidence adduced by Thissen is tests of invariance, and in every instance, the linkage failed at least one of them. These include failures of invariance across countries, across states within countries, across gender and race/ethnicity within states, and, especially, over time. The two obvious questions raised by these failures are the magnitude of the instability in linking functions and its causes. Thissen provided only limited information about the magnitude of the failures of invariance, but in at least several cases, the failure was large. Thissen or those he cited attributed these failures to differences in content, format, motivation, test-specific learning, learning with lagged effects on other tests, and test use. In a later section of these comments, I will argue that these various causes of instability of the linking function are not equivalent—specifically, that the implications of the instability of linkages over time for the validity of certain inferences about performance on the focal test depend on which factors induce it.

Thissen used two other types of evaluative evidence as well, albeit with much less emphasis: correlations between the two linked tests and between each of the tests and nontest variables. The lesser prominence of this sort of evidence in Thissen's chapter mirrors the field; few of the studies of aggregate linkages have included it. The linkage of the North Carolina end-of-grade (NC EOG) assessments with NAEP was unusual in that matched student-level scores were available. Thissen made use of this fact to provide both student-level correlations between the tests and a comparison of standardized mean differences between two racial/ethnic groups. The student-level correlation was .73, which is low relative to the reliabilities of the two tests, and the standardized mean difference was substantially larger for NC EOG than for NAEP.[2] Thissen noted that these findings indicated that the two tests did not measure precisely the same thing and that, therefore, neither equating nor calibration would be appropriate. Projection was used instead. The implications of these findings for aggregate linkages, however, go beyond the choice of linking method, particularly in the case of the equipercentile methods that predominate in aggregate linking. Depending on the specific inferences based on the link, low correlations such as these have important implications for validity, and this should be one focus of future work evaluating aggregate linkages.

---

[2] Dorans (2004d) maintained that correlations of .87 or higher or reductions in uncertainties of 50% or higher are desirable for scores that are to be equated or linked. He also used differences between measures in standardized mean differences between groups to evaluate whether it is sensible to perform a concordance between two measures.

18.2. Comments on Braun and Qian

The chapter by Braun and Qian focuses only on one class of links: those between NAEP scale scores and state assessment results reported in terms of a PAC (the percentages above various state performance standards, particularly the "proficient" standard that is the crux of the No Child Left Behind accountability system). Unlike Thissen, Braun and Qian focused on the statistical nuts and bolts of these linkages. The chapter is more optimistic in tone than Thissen's, offering several positive conclusions about both the feasibility and utility of these methods.

Braun and Qian's work is an effort to address the widespread interest in comparing PACs and changes in PACs across states, a concern that has been intensified by No Child Left Behind. They noted the pessimistic conclusions of the National Research Council Committee on Equivalency and linkage of Educational Tests (Feuer, Holland, Green, Bertenthal, & Hemphill, 1999) about the feasibility of linking the results of disparate state tests, and they specifically noted that differences in tests, standard-setting methods, and the stringency of standards hinder the creation of useful links expressed in terms of PACs. Nonetheless, they draw a fairly strong inference from their linkage: "We then assert that most of the observed differences among states in the proportions of students meeting states' proficiency standards are the result of differences in the stringency of their standards."

Although their method is an improvement over earlier ones and could have numerous uses, I am unconvinced that this strong inference is warranted. It would strain credulity to argue that between-state differences in the severity of standards do not contribute to Braun and Qian's findings, and I am not making that argument here. Indeed, if we could ascertain the contribution of differences in the severity of standards, I would wager that its impact is large. My argument is that Braun and Qian's method cannot fully answer this question. Moreover, exploring the uncertainties left by their findings helps clarify an inherent ambiguity in the meaning of "severe" or "lenient" standards.

Braun and Qian's work was an effort to improve methods that McLaughlin devised earlier for linking state assessments to NAEP (McLaughlin, 2000; McLaughlin & Bandeira de Mello, 2002, 2003). They noted that their method differs from McLaughlin's in three respects:

1. The use of reported NAEP distributions rather than the NAEP full population estimates.
2. The linking of weighted statewide distributions rather than the mean of within-school links.

3. The use of NAEP methods for estimating sampling and measurement error rather than simple random sampling methods.

Braun and Qian discussed a number of criteria for evaluating their linkages, including (a) estimated versus actual PACs, (b) comparisons of their estimates to McLaughlin's, (c) state-level correlations between PACs and corresponding mapped NAEP scale scores, and (d) state-level correlations between mean NAEP scale scores and mapped NAEP scale scores. I will comment on criteria (b)–(d).

The major effect of these differences in method was on estimated error variances. As one would expect, Braun and Qian's estimates of variances, which take into account the clustering of the NAEP sample, are substantially larger than McLaughlin's simple random sampling (SRS) estimates. Differences between the two methods in point estimates, on the other hand, were generally small and inconsistent. This implies that it is criterion (c) of the above differences between their method and McLaughlin's that matters most. Given that Braun and Qian's variance estimation reflects the specific design of the NAEP survey—the use of random draws from the posterior distribution to estimate proficiency as well as the clustered sample—they are on strong ground in arguing that, at least with respect to criterion (c) of their differences, their method is an improvement over McLaughlin's.

Braun and Qian's interpretation of their linkage depends substantially on a very high negative correlation (approximately –.95) between state percents above proficient and their corresponding mapped NAEP scale scores in mathematics (Figure 17.3). This correlation indeed seems striking, even counterintuitive. Given that we already know that states use substantially different tests and that they impose substantially different standards, one might expect the correlation to be lower. Examined more closely, however, this correlation is less surprising than it first seems, and in my opinion, its interpretation is correspondingly murkier than Braun and Qian suggested.

To interpret the correlation found by Braun and Qian, it is first necessary to explore the impact of the equipercentile link that is at the core of their method and McLaughlin's. To see this, it is helpful to break their approach into logical steps that are quite different from the steps of the actual procedure that they employed. This alternative presentation is a simplification of their approach, but the analogy is close enough to highlight the importance of linking method. As a first step, consider the correlation one would obtain from a simple equipercentile linkage of the PACs on the two tests, assuming census testing. This correlation is, of course, perfect by construction. This is represented by the first row of Table 18.1. As a second step, still assuming census testing, we map the

NAEP PAC to a NAEP scale score, represented by the equation in the second row of Table 18.1. This appears to have a trivial effect on the correlation, which is exactly as one would expect. The distribution of NAEP scores is roughly normal, and the set of PACs includes no values in the tails, where the mapping of p to z is substantially nonlinear. Finally, in the third row of Table 18.1, we add the estimation of both quantities from sample data. The impact of this on the correlation is unknown a priori, but it turned out to be very small.

Table 18.1. Reduction of a perfect correlation between NAEP and state performance estimates in the Braun-Qian approach

Logical step	NAEP value (z)	State test value (y)	Reduction of correlation
Equipercentile linking	$p_z = p_y$	p_y	NA
Nonlinear transformation	$z = F^{-1}\left(1 - p_y\right)$	p_y	Trivial
Estimation from sample	$\hat{z}_{\text{WAM}} = F^{-1}\left(1 - \hat{\bar{p}}_w\right)$	$\hat{\bar{p}}_w$	?

The fact that the levels of states' standards does not enter into this process might seem counterintuitive, but a thought experiment helps clarify why they do not. To generate a minimal contrast, imagine a case in which two states are nothing but random samples from one state population, stratified by variables (such as major differences in curriculum) that substantially affect the alignment of the test with instruction. Further assume that that both states are administered the same test. However, the first state sets a low performance standard, whereas the second sets a higher one. This is an approximately minimal contrast for the severity of the standard. The equipercentile link in Braun and Qian's method would make this difference in the level of standards largely irrelevant, unless one of the standards was very high or low, outside the range within which the mapping of p to z is almost linear. If you assume that the low state is on the regression line when the NAEP-mapped score is regressed on state PACs, the harder standard would move the data point to the left and up, keeping it close to the same line. These two states would show approximately the same fit to the regression line, regardless of the levels of the standards they set.

One might object that this thought experiment compares two halves of a state using the identical test, whereas the actual data compare states that use different tests. Would not one expect differences among state tests to lower the between-state correlation, making the observed, nearly perfect correlation all the more remarkable? This objection raises a second primary source of the ambiguity in the interpretation of Braun and Qian's nearly perfect correlation: the indeterminacy of the joint state-level distribution of NAEP and state test scores. Because states use different tests and different scales, this joint distribution is latent and can only be made manifest by means of a linkage. Thus, asking what effect the state-level joint distribution of scores on NAEP and state tests would have on Braun and Qian's results is, to some degree, putting the cart before the horse. The more important question is the reverse: What effects does the linking method used by Qian and Braun have on the *observed* joint distribution? This brings us back to the equipercentile link, which helps generate the very high correlation that Braun and Qian found.

I will give another example, but first I should comment on a less central but related point: Braun and Qian's citation of Kingsbury et al. (2003). Within-state correlations between two tests, regardless of whether they are at the student or school level, do not help resolve the indeterminacy of the state-level joint distribution. Inferring between-state correlations from within-state relationships could be called the ecological fallacy in reverse. Any number of scenarios can be used to show that the between-state relationship can be fundamentally different than the within-state relationships, and these are not all hypothetical. For example, Koretz and Barron (1998) found that during the first years of Kentucky's high-stakes KIRIS program, the state's mean scores on the math component of the ACT® (the dominant college-admissions test in Kentucky) remained unchanged at the same time that the mean on the state test increased by about .7 standard deviation, a disparity that Koretz and Barron interpreted as evidence of score inflation on the state test. (Trends on the state test were nearly identical for the state as a whole and for the subset of students who took the ACT.) The effect of this sort of pattern, if nonuniform across states, would obviously be to reduce the state-level correlation between the ACT and state tests, if the state tests were on a common scale so that the correlation could be computed. Yet, Koretz and Barron found that the within-state student- and school-level correlations between the two tests remained largely stable over this period. Schools did not move up in lockstep on the state test; but correlations in the range that we found (around .7) do not necessitate that. As schools found ways to pump up their KIRIS scores, the general tendency for high-scoring students and schools to do better on both tests persisted.

Braun and Qian noted that one could construct alternative explanations of the nearly perfect correlation that they found and then argued that one of them—a particular type of difference in the content of the state tests and NAEP—is implausible. Perhaps, although I am not convinced; there are a great many potential differences in alignment that could have a variety of effects. However, one other example is sufficient, I believe, to illustrate the ambiguity in the interpretation of their findings.

Start with a scenario in which all states administer the same test. Content differences between NAEP and the single state test are relatively minor and have no significant effects on scores that are differential across states. States use identical methods to set standards on the common state test but set them at various levels. Population differences among states have little effect on the distribution of scores beyond the first moment. There is no inflation of scores. Call this Year 1.

In this case, one would obtain a graph similar to Figure 17.3. Because there are no differences among states beyond the first moment, the impact of substituting y for $\bar{p}_w$ in Figure 17.3 would be trivial, and the result would be a very high negative correlation between the mapped NAEP score and P. Additionally, by construction, Braun and Qian's interpretation would be correct: This correlation would be attributable to differences in severity of standards.

However, now add a single change in Year 2: Assume that there is severe inflation on the state test in several states, which is certainly not an unrealistic scenario given the sparse but consistent research on the topic. Call the states with inflation Group 1. Mean scores on the state test, P, and $\bar{p}_w$ go up in Group 1 states relative to the level warranted by mastery of the domain. The between-state correlation between NAEP and state-test *means* drops relative to what one would obtain in the absence of score inflation: The means on the state test for Group 1 move up relative to those of other states relative to what one would find in the absence of inflation, whereas their means on NAEP do not. (The within-state correlations need not be changed.)

However, the between-state correlation between P and y shown in Figure 17.3 would be preserved in Year 2. Group 1 states would move to the right on the abscissa because of the score inflation, but they would also move down on the ordinate, despite their lack of improvement on NAEP. The equipercentile link maintains their position in the joint distribution.

In this case, what can we say about the "stringency" of the standards in Group 1 states? Braun and Qian's procedure would lead to the conclusion that the standards in Group 1 states had become more lenient between

Year 1 and Year 2. In one very circumscribed sense, this is true: It has become easier for students to cross the cut-score. However, most people would use "more lenient standards" to mean "lowered expectations," and in that sense, Braun and Qian's inference would not be warranted. There has been no convening of new panels to redo the standards. There has been no post hoc adjustment by policy makers concerned that the previous panel set the standards too high. No one has decided to expect less of students. All that has happened is that some teachers have cut corners in preparing students for the test. Thus, in a substantive sense, the performance standards have not changed; what has change is the observed manifestation of the standard in the distribution, and this observed change represents a bias in scores on the state test, not an improvement in performance.

This scenario does not imply that Braun and Qian's interpretation of Figure 17.3 is wrong, but it does imply that their interpretation is insufficiently justified. The scenario illustrates that the high correlation is largely preordained by the equipercentile link and does not warrant the inference about differences in severity of standards that Braun and Qian offered and that users will want to make. Additional data would be needed to support that inference.

Perhaps more important for common inferences is the comparison Braun and Qian provided between states' mean NAEP scale scores and their mapped NAEP scores. The correlation is nearly zero. Braun and Qian argued that this shows that between-state differences in PACs reflect differences in the severity of standards rather than differences in mathematics proficiency, as measured by NAEP. They could go further. If one simply correlates state means and PACs—either actual PACs or estimates obtained from sample data using Braun and Qian's method—one finds small but nonzero correlations (about 0.4 in the two I calculated). Thus, the raw data suggest that a very modest impact of differences in mean mathematics proficiency on PACs might be plausible, but their linkage provides evidence suggesting that the raw data overstate this possibility. That is a valuable use of their method.

In sum, I would argue that the inferences warranted by Braun and Qian's work are as follows:

- In 2000, between-state differences in PACs in mathematics did not reflect differences in proficiency as measured by NAEP, despite a modest correlation in the raw data.
- The linkages do not clarify which other factors might contribute to differences in PACs. These might include differences in the severity of standards setting, content differences, and score inflation.

- Inferences based on these links about years other than the one in which the link is calculated are not warranted because of likely failure of invariance of the linking functions over time.

The first of these is important, but I suspect that most consumers of the linkages would like to go well beyond it, drawing inferences (such as those indicated by the second and third items) that the results do not justify.

18.3. More on Failures of Invariance over Time

I would like to extend Thissen's chapter by addressing three questions about the failure of aggregate linkages over time: its severity, its causes, and the implications of these causes for validity.

Information on failures of invariance over time can be found in an additional literature: research on the validity of gains obtained under high-stakes conditions. Although there are only a handful of good studies of possible score inflation in high-stakes contexts, most contrast trends on high-stakes tests to trends on other measures designed to support similar inferences. In a few instances (Thissen, Chapter 16, provided one), a formal aggregate linkage was conducted and one could evaluate the stability of that link over time. In other studies, there was not a formal linkage at the outset, but one could evaluate, post hoc, the degree to which performance on a target measure (the high-stakes test) remained consistent with the aggregate patterns one would predict based on the relationship observed at the beginning of the study period. Most of these few studies showed a rapid divergence of means on the two tests, sometimes at a rate of more than one-fourth of a standard deviation per year. I will give only two examples. Both are from Kentucky's KIRIS assessment program of the 1990s, which was also one of Thissen's examples, but other results of other studies have been similar.

During the first 2 years after the KIRIS assessment was first administered, fourth-grade reading scores went up a stunning three-fourths of a standard deviation. During that same 2-year period, however, the state's mean score in fourth-grade reading on NAEP remained constant (Hambleton et al., 1995; see Table 18.2). This contrast was particularly important given that the frameworks for the state's assessments in reading and mathematics were explicitly made similar to those of the NAEP. Results in fourth- and eighth-grade mathematics over 4 years told a similar but less extreme story: Gains on KIRIS were again very large, although not as rapid as in reading, whereas NAEP means increased at about one-fourth the rate of KIRIS scores (Koretz & Barron, 1998). The implications of these results seem inescapable: Gains on KIRIS were substantially inflated; that is, they were considerably larger than improvements in the mastery of the domain about which inferences were drawn.

Table 18.2. Changes in fourth-grade reading proficiency in Kentucky, KIRIS, and NAEP

	Raw change	Standardized change
KIRIS	18.8	0.76
NAEP	−1	−0.03

Source: Hambleton et al., 1995.

As noted earlier, 11th-grade mathematics scores on KIRIS also showed a rapid gain that appeared not to generalize. In this case, Koretz and Barron (1998) used the ACT as an audit test, restricting the comparison to students who took both tests and who attended schools in which at least 10 students took both in order to control for changing selectivity bias. In this restricted sample, the mean score on KIRIS increased about 0.7 standard deviation in the space of only 3 years (roughly the increase shown in the entire state), whereas ACT scores remained flat (Figure 18.1).

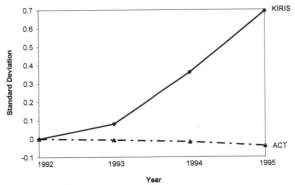

Figure 18.1. Trends in 11th-grade mathematics in Kentucky, KIRIS, and ACT. (Source: Koretz & Barron, 1998)

When the divergence in trends—the failure of invariance—is as egregious as in these cases, the implications for interpretation of gains on the high-stakes test seem clear. For example, the comparison of KIRIS with the ACT is harder to interpret than the comparison with NAEP because the frameworks and formats of the ACT and KIRIS were quite different, but Koretz and Barron (1998) argued that the overlap both in the frameworks and in the intended inferences about proficiency were, nonetheless, large, more than sufficient to make this divergence evidence of inflated gains on KIRIS.

Regardless of whether Koretz and Barron's (1998) argument was correct in that particular instance, the more revealing case is one in which the failure of invariance is less marked and its interpretation correspondingly more ambiguous. When the failure of invariance is modest, what is the implication for the validity of inferences about change on the high-stakes test? What is the relevance of the causes of the divergence?

Koretz and Barron (1998) offered the Venn diagram in Figure 18.2 to illustrate the problem. The rectangle in the diagram represents total gains on the high-stakes test and the partially overlapping oval represents gains on the audit test—in this case, NAEP. The area of overlap represents gains that are unambiguous in that they generalize across tests. The upper left-hand corner represents gains that arise from score inflation. The lower left-hand area represents gains on the state test that fail to generalize but are meaningful regardless, because they represent improvements relevant to the intended inferences from the state test but not from NAEP. If this subset of gains is substantial, the simple divergence in trends would overstate score inflation. The final section, the portion of the oval on the right that is outside of the area of intersection, represents gains on NAEP that do not generalize to the state test because of improved mastery of content that does not appear on the state test and is not relevant to the inferences based on it. If this area is sufficiently large, the divergence in trends could understate the degree of inflation, but for purposes of discussion, assume that this area is negligible and that the lower left-hand area, nongeneralizable real gains on the state test, is appreciable.

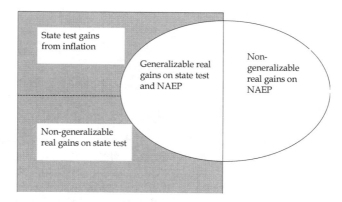

Figure 18.2. A schematic representation of partial generalizability of score gains. (Source: Koretz & Barron, 1998)

Thus, the task is to apportion the divergence of trends into two parts: score inflation and nongeneralizable but meaningful gains. Although this allocation is essential for validating aggregate gains obtained under high-stakes conditions—arguably the single most important class of inferences based on large-scale assessments in the United States today—the field, as yet, lacks good methods for undertaking it. To make progress on this front, we need to consider the causes of failures of invariance over time.

Failures of invariance of the linking functions between the tests over time could stem from all manner of factors. One set of possible causes comprises characteristics of the tests, for example, differences in content, format and item style (Koretz, 2002), difficulty, context (in particular, differences in the stakes attached to the two tests), scoring rubrics, administrative conditions, and timing of administration. A second set could be labeled behavioral responses to testing and includes several types of inappropriate test preparation that leads to score inflation: simple cheating, some forms of reallocation, and many forms of coaching (Koretz, McCaffrey, & Hamilton, 2001). These two sets overlap. For example, inappropriate test preparation can focus on specific details of content or scoring rubrics. Kolen (Chapter 3, Section 3.2) explicitly included these kinds of factor under the heading *conditions of measurement* in his discussion of equating requirements. In addition, characteristics of the population can also lead to a lack of invariance of linkages, as indicated by Thissen (Chapter 16).

Early in the evolution of the No Child Left Behind legislation, it appeared as though NAEP might become the measure for auditing gains on the tests used in the new accountability system, and the National Assessment Governing Board convened an ad hoc panel to advise it on how NAEP should be used in this regard. The panel concluded that "any amount of growth on the National Assessment should be sufficient to 'confirm' growth on state tests" (Ad Hoc Committee on Confirming Test Results, 2001, p. 9). One reason for the panel's conclusion was their focus on the first class of possible causes of divergence, such as content, format, difficulty, standard setting, and student motivation, which they maintained "limit the convergence between NAEP and state test results" (p. 8). Divergence between state tests and NAEP should be seen as problematic only "when there is consistent, compelling contrary evidence from the National Assessment that cannot be explained simply by the differences between the two tests or other relevant factors" (p. 9).

This argument is incorrect: Differences between a high-stakes test and an audit test do not necessarily excuse a divergence of trends. The implications of the failure of invariance depend on which specific differences between the tests contributed to the divergence. Before considering the general explanation, recall the classic example from New Jersey test results offered by Shepard (1988) nearly 20 years ago:

> When students were asked to add decimals in vertical format, the state percent passing was 86 percent. In horizontal format for identically difficult decimals, the percent passing was 46 percent. For subtraction of decimals in the two formats the passing rates were 78 percent and 30 percent, respectively. (p. 4)

So now imagine a hypothetical high-stakes test that included only subtraction-of-decimals problems in the vertical format, paired with an audit test that included only problems in the horizontal format. Would one conclude that the disparity in performance on the two tests is unimportant because it can be explained by a difference between the tests, specifically the difference in formats? Clearly not.

The key lies in examining the relationship between the aspects of the test that cause the divergence in performance and the inferences based on the test. Koretz et al. (2001) suggested a framework for doing so. They suggested conceiving of a test as comprising many performance elements. This is a deliberately vague term intended to subsume the diverse aspects of a test that contribute to variations in performance. These are both substantive (e.g., skills and knowledge relevant to the intended inferences) and nonsubstantive (e.g., many aspects of format and item style). The construction and scaling of a test assigns an "effective test weight" to each element, which is simply the partial derivative of scores with respect to performance on that element. The inferences based on scores reflect a similar but generally vague and tacit set of weights signaling the importance of each performance element to the inferences. The effective test weights of many performance elements important to the inferences are zero because of the necessity of omitting content to stay within time and budget constraints. The validity of gains hinges on the correspondence between changes in performance on elements with substantial test weights and changes in performance on the elements with substantial inference weights, even if the latter are unmeasured; that is, even if they have zero or trivial test weights.

In Shepard's (1988) example, the performance element accounting for the disparity in results—the particular aspect of item format in terms of which the tests differed—has a near zero inference weight. One can hardly imagine a group of New Jersey parents saying, "Oh, that's OK. When I concluded that our kids were doing better in subtraction, I only had in mind subtraction in the vertical format. In real life in New Jersey, we never encounter the horizontal format." The substantive performance element (subtraction of decimals), however, does not have a trivial inference weight. The result is an invalid inference based on performance on the high-stakes test.

Thus, failures of invariance between a high-stakes test and an audit test might undermine the validity of inferences based on the former even if we can fully explain the disparity by reference to characteristics of the test. One circumstance in which validity is undermined is when there is a failure of generalizability on a performance element with a substantial inference weight (subtraction) across levels of a performance element that is not relevant to the inference (horizontal vs. vertical format). Other cases might be less unambiguous. This example, however, makes it clear that one key to the puzzle is the importance of the performance elements involved in the failure of generalizability to the major inferences based on scores.

18.4. Conclusion

As Thissen's chapter and this discussion showed, aggregate linkages often fail to show invariance over time. This is hardly surprising, given the current incentives for educators and students to behave in ways that inflate test scores. This instability precludes many of the inferences about performance on unadministered tests that users would like to base on the linkages. The silver lining in this cloud is that failures of invariance also hold a key to evaluating the validity of gains on the tests administered for accountability.

For purposes of validation, it is not enough to identify the cases in which score inflation is egregious. To provide useful formative feedback and to evaluate cases in which the failure of invariance is moderate in size, we need to be able to identify the sources of the instability of the linking function and relate them to the specific inferences users base on scores. This will require close examination of the performance on the linked tests, more careful specification of users' major inferences, and a better analytical toolkit than we currently have available for this purpose.

19 Postscript

19.1. The Descent of Linking

As we progressed from Part 2 to Part 6 in this volume, we moved from ideal linking conditions in which ample samples of motivated examinees are administered reliable tests that are built to the same set of specifications, to less than ideal conditions, in which content, examinees, testing conditions, or reliability might differ across the measures that we are attempting to link. A linkage conducted under ideal conditions is of such high quality that scores can be treated as interchangeable across linked forms. As we deviate from ideal linking conditions, the interpretation and usage of linked scores must shift to reflect the conditions under which the linkage is conducted. The assumption of score interchangeability might no longer be tenable.

In equating, as indicated in Part 2, concerns are important but relatively mundane: definition of population, small sample sizes, and the adequacy of the anchor, to name a few. When tests are undergoing a systematic transition, as demonstrated in Part 3, linking becomes more challenging, but equatable scores can still be approximated if the transition is controlled. With concordances, the focus of Part 4, the tests differ but the scores produced by them might order individuals from a population in much the same way. Vertical scaling deviates from the ideal standards of equating in two important ways, as noted in Part 5. Not only are the tests different in content and difficulty, but the groups of examinees differ as well. Finally, the challenges associated with linking state assessments designed to assess proficiencies of individuals to a group-based national-report-card assessment are manifold, as a reading of the chapters in Part 6 reveals: Content differs, instructions differ, reliability differs, and difficulty differs.

If equating can be thought of as the apex of linking, each of these weaker forms of linking can be viewed as slipping down a slope from the apex. With tests in transition, it might be changes in content and statistical specifications or changes in mode of administration that lead to the slippage. If the slope is shallow, then equating might remain within reach. Concordances are limited by the test differences in content and statistical specifications and enough slippage is expected to ensure loss of the interchangeability associated with equated scores. Vertical scales are unlikely to produce interchangeable scores because of differences in the tests and, more importantly, in the populations. Slippage due to content shifts is accompanied by slippage due to large differences in populations. Finally, the linking of a state assessment to a group measure like NAEP slips in several directions. Content differences, difficulty differences, reliability differences, examinee proficiency differences, and differences in motivation between the samples taking the state assessment and those taking the group assessment all conspire to make claims of interchangeability implausible.

19.2. Extreme Linkages

The appetite for applied linkages is not limited to the applications discussed in this volume. There is at least one area where linkages are developed under conditions that might be more challenging than those discussed here. For example, linking scores obtained from tests administered in different languages or *test adaptation* (Hambleton, Merenda, & Spielberger, 2005) is a very difficult challenge. Assessing issues like differential reliability and differential test difficulty are problematic when examinees who speak different languages are confronted by questions expressed in different languages and given under different conditions. It is reasonable to expect a test in one's own language to be easier and more reliable than a test in another language. This fact makes it virtually impossible to compare groups who take tests in different languages via an anchor-test design. The use of bilingual examinees as an equivalent group is also problematic: This group is unlikely to be representative of either monolingual group. The use of a universal language is also problematic because it is hard to conceptualize thinking independently of language. Linking can slip down many slippery slopes from the apex of equating in this domain. Any attempts to link across languages should be done with great caution and low expectation.

A quality linking cannot occur without adequate data. Methodological attempts to compensate for poor data collections, whether weakly linked test forms, small or unrepresentative samples, unmotivated examinees, or out-of-level testing, will continue to be made and continue to be problematic.

19.3. IRT: Tool Versus Theory

To some, linking refers to a process for putting item parameters on the same scale. In this volume, we have used linking to refer as a process for putting scores on the same scale. Item response theory (IRT) has been primarily treated in this volume as a tool in the service of score linking, not as a model for item performance. This has been intentional. As with other linking methods, IRT needs to be evaluated in terms of the quality of what it produces and the appropriateness of its assumptions.

Linking results agree across different methods when they are based on strong data collections, such as equivalent groups and nonequivalent groups with anchor test (NEAT) designs, in which ability differences on the anchor test are small. In such cases, IRT might be viewed as unnecessary. Indirect linking of scores via the item-level modeling of IRT is less parsimonious than directly linking scores.

However, with incomplete, poorly connected item response data, IRT methods might be the only way to link scores. Compared to the observed score linking procedures, model-based IRT linking procedures possess the potential for addressing complex linking problems. Here the strong assumptions of IRT enable it to replace data with assumptions to provide an answer that might be a solution to an otherwise intractable problem.

In the context of score linking, it is helpful to think of using an item response *tool* rather than employing an item response *theory* that explains examinee performance on items.

19.4. Future Trends

Each year, millions of students take our tests, trusting that the score they receive will be an accurate reflection of their capabilities. As such, we are alarmed to note what appears to be a trend toward increased incidences of scoring errors that negatively impact students' lives. Perhaps this perceived "trend" is simply an illusion, triggered by an ever-vigilant media poised to pounce on any missteps by what is perceived to be an indifferent industry. It is also feasible, however, that the trend reflects the reality of an increasingly market-driven industry. As government-mandated statewide testing forges ahead, the competition for state contracts leads marketers to make promises that the psychometricians cannot keep. In our haste to get products out the door, quality control suffers and costly mistakes happen.

Another alarming trend is the increased demand for linkages between tests that were not designed with the intention of being linked. It is difficult to pinpoint when exactly Pandora's box was opened, but it is now wide open. Score users often mandate linkages that are of questionable validity. Just because we have the capability of conducting a linkage does not mean that we should actually do it. Just because we have a linkage between two sets of scores does not make it meaningful. As Feuer (2005) noted in *E Pluribus Unum: Linking Tests and Democratic Education*, test score linking will require psychometricians to address the question of *how much* score meaning is compromised under various types of linking, rather than merely pointing out that it is compromised. The chapters in this volume should help clarify conditions under which different types of linkage are appropriate. In addition, tools have been presented that might be used to quantify the degree of compromise.

19.5. Closing Comments

In the first part of this volume, Kolen noted that the same data collection designs and methods can be applied to produce different types of linkage. Holland presented a framework for linking that helps us make distinctions among the different types of linking, which are described in Parts 2–6. As practitioners, we are gradually becoming aware of the importance of making finer distinctions among linkage types and linking scenarios that on the surface appear to be essentially the same.

Many people who take tests, use test scores, or write about trends in test scores lack an awareness and an appreciation for some of the distinctions made in this volume. It is important for us as practitioners to understand these distinctions and to convey them in simple language to the nonpractitioners. Testing appears to be receiving more attention from the press these days (positive and negative), which results in a greater need for us to explain our obscure craft to the growing number of people who (often unknowingly) rely on it.

In the last 100 years of testing, we have seen substantial changes in linking practices. Vast improvements in technology and the ready availability of sophisticated software have removed many technical limitations that hindered psychometricians 50 years ago. It is hard to believe in today's computer-centric society that equatings were once conducted by hand. We interact with a worldwide testing community that exchanges ideas through international conferences, journals, and the Internet. Our field has benefited from the merging of expertise across diverse fields such as statistics, biostatistics, mathematics, cognitive psychology, educational psychology, computer science, and human-computer interactions. The testing industry is expanding and evolving at a rapid rate.

As such, it is an exciting time to be a psychometrician and a participant in the growing discussion of the linking paradigm. The continuity of scores and scales is the crux of testing. If a linking fails, some validity goes out the window. Each part of this volume presented multiple perspectives of experienced practitioners on different linkage scenarios and linkage types. Although the chapters in this book reflected state-of-the-art linking attitudes and practices, Holland in Chapter 2 suggested that, in reality, the art of linking is still young. There is much growth yet to be exhibited in the field.

In closing, we emphasize that the communication of linking issues to users is a critical component to ensuring the validity of a linkage. Parsimony of explanation is essential to meeting our goal of helping policy makers appreciate the different meanings that can be attached to different linkages and the necessary requirements to achieve solid linkages. Correctness of explanation is also critical. We should present linking issues in as simple terms as possible, but no simpler.

References

ACT. (1989). *The enhanced ACT assessment: Using concordance tables (postsecondary)*. Iowa City, IA: Author.

ACT. (1997a). *ACT assessment technical manual*. Iowa City, IA: Author.

ACT. (1997b). *The high school profile report (High school graduating class 1997)*. Iowa City, IA: Author.

ACT. (1999). *PLAN technical manual*. Iowa City, IA: Author.

ACT. (2000). *ACT educational planning and assessment system*. Iowa City, IA: Author.

Ad Hoc Committee on Confirming Test Results. (2001). *Using the National Assessment of Educational Progress to confirm state test results*. Washington, DC: National Assessment Governing Board.

Adams, R. J., Wilson, M., & Wang, W. (1997). The multidimensional random coefficients multinomial logit model. *Applied Psychological Measurement, 21*, 1–23.

Akaike, H. (1987). Factor analysis and AIC. *Psychometrika, 62*, 317–332.

Allen, N., Donoghue, J., & Schoeps, T. (2001). *The NAEP 1998 technical report* (NCES 2001-509). Washington, DC: National Center for Education Statistics.

American Educational Research Association, American Psychological Association, & National Council on Measurement in Education. (1999). *Standards for educational and psychological testing*. Washington, DC: American Educational Research Association.

Andrews, K. M. (1995). *The effects of scaling design and scaling method on the primary score scale associated with a multi-level achievement test*. Unpublished doctoral dissertation, University of Iowa, Iowa City.

Angoff, W. H. (1962). *The equating of nonparallel tests* (ETS Research Memorandum No. RM-62-02). Princeton, NJ: Educational Testing Service.

Angoff, W. H. (1971). Scales, norms and equivalent scores. In R. L. Thorndike (Ed.), *Educational measurement* (2nd ed., pp. 508–600). Washington, DC: American Council on Education.

Angoff, W. H. (1984). *Scales, norms, and equivalent scores*. Princeton, NJ: Educational Testing Service.

Angoff, W. H., & Cook L. L. (1988). *Equating the scores on the "Prueba de Aptitud Academica" and the "Scholastic Aptitude Test"* (College Board Rep. No. 88-2). New York: The College Board.

Angoff, W. H., & Cowell, W. R. (1986). An examination of the assumption that the equating of parallel forms is population-independent. *Journal of Educational Measurement, 23*, 327–345.

Arce-Ferrer, A., Frisbie, D. A., & Kolen, M. J. (2002). Standard errors of proportions used in reporting changes in-group performance with achievements levels. *Educational Assessment, 8*, 59–75.

Barron, S. I., & Hoover, H. D. (2001, April). *The impact of context effects in test linking based on common items.* Paper presented at the annual meeting of the National Council in Measurement in Education, Seattle, WA.

Beaton, A. E., & Gonzalez, E. J. (1993). Comparing the NAEP trial state assessment results with the IAEP international results. In L. A. Shepard, R. Glaser, R. Linn, & G. Bohrnstedt (Eds.), *Setting performance standards for student achievement: Background studies.* Stanford, CA: The National Academy of Education.

Beaton, A. E., & Zwick, R. (1992). Overview of the National Assessment of Educational Progress. *Journal of Educational Statistics, 17*, 95–109.

Béguin, A. A., & Glas, C. A. (2001). MCMC estimation and some model-fit analysis of multidimensional IRT models. *Psychometrika, 66*, 541–561

Birkes, D., & Dodge, Y. (1993). *Alternative methods of regression.* New York: Wiley.

Birnbaum, A. (1968). Some latent trait models and their use in inferring an examinee's ability. In F. M. Lord & M. R. Novick, *Statistical theories of mental test scores.* Reading, MA: Addison-Wesley.

Bishop, N. S., & Omar, M. H. (2002, April). *Comparing vertical scales derived from dichotomous and polytomous IRT models for a test composed of testlets.* Paper presented at the annual meeting of the National Council on Measurement in Education, New Orleans, LA.

Blackwell, D., & Girshick, M. A. (1954). *The theory of games and statistical decisions.* New York: Wiley.

Bloxom, B., Pashley, P., Nicewander, A., & Yan, D. (1995). Linking to a large-scale assessment: An empirical evaluation. *Journal of Educational and Behavioral Statistics, 20*, 1–26.

Bock, R. D. (1983). The mental growth curve reexamined. In D. J. Weiss (Ed.), *New horizons in testing* (pp. 205–209). New York: Academic Press.

Boughton, K. A., Lorie W., & Yao L. (2005, April). *A multidimensional multi-group IRT model for vertical scales with complex test structure: An empirical evaluation of student growth using real data.* Paper presented at the annual meeting of the National Council on Measurement in Education, Montreal, Canada.

Braswell, J., Lutkus, A., Grigg, W., Santapau, S., Tay-Lim, B., & Johnson, M. (2001). *The nation's report card: Mathematics 2000.* Washington, DC: National Center for Education Statistics.

Braun, H. I. (1988). A new approach to avoiding problems of scale in interpreting trends in mental measurement data. *Journal of Educational Measurement, 25*, 171–191.

Braun, H. I. (2005). *Using student progress to evaluate teachers: A primer on value-added models* (ETS Policy Information Perspective). Princeton, NJ: Educational Testing Service.

Braun, H. I., & Holland, P. W. (1982). Observed-score test equating: A mathematical analysis of some ETS equating procedures. In P. W. Holland & D. B. Rubin (Eds.), *Test equating* (pp. 9–49). New York: Academic Press.

Braun, H. I., & Mislevy, R. J. (2005, March). Intuitive test theory. *Phi Delta Kappan, 86,* 489–497.

Braun, H. I., & Qian, J. (2006). *Mapping state performance standards on to the NAEP scale.* Manuscript in preparation.

Brennan, R. L. (1981). *Some statistical procedures for domain-referenced testing: A handbook for practitioners* (ACT Tech. Bulletin No. 38). Iowa City, IA: ACT.

Brennan, R. L. (Ed.). (1989). *Methodology used in scaling the ACT assessment and PACT+.* Iowa City, IA: ACT.

Brennan, R. L. (2006). A discussion of population invariance. In A. A. von Davier & M. Liu (Eds.), *Population invariance of test equating and linking: Theory extension and applications across exams* (ETS Research Rep. No. RR-06-31, pp. 171–190). Princeton, NJ: Educational Testing Service.

Brennan, R. L., & Kolen , M. J. (1987). Some practical issues in equating. *Applied Psychological Measurement, 11,* 279–290.

Burket, G. R. (1984). Response to Hoover. *Educational Measurement: Issues and Practice, 3,* 15–16.

Camilli, G. (1988). Scale shrinkage and the estimation of latent distribution parameters. *Journal of Educational Statistics, 13,* 227–241.

Carey, P. A. (1999, April). *The use of linear-on-the-fly testing (LOFT) for TOEFL Reading.* Paper presented at the annual meeting of the National Council on Measurement in Education, Montreal, Canada.

Childs, R. A., & Chen, W.-H. (1999). Software Note. Obtaining comparable item parameter estimates in MULTILOG and PARSCALE for two polytomous IRT models. *Applied Psychological Measurement, 23,* 371–379.

Clemans, W. V. (1993). IRT, vertical scaling, and something's awry in the state of test mark. *Educational Assessment, 1,* 329–347.

The College Board. (1997). *1997 college-bound seniors, national report.* Retrieved May 11, 2006, from http://www.collegeboard.com/sat/cbsenior/yr1997/nat/cbtbk397.html

The College Board. (2005). *The new SAT®: A guide for admission officers.* New York: Author.

Cochran, W. G. (1977). *Sampling techniques* (3rd ed.). New York: John Wiley & Sons.

Cook, L. L. (1984). *Equating refurbished achievement tests.* Unpublished manuscript.

Cook, L. L., Eignor, D. R., & Taft, H. (1985). *A comparative study of curriculum effects on the stability of IRT and conventional item parameter estimates* (ETS Research Rep. No. RR-85-38). Princeton, NJ: Educational Testing Service.

Cook, L. L., Eignor D. R., & Taft, H. (1988). A comparative study of the effects of recency of instruction on the stability of IRT and conventional item parameter estimates. *Journal of Educational Measurement, 25*(1), 31–45.

Cook, L. L., & Petersen, N. S. (1987). Problems related to the use of conventional and item response theory equating methods in less than optimal circumstances. *Applied Psychological Measurement, 11*(3), 225–224.

Cramér, H. (1946). *Mathematical methods of statistics*. Princeton, NJ: Princeton University Press.

Crichton, M. (1999). *Timeline*. New York, NY: A. A. Knopf.

Crocker, L., & Algina, J. (1986). *Equating scores from different tests. Introduction to classical and modern test theory*. New York: Holt, Rinehart, and Winston.

CTB/McGraw-Hill. (1979). *California Achievement Tests, Forms C and D, Technical Bulletin 1*. Monterey, CA: Author.

CTB/Macmillan/McGraw-Hill. (1993a). *California Achievement Tests, Technical Bulletin 2* (5th ed.). Monterey, CA: Author.

CTB/McGraw-Hill. (1993b). *California Achievement Tests, Form E*. Monterey, CA: Author.

CTB/McGraw-Hill. (1993c). *The comprehensive tests of basic skills* (4th ed.). Monterey, CA: Author.

Divgi, D. R. (1981, December). *Two direct procedures for scaling and equating tests with item response theory*. Paper presented at the annual meeting of the American Educational Research Association, Los Angeles.

Donlon, T. F., & Angoff, W. A. (1971). The Scholastic Aptitude Test. In W. A. Angoff (Ed.), *The College Board Admissions Testing Program: A technical report on research and development activities relating to the Scholastic Aptitude Test and Achievement Tests* (pp. 15–45). New York: The College Board.

Dorans, N. J. (1990a). Equating methods and sampling designs. *Applied Measurement in Education, 3*, 3–17.

Dorans, N. J. (Ed.). (1990b). Selecting samples for equating: To match or not to match [Special issue]. *Applied Measurement in Education, 3*(1).

Dorans, N. J. (1999). *Correspondences between ACT and SAT I scores* (College Board Rep. No. 99-1). New York: The College Board.

Dorans, N. J. (2000). *Distinctions among classes of linkages* (College Board Research Note No. RN-11). New York: The College Board.

Dorans, N. J. (2002). Recentering and realigning the SAT score distributions: How and why. *Journal of Educational Measurement, 39*, 59–84.

Dorans, N. J. (Ed.). (2004a). Assessing the population sensitivity of equating functions [Special Issue]. *Journal of Educational Measurement, 41*(1).

Dorans, N. J. (2004b). *A conversation with Ledyard R Tucker*. Retrieved from the Educational Testing Service Web site September 25, 2006: http://www.ets.org/Media/Research/pdf/TUCKER.pdf

Dorans, N. J. (2004c). Editor's introduction to special issue: Assessing the population sensitivity of equating functions. *Journal of Educational Measurement, 41*(1), 1–2.

Dorans, N. J. (2004d). Equating, concordance and expectation. *Applied Psychological Measurement, 28*(4), 227–246.

Dorans, N. J. (2004e). Using subpopulation invariance to assess test score equity. *Journal of Educational Measurement, 41*(1), 43–68.

Dorans, N. J., & Feigenbaum, M. D. (1994). Equating issues engendered by changes to the new SAT and PSAT/NMSQT. In I. M. Lawrence, N. J. Dorans, M. D. Feigenbaum, N. J. Feryok, A. P. Schmitt, & N. K. Wright (Eds.), *Technical issues related to the introduction of the new SAT and PSAT/NMSQT* (ETS Research Memorandum No. RM-94-10). Princeton, NJ: Educational Testing Service.

Dorans, N. J., & Holland, P. W. (2000). Population invariance and the equatability of tests: Basic theory and the linear case. *Journal of Educational Measurement, 37*, 281–306.

Dorans, N. J., Holland, P. W., Thayer, D. T., & Tateneni, K. (2003). Invariance of score linking across gender groups for three Advanced Placement Program examinations. In N. J. Dorans (Ed.), *Population invariance of score linking: theory and applications to Advanced Placement Program examinations* (ETS Research Rep. No. RR-03-27, pp. 79–118). Princeton, NJ: Educational Testing Service.

Dorans. N. J., Lyu, C. F., Pommerich, M., & Houston, W. M. (1997). Concordance between ACT assessment and recentered SAT I sum scores. *College and University, 73*(2), 24–34.

Educational Testing Service. (1999). *Score change for PSAT/NMSQT test takers* (ETS Statistical Rep. No. SR-99-68). Princeton, NJ: Author.

Educational Testing Service. (2005). *The Comprehensive English Language Learning Assessment: Technical report.* Princeton, NJ: Author.

Educational Testing Service. (2006). KE-software [Computer software]. Princeton, NJ: Author.

Eignor, D. R. (1993). *Deriving comparable scores for computer adaptive and conventional tests: An example using the SAT* (ETS Research Rep. No. RR-93-55). Princeton, NJ: Educational Testing Service.

Eignor, D. R., & Schaeffer, G. A. (1995, April). *Comparability studies for the GRE General CAT and the NCLEX using CAT.* Paper presented at the annual meeting of the National Council on Measurement in Education, San Francisco.

Eignor, D. R., Stocking, M. L., Way W. D., & Steffen, M. (1993). *Case studies in computer adaptive test design through simulation* (ETS Research Rep. No. RR-93-56). Princeton, NJ: Educational Testing Service.

Eignor, D. R., Way, W. D., & Amoss, K. E. (1994, April). *Establishing the comparability of the NCLEX using CAT with traditional NCLEX examinations.* Paper presented at the annual meeting of the National Council on Measurement in Education, New Orleans, LA.

Ercikan, K. (1997). Linking statewide tests to the National Assessment of Educational Progress: Accuracy of combining test results across states. *Applied Measurement in Education, 10*, 145–159.

Feuer, M. J. (2005). E pluribus unum: Linking tests and democratic education. In C. A. Dwyer (Ed.), *Measurement and research in the accountability era* (pp. 165–183). Mahwah, NJ: Lawrence Erlbaum Associates.

Feuer, M. J., Holland, P. W., Green, B. F., & Bertenthal, M. W., & Hemphill, F. C. (1999). *Uncommon measures: Equivalence and linkage among educational tests* (Report of the Committee on Equivalency and Linkage of Educational Tests, National Research Council). Washington, DC: National Academy Press.

Fischer, G. H. (1995). Some neglected problems in IRT. *Psychometrika, 60,* 459–487.

Fitzpatrick, A. R. (1994). *Two studies comparing parameter estimates produced by PARDUX and BIGSTEPS.* Unpublished manuscript.

Flanagan, J. C. (1939). *The cooperative achievement tests: A bulletin reporting the basic principles and procedures used in the development of their system of scaled scores.* New York: American Council on Education Cooperative Test Service.

Flanagan, J. C. (1951). Units, scores, and norms. In E. F. Lindquist (Ed.), *Educational measurement* (1st ed., pp. 695–763). Washington, DC: American Council on Education.

Flanagan, J. C. (1964). Obtaining useful comparable scores for non-parallel tests and test batteries. *Journal of Educational Measurement, 1,* 1–4.

Galton, F. (1888). Co-relations and their measurements, chiefly from anthropological data. *Proceedings of the Royal Society of London, 45,* 135–145.

Glaser, R., & Linn, R. (Eds.). (1993). *The Trial State Assessment: Prospects and realities.* Stanford, CA: National Academy of Education.

Green, B. F. (2003). Comments on population invariance in score linking. In N. J. Dorans (Ed.), *Population invariance in score linking: Theory and applications to Advanced Placement Program examinations* (ETS Research Rep. No. RR-03-27, pp. 127–130). Princeton, NJ: Educational Testing Service.

Gulliksen, H. (1950). *Theory of mental tests.* New York: Wiley.

Hambleton, R. K., Jaeger, R. M., Koretz, D., Linn, R. L., Millman, J., & Phillips, S. E. (1995). *Review of the measurement quality of the Kentucky Instructional Results Information System, 1991–1994.* Frankfort, KY: Office of Education Accountability, Kentucky General Assembly.

Hambleton, R. K., Merenda, P. F., & Spielberger, C. D. (Eds.). (2005). *Adapting educational and psychological tests for cross-cultural assessment.* Mahwah, NJ: Lawrence Erlbaum Associates.

Hambleton, R. K., Swaminathan, H., & Rogers, H. J. (1991). *Fundamentals of item response theory.* Newbury Park, CA: Sage.

Han, N., Li, S., & Hambleton, R. (2005, April). *Comparing kernel and IRT equating methods.* Paper presented at the annual meeting of the National Council on Measurement in Education, Montreal, Canada.

Hanson, B. A. (1991). A note on Levine's formula for equating unequally reliable tests using data from the common item nonequivalent groups design. *Journal of Educational Statistics, 16,* 93–100.

Hanson, B. A. (1996). Testing for differences in test score distributions using log-linear models. *Applied Measurement in Education, 9,* 305–321.

Hanson, B. A., & Béguin, A. A. (2002). Obtaining a common scale for IRT item parameters using separate versus concurrent estimation in the common item nonequivalent groups equating design. *Applied Psychological Measurement*, *2*(1), 3–24.

Hanson, B. A., Harris, D. J., Pommerich, M., Sconing, J. A., & Yi, Q. (2001, February). *Suggestions for the evaluation and use of concordance results* (ACT Research Rep. No. 2001-1). Iowa City, IA: ACT.

Harcourt Educational Measurement. (1985). *Stanford Achievement Test series. Technical data report*. San Antonio, TX: Author.

Harris, D. J. (1991). A comparison of Angoff's Design I and Design II for vertical equating using traditional and IRT methodology. *Journal of Educational Measurement, 28*, 221–235.

Harris, D. J. (1993, April). *Practical issue in equating*. Paper presented at the annual meeting of the American Educational Research Association, Atlanta, GA.

Harris, D. J., & Crouse, J. D. (1993). A study of criteria used in equating. *Applied Measurement in Education 6*, 195–240.

Harris, D. J., Hendrickson, A. B., Tong, Y., Shin, S.-H., & Shyu, C.-Y. (2004, April). Vertical scales and the measurement of growth In D. J. Harris (Organizer), *Methods of establishing vertical scales and their impact on measuring growth*. Symposium conducted at the 2004 annual meeting of the National Council on Measurement in Education, San Diego, CA.

Harris, D. J., & Hoover, H. D. (1987). An application of the three-parameter IRT model to vertical equating. *Applied Psychological Measurement, 11*, 151–159.

Harris, D. J., & Kolen, M. J. (1986). Effect of examinee group on equating relationships. *Applied Psychological Measurement, 10*, 35–43.

Hendrickson, A. B., Kolen, M. J., & Tong, Y. (2004, April). *Comparision of IRT vertical scaling from scaling-test and common item designs*. Paper presented at the annual meeting of the American Educational Research Association, San Diego, CA.

Hendrickson, A. B., Wei, H., Kolen, M. J., & Tong, Y. (2005, April). *Dichotomous and polytomous scoring for IRT vertical scaling from scaling-test and common-item designs*. Paper presented at the annual meeting of the National Council for Measurement in Education, Montreal, Canada.

Henrysson, S. (1971). Gathering, analyzing, and using data on test items. In R. L. Thorndike (Ed.), *Educational measurement* (2nd ed., pp. 130–139). Washington, DC: American Council on Education.

Holland, P. W. (2002). Two measures of change in the gaps between CDFs of test-score distributions. *Journal of Educational & Behavioral Statistics, 27*, 3–18.

Holland, P. W., & Dorans, N. J. (2006). Linking and equating. In R. L. Brennan (Ed.), *Educational measurement* (4th ed., pp. 187–220). Westport, CT: Praeger Publishers.

Holland, P. W., Dorans, N. J., & Petersen, N. S. (2006). Equating test scores. In C. R. Rao & S. Sinharay (Eds.) *Handbook of statistics, Vol. 26. Psychometrics*. Amsterdam: Elsevier.

Holland, P. W., & Hoskens, M. (2003). Classical test theory as a first-order item response theory: Application to true-score prediction from a possibly nonparallel test. *Psychometrika, 68*, 123–149.

Holland, P. W, Liu, M., & Thayer, D. T. (2005, April). *Exploring the population sensitivity of linking functions to differences in test constructs and reliability using the Dorans-Holland measures, kernel equating and data from the LSAT.* Paper presented at the annual meeting of the National Council on Measurement in Education, Montreal, Canada.

Holland, P. W., & Rubin, D. B. (Eds.) (1982). *Test equating.* New York: Academic Press.

Holland, P. W., & Thayer, D. T. (1987). *Notes on the use of log-linear models for fitting discrete probability distributions* (ETS Research Rep. No. RR-87-31). Princeton NJ: Educational Testing Service.

Holland, P. W., & Thayer, D. T. (1989). *The kernel method of equating score distributions* (ETS Research Rep. No. RR-89-7). Princeton: Educational Testing Service.

Holland, P. W., & Thayer, D. T. (1990, April). *Kernel equating and the counterbalanced design.* Paper presented at the annual meeting of the American Educational Research Association, Boston.

Holland, P. W., & Thayer, D. T. (2000). Univariate and bivariate loglinear models for discrete test score distributions. *Journal of Educational and Behavioral Statistics, 25,* 133–183.

Holmes, S. E. (1982). Unidimensionality and vertical equating with the Rasch model. *Journal of Educational Measurement, 19,* 139–147.

Hoover, H. D. (1984a). The most appropriate scores for measuring educational development in the elementary schools: GE's. *Educational Measurement: Issues and Practice, 3,* 8–18.

Hoover, H. D. (1984b). Rejoinder to Burket. *Educational Measurement: Issues and Practice, 3,* 16–18.

Hoover, H. D., Dunbar, S. D., & Frisbie, D.A. (2001). *The Iowa Tests of Basic Skills: Interpretative guide for teachers and counselors. Forms A and B, Levels 9-14.* Itasca, NY: Riverside Publishing.

Hoskens, M., Lewis, D. M., & Patz, R. J. (2003, April). *Maintaining vertical scales using a common item design.* Paper presented at the annual meeting of the National Council on Measurement in Education. Chicago.

Houston, W., & Sawyer, R. (1991). Relating scores on the Enhanced ACT assessment and the SAT test batteries. *College and University, 66,* 195–200.

Hull, C. L. (1922). The conversion of test scores into series which shall have any assigned mean and dispersion. *Journal of Applied Psychology, 6,* 298–300.

Iowa Test of Basic Skills. (2003). *Scaling, norming, and equating the Iowa Tests.* Iowa City, IA: University of Iowa.

Jaeger, R. M. (1981). Some exploratory indices for selection of a test equating method. *Journal of Educational Measurement, 18,* 23–38.

Jiang, H. (1999, April). *Estimation of score distributions for TOEFL concordance tables.* Paper presented at the annual meeting of the National Council on Measurement in Education, Montreal, Canada.

Jodoin, M., Keller, L., & Swaminathan, H. (2003). A comparison of linear, fixed common item, and concurrent parameter estimation equating procedures in capturing academic growth. *The Journal of Experimental Education, 71,* 229–250.

Johnson, E. G. (1998). *Linking the National Assessment of Educational Progress and the Third International Mathematics and Science Study: A technical report* (NCES-98-499). Washington, DC: National Center for Education Statistics.

Johnson, E. G., & Allen, N. L. (Eds.) (1992). *The 1990 NAEP technical report* (Rep. No. 21-TR-20, pp. 143–158). Washington, DC: U.S. Department of Education.

Johnson, E. G., & Siegendorf, A. (1998). *Linking the National Assessment of Educational Progress and the Third International Mathematics and Science Study: Eighth-grade results* (NCES-98-500). Washington, DC: National Center for Education Statistics.

Jones, L. V. (1996). A history of the National Assessment of Educational Progress and some questions about its future. *Educational Researcher, 25*, 15–22.

Jones, L. V. (1997). The National Assessment of Educational Progress, origins and prospects. In R. Glaser, R. L. Linn, & G. Bohrnstedt (Eds.), *Assessment in transition: Monitoring the nation's educational progress, background studies* (pp. 1–18). Stanford, CA: National Academy of Education.

Jones, L. V., & Olkin, I. (2004). *The nation's report card: Evolution and perspectives*. Bloomington, IN: Phi Delta Kappa Educational Foundation.

Karkee, T., Lewis, D. M., Hoskens, M. Yao, L., & Haug, C. (2003, April). *Separate versus concurrent calibration methods in vertical scaling.* Paper presented at the annual meeting of the National Council on Measurement in Education. Chicago.

Keeves, J. (1988). Scaling achievement test scores. In T. Husen & T. N. Postlethwaite (Eds.), *International encyclopedia of education.* Oxford: Pergamon.

Kelley, T. L. (1914). Comparable measures. *Journal of Educational Psychology, 5*, 589–595.

Kelley, T. L. (1923). *Statistical methods.* New York: Macmillan.

Kelley, T. L. (1927). *Interpretation of educational measurements.* New York: World Book Co.

Kentucky Department of Education. (1993). *Kentucky Instructional Results Information System 1991-92 technical report.* Frankfort, KY: Author.

Kim, D., Brennan, R. L., & Kolen, M. J. (2005). A comparison of IRT equating and beta 4 equating. *Journal of Educational Measurement, 42*, 77–99.

Kim, S., & Cohen, A. S. (1998). A comparison of linking and concurrent calibration under item response theory. *Applied Psychological Measurement, 22*(2), 131–143.

Kim, S., von Davier, A. A., & Haberman, S. (2006). *Equating with small samples.* Princeton, NJ: Educational Testing Service.

Kingsbury, G. G., & Hauser, C. (2004 April). *Computerized adaptive testing and No Child Left Behind.* Paper presented at the annual meeting of the American Educational Research Association, San Diego.

Kingsbury, G. G., Olson, A., Cronin, J., Hauser, C., & Houser, R. (2003). *The state of state standards: Research investigating proficiency levels in fourteen states.* Portland: OR: Northwest Evaluation Association.

Kish, L. (1965). *Survey sampling.* New York: John Wiley & Sons.

Klein. L. W., & Jarjoura, D. (1985). The importance of content representation for common-item equating with nonrandom groups. *Journal of Educational Measurement, 22*, 197–206.

Klein, L. W., & Kolen, M. J. (1985 April). *Effect of number of common items in common-item equating with nonrandom groups.* Paper presented at the annual meeting of American Educational Research Association, Chicago.

Kolen, M. J. (1981). Comparison of traditional and item response theory methods for equating tests. *Journal of Educational Measurement, 18*, 1–11.

Kolen, M. J. (1990). Does matching in equating work? A discussion. *Applied Measurement in Education, 3*(1), 97–104.

Kolen, M. J. (2001). Linking assessments effectively: Purpose and design. *Educational Measurement: Issues and Practice, 20*, 5–9.

Kolen, M. J. (2003, April). *Equating and vertical scaling: Research questions.* Paper presented at the annual meeting of the National Council on Measurement in Education, Chicago.

Kolen, M. J. (2004a). Linking assessments: Concept and history. *Applied Psychological Measurement, 28*, 219–226.

Kolen, M. J. (2004b). Population invariance in equating and linking: Concept and history. *Journal of Educational Measurement, 41*, 3–14.

Kolen, M. J. (2006). Scaling and norming. In R. L. Brennan (Ed.), *Educational measurement* (4th ed., pp. 155–186). Westport, CT: Praeger Publishers.

Kolen, M. J., & Brennan, R. L. (2004). *Test equating, scaling, and linking. Methods and practices* (2nd ed.). New York: Springer.

Kolen, M. J., & Jarjoura, D. (1987). Analytic smoothing for equipercentile equating under the common item nonequivalent populations design. *Psychometrika, 52*, 43–59.

Koretz, D. (2002, September). *Believe me, it is not cheating, but some strange method.* Invited presentation at the annual meeting of the Center for Research on Evaluation, Standards, and Student Testing, Los Angeles.

Koretz, D. M., & Barron, S. I. (1998). *The validity of gains in scores on the Kentucky Instructional Results Information System (KIRIS)* (MR-1014-EDU). Santa Monica, CA: RAND.

Koretz, D. M., Bertenthal, M. W., & Green, B. F. (1999). *Embedding questions: The pursuit of a common measure in uncommon tests* (Report of the Committee on Embedding Common Test Items in State and District Assessments, National Research Council). Washington DC: National Academy Press.

Koretz, D., McCaffrey, D., & Hamilton, L. (2001). *Toward a framework for validating gains under high-stakes conditions* (CSE Tech. Rep. 551). Los Angeles: Center for the Study of Evaluation.

Lane, S. (2004). 2004 NCME presidential address: Validity of high-stakes assessments: Are students engaged in complex thinking? *Educational Measurement: Issues and Practice, 23*(3), 6–14.

Lavergne, G., & Walker, B. (2001). *Revising multiple regression equations for calculating predicted freshman year grade point average at the University of Texas at Austin.* Austin: The University of Texas at Austin, Office of Admissions Research.

Lawrence, I. M., & Dorans, N. J. (1990). Effect on equating results of matching samples on an anchor test. *Applied Measurement in Education, 3*(1), 19–36.

Lawrence, I. M., & Feigenbaum, M. (1997). *Linking scores for computer-adaptive and paper-and-pencil administrations of the SAT* (ETS Research Rep. No. RR-93-55). Princeton, NJ: Educational Testing Service.

Lawrence, I. M., Rigol, G. W., Van Essen, T., & Jackson, C. A. (2003). A *historical perspective on the content of the SAT* (College Board Research Rep. No. 2003-1). New York: The College Board.

Leahy, P. (n.d.). *Major issues: No child left behind.* Retrieved August 30, 2006, from http://leahy.senate.gov/issues/education/nochildleftbehind.html

Levine, R. S. (1955). *Equating the score scales of alternate forms administered to samples of different ability* (ETS Research Bulletin No. RB-55-23). Princeton, NJ: Educational Testing Service.

Lewin, T. (2005, March 4). Strivers sharpen no. 2's for different college test. *The New York Times* Retrieved August 30, 2006, from http://www.nytimes.com/2005/03/04/education/04SAT.html

Lewis, D. M., Mitzel, H., & Green, D. R. (1996). Standard setting: A bookmark approach. In D. R. Green (Chair), *IRT-based standard-setting procedures utilizing behavioral anchoring.* Symposium presented at the 1996 Council of Chief State School Officers National Conference on Large-Scale Assessment, Phoenix, AZ.

Lindquist, E. F. (1964, February). *Equating scores on non-parallel tests.* Paper presented at the annual meeting of the American Educational Research Association, Chicago.

Linn, R. L. (1993). Linking results of distinct assessments. *Applied Measurement in Education, 6*(1), 83–102.

Linn, R. L. (2003). Accountability: Responsibility and reasonable expectations. *Educational Researcher, 32,* 3–13.

Linn, R. L., & Kiplinger, V. L. (1994). *Linking statewide tests to the National Assessment of Educational Progress: Stability of results* (CSE Tech. Rep. 375). Los Angeles: National Center for Research on Evaluation, Standards, and Student Testing.

Liou, M., Cheng, P.E., & Li, M.Y. (2001). Estimating comparable scores using surrogate variables. *Applied Psychological Measurement, 25,* 197–207.

Lissitz, R. W., & Huynh, H. (2003). Vertical equating for state assessments: Issues and solutions in determination of adequate yearly progress and school accountability. *Practical Assessment, Research & Evaluation, 8*(10). Retrieved August 31, 2006, from http://pareonline.net/getvn.asp?v=8&n=10

Liu, J., Cahn, M. F., & Dorans, N. J. (2006). An application of score equity assessment: Invariance of linkage of new SAT to old SAT across gender groups. *Journal of Educational Measurement, 43,* 113–129.

Liu, J., Feigenbaum, M., & Cook, L. (2004). *A simulation study to explore configuring the SAT I: Verbal Test without analogy items* (College Board Research Rep. No. 2004-2). New York: The College Board.

Liu, J., Feigenbaum, M., & Dorans, N. J. (2005). *Invariance of linkings of the revised 2005 SAT Reasoning Test to the SAT I: Reasoning Test across gender groups* (College Board Research Rep. No. 2004-6). New York: The College Board.

Liu, M., & Holland, P. W. (2006). Exploring the population sensitivity of linking functions across test administrations using LSAT sub-populations. In A. A. von Davier & M. Liu (Eds.), *Population invariance of test equating and linking: Theory extensions and applications across exams* (ETS Research Rep. No. RR-06-31, pp. 29-57). Princeton, NJ: Educational Testing Service.

Livingston, S. A. (1993). Small-sample equating with log-linear smoothing. *Journal of Educational Measurement, 30*, 23–39.

Livingston, S. A. (2004). *Equating test scores (without IRT)*. Princeton, NJ: Educational Testing Service.

Livingston, S. A., Dorans, N. J., & Wright, N. K. (1990). What combination of sampling and equating methods works best? *Applied Measurement in Education, 3*(1), 73–95.

Lord, F. M. (1950). *Notes on comparable scales for test scores* (ETS Research Bulletin No. RB-50-48). Princeton, NJ: Educational Testing Service.

Lord, F. M. (1955). Equating test scores: A maximum likelihood solution. *Psychometrika, 20*, 193–200.

Lord, F. M. (1980). *Applications of item response theory to practical testing problems*. Hillsdale, NJ: Lawrence Erlbaum Associates.

Lord, F. M. (1982). The standard error of equipercentile equating. *Journal of Education Statistics, 7*, 165–174.

Loyd, B. H., & Plake, B. S. (1987). *Vertical equating: Effects of model, method, and content domain*. Paper presented at the annual meeting of the American Educational Research Association, Washington, DC.

Lunz, M. E., & Bergstrom, B. A. (1995, March). *Equating computerized adaptive certification examinations: The Board of Registry series of studies*. Paper presented at the annual meeting of the National Conference on Measurement in Education, San Francisco.

Mao, X., von Davier, A. A., & Rupp, S. (2006). *Comparisons of the kernel equating method with the traditional equating methods on PRAXIS data* (ETS Research Rep. No. RR-06-30). Princeton, NJ: Educational Testing Service.

Marco, G. L., & Abdel-fattah, A. A. (1991). Developing concordance tables for scores on the Enhanced ACT assessment and the SAT. *College and University, 66*, 187–194.

Marco, G. L., Abdel-fattah, A. A., & Baron, P. A. (1992). *Methods used to establish score comparability on the enhanced ACT assessment and the SAT* (College Board Rep. No. 92-3). New York: The College Board.

Marco, G. L., Petersen, N. S., & Stewart, E. E. (1983). *A large-scale evaluation of linear and curvilinear score equating models* (ETS Research Memorandum No. RM-83-2). Princeton, NJ: Educational Testing Service.

Mazzeo, J., Druesne, B., Raffeld, P. C., Checketts, K. T., & Muhlstein, A. (1991). *Comparability of computer and paper-and-pencil scores for two CLEP General Examinations* (College Board Report No. 91-5). The College Board, New York.

Mazzeo, J., & Harvey, A. L. (1988). *The equivalence of scores from automated and conventional educational and psychological tests* (College Board Report No. 88-8). New York: The College Board.

McBride, J. R., Corpe, V. A., Wing, H. (1987, August). *Equating the computer adaptive edition of the Differential Aptitude Tests.* Paper presented at the annual meeting of the American Psychological Association, New York.

McGaw, B. (1977). The use of rescaled teacher assessments in the admission of student to tertiary study. *Australian Journal of Education, 21,* 209–225.

McLaughlin, D. (2000). *Protecting state NAEP trends from changes in SD/LEP inclusion rates* (Tech. Rep.). Palo Alto, CA: American Institutes for Research.

McLaughlin, D., & Bandeira de Mello, V. (2002, April). *Comparison of state elementary school mathematics achievement standards using NAEP 2000.* Paper presented at the annual meeting of the American Educational Research Association Annual Meeting, New Orleans, LA.

McLaughlin, D., & Bandeira de Mello, V. (2003, June). *Comparing state reading and math performance standards using NAEP.* Paper presented at the National Conference on Large-Scale Assessment, San Antonio, TX.

McLaughlin, D. H. (1998a, April). *Linking state assessments of NAEP: A study of the 1996 mathematics assessment.* Paper presented to the American Educational Research Association, San Diego.

McLaughlin, D. H. (1998b). *Study of the linkages of 1996 NAEP and state mathematics assessments in four states.* Washington, DC: National Center for Education Statistics.

Mead, A. D., & Drasgow, F. (1993). Equivalence of computerized and paper-and-pencil cognitive ability tests: A meta-analysis. *Psychological Bulletin, 114,* 449–458.

Mislevy, R. J. (1984). Estimating latent distributions. *Psychometrika, 44,* 358–381.

Mislevy, R. J. (1985). Estimation of latent group effects. *Journal of the American Statistical Association, 80,* 993–997.

Mislevy, R. J. (1990). Scaling procedures. In E. G. Johnson & R. Zwick (Eds.), *Focusing the new design: The NAEP 1988 technical report* (NAEP Rep. No. 19-TR-20). Princeton, NJ: Educational Testing Service.

Mislevy, R. J. (1992, December). *Linking educational assessments: Concepts, issues, methods, and prospects* (Policy Information Report). Princeton, NJ: Educational Testing Service.

Mislevy, R. J., Johnson E. G., & Muraki, E. (1992). Scaling procedures in NAEP. *Journal of Educational Statistics, 17,* 131–154.

Mislevy, R. J., Sheehan, K. S., & Wingersky, M. S. (1993). How to equate tests with little or no data. *Journal of Educational Measurement, 30,* 1, 55-78.

Mitzel, H. C., Lewis, D. M., Patz, R. J., & Green, D. R. (2001). The bookmark procedure: Psychological perspectives. In G. J. Cizek (Ed.), *Setting performance standards: Concepts, methods, and perspectives* (pp. 249–281). Mahwah, NJ: Lawrence Erlbaum Associates.

Moore, D. S., & McCabe, G. P. (1999). *Introduction to the practice of statistics* (3rd ed.). New York: W. H. Freeman.

Morris, C. N. (1982). On the foundations of test equating. In P. W. Holland & D. B. Rubin (Eds.), *Test equating* (pp. 169–191). New York: Academic Press.

Moses, T. P. (2006). *Using the kernel method of test equating for estimating the standard error of population invariance measures* (ETS Research Rep. No. RR-06-20) Princeton, NJ: Educational Testing Service.

Moses, T. P., & Holland, P. W. (in press). *Notes on the general framework for observed score equating.* Princeton, NJ: Educational Testing Service.

Moses, T. P., Yang, W.-L., & Wilson, C. (2005, April). *Using kernel equating to check the statistical equivalence of nearly identical test editions.* Paper presented at the annual meeting of the National Council on Measurement in Education, Montreal, Quebec, Canada.

Mullis, I. V. S., Martin, M. O., Beaton, A. E., Gonzalez, E. J., Kelly, D. L., & Smith, T. A. (1997). *Mathematics achievement in the primary school years: IEA's Third International Mathematics and Science Study (TIMSS).* Chestnut Hill, MA: Boston College, TIMSS International Study Center.

Muraki, E. (1992). A generalized partial credit model: Application of an EM algorithm. *Applied Psychological Measurement, 16*(2), 159–176.

Musick, M. D. (1996). *Setting education standards high enough.* Unpublished manuscript.

No Child Left Behind Act of 2001, 20 U.S.C. § 6301 et seq. (2002).

Omar, M. H. (1997, March). *Objective achievement growth rate as measured by IRT scales: An analysis when the scaling model is appropriate.* Paper presented at the annual meeting of the American Educational Research Association, Chicago.

Omar, M. H., & Hoover, H. D. (1997, March). *An investigation into the reasons why IRT theta scale shrinks for higher achieving groups.* Paper presented at the annual meeting of the National Council on Measurement in Education, Chicago.

Otis, A. S. (1916). The reliability of spelling scales, including a 'deviation formula' for correlation. *School and Society, 4*, 96–99.

Otis, A. S. (1918). An absolute point scale for the group measurements of intelligence. Part I. *Journal of Educational Psychology, 9*, 239–260.

Otis, A. S. (1922). The method for finding the correspondence between scores in two tests. *Journal of Educational Psychology, 13*, 529–545.

Parzen, E. (1960). *Modern probability theory and its applications.* New York: Wiley.

Pashley, P. J., & Phillips, G. W. (1993). *Toward world-class standards: A research study linking international and national assessments.* Princeton, NJ: Educational Testing Service.

Patz, R. J., & Hanson, B. (2002, April). *Psychometric issues in vertical scaling.* Paper presented at the annual meeting of the National Council on Measurement in Education. New Orleans, LA.

Patz, R. J., & Junker, B. W. (1999a). A straight forward approach to Markov chain Monte Carlo methods for item response models. *Journal of Educational and Behavioral Statistics, 24,* 146–178.

Patz, R. J., & Junker, B. W. (1999b). Applications and extensions of MCMC in IRT: Multiple item types, missing data, and rated responses. *Journal of Educational and Behavioral Statistics, 24,* 342–346.

Patz, R. J., & Yao, L. (2006). Vertical scaling: Statistical models for measuring growth and achievement. In C. R. Rao & S. Sinharay (Eds.), *Handbook of statistics: Vol. 26. Psychometrics.* Amsterdam: Elsevier.

Patz, R., Yao, L., Chi, M., Lewis, D., & Hoskens, M. (2003, April). *Hierarchical and multidimensional models for vertical scaling.* Paper presented at the annual meeting of the National Council on Measurement in Education, Chicago.

Petersen, N. S., Cook, L. L., & Stocking, M. L. (1983). IRT versus conventional equating methods, A comparative study of scale stability. *Journal of Educational Statistics, 8*(2), 137–156.

Petersen, N. S., Kolen, M. J., & Hoover, H. D. (1989) Scaling, norming, and equating. In R. L. Linn (Ed.), *Educational measurement* (3rd ed., pp. 221–262). New York: Macmillan.

Petersen, N. S., Marco, G. L., & Stewart, E. E. (1982). A test of adequacy of linear score equating models. In P. W. Holland & D. B. Rubin (Eds.), *Test equating* (pp. 71–135). New York: Academic Press.

Phillips, S. E. (1983). Comparison of equipercentile and item response theory equating when the scaling test method is applied to a multilevel achievement battery. *Applied Psychological Measurement, 7,* 267–281.

Pinter, R. (1914). A comparison of the Ayres and Thorndike handwriting scales. *Journal of Educational Psychology, 5,* 525–536.

Pitoniak, M. J., & Mead, N. A. (2003). *Statistical methods to account for excluded students in NAEP: 2002 reading and writing assessments.* Princeton, NJ: Educational Testing Service.

Poggio, J., Glasnapp, D. R., Yang, X., & Poggio, A. J. (2005). A comparative evaluation of score results from computerized and paper and pencil mathematics testing in a large scale state assessment program. *Journal of Technology, Learning, and Assessment, 3*(6). Retrieved August 30, 2006, from http://escholarship.bc.edu/jtla/vol3/6/

Pommerich, M. (2004). Developing computerized versions of paper-and-pencil tests: Mode effects for passage-based tests. *Journal of Technology, Learning, and Assessment, 2*(6). Retrieved August 30, 2006, from http://escholarship.bc.edu/jtla/vol2/6/

Pommerich, M., & Dorans, N. J. (Eds.). (2004). Concordance [Special issue]. *Applied Psychological Measurement 28*(4).

Pommerich, M., Hanson, B. A., Harris, D. J., & Sconing, J. A. (2000). *Issues in creating and reporting concordance results based on equipercentile methods* (ACT Research Rep. No. 2000-1). Iowa City, IA: ACT.

Pommerich, M., Hanson, B. A., Harris, D. J., & Sconing, J. A. (2004). Issues in conducting linkages between distinct tests. *Applied Psychological Measurement, 28,* 247–273.

Pomplun, M., Omar, M. H., & Custer, M. (2004). A comparison of Winsteps and Bilog-MG for vertical scaling with the Rasch model. *Educational and Psychological Measurement, 64,* 600–616.

The Psychological Corporation. (1988). *Metropolitan Achievement Tests. MAC 6: Technical manual.* San Antonio, TX: Author.

Qian, J., Kaplan, E., Johnson, E., Krenzke, T., & Rust, K. (2001). State weighting procedures and variance estimation. In N. Allen, J. Donoghue, & T. Schoeps (Eds.), *The NAEP 1998 technical report* (NCES 2001-509, pp. 193–226). Washington, DC: National Center for Education Statistics.

Raju, N. S., Edwards, J. E., & Osberg, D. W. (1983, April). *The effect of anchor test size in vertical equating with the Rasch and three-parameter models.* Paper presented at the annual meeting of the American Educational Research Association, Montreal, Canada.

Rasch, G. (1960). *Probabilistic models for some intelligence and attainment tests.* Copenhagen: Danish Institute for Educational Research.

Reckase, M. D. (1985). The difficulty of test items that measure more than on ability. *Applied Psychological Measurement, 9,* 401–412.

Reckase, M. D. (1997). The past and future of multidimensional item response theory. *Applied Psychological Measurement, 21,* 25–36.

Reckase, M. D., & McKinley, R. L. (1991). The discriminating power of items that measure more than one dimension. *Applied Psychological Measurement, 15,* 361–373.

Rogers, A. M. (1991). NAEP MGROUP: Enhanced version of Sheehan's software for the estimation of group effects in multivariate models [Computer software]. Princeton, NJ: Educational Testing Service.

Sanders, W., Saxton, A., & Horn, B. (1997). The Tennessee value-added assessment system: A quantitative outcomes-based approach to educational assessment. In J. Millman (Ed.), *Grading teachers, grading schools: Is achievement a valid measure?* Thousand Oaks, CA: Corwin.

Sawyer, R. (2007). Indicators of usefulness of test scores. *Applied Measurement in Education, 20*(3).

Schaeffer, G. A., Reese, C. M., Steffen, M., McKinley, R. L., & Mills, C. N. (1993). *Field test of a computer-based GRE General Test* (ETS Research Rep. No. RR-93-07). Princeton, NJ: Educational Testing Service.

Schaeffer, G. A., Steffen, M., Golub-Smith, M. L., Mills, C. N., & Durso, R. (1995). *The introduction and comparability of the computer adaptive GRE General Test* (GRE Board Professional Rep. No. 88-08a). Princeton, NJ: Educational Testing Service.

Schulz, E. M., Perlman, C., Rice, W., & Wright, B. (1992). Vertically equating reading tests: An example from Chicago public schools. In M. Wilson (Ed.), *Objective measurement: Theory into practice* (pp. 138–156). Norwood, NJ: Ablex.

Segall, D. O. (1995, April). *Equating the CAT-ASVAB: Experiences and lessons learned.* Paper presented at the annual meeting of the National Council on Measurement in Education, San Francisco.

Segall, D. O., & Carter, G. (1995, April). *Equating the CAT-GATB: Issues and approach.* Paper presented at the annual meeting of the National Council on Measurement in Education, San Francisco.

Sheehan, K. M. (1985). MGROUP: *Estimation of group effects in multivariate models* [Computer software]. Princeton, NJ: Educational Testing Service.

Shepard, L. A. (1988, April). *Should instruction be measurement driven? A debate.*. Paper presented at the annual meeting of the American Educational Research Association, New Orleans, LA.

Simmons, T. (1995, July 4). State rankings please parents, but annoy some educators. *The News & Observer*, pp. 1–4.

Singer, J. D. (1998). Using SAS PROC MIXED to fit multilevel models, hierarchical models, and individual growth models. *Journal of Educational and Behavioral Statistics, 24*, 323–355.

Singer, J. D., & Willet, J. D. (2003). *Applied longitudinal data analysis: Modeling change and event occurence*. London: Oxford University Press.

Sinharay, S., & Holland, P.W. (2006). *The correlation between the scores of a test and an anchor test* (ETS Research Rep. No. RR-06-04). Princeton, NJ: Educational Testing Service.

Sitter, R. R. (1992a). A resampling procedure for complex survey data. *Journal of the American Statistical Association, 87*, 755–765.

Sitter, R. R. (1992b). Comparing three bootstrap methods for survey data. *The Canadian Journal of Statistics, 20*, 135–154.

Skaggs, G. (1990). To match or not to match samples on ability for equating: A discussion of five articles. *Applied Measurement in Education, 3*, 105–113.

Skaggs, G. (2004, April). *Passing score stability when equating with very small samples*. Paper presented at the annual meeting of the National Council on Measurement in Education, San Diego.

Skaggs, G., & Lissitz, R. W. (1986). IRT test equating: Relevant issues and a review of recent research. *Review of Educational Research, 56*(4), 495–529.

Skaggs, G., & Lissitz, R. W. (1988). Effect of examinee ability on test equating invariance. *Applied Psychological Measurement, 12*, 69–82.

Slinde, J. A., & Linn, R. L. (1979). A note on vertical equating via the Rasch model for groups of quite different ability and tests of quite different difficulty. *Journal of Educational Measurement, 16*, 159–165.

Smirnov, N. V. (1948). Table for estimating the goodness of fit of empirical distributions. *Annals of Mathematical Statistics, 19*, 279–281.

Smith, R. L., & Yen, W. M. (2006). Models for evaluating grade-to-grade growth. In R. W. Lissitz (Ed.), *Longitudinal and value added modeling of student performance* (pp. 82–94). Maple Grove, MN: JAM Press.

Starch, D. (1913). The measurement of handwriting. *Journal of Educational Psychology, 4*, 445–464.

Stigler, S. M. (1986). *The history of statistics: The measurement of uncertainty before 1900*. Cambridge, MA: Harvard University Press.

Stocking, M. L., & Lord, F. M. (1983). Developing a common metric in item response theory. *Applied Psychological Measurement, 7*, 201–210.

Stocking, M. L., & Swanson, L. (1993). A method for severely constrained item selection in adaptive testing. *Applied Psychological Measurement, 17*, 277–292.

Student Testing Flexibility Act of 2003. S. 956, 108th Cong. (2003).

Sykes, R. C., & Ito, K. (1997). The effects of computer administration on scores and item parameter estimates of an IRT-based licensure examination. *Applied Psychological Measurement, 21*, 51–63

Terman, L. M., & Merrill, M. A. (1937). *Measuring intelligence*. Boston: Houghton Mifflin.

Thissen, D., & Wainer, H. (Eds.) (2001). *Test scoring*. Mahwah, NJ: Erlbaum.

Thomas, N. (1993a). Asymptotic corrections for multivariate posterior moments with factorial likelihood functions. *Journal of Computing and Graphical Statistics, 2*, 309–322.

Thomas, N. (1993b, November). *The E-step of the MGROUP EM algorithm* (ETS Tech. Rep. TR-93-37). Princeton, NJ: Educational Testing Service.

Thorndike, E. L. (1922). On finding equivalent scores in tests of intelligence. *Journal of Applied Psychology, 6*, 29–33.

Tomkowicz, J., & Schaeffer, G. A. (2002). *Vertical scaling for custom criterion-referenced tests*. Paper presented at the annual meeting of the National Council on Measurement in Education, New York.

Tong, Y. (2005). *Comparisons of methodologies and results in vertical scaling for educational achievement tests*. Unpublished doctoral dissertation, University of Iowa, Iowa City.

Tong, Y., & Kolen, M. J. (2005). *Comparison of methodologies and results in vertical scaling of educational achievement tests*. Paper presented at the annual meeting of the National Council on Measurement in Education, Montreal, Quebec.

Triplett, S. (1995, May 12). *Memorandum to North Carolina LEA Superintendents*. Raleigh, NC: Department of Public Instruction.

Uebersax, J. S. (2006). *Statistical methods for rater agreement*. Retrieved May 11, 2006, from http://ourworld.compuserve.com/homepages/jsuebersax/agree.htm

U.S. Congress. Office of Technology Assessment. (1992). *Testing in American schools: Asking the right questions*. Washington, DC: U.S. Government Printing Office.

U.S. Department of Defense. (1982, March). *Profile of American youth: The 1980 nationwide administration of the Armed Services Vocational Aptitude Battery*. Washington, DC: Office of the Assistant Secretary of Defense (Manpower, Reserve Affairs and Logistics).

U.S. Department of Education. (2006, May 17). Secretary Spellings approves Tennessee and North Carolina growth model pilots for 2005–2006. Retrieved August 30, 2006 from http://www.ed.gov/news/pressreleases/2006/05/05172006a.html

van der Linden, W. J. (2000). A test-theoretic approach to observed-score equating. *Psychometrika, 65*, 437–456.

van der Linden, W. J., & Reese, L. M. (1998) A model for optimal constrained adaptive testing. *Applied Psychological Measurement, 22*, 259–270.

von Davier, A. A. (2003). *Notes on linear equating methods for the non-equivalent groups design* (ETS RR-03-24). Princeton, NJ: ETS.

von Davier, A. A., Fournier-Zajac, S., & Holland, P. W. (in press). *Introducing a non-linear Levine observed-score equating method*. Princeton, NJ: Educational Testing Service.

von Davier, A. A., Holland, P. W., Livingston, S. A., Casabianca, J., Grant, M. C., & Martin, K. (2006). *An evaluation of the kernel equating method. A special study with pseudotests constructed from real test data* (ETS Research Rep. No. RR-06-02). Princeton, NJ: Educational Testing Service.

von Davier, A. A., Holland, P. W., & Thayer, D. T. (2003). Population invariance and chain versus post-stratification methods for equating and test linking. In N. Dorans (Ed.), *Population invariance of score linking: Theory and applications to Advanced Placement Program Examinations* (ETS Research Rep. No. RR-03-27, pp. 19_36). Princeton, NJ: Educational Testing Service.

von Davier, A. A., Holland, P. W., & Thayer, D. T. (2004a). The chain and post-stratification methods for observed-score equating: Their relationship to population invariance. *Journal of Educational Measurement, 41*(1), 15–32.

von Davier, A. A., Holland, P. W., & Thayer, D. T. (2004b). *The kernel method of test equating.* New York: Springer.

von Davier, A. A., & Liu, M. (Eds.). (2006). *Population invariance of test equating and linking: Theory extension and applications across exams.* Princeton, NJ: Educational Testing Service.

von Davier, A. A., & Kong, N. (2005). A unified approach to linear equating for the nonequivalent groups design. *Journal of Educational and Behavioral Statistics, 30*(3), 313–342.

von Davier, A. A., & Manalo, J. (2006). *Theoretical and empirical standard errors for two population invariance measures in the linear equating case.* Paper presented at the NCME, San Francisco, CA.

von Davier, A. A., & Wilson, C. (2005). *A didactic approach to the use of IRT true-score equating* (ETS Rep. No. RR-05-19) Princeton, NJ: Educational Testing Service.

von Davier, A. A., & Wilson, C. (2006). Population invariance of IRT true score equating. In A. A. von Davier & M. Liu (Eds.), *Population invariance of test equating and linking: Theory extensions and applications across exams* (ETS Research Rep. No. RR-06-31, pp. 1-28). Princeton, NJ: Educational Testing Service.

Wainer, H. (1993). Measurement problems. *Journal of Educational Measurement, 30*, 1–21.

Wainer, H., Vevea, J. L., Camacho, F., Reeve, B. B., Rosa, K., Nelson, L., et al. (2001). Augmented scores—"Borrowing strength" to compute scores based on small numbers of items (pp. 343–383). In D. Thissen & H. Wainer (Eds.), *Test scoring.* Mahwah, NJ: Lawrence Erlbaum Associates.

Walker, M., & Liu, J. (2002). *Sample size considerations for the spring 2003 new SAT field trial.* Unpublished manuscript.

Waltman, K. K. (1997). Using performance standards to link statewide achievement results to NAEP. *Journal of Educational Measurement, 34*, 101–121.

Wang, J., & Smith, R. (2003). *NYSESLAT Calibration and Linking Summary.* Princeton, NJ: Educational Testing Service.

Wang, T. (2004). *An alternative continuization method to the kernel method in von Davier, Holland, and Thayer's (2004) test equating framework* (CASMA Research Rep. No. 11). Iowa City, IA: University of Iowa, Center for Advanced Studies in Measurement and Assessment.

Wang, T., & Kolen, M. J. (2001). Evaluating comparability in computerized adaptive testing: Issues, criteria, and an example. *Journal of Educational Measurement, 38,* 19–49.

Way, W. D., Eignor, D. R., & Gawlick, L. A. (2001). *Scoring alternatives for incomplete computerized adaptive tests* (ETS Research Rep. No. RR-01-20). Princeton, NJ: Educational Testing Service.

Way, W. D., Twing, J. S., & Ansley, T. N. (1988). *A comparison of vertical scalings with the three-parameter model using LOGIST and BILOG and two different calibration procedures.* Paper presented at the annual meeting of the National Council of Measurement in Education, New Orleans, LA.

Weiss, A. P. (1914). A modified slide rule and the index method of individual measurements. *Journal of Educational Psychology, 5,* 511–524.

Weiss, D. J. (Ed.). (1983). *New horizons in testing.* New York: Academic Press.

Wells, H. G. (1895). *The time machine.* London: Heinemann.

Willet, J. B. (1994). Measurement of change. In T. Husen & T. N. Postlethwaite (Eds.), *International encyclopedia of education* (2nd. ed., pp. 671–678). Oxford: Elsevier Science Press.

Williams, V. S. L., Pommerich, M., & Thissen, D. (1998). A comparison of developmental scales based on Thurstone's methods and item response theory. *Journal of Educational Measurement, 35,* 93–107.

Williams, V. S. L., Rosa, K. R., McLeod, L. D., Thissen, D., & Sanford, E. E. (1998). Projecting to the NAEP scale: Results from the North Carolina End-of-Grade Testing Program. *Journal of Educational Measurement, 35,* 277–296.

Wilson, D., Wood, R., & Gibbons, R. D. (1987). TESTFACT: Test scoring, item statistics, and item factor analysis [Computer software]. Mooresville IN: Scientific Software.

Winchester, S. (1998). *The professor and the madman.* New York: Harper Collins.

Wise, L., & Alt, M. (2006). *Assessing vertical alignment.* Washington, DC: Council of Chief State School Officers.

Wolf, L. F., & Smith, J. K. (1995). The consequence of consequence: Motivation, anxiety, and test performance. *Applied Measurement in Education, 8,* 227–242.

Wolter, K. (1985). *Introduction to variance estimation.* New York: Springer-Verlag.

Woodworth, R. S. (1912). Combining the results of several tests: A study in statistical method. *Psychological Review, 19,* 97–123.

Wright, N. K., & Dorans, N. J. (1993). *Using the selection variable for matching or equating* (ETS Research Rep. No. RR-93-04). Princeton, NJ: Educational Testing Service.

Yamamoto, K., & Mazzeo, J. (1992). Item response theory scale linking in NAEP. *Journal of Educational Statistics, 17,* 155–173.

Yang, W.-L. (2004). Sensitivity of linkings between AP multiple-choice scores and composite scores to geographical region: An illustration of checking for population invariance. *Journal of Educational Measurement, 41,* 33–41.

Yao, L. (2003). BMIRT. Bayesian multivariate item response theory estimation. [Computer software]. Monterey, CA: CTB/McGraw-Hill.

Yen, W. M. (1986). The choice of scale for educational measurement: An IRT perspective. *Journal of Educational Measurement, 23*, 299–325.

Yen, W. M. (1993). Scaling performance assessments: Strategies for managing local item independence. *Journal of Educational Measurement, 30*, 187–213.

Yen, W. M., & Burket, G. R. (1997). Comparison of item response theory and Thurstone methods of vertical scaling. *Journal of Educational Measurement, 34*(4), 293–313.

Yen, W. M., Burket, G. R., & Fitzpatrick, A. R. (1996). Response to Clemans. *Educational Assessment, 3*, 181–190.

Yen, W. M., & Fitzpatrick, A. R. (2006). Item response theory. In R. L. Brennan (Ed.), *Educational measurement* (4th ed., pp. 111–154). Westport, CT: Praeger Publishers.

Yin, P., Brennan, R. L., & Kolen, M. J. (2004). Concordance between ACT and ITED scores from different populations. *Applied Psychological Measurement, 28*, 274–289.

Yoakum, C. S., & Yerkes, R. M. (1920). *Army mental tests.* New York: Henry Holt & Co.

Author Index

Subject Index

Printed in the United States of America.